WORLD*fOCUS*

Mexico

ROB ALCRAFT
SEAN SPRAGUE

Contents

The country

Introduction 2

The people 4

Where do people live? 6

Agriculture 8

Industry 10

The rich and the poor 12

A closer look at La Trinidad

La Trinidad 14

Village life 16

School 18

Spare time 20

A day with the Ugalde family 22

Travel around La Trinidad 24

Journeys 26

Looking at Mexico 28

Glossary 30

Index 31

Introduction

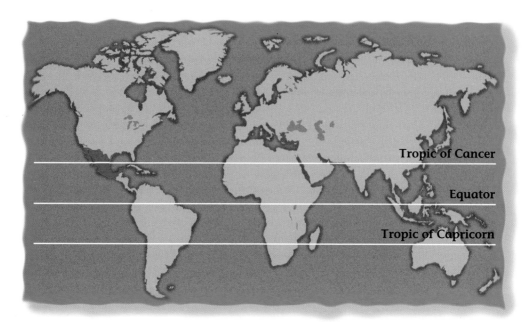

Tropic of Cancer

Equator

Tropic of Capricorn

Think of Mexico and maybe you think of chilli peppers, tortilla chips and sombreros. You might have heard of Acapulco or Cancun, where tourists bake on white sand beaches. Or perhaps you know something about the **Aztec** and the **Maya** Indians, who ruled Mexico long before Europeans even knew it was there. But there's more to Mexico than these few, familiar things.

△ **Where is Mexico?**

People and wealth

Eighty seven million people live in Mexico. The population has grown quickly, doubling in the last 20 years. Today half of all Mexicans are under fifteen years old. Most Mexicans are of part European and part Indian descent. Around 10 million are pure-blood Indians, and there are still some 50 different Indian peoples, like the Maya, the Nahua and the Zapotec.

Mexicans are proud of their Indian history, but Indians themselves are often among the poorest and most disadvantaged people in Mexico. Yet in some ways Mexico is a rich country. There are industries and oil refineries, car plants and textile factories. Mexico City, the country's capital, is one of the largest cities in the world – twice as big as London.

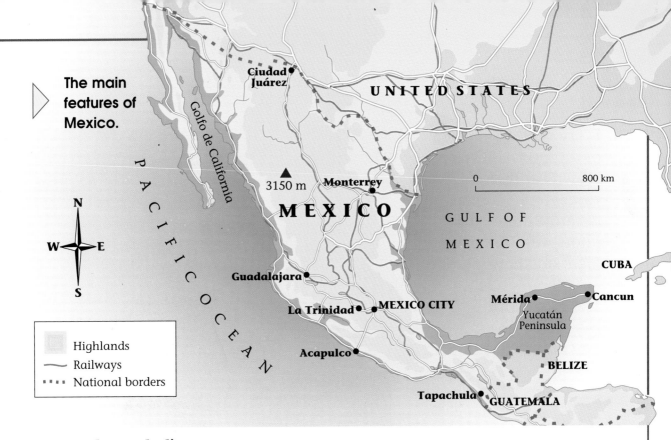

The main features of Mexico.

UNITED STATES

Ciudad Juárez

▲ 3150 m   Monterrey

MEXICO

0 ——————— 800 km

Golfo de California

PACIFIC OCEAN

N
W – E
S

Highlands
Railways
National borders

Guadalajara

La Trinidad   **MEXICO CITY**

Acapulco

GULF OF MEXICO

CUBA

Mérida   Cancun

Yucatán Peninsula

BELIZE

Tapachula   **GUATEMALA**

Geography and climate

More than half of Mexico is 1000 metres or more above sea level. A high **plateau** runs roughly north to south through the centre of the country. To the north, it is low and dry, a semi-desert of cactus and scrub. In the south the land rises and becomes mountainous.

▽ Thunderstorm clouds gather over volcanic mountains in southern Mexico.

The climate changes with altitude. On the flat coastal plains there is little rain, and it is hot – above 20° C all year. In the central highlands it is cooler and wetter – a **temperate** climate.

Half of Mexico is **arid**. There are often droughts, and only about a tenth of Mexico has rain all year round.

The people

Every year, on the Day of the Dead, Mexicans remember their **ancestors**. Families decorate graves and altars with flowers and food, and have parties.

The Maya and the Aztec

The ancestors that people celebrate on the Day of the Dead can be traced back to the original Indian peoples of Mexico. Two of the most powerful were the **Maya** and the **Aztec** who settled in the highlands of Mexico and Central America more than 1000 years ago. They were warrior peoples, but they also traded and farmed and built great cities, the ruins of which can still be seen today.

Europeans arrive

About 500 hundred years ago, just after Columbus sailed to the Americas, Spanish soldiers led by Hernán Cortés began the conquest of Mexico. In three years, between 1519 and 1521, they destroyed the Aztec empire, claiming Mexico as a Spanish **colony**. They took the Indians as slaves, and ruined most of their pyramids and cities. Millions of Indians died, either killed by soldiers, or by diseases introduced to the area by the Europeans.

△ Knowing how to farm and cook maize allowed the Aztec and Maya to flourish.

Spanish culture and civil war

It was the beginning of 300 years of rule from Spain. Spanish **culture** spread. Priests came and converted the Indians to Catholicism. New cities were built in the Spanish style with a **plaza** at their centre and a Catholic church. Spanish became the national language.

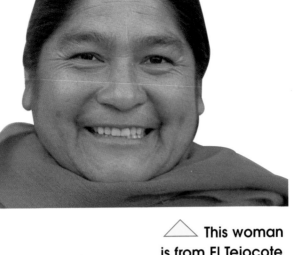

△ This woman is from El Tejocote in the state of Queretaro.

After independence was won from Spain in 1810, Mexico descended into 100 years of turmoil and war and lost almost half its territory (including Texas) to the USA.

The Mexican Revolution

By 1917 many ordinary Mexicans united in a **revolution**. They fought for the right to rule themselves, and to create a country where they could own their own land and in which there would be health care and education for all. This was the Mexican Revolution, and it was the birth of modern Mexico with its 31 states and **constitution**.

▽ Chocolate skulls go on sale for the Day of the Dead.

Many Mexicans feel the ideals people fought for then have been betrayed, and today the majority of Mexicans are poor. But life is not always grim. There are many **fiestas** or parties. At least once a year whole villages or towns will join in, dressing up, dancing, eating and drinking.

Where do people live?

Thirty years ago most Mexicans lived in the countryside. Now three-quarters of the population live in cities like Mexico City, Guadalajara and Monterrey.

City life

More than 20 million people live in Mexico City, a vast, bustling place. The centre is smart and modern. There are buses and an underground metro. Brightly painted taxis hurtle along the wide boulevards, among office blocks, pleasant houses and expensive shops.

But take a bus a few miles along one of the main motorways and you arrive in the slums. Millions of people live here. The roads are dirt tracks which turn to mud when it rains. Houses have one or two rooms, and are often built with old bits of corrugated iron, wood and plastic. Living is cramped and unhealthy. If there is running water it comes from a shared outside tap.

▽ This is Mexico City. In the distance you can see volcanoes.

△ Most people live in small, cheaply built houses.

Life in the countryside

The rainfall and soil needed for successful farming are best in Mexico's central highlands. Many Mexicans live here. Many other regions are sparsely populated, such as the north, which is **arid**, and the plains and scrubland of the Yucatán.

Most Mexicans who live in the countryside farm pieces of land not much bigger than one or two football pitches. Some people own or rent land, but since the **revolution** millions of families live on communal land. This is land everyone in a community agrees to use together. Selling communal land was once unthinkable. But now the government is trying to change agriculture and the laws protecting this land have been altered. Some of it is being sold to companies which grow **cash crops** for **export**. Once the land is sold, people have no way to feed themselves, and have to work on the new farms, or leave to find work in one of the big cities.

Agriculture

Good farmland is scarce in Mexico. Some of the land is too **arid** for crops. Other land is difficult to farm because it covers mountains and steep slopes. In some areas, such as the Yucatán, the soils are too thin to farm. **Soil erosion** is also a huge problem. Once the soil erodes, growing crops becomes more difficult than ever. But people have no other means of supporting themselves, and so they farm it anyway.

Land

What land there is is shared out unfairly, and there has often been fighting over who owns it. This was one of the causes of the 1917 **revolution**. By law, privately owned land must be divided between children when the parents die.

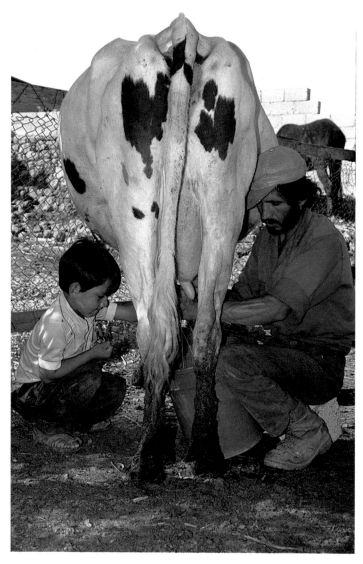

△ Many farmers keep a few animals.

Consequently farm sizes have become smaller over the generations as land is divided.

Sometimes the family of one brother or sister will keep the land, while the others leave to work in the cities. The farming family will eat what they grow, which is mostly maize and beans. What is left over will be sold at the local market, and they will spend the money on essentials like soap, sugar and cooking oil. These families are known as **subsistence farmers**. Sometimes they will grow a **cash crop** like coffee for money.

Big farms and imports

The wealthier farmers and companies have a lot of good land. Where there isn't enough rain, they can afford to use **irrigation**. They use machinery and grow many different crops for **export,** such as cotton, coffee and fruit. Raising cattle for beef is also important, especially in the dry north of Mexico.

However, as more export crops are grown and use up farmland, more food must be **imported** from abroad. Many Mexicans could afford to eat more healthily when Mexico grew all its own maize and beans.

Maize

Maize is Mexico's most important crop. Maize is a staple food – just as bread, potatoes or rice are for us. Everyone eats it and it has been grown there for 7000 years. Often it is ground, and the flour used to make 'tortillas' – flat maize pancakes. We even eat them here – cut into quarters, then fried and sold as tortilla chips.

▽ Not all farmers can afford machinery so land is often ploughed using horses.

Industry

Mexico has a rich economy. There are modern industries and plentiful **raw materials**.

▽ A young dancer in an Aztec-style costume earns money from tourists.

Tourism and modern industry

Tourism is one of Mexico's biggest industries. More than 6 million holidaymakers visit every year, spending millions of pounds in hotels, restaurants and beach resorts like Acapulco. They come mainly for the sun, but also to visit the temples and pyramids that remain from the **Aztec** and **Maya** empires.

Most of Mexico's modern industry is in Mexico City, Guadalajara and Monterrey, and in a 20-kilometre wide strip along the border with the USA. Here there are more than 2000 factories making cars, televisions and computers for **export** to the USA.

Mexico uses iron ore to make steel. It uses cotton to make textiles. It has oil and makes chemicals. The land is also rich in minerals such as silver, gold and copper. Mexico's most valuable exports are cars, machinery and chemicals.

△ Small-scale industries, like making breeze blocks, use simple, cheap technology.

Trade

A new trade deal, known as NAFTA, has been signed between Mexico, the USA and Canada. The plan is that more trade will create more money and jobs for Mexico. But groups which represent farmers and poor people fear that the companies which come to Mexico may simply take advantage, treat workers badly, and pollute the environment. Another concern is that US government **subsidies** to American maize farmers will mean that Mexico will **import** US maize instead of buying from Mexican peasant farmers. Wages are already very low in Mexico (about £2 a day).

Making a living

Many Mexicans have little to do with modern industry. They work for themselves as street traders selling clothes, tortillas, beans and hot snacks and crafts. Gloria Bautista's son is ten years old. He goes out to collect rubbish to sell for recycling. He may only bring home five to seven pesos (about a pound), but he uses that to buy his things for school.

The rich and the poor

Lots of children in Mexico have to work to earn money for their families.

Mexico, as we have seen, is a rich country. It has oil and industry. It makes cars and computers. However, this wealth is not shared equally among its people. The 35 richest families in Mexico have as much wealth between them as the 15 million poorest people.

Poverty and debt

More than half of all Mexicans are very poor. They die sooner, earn less and eat less than rich Mexicans. They live in bad housing and are lucky if they can afford hospitals or schools.

This startling difference between the way people live in Mexico is the country's biggest challenge. Unfortunately in the last few years this difference has increased.

Part of the problem is that Mexico borrowed billions of dollars to build new industries. Now it has to pay the money back, and there is not enough left over for schools and hospitals. 'There are many economic problems,' says Eliazar Nieto from the village of La Trinidad. 'Everything changes quickly: the price of petrol and food is always rising and we don't know what to do from one day to the next.'

The southern state of Chiapas, is one of the poorest states. Here Indian farmers are fighting the army and gunmen hired by the big landowners, for land the Indians believe is rightfully theirs.

Emigration and families

In the north of Mexico thousands of Mexicans cross the border into the USA. Some **emigrate** legally, but many can't get **work visas** so have to climb the border fences and make a run for it during the night. Even the worst jobs in the USA will pay more than work they can get in Mexico.

Many of those who do have jobs still find life hard.

The only way people survive is by relying on each other. In families, everybody from cousins to grandparents, will help each other. Those with a job, or who emigrate to the USA, help support family and relatives back home.

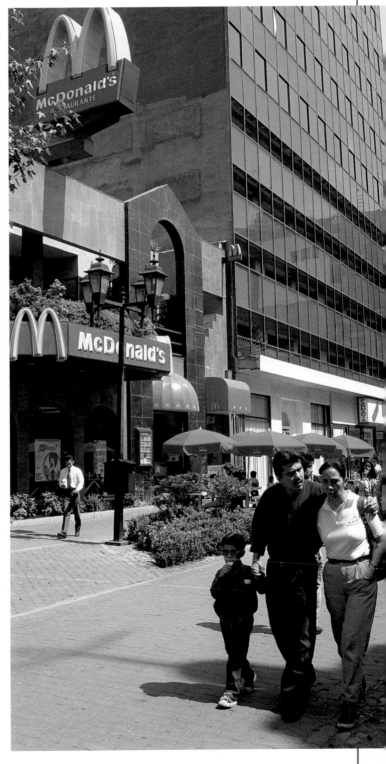

▽ If you have money, there is everything you could want in Mexico.

La Trinidad

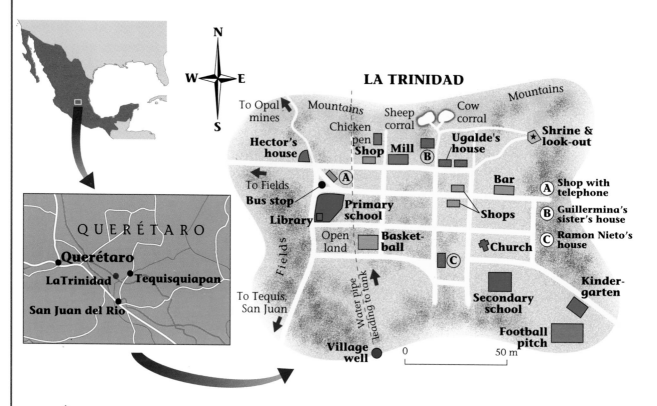

LA TRINIDAD

To Opal mines
Mountains
Chicken pen
Sheep corral
Cow corral
Mountains
Hector's house
Shop
Mill
Ugalde's house
(B)
Shrine & look-out
To Fields
Bus stop
Library
(A)
Primary school
Bar
Shops
(A) Shop with telephone
(B) Guillermina's sister's house
(C) Ramon Nieto's house
Fields
Open land
Basket-ball
(C)
Church
To Tequis, San Juan
Water pipe heading to tank
Secondary school
Kinder-garten
Football pitch
Village well
0
50 m

QUERÉTARO

Querétaro
LaTrinidad
Tequisquiapan
San Juan del Rio

The village of La Trinidad.

La Trinidad is a village in the state of Querétaro in central Mexico. There are some small shops, a church, a public telephone, a library, and a mill where the women go to grind maize. The land around is fertile, part of a wide valley that slopes down to the San Juan River. In summer the valley is hot and dry and, up behind the village, cacti grow on the rocky cliffs.

A dusty road leads out of La Trinidad to the nearest town, Tequisquiapan, or 'Tequis' for short, eleven kilometres away.

Homes and families

About 2000 people live in La Trinidad. The houses are small and built of stone or breeze blocks with roofs of tiles and grey asbestos sheeting.

The Ugalde family live in La Trinidad. They are Juan and Guillermina, and their seven children, aged between seven and seventeen. Their house has three rooms; one is a kitchen and living room, and the other two are bedrooms.

The children share one bedroom, sleeping head-to-toe in two double beds. The family also has a bathroom, a store room and a garden for flowers, vegetables, tomatoes and chilli peppers.

Water, electricity and roads

La Trinidad, like many villages in Mexico, is changing quickly. Organized by their village council, the people of La Trinidad have laid cobbled streets where there used to be only dirt tracks. They've persuaded the government to put in mains electricity, so most houses now have fridges, televisions and electric light.

Villagers also persuaded the federal government to help them build a water and sewerage system. Now there are flush toilets, and piped water from a deep well bored below the village. It's a lot easier than carrying water in buckets from the old well.

△ Mrs Ugalde with three of her children.

 Juan Ugalde looks out over La Trinidad.

Village life

La Trinidad is a farming community. Nearly every family in the village owns a few acres of land.

Farming and animals

Juan Ugalde is a farmer. From April he's busy in the fields, ploughing and planting the seeds, which he saved from the previous year's harvest. Juan still uses horses for ploughing, though some farmers hire tractors.

There's no **irrigation** in La Trinidad so everyone makes the most of the rain. Planting begins with the rainy season in May. Juan grows maize and beans – not to sell, but for the family to eat. He usually harvests enough to last the year, and stores it in the village.

▽ Juan and his son Manuel groom their horses and donkey.

△ Hector Montes cuts, polishes and sells opals found in the mines.

Juan's neighbour, Martin Nieto, keeps eleven dairy cows. The cows were expensive and Martin had to borrow from a savings club to buy them. He earns enough selling the milk to keep his family going, though he still has a lot of debt. Most families keep some smaller animals – chickens, sheep or pigs. They're not so expensive to buy and are easier to look after.

Earning a living

As well as farming most people have to do another job just to make a living. When Juan Ugalde isn't farming he supports his family by labouring on building sites around the village. When there's no labouring work he goes to the **opal** mines.

The mines are a series of caves and rock faces, an hour's walk from La Trinidad. Anyone is free to try their luck, but the work is hard and boring. Often, after a long day spent cracking rocks looking for the small white opals, Juan will still come home empty-handed. At weekends his sons sometimes help him.

School

In Mexico schooling is free, though parents have to pay for some of the books needed for lessons and the school uniform. Nearly all children go at least to primary school because everyone feels it's important. Juan Ugalde says 'My dream is for the children to go to school and learn well, or they will have no future.'

Today more Mexican children have the opportunity to learn than in the past. In Juan's childhood fewer than one in ten children in the village could read or write. But even now teenagers often drop out of school because their families need the money they can earn.

▽ Rosio's sister, seven-year-old Marisol enjoys school.

Schools in La Trinidad

In La Trinidad there are three schools: a kindergarten for under-fives, a primary school for six to twelve-year-olds and the secondary school. The school buildings are modern, and there are sports fields and playgrounds.

School starts at 8 a.m., and finishes at 12.30 p.m., or 2 p.m. in the secondary school.

 Rosio Ugalde at the secondary school with her friends.

Marisol and Miguel-Angel Ugalde set off for school with their cousin.

Lessons

The primary school has 230 pupils spread among six classes. Here Marisol Ugalde learns to read and write, and studies Spanish, history, maths, science, art and PE.

Lessons at the secondary school begin with fifteen minutes of educational television, beamed in via a satellite dish on the roof. The broadcasts cover the national curriculum for schools all over Mexico.

There are three classes in the secondary school and most students are aged between twelve and fifteen. The subjects would all be familiar to students in the UK, except with Spanish instead of English. But the school also has a vegetable garden, and students study agriculture.

If young people want to go to college they must pay to travel to the towns of Tequis or San Juan to study. Very few ever do because it is too expensive for most families.

Spare time

Men sit and talk and play dominoes.

Spare time for young people like the Ugalde children, is often spent helping out – with the animals, around the house, or looking for **opals** with their father.

There are always chores to do – but is it just work? For Manuel Ugalde who rides the donkey to the stream to drink, or for his brother who herds the sheep, it is hard to say whether it's work or play.

Sport

When it comes to sport, football and basketball are the favourites of the village and the whole of Mexico. La Trinidad has one of the best football teams in the area, and there are matches against other village teams on Saturdays. In the cool of the evenings Rosio Ugalde plays basketball with her friends on concrete courts in the village.

The Church

The Catholic Church is very important to Mexicans. On Sundays the whole family puts on their best clothes for mass at the local church. On Saturdays younger children go to **catechism** class, led by teenagers from La Trinidad.

Television has become very much a part of Mexican life. Soap operas, or 'novelas', have millions of devoted viewers. Most of the other television programmes are imported from the USA, and dubbed into Spanish.

The Ugalde children read comics or 'photo-novelas' – romance or adventure stories which have real photos set out like comic strips.

In large towns like Tequis, or San Juan, there are different things to do – and better facilities. Roller-bladers and cyclists whizz around the smooth pavements and squares. There are video arcades, parks, swimming pools, cinemas and bookshops.

▽ Edgar Ugalde and his cousin herd sheep to pasture. It's work but it can be fun as well.

A day with the Ugalde family

▽ **Guillermina makes tortillas every day.**

Guillermina Ugalde has ten brothers and sisters, all living nearby, and Juan has eight. Their brothers and sisters also have children, so the Ugaldes' children have many aunts, uncles and cousins to visit or stay with.

Manuel Ugalde, aged nine, usually lives with his aunt. His brother, sixteen-year-old Adrian, sleeps at his grandmother's next door.

Morning

The family gets up at 6 a.m. Guillermina is first up. She cooks breakfast. There are scrambled eggs and beans on the stove, tortillas roasting, and the smell of coffee and hot chocolate. Edgar feeds the budgie. Miguel-Angel gets the eggs from the hens in the garden. The kitchen is crowded and loud music is playing on the radio to wake everyone up.

By 7.50 a.m. the children have packed a mid-morning snack and set off to school. Then it's Juan's turn to have breakfast.

Guillermina carries a bucket of soaked maize to the mill two streets away. She waits with the other women to have her corn ground into a thick paste to make tortillas.

She roasts the tortillas at her sister's house. She makes a large pile – enough for the day and the following day's breakfast. Then it's home to wash the dishes at the tap in the yard. Later she hand-washes clothes and hangs them on the line to dry.

Afternoon

By 2 p.m. everyone is back home for the main meal of the day. Once or twice a week the Ugaldes eat chicken, and every day there are beans, tortillas, rice and tomatoes. Sometimes there are treats like 'chili rellenos', which are peppers stuffed with cheese.

△ Marisol does her homework in the afternoon.

◁ Breakfast time in the Ugalde household.

The Ugaldes have twelve sheep, and in the afternoon Edgar takes them from the corral under the cliff to graze on the hillside. Marisol and Miguel-Angel do their homework. Manuel's special job is riding the family's donkey down to the stream to drink, and giving it hay.

Everyone is home again by the evening, when the family sits down for a meal together. There are leftovers from lunch, and bread and warm milk.

Travel around La Trinidad

Few people in La Trinidad can afford a car or a pick-up truck. To get to work they walk to their fields or to the **opal** mines. Most things people need are within walking distance. The shops, the clinic, the school and many of their relatives are all close by. Occasionally a travelling salesman, or a shoe repairer calls at the village.

Ramon Nieto has a pick-up truck. He sells milk around the village, and loads up **alfalfa** for animals. The truck is his livelihood.

Travelling beyond La Trinidad

To travel farther, to Tequis or San Juan, people take a taxi or the bus. From San Juan it's a two-hour bus ride to Mexico City. There's a train too, but it's slower. However it's not often that any of the villagers can afford or need to go that far.

Villagers from La Trinidad travel to the bustling daily market in Tequis.

Only the younger villagers travel a lot. They go to work in the factories in the industrial town of San Juan about 20 kilometres away. Sometimes they go even farther, north to the USA. Leopoldo is 29. Every year he works for nine months on the big farms in California. 'I prefer to work in the USA,' says Leopoldo. 'I can earn much more money to send home to my family. But it's getting more difficult to cross the border.'

△ A street trader makes a living selling pots in Tequis.

Tequis

Tequis is the place people from La Trinidad most often visit. There's a daily market with stalls selling everything from kitchen utensils to radios and cassettes, seeds and fertilizer, fruit and wine. There are also chemists and a hospital. Several buses go each day and the round trip costs about 20 pence.

At weekends Tequis' central square comes alive. Sometimes on Sundays there is an open-air mass in front of the cathedral. Hundreds of people gather for the service. Afterwards dancers perform in fantastic **Aztec** costumes for the tourists. On the other side of the square a brass band blasts away, while townspeople and tourists mingle and relax.

Journeys

Going by bus

Most Mexicans travel by bus. Buses are cheap and they go everywhere. On the long-distance routes you can travel first-class in gleaming buses with air conditioning and toilets. If you don't have much money you go third-class. It's slower and less comfortable but you still get to where you want to go. Distances are vast, and journeys from Mexico City to Mérida in the Yucatán, or to Tapachula in Chiapas, will take more than 24 hours.

Even small towns have their own bus station, or street or square, called 'la central', where the buses pull in and out. These are favourite places for food sellers and you can buy tortillas, roasted maize or beans, to keep you going on your journey.

In the countryside many of the roads are only dirt or gravel and so they are very bumpy. Buses here are old, and they rattle and shake with their cargoes of farmers and families travelling to market, or to see relatives.

△ When there isn't a bus you can usually hitch a lift on a pick-up truck to finish your journey.

Donkeys, bicycles and the metro

Horses and donkeys are used to transport farm produce and firewood. This is slow but cheap, and it is also good for mountain tracks. Many people also walk long distances, carrying heavy loads.

On Mexico City's metro there's only one fare, wherever you go. More than 4 million travellers use the metro each day, and at rush hour the carriages are crammed. Up above ground buses, taxis and cars spew fumes into the thin mountain air. There are more than 3 million private cars, and many thousands of buses which cause snake-like traffic jams across the city.

▽ In Mexico City the metro underground railway is usually crowded with travellers.

Bikes and motor bikes are used widely, often loaded with as many people or as much luggage as possible. One motorbike might carry three or four people, or a bike a whole stack of newspapers almost three metres high.

Looking at Mexico

△ **A saint's day procession in Tequis.**

▽ **Enjoying a day out in Chapultapec Park, Mexico City.**

Mexico City is a reminder of just how different the whole country of Mexico can be. You see the old and the new. You can see Indian **culture** and Spanish-speaking culture mixing in languages, clothes and customs. Walk through Mexico City and you see huge contrasts. You can see the ruins of great Aztec pyramids beside modern high-rise buildings.

These differences make Mexico an exciting place to be. You can enjoy the food – the spicy flavours, the beans and the tortillas. You can see colourful processions and visit the markets and **fiestas**.

The challenge for the future

But as we have seen in this book, one of the most striking differences is between the lives of the rich and the poor.

Mexicans see these differences too. Many work very hard to try to ensure that everyone gets a chance to enjoy what's good about Mexico, not just a lucky few. For example 'Super Barrio', a community leader dressed up as a comic book super hero, leads campaigns by poor people to get water or rubbish collection in the slums.

△ Playing on the beach at Zihuatanejo on the Pacific coast.

▽ Soldiers on parade on the Zocalo, the central square in Mexico City.

Mexicans face hard choices about how the country's wealth can be shared more equally, and how to provide a better future for the young people that make up over half the population.

Glossary

Alfalfa A green, leafy plant used for animal feed.

Ancestors The people from whom you are descended – your grandparents, their parents and grandparents before them, and so on.

Arid An arid climate is very dry with little rain.

Aztec The Aztec settled in central Mexico from about AD900. They began to build up a civilization and construct cities in the 1300s. They were constantly at war with neighbouring peoples and made many enemies. The Spanish used these enemies to help them defeat the Aztecs.

Cash crops Crops which are grown to be sold, rather than eaten.

Catechism A way of learning about a religion in a question-and-answer form.

Colony When settlers take over a country, and claim it as their own or for their own country they colonize it.

Constitution The set of basic laws by which a state is governed.

Culture A people's whole way of life. This includes their ideas, beliefs, language, values, knowledge, customs and the things they make.

Emigrate To move to, and settle in another country.

Exports Goods that are sold to, or traded with another country.

Fiesta A spanish word for a party or celebration.

Imports Goods brought in from another country.

Irrigation A way of providing water for plants with channels or pipes.

Maya One of the world's great civilizations. The Maya ruled several city states in southern Mexico. They were the first people in this part of the world to invent writing.

Opal A white, semi-precious stone used in jewellery making.

Plateau A high, flat area of land.

Plaza The Spanish word for town square.

Raw materials The basic materials, like cotton or iron ore, from which finished goods are made.

Revolution A change to government or the way a country is run, often achieved by force.

Soil erosion When soil is washed away by rain or wind. Farming makes this more likely by breaking up the soil and removing the trees or plants that helped to keep it in place.

Subsidy Government money given to keep down the price of products.

Subsistence farmers Farmers who produce only enough to support their households.

Temperate A temperate climate is one that is neither hot nor cold. The UK has a temperate climate.

Work visa Permission to work in another country.

Index

Acapulco 2, 10
Aztecs 2, 4, 10, 25

Buses 25, 26, 27

Cancun 2
Chiapas 13, 26
Cities 2, 4, 6, 10
Climate 3, 7
Columbus,
    Christopher 4
Cortes, Hernan 4
Crops 8, 9, 15, 16
Culture 2, 5, 28

Day of the Dead 4, 5
Disease 4

Emigration 13
Exports 7, 9, 10

Family life 11, 13,
    14–15, 22–23
Farming 4, 7, 8–9, 16,
    17, 19, 23
Food 4, 8, 9, 15, 22, 23,
    26, 28

Government 7, 15
Guadalajara 6, 10

History 2, 4
Houses 6, 14

Imports 9
Industry 10–11, 12, 13,
    25

La Trinidad 13, 14, 15,
    16, 17, 18, 20, 24,
    25

Maize 4, 8, 9, 14, 16,
    23, 26
Markets 25, 28
Maya 2, 4, 10
Merida 26
Mexican Revolution 5,
    7, 8
Mexico City 2, 6, 10,
    24, 26, 27, 28
Minerals 10
Monterrey 6, 10

Opals 17, 20, 24

Pollution 11
Population 2, 6
Poverty 5, 6, 12, 13, 28,
    29

Queretaro 14

Religion 5, 20, 25, 26
Roads 6, 15

San Juan 19, 21, 25
School 11, 18–19, 23
Soap operas 21
Spain 4, 5, 28
Sport 20

Tapachula 26
Television 19, 21
Tequisquiapan 14, 19,
    21, 25
Tourism 2, 10, 25
Trade 11
Transport 6, 24–25,
    26–27

Ugalde family 14, 15,
    16, 17, 18, 19, 20,
    21, 22–23
USA 5, 10, 11, 13, 21,
    25

Yucatan 7, 8, 26

About Oxfam in Mexico

The international family of Oxfams works with poor people and their organizations in over 70 countries. Oxfam believes that all people have basic rights: to earn a living, and to have food, shelter, health care, and education. Oxfam provides relief in emergencies, and gives long-term support to people struggling to build a better life for themselves and their families.

Oxfam UK and Ireland's programme in Mexico concentrates on training and supporting local organizations – helping people to defend their interests and improve incomes. In urban areas Oxfam funds training to help people participate in community planning – and legal training for women, often vulnerable and unaware of their rights. Oxfam also promotes networks of groups working with the poor – from farmers to academics – in an effort to influence and propose alternatives that will benefit poor communities.

The publishers would like to thank the following for their help in preparing this book: Larry Boyd, Pauline Martin and Eduardo Klein of Oxfam's Latin American programme; the Ugalde family and the people of La Trinidad; Tracey Hawkins of Oxfam's photo library.

The Oxfam Education Catalogue lists a range of other resources on economically developing countries, including Mexico, and issues of development. These materials are produced by Oxfam, by other agencies, and by Development Education Centres. For a copy of the catalogue contact Oxfam, 274 Banbury Road, Oxford OX2 7DZ, phone (01865) 311311, or your national Oxfam office.

Photographic acknowledgements
The author and publishers wish to acknowledge, with thanks, the following photographic sources:

GSF Picture Library p3. Buzz Mitchell p5 bottom. All other photographs Sean Sprague.

The publishers have made every effort to trace the copyright holders, but if they have inadvertently overlooked any, they will be pleased to make the necessary arrangement at the first opportunity.

Cover photograph: Liba Taylor, Hutchison Library

Note to the reader - In this book there are some words in the text which are printed in **bold** type. This shows that the word is listed in the glossary on page 30. The glossary gives a brief explanation of words which may be new to you.

First published in Great Britain by Heinemann Library, an imprint of Heinemann Publishers (Oxford) Ltd Halley Court, Jordan Hill, Oxford OX2 8EJ

OXFORD LONDON EDINBURGH MADRID ATHENS BOLOGNA PARIS MELBOURNE SYDNEY AUCKLAND SINGAPORE TOKYO IBADAN NAIROBI HARARE GABORONE PORTSMOUTH NH (USA)

© 1996 Heinemann Publishers (Oxford) Ltd.

00 99 98 97 96
10 9 8 7 6 5 4 3 2 1

British Library Cataloguing in Publication Data
Alcraft, Rob
  Mexico. – (Worldfocus Series)
  I. Title II. Sprague, Sean III. Series
  972

ISBN 0 431 07247 7 (Hardback)

ISBN 0 431 07242 6 (Paperback)

Designed and produced by Visual Image
Cover design by Threefold Design
Printed and bound in Britain by Bath Press Colourbooks, Glasgow

A 5% royalty on all copies of this book sold by Heinemann Publishers (Oxford) Ltd will be donated to Oxfam (United Kingdom and Ireland), a registered charity number 202918.

Modern Art, Britain and the Great War

Modern Art, Britain and the Great War

witnessing, testimony and remembrance

Sue Malvern

Published for
The Paul Mellon Centre for Studies in British Art
by Yale University Press
New Haven and London

Designed by Laura Bolick

Printed in China

100555 3714

Library of Congress Cataloging-in-Publication Data

Malvern, Sue, 1951–
Modern Art, Britain, and the Great War: witnessing,
testimony, and remembrance / Sue Malvern.
p. cm.
Includes bibliographical references and index.
ISBN 0-300-10576-2 (cl : alk. paper)
1. Art, British – 20th century. 2. World War, 1914-1918 –
Art and the war.
3. Art and war. 4. Propaganda in art. 1. Title.
N6768.M26 2004
709'.41'09041–dc22
2004002268

A catalogue record for this book is available from
The British Library

frontispiece C. R. W. Nevinson, *The Harvest of Battle* (detail of fig. 71), 1919,
Imperial War Museum, London

contents

Acknowledgements   vii

Introduction   I
Masculine Modernism and Avant-Gardes   I
The Myth of Self-Regeneration and the
    Cult of Renaissance   5
Official War Artists   13

one   Art, Propaganda and Persuasion
at Wellington House   17
Liberalism and 'Englishness'   17
The Western Front   24
British Artists at the Front   29

two   Realism, Representation and
Censorship   37
War and Truth   37
Patronage and Censorship   49
Images and Perceptions   55

three   Making History: The British War
Memorials Committee   69
Founding the Ministry of Information
    and Funding a War Memorial   69
Canons, Subjects, Money   75
Commissioning History Paintings   85

four   Modern Art, Modern War and the
Impossible Project of History
Painting   91
Representing the Unrepresentable   91
Public and Private in the Nation's
    War Paintings   92
Veterans and Soldier–Artists   98
The Forms of the Pictures   100
The Critical Response   106

five   Post-War Modernisms: William
        Roberts, David Bomberg,
        Wyndham Lewis and
        C. R. W. Nevinson   109
        Modernism and War   109
        The Ethics of Art-Making: Bomberg
           and Roberts   114
        The Politics of Art: Lewis and Nevinson   132
        War Artists and the 1930s   145

six   Redeeming the War: 'Englishness'
        and Remembrance   151
        Remembering the Great War   151
        Arcadia and Paul Nash   154
        Stanley Spencer and Burghclere   162
        Allegories of Remembrance   165
        Postscript   177

        Appendices   178
        British War Memorials
           Committee of Painting and Sculpture:
           Artists Commissioned and Employed.   178
        War Artists Involved in
           First World War Schemes   181

        Notes   200
        Photograph Credits   225
        Index   226

Acknowledgements

This book has been some years in gestation and I have had support and help from numerous individuals and institutions. In 2002, the Arts and Humanities Research Board provided a research leave that made it possible for me to complete the manuscript, and the Yale Center for British Art, New Haven, a research fellowship that gave me space to think, for which I am grateful. Among staff in archives and museums, I thank Jenny Wood, Pauline Allwright, Vivienne Crawford and Robert Crawford at the Imperial War Museum, Adrian Glew at Tate Archives, Rosemary Holmes of the National Gallery of Canada for her energetic work tracking down works of art in store, and Laura Brandon of the Canadian War Museum for her generosity with sources and papers. I am especially grateful to Mike Moody at the Imperial War Museum for friendship and help from the very beginning. Amongst friends and colleagues, for conversations, advice and support, I thank Brandon Taylor, Will Vaughan, Jon Wood, Jo Anna Isaak, Reesa Greenberg, Tim Barringer, Leah Sherman, Mike Biddiss and Cedric Brown, and for their exceptional warmth and friendship, Paul Davies and Andrew Stephenson. Although neither lived to see this book published, both Peter Fitzgerald and Joe Darracott were adamant that this was a project worth doing, and I am indebted to the rigour of the advice they gave me.

In recent years, I have given research papers on art and the First World War in Britain and the United States and I am grateful to Tate Britain, the Paul Mellon Center for British Art at Yale University, Andrew Hemingway, Brandon Taylor and David Peters Corbett for their invitations. Parts of the introduction and chapters one and six were first published in *Art History* (vol. 9. no. 4, 1986 and vol. 23. no. 2, 2000) and *Oxford Art Journal* (vol. 24. no. 1, 2001). I thank Gillian Malpass for exemplary editorial support in seeing this book into print, Sandy Chapman for her great care with copy editing, and Laura Bolick for her design and enthusiasm.

Finally, for their great love and infinite patience, my thanks to my family, David and Esther.

Introduction

> The body in duress. . . . The body in uniform. The body under fire. Bodies
> maimed, wounded and killed. Bodies sexed and unsexed by war . . . The Corps.
> . . . Bodies of bodies. . . . Dying bodies. . . . Arms without bodies. Cannon fodder
> . . . War babies. . . . Foreign bodies. . . . Artificial limbs and prosthetic devices. . . .
> The body numb. The body abject and the body erect, killing and being killed . . .
>
> Jane Marcus 1989.[1]

Masculine Modernism and Avant-Gardes

Jacob Epstein's innovative sculpture *Rock Drill* was first exhibited in March 1915 as a robotic figure mounted on a real rock drill. By the time of its second showing in 1916, however, the artist had cut it down to a torso, removing the drill, part of the operating arm and lower body (fig. 3). This reduction has been read as an emasculation that exemplifies the demise of the avant-garde and symbolises a crisis about the male body, both instigated by the First World War. It has often been remarked that the war put an end to avant-garde art in Britain, a disruption said to have lasted until the 1930s when new avant-gardes emerged.[2] The First World War was a young man's war and, inevitably, significant numbers of British avant-garde artists, by and large in their twenties at its outbreak, volunteered. Over its four-year period of largely static and entrenched fighting, the young male population of Europe was decimated, and the war has sometimes been described as one that provoked a crisis in masculinity, meaning that expectations of virile manliness were first invoked in its prosecution and then confounded in the experience of its futility.[3] Avant-garde art and masculinity have been described in parallel and

overlapping narratives of loss and dismemberment.[4] Epstein's amendment of *Rock Drill* from predatory and sinister robotic machine of 1915 to maimed and incapacitated torso in 1916 looks emblematic; the fate of the sculpture, the national fate. It represents British war experience and it is what happened to the avant-garde. The male body was cut short, dismembered, victimised and rendered defenceless.

The first version of *Rock Drill* was the most radical modernist sculpture in Britain when it was seen at the second London Group exhibition, a show dominated by the most innovative artists working on the British art scene. The whole ensemble stood as a modernist icon for potent and phallic masculinity. It exemplified the kind of modern sculpture Henri Gaudier-Brzeska called in 1914 'this virile art', identified with carving hard machine-like forms in contrast to 'light voluptuous modelling'.[5] The work also functioned as a metaphor for the carver–sculptor as a self-creating, self-realising individual.[6] The second, dissected version appeared at a London Group exhibition in June 1916 which was virtually denuded of avant-garde artists. By then there was no avant-garde in London; most artists had joined up.[7] In retrospect, the surviving fragment of upper torso and head has been understood as

1 C. R. W. Nevinson, *Returning to the Trenches*, 1914–15, oil on canvas, 51.2 × 76.8, National Gallery of Canada, Ottawa

2 Luigi Russolo, *La Revolta*, 1912, oil on canvas, 150 × 230, Gemeentemuseum The Hague

3 Jacob Epstein, *Torso in Metal from 'The Rock Drill'*, 1913–14, bronze, 70.5 × 58.4 × 44.5, Tate, London

4 C. R. W. Nevinson, *The Arrival*, c.1913 or 1914, oil on canvas, 76.2 × 63.5, Tate, London, presented by the artist's widow 1956

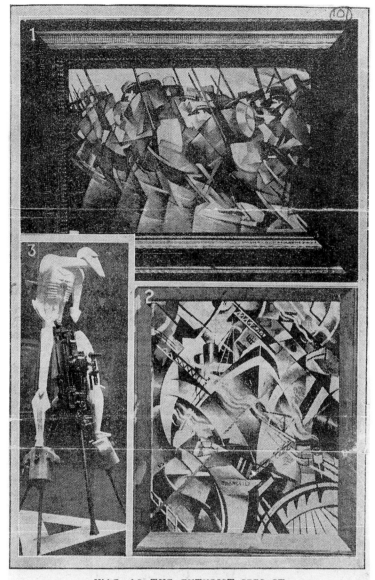

WAR AS THE FUTURIST SEES IT.

Mr. C. R. W. Nevinson, the Futurist artist, has paid a visit to the front. Some of his impressions are now to be seen at the second exhibition of works by members of the London Group at the Goupil Gallery, Regent Street. 1. "Returning to the Trenches." 2. "My Arrival at Dunkirk." 3. "Rock Drill," a piece of Futurist sculpture by Mr. Jacob Epstein ("Daily Graphic" photographs.)

5 War as the Futurist Sees it, *Daily Graphic*, 5 May 1915, showing C. R. W. Nevinson's *Returning to the Trenches*, *My Arrival at Dunkirk* and Jacob Epstein's *Rock Drill* at the London Group, Goupil Gallery, 1915

mirroring the fragmentation of male bodies on the battlefields of the First World War. It is the 'castrated victim of the mechanical age'.[8] It is 'impotent, armoured in futility'.[9] The two versions, recurring in quick succession in the first years of the war, apparently parallel an early phase of optimism and patriotism followed by disillusionment with mounting casualties and no end to war in sight. Consequently, the work gets described as 'pivotal', 'summarizing' the

English avant-garde organised around artists associated with Vorticism in 1914–15 'as it ushers in the disenchantment . . . that led to the Vorticists' downfall'.[10] As a radical virile work, 'Rock Drill' was a challenge to other avant-garde artists, in particular, Gaudier-Brzeska. Accompanied by Ezra Pound, he viewed the whole ensemble when it was set up in 1913 in Epstein's studio, a visit that resulted in the poet commissioning the artist to carve a portrait head,[11] shown at the

Whitechapel Art Gallery's *Twentieth-Century Art: A Review of Modern Movements* exhibition in 1914 and reproduced in the second 'War Number' of Wyndham Lewis's key avant-garde journal *Blast: A Review of the Great English Vortex*. This issue, the last, was also a memorial to Gaudier-Brzeska 'MORT POUR LA PATRIE' at Neuville St. Vaast on 5 June. Reducing 'Rock Drill', mutilating the sculpture in 1916, might have been a homage to Gaudier-Brzeska, the avant-garde's earliest martyr and the mythical artist–hero sacrificed to the cause of both modern art and modern war.[12] Later Epstein would claim his untimely death made the myth: 'His early death . . . gave him . . . immediate status'.[13]

Nation and national destiny, modern and avant-garde art, and modern artists are all mapped onto one work of art, and read as a narrative for the vicissitudes of masculinity. Making an analogy between *Rock Drill* and the fate of the avant-garde, however, rests on the assumption that the first version is a complete, unified whole that can then become a fragmented body in pieces, just as the avant-garde is also being viewed as a homogenous and unified totality that can then be shattered by war experience. The original *Rock Drill*, however, was not seen by its contemporary audiences as integrated. Instead the combination of sculpture/figure and machine/drill was read for its lack of fit. Wyndham Lewis noted how it disconcerted, writing 'I feel the combination of the white figure and the rock-drill is rather unfortunate and ghost-like. But its lack of logic has an effectiveness of its own.'[14] Lack of congruity was the dominant reading in both sympathetic and hostile reviews. The *Guardian*, which was supportive, called attention to the 'incongruity' of machine and synthetic man. P. G. Konody, who abhorred the work, identified its 'lack of cohesion'.[15] Such terms suggest defamiliarisation or making strange, a crucial avant-garde strategy at precisely this historic moment. In the circles around Gaudier and Epstein, carving was intended to be a rejection of classical Greek tradition, and involved the disaffirmation of effeminacy and homosexuality. Modernist carving was to overturn a Renaissance humanist tradition and, with this, any notion of an integrated self. Wyndham Lewis wrote in his 'Vortex' in 1915, 'Be Thyself' that 'For the Individual, the single object, and the isolated is, you will admit, an absurdity. Why try and give the impression of a consistent and indivisible personality?'[16] Notions

of fractured subjectivities, involving the loss of the body and the dismemberment of classical tradition, were already at work well before the war.

To say the avant-garde declined because of the First World War is to suggest imagining, counter-factually and impossibly, works of art not made, positions not consolidated and new avant-gardes not inaugurated because a war took place. At the very least, such a simple case of cause and effect ignores how the boundaries of the war were permeable, and fails to recognise that the relationship of war and art is not unidirectional. The experience of war was itself shaped in representation and the conflict was thought and imagined before it was fought in ways that prepared the ground for the unimaginable to take place.[17] In his examination of avant-garde art and war, Hal Foster does not assume that modern art traces some sort of predictable trajectory, but characterises avant-garde activism as a shifting, dynamic process, as a campaign with endlessly adjusted targets. Writing about Marinetti and Wyndham Lewis, he argues for how the body was reconceived in modern art under the pressure of war as a process articulated between and across cultural fields: 'The 1920s were dominated by two tendencies: on the one hand, various returns to the figure, often neo-classical in nature, most of which were reaction-formations against the mutilated bodies of World War I as well as the fragmented figures of high modernism; and, on the other hand, various machinic modernisms, most of which were also concerned to make over this body-ego image that had been damaged in reality and representation alike.'[18]

An equation between modern art and the national body, what Paul Peppis has termed 'dissenting patriotism',[19] was engendered by avant-garde artists themselves. When the Vorticists had their one and only London showing at the Doré Gallery in June 1915, they declared themselves 'necessary to this country' and, by implication, to the war effort.[20] The Vorticists were avant-garde warriors, primitive mercenaries of the modern world, or as Raymond Williams puts it 'militants of a creativity to revive and liberate humanity.'[21] The opening 'Blast' and 'Bless' section of the Vorticist manifesto, published in the first issue of *Blast* in July 1914, cursed England's climate – 'Dismal symbol, set around our bodies, of effeminate lout within . . .'[22] – and set up an equivalence between the masculine body and the nation-state; masculine destiny became the national destiny. Periods of war are times when the gender identifications and roles of men and women are most visibly prescribed and marked, ritually segregating communities into (male) defender and (female) defended. At the same time, the experience of war often reverses and always destabilises assumptions about fixed masculinities and femininities. Questions about gendered identities and singular or stable subjectivities had already appeared in the pre-war avant-garde, making the impact of war experience on such issues much more elusive and difficult to unpick, and certainly more complex than a simple case of cause and effect.

An alternative model substitutes a simple binarism for cause and effect. On the one hand, total war subordinated all aspects of civil society, including art, to the needs of the State. On the other hand, the war opened up a cultural space for the expression of avant-garde artists' disillusionment or 'a bitter truth'.[23] This will not do either, however, as this notion must repress the ways in which ironic or disenchanted images could also be recruited in the promulgation of a just war viewed as honourable and necessary, or fatalistically as inevitable.[24] The idea that avant-garde artists, simply by virtue of being avant-garde, were bound to paint truthful images of disillusion is made unsustainable in Britain by the recruitment of a substantial proportion as official war artists. Various schemes dating from 1916 culminated in a large project that commissioned commemorative history paintings from artists such as Wyndham Lewis, William Roberts and C. R. W. Nevinson. These were shown at the Royal Academy in 1919 as *The Nation's War Paintings*, a year after the exhibition of memorial canvases for a Canadian scheme to which these artists, together with David Bomberg and Edward Wadsworth, also contributed. What I will argue here is that closer examination of official employment, war service and the cultural meanings of the war will present a more complex narrative in which some questions of being modern, being avant-garde and going to war presented paradoxical and irresolvable issues for artists and critics alike. After 1917, avant-garde art struck out in contradictory and volatile political directions, including identifications with fascism and communism. When it came to settling accounts after the war and re-establishing continuities with pre-war concerns, artists, as well as their audiences, found that the events of the war had brought into focus problematic

issues concerning avant-gardism and modernism, incorporation and opposition, continuity and discontinuity, art and its function in society.[25]

The Myth of Self-Regeneration and the Cult of Renaissance

At the 1915 London Group exhibition where Epstein showed *Rock Drill*, C. R. W. Nevinson and Henri Gaudier-Brzeska were the only artists with front-line experience (Nevinson as an voluntary ambulance driver and orderly, Gaudier in the French army) and only they showed work about the war (figs. 1 5, 9, and 10). Reviewers, habitually hostile to modern art, characterised the other works not only as an irresponsible failure of duty and unpatriotic but almost as enemy action. *The Times* declared that Wadsworth, Roberts, and Lewis were 'Prussian in . . . spirit. These painters seem to execute a kind of goose-step, where other artists are content to walk more or less naturally.'[26] The idea that modern art was an alien presence within the nation was already a well-used notion, however. By being popularly associated with degeneracy and insanity,[27] modern art was said to distort 'normal' vision, a 'normality' often identified with an academic tradition for narrative subject paintings. The look of a modern painting could not be confirmed by judgements appealing to a tradition for empirically verifiable evidence.[28] Empiricism equated truth and beauty in art with the health and wholeness of the nation. The so-called deviancy of modern art was then linked to politics, including anxieties about the maintenance of class boundaries and fears for the fragmentation of national coherence. Conservative critics assumed that national artistic heritage was an integrated whole under threat from the contamination of foreign influence and in need of protection. When war broke out, critical language adopted anti-German rhetoric to identify modern art with an enemy or outsider, but the war did not invent the tendency to conceive experimentation in art as alien to national interests.[29] Critical reaction being extreme, however, was symptomatic of a feeling that there was such a thing as an essential national identity vulnerable to fracture. The identity of a nation has no fixed essence and supplements this lack with the labour of continuous self-representation. Nationhood is formed by telling stories, manufacturing fictions, and inventing traditions in a ceaseless and selective process of inclusion and exclusion, remembering and forgetting. Art, incorporated into national collections and displayed in exhibitions, is one of the means for the self-representation of the nation. The Great War defined a national mission and made subscribing to the fiction of a unified nation a patriotic obligation.

The excess of critical attacks on modern art also indicates how much academic traditions were threatened with being marginalised and superseded. Reviewers sympathetic to modern art did not so much adopt an antagonistic defence of its value as pursue a logic of moderation, a middle ground predicated on maintaining a sense of proportion. In contrast to those who vilified modern art as 'German', the *Manchester Guardian*, commenting on the London Group in March 1915, noted that the war had weakened the idea of art as defiance, not least because men under forty were disappearing from civilian life. Being young, healthy and still civilian did not suggest that a man was either 'daring' or 'remarkable'. Once the 'enemy' had been convention, but real warfare had made it 'difficult at the moment to see any art as daring and as strange.'[30] Rather than attributing the stereotypes of a national enemy to modern art, the paper was proposing that set against matters of life and death, avant-garde politics were insignificant. The crisis had brought humanitarian issues into focus and national priorities had changed. The importance of the practice of art as a site for contention had diminished. Later that year, Ford Madox Hueffer deplored the continuance of attacks on Gaudier-Brzeska's art, once the artist had lost his life at the Front, and began to promote an idea that would find wider acceptance; the war had given rise to a debt to youth.[31]

The question of what position to take up in the war was an issue for modern artists and questions of modern art, national interest and war are made more difficult to disentangle by the stance of radical British artists themselves.[32] The belligerence of artists like Nevinson and Lewis has led to the view that the avant-garde was itself implicated in the causes of the First World War. Going to war was seen as purgative and beneficial by many, and members of the European avant-garde welcomed the conflict as a culmination of calls for the renewal of culture. It also created opportunities for making literal and metaphorical capital and it offered a new subject matter for art.[33] Nevinson declared, on his return to London after three months in Flanders, that going to the front was a necessary test of virility for artists who would 'strengthen their art by a worship of physical and moral courage and a fearless desire of adventure, risk and daring, and free themselves from the canker of professors, archaeologists, cicerones, antiquaries, and beauty-worshippers'.[34]

Nevinson's work at the London Group, which included his first major war image *Returning to the Trenches* (fig. 1), was described as the beginning of a 'return from the barren wilderness of abstraction'[35] and as 'a very oasis of intellectual clearness among a babel of artistic gibberish.'[36] *Returning to the Trenches* depicts French troops caught up in the momentum and anonymity of total war. Glimpses of particular men emerge here and there from the huddle and it is usually read as a symbol for the immersion of the individual in the totality of a war machine. The painting derives from Luigi Russolo's *La Revolta* (fig. 2), which was shown in the Italian Futurist exhibition at the Sackville Gallery in 1912 and reproduced in the catalogue. Rifles replace the raised fists of Russolo's canvas. *La Revolta* was described in the Sackville catalogue as 'The collision of two forces, that of the revolutionary element made up of enthusiasm and red lyricism against the forces of inertia and reactionary resistance of tradition.'[37] In Nevinson's composition, the rushing soldiers sweep away from the picture plane diminishing in scale towards an unknown point. An alternative reading, and consonant with Nevinson's own pronouncements, would suggest that it is an icon for war as purgative and cleansing. Nevinson's war paintings suggested that because avant-garde art broke with a tradition for representation based on what could be empirically verified, it was particularly well adapted to depict sights without precedence in the life of a nation. Avant-garde art had the potential to fulfil a role of national significance. The works were described as impressions 'of the utter indifference and vacuity which come through fatigue, squalor, bursting shrapnel, hunger, and cold wet weather.'[38] The forms of the paintings were said not to be something wilfully imposed on an audience by an artist out to shock, but the effect of inhuman sights. Claude Phillips, who had called modern art shown at the Whitechapel Art Gallery in 1914 an infection that needed to be purged, wrote about Nevinson's *A*

6 C. R. W. Nevinson, *Flooded Trench on the Yser*, 1915, oil on canvas, 50 × 61 private collection

Deserted Trench (subsequently known as *Flooded Trench on the Yser*) (fig. 6) shown at the London Group in autumn 1915, that its formal means were strange and yet it arrived at 'a poignant impression of utter desolation.' Here Cubism was 'of some use in the rendering of the vast sky, chill grey yet vibrant, that dominates a scene in which dead earth and wan water seem one.'[39]

Throughout 1915, Nevinson participated in most major exhibitions including contributions to the first Vorticist exhibition and the second issue of *Blast*. In the early years of the war the art market retrenched,

only beginning to show signs of revival in 1916, but with a new demand for persuasive images of modern war.[40] By 1916, Nevinson was virtually the only avant-garde artist still showing in London and capitalised on his unique position with a highly successful one-person show entirely of war paintings held in the autumn at London's premier modern art dealers, the Leicester Galleries, together with a book of reproductions with a text by P. G. Konody, *Modern War Paintings by C. R. W. Nevinson*, published early in 1917. Some of his most successful motifs, such as *Bursting Shell* of 1915 (fig. 7), which he reiterated in numerous variants,

7

7 (*left*) C. R. W. Nevinson, *Bursting Shell*, 1915, oil on canvas, 76 × 56, Tate, London

8 (*facing page*) C. R. W. Nevinson, *La Mitrailleuse*, 1915, oil on canvas, 61 × 50.8, Tate, London, presented by the Contemporary Art Society 1917

9 (*below left*) Henri Gaudier-Brzeska, *One of our Shells Exploding*, 1915, pencil on paper, 22 × 28.5, Musée National d'Art Moderne, Paris

10   Henri Gaudier-Brzeska, *A Mitrailleuse in Action*, 1915, pencil on paper, 28.5 × 22, Musée National d'Art Moderne, Paris

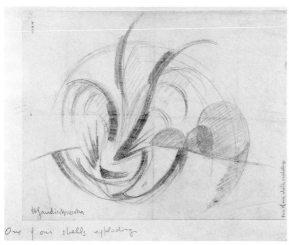

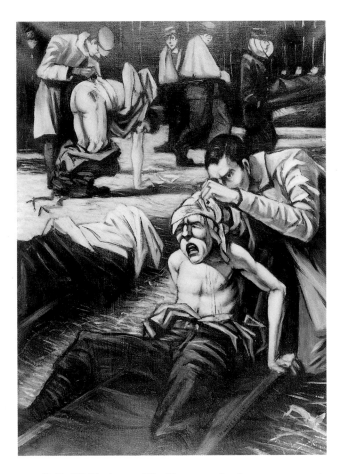

11 C. R. W. Nevinson, *The Doctor*, 1916, oil on canvas, 57.15 × 41.27, Imperial War Museum, London

and *La Mitrailleuse* of 1915 (fig. 8), purchased by the Contemporary Art Society and presented to the Tate in 1917, were suggested by the two front-line drawings Gaudier had sent to the London Group in 1915, *One of our Shells Exploding* (fig. 9) and *A Mitrailleuse in Action* (fig. 10). When Nevinson's *La Mitrailleuse* was shown at the Allied Artists Association (under the title *Mitrailleuse: An Illustration*) with two other works, now lost (*Violence: An Abstraction* and *Night; Light; Crowd: An Interpretation*), Frank Rutter applauded the work, 'It is one of the best of war paintings I have seen this year, sufficiently "futurist" to be piquant and distinguished, yet not so relentlessly futurist, as are his other two paintings, as to be bewilderingly disintegrated.'[41] It satisfied the demand for work that could be described as 'illustration' and yet also be modern; for work that revealed the reality of war but was art, not mere reportage.[42] By the time of his first major exhibition

in 1916, Nevinson had produced images such as *The Doctor* (fig. 11) revealing a new wartime realism that seemed the vision of soldier and artist combined.[43]

In his book *Modern War Paintings*, Konody placed Nevinson's work in a tradition of war art stretching back to the Greeks. He summarised how heroic depictions of war, including a decorative renaissance tradition exemplified by Uccello, had been replaced since the nineteenth century with an emphasis on commonplace suffering and deprivation in the realism of Goya and the Russian Vereshchagin. The Great War had involved all European nations and their populations in a total war experience and it needed a new kind of art and a new tradition. Rebellious experimentation and modern art had prefigured the events of the war to come. Konody cited, as evidence, Michael Sadler's lecture 'Premonitions of the War in Modern Art', read in Leeds in October 1915.[44] Konody's biography of Nevinson demonstrated the events and meaning of modernism before the conflict, but, as he explained, real war had shattered illusions. What had now emerged in Nevinson's work, and which was of particular significance in justifying and rationalising avant-garde experimentation, was moderation in the form of 'a tactful compromise between geometric abstraction and frank – sometimes brutally frank – illustration.' It was the result of a desire to communicate having 'its root in the sober recognition of the futility of experiments unintelligible to everybody but the artist himself.'[45] By the simple strategy of reversing the chronology of Nevinson's paintings, Konody tried to demonstrate to the reader how Nevinson hoped, by proceeding from realism to abstraction, to educate the reader's vision. By 1917, when he became an official war artist, Nevinson's work exemplified a spirit of consensus, capable of recognising a debt to youth by accommodating the experimentation of more radical artists as necessary to give meaningful form to war experience.

C. Lewis Hind noted in autumn 1916 that the war was a matter for youth not just at the front but also in the studio. Eric Kennington, a relatively unknown artist, had volunteered for the London Regiment and served in France until discharged unfit in January 1915. He showed his tribute to his platoon, *The Kensingtons at Laventie* (fig. 12), in April/May 1916 at the Goupil Gallery and Hind rated him and Nevinson the two finest painters of the war.[46] *The Kensingtons at Laventie*

12   Eric Kennington, *The Kensingtons at Laventie*, 1915–6, oil on glass, 139.7 × 152.4, Imperial War Museum, London

is a distinctive work painted on glass in a technique called *Hinterglasmalerie*. Highlights are laid in first and the work is painted foreground to background. Kennington's tribute is something of a tour de force, emphasised by the way the *pickelhaube*, carried as a trophy by one of the soldiers, is foreshortened. The subject is meticulously specified. These are obviously serving soldiers and evidently battle-worn. Each figure can be identified, including Kennington himself on the left wearing a balaclava. The viewpoint is low so that the figures rise frieze-like dominating the spectator,

and because painting on glass makes it a problem to transport, Kennington probably intended the work to be fixed permanently, possibly in a public location. Like Nevinson's work, the painting was well-received. It was clearly an image based on first-hand experience, with attention given to the detritus and accoutrements of warfare and authenticated by the presence of his self-portrait. Rather than glorifying or romanticising war, it stressed instead the deprivations experienced by a then still volunteer army. It was also a mediated image that synthesised what it had to report into a memorable and monumental work of art, reworking a chivalric ideal of soldiers into a modern and democratic vision. The separation of the officer from the other men and the soldier fallen from exhaustion emphasised a humanitarian identification with its subject matter.

Nevinson's popular success as a war artist meant that he supplied a measure for other young painters seeking to give form to war experience. Paul Nash wrote to his wife from the front in March 1917 asking her to send an example of Nevinson's work.[47] In June, while convalescing from an injury, Nash held a small exhibition of modestly priced war drawings at the Goupil Gallery. The work was admired because it was the work of a soldier–artist, in this case one who specialised in landscape scenes that seemed to be naively but sincerely drawn. The work was perceived by reviewers as being haunted with 'a kind of brooding vision, with a sense of hurt in the landscape – even the sky in one of these drawings has a bruised and livid tinge.'[48]

Dating from around 1916, a notion began to emerge that the war would give rise to a national renaissance in visual art. For example, Claude Phillips wrote in the *Daily Telegraph* that 'When the world is once for all freed from the strangling coils of the monstrous serpent now seeking to enfold and paralyse it, there may be expected a great and joyous artistic upheaval, both at home and abroad.'[49] On 5 May 1916, a lengthy editorial called 'Artists and the War' appeared in *The Times*. This proposed a resolution to the question of art and its national role in wartime. The writer noted two conditions: first, the war was all consuming in terms of national resources of 'men, materials and *moral*'; second, the nation possessed a number of vigorous, worthy artists, representing a significant national asset. It was a matter of bringing these two things together, creating both openings for artists and a lasting national heritage that would invent 'for ourselves and our children worthy and lasting memorials of awful happenings and also of deeds that do honour to our race'. The matter of art and war was a special case. Part of the function of art was to record momentous events, but it had a different and more telling role than photography. Work was needed from artists 'who have seen with their own eyes, and have brought the emotion of the artist into touch with the grim or noble realities of war.' *The Times* advocated 'a carefully prepared scheme' using a few selected artists to visit the front and collect material and studies. The circumstances of a nation at war

meant recognising the necessity for military control of the artists and the right of the military authorities to censor work. The editorial concluded: 'Then the studies would, in time, become pictures, some of them, no doubt, great pictures . . . In a word Britain might thus become possessed of worthy memorials of the greatest epoch in the country's history, and a true Renaissance of Art might be brought about under the stress of a noble and all-pervading emotion.'

'Artists and the War' clearly reveals how the conflict, in the process of becoming all consuming, had altered a number of parameters for art. No longer a matter of private activity, the market and artistic autonomy, art could now be an instrument of the state and nation at war. A role of unprecedented significance was on offer at the cost of submitting artistic licence and independence to military and state supervision. Art would therefore find a status under the same conditions as most other aspects of daily civilian life. Instead of peaceful coexistence alongside a war that was taking place elsewhere, art would take up a function within a total effort. The reward would be the production of a post-war, national renaissance of art. The reference to 'Renaissance' by *The Times*, echoed elsewhere, for instance by Phillips, is both revealing and complex. Owing much to nineteenth-century writings such as Jules Michelet's *Histoire de France*, 1855, and Burckhardt's *Civilization of the Renaissance in Italy*, 1860, the term had become specific to a chronological period and particular to a place or location. It was possible to speak of a national renaissance in the arts. The idea of 'renaissance' was associated with prestige, with civilised and civilising values opposed to unreason and darkness, and with a triumph of individual values and achievements dedicated to civic and public ends. It also meant a fresh start, a new beginning, and a rebirth with previous failures and disillusions annulled. The idea of a national renaissance was repeated in the critical reception of *The Nation's War Paintings* at the Royal Academy in 1919 and the triumph of the exhibition was attributed to the work of younger and radical artists such as Wyndham Lewis, C. R. W. Nevinson and William Roberts.

Although at the beginning of the war, modern art was called treasonous, the interesting issue is not the existence of this sort of hostility but that the period also gave rise to calls for moderation and accommodation, a new tolerance of experimental art in the life of the nation which predated official employment. In the first years of the war, perceptions of the avant-garde altered, the art market changed, and there were calls for a national role for art. In this process, ideas about the nation and its art were continuously renegotiated and the notion of a consensus, capable of accommodating established artists and an experimental avant-garde together, began to appear. By 1919, that a national art was consensual and capable of absorbing innovative art had become the dominant view.

Official War Artists

The Glaswegian printmaker and New English Art Club Member Muirhead Bone is now mostly remembered, if at all, as Britain's first official war artist. Accounts by Bone's family and friends are anecdotal, stressing the coincidences and good luck that brought him to the attention of a propaganda organisation called Wellington House just when he was about to be called up. The story goes that in May 1916, at a sale of blank canvases in aid of the Red Cross, the literary agent, A. S. Watt, purchased an option on a work by Bone. He was told by the artist, who was almost forty-one, to settle on the subject matter quickly before Bone was conscripted. Watt worked for Wellington House negotiating with publishers and editors, and suggested employing Bone, sending a letter of reference from Campbell Dodgson, Keeper of Prints and Drawings at the British Museum.[50] Bone's appointment, in July 1916, had some far-reaching, almost extravagant ramifications, leading by the end of 1918 to the inclusion of nearly every significant avant-garde artist in Britain, alongside more enterprising representatives from an older generation, in one sort of official war artist scheme or another. These schemes gave unprecedented scope to modern artists to address their work to the needs of the modern nation state and create new audiences for their art. My concern here is how all this came about, the purposes imagined for the work generated – some 3,000 paintings, drawings and sculptures by 1919–20, including some of the most important British war art in the twentieth century – and what all this might mean for British art.

Bone's position carried a salary of £500 per annum and, so that he could go to the front and see for himself, an honorary commission as a second lieu-tenant because GHQ agreed to receive him as a visitor only if he came in uniform. The plan was for the artist to make drawings for use in propaganda there and then, and as a historical record for the future. The right to reproduce his work was assigned to the Government for the duration of the conflict, while Dodgson was to select drawings for the museum's permanent collection, which incidentally led to Dodgson's participation in almost all the schemes that followed. The Treasury, as ever the principle instrument, sometimes the main obstacle, for making any of the schemes actually happen, sanctioned the expenditure, based on arguments about Bone's altruism in sacrificing his potential earnings as a freelance artist in order to serve his country and the possible gain to the nation's art collections for minimal expense. In August 1916, Bone arrived at the front in France, attached to Intelligence at GHQ.

Wellington House, the organisation that became Bone's employer, was a Propaganda Bureau established in August 1914 to disseminate British views on the war to neutral, and later allied, countries.[51] It was run by the Liberal politician, C. F. G. Masterman, Chancellor of the Duchy of Lancaster and Chairman of the National Health Insurance Commission, who based his Bureau at the offices of the Commission at Wellington House, Buckingham Gate.[52] Masterman, forty years old when war broke out, had had a distinguished political career. Frank Rutter, his contemporary at Cambridge, later recollected that when Masterman was still a student, it was widely supposed he would one day become Prime Minister.[53] He had spent some years as a social worker, university extension lecturer and journalist in London, joining the fashion for slumming it as one of Arnold Toynbee's evangelical student-citizens, Oxford and Cambridge graduates who worked in the often all-male communities of the university settlement houses, in Masterman's case around Camberwell. Their mission, an obligation of privilege, was the advocacy of a citizenship of national culture, uniting all classes in a national community, part of the same philanthropic impulse that fuelled Canon and Henrietta Barnett's Whitechapel Art Gallery established in 1903, itself an extension of the programme at Toynbee Hall, which Masterman knew well. A network of social reformers, with a shared background in the settlement houses and social work, later built the early welfare state when an unprecedented range of social legislation was enacted following the Liberal landslide of 1906, the point when Masterman first entered Parliament as one of the New Liberals. Masterman is now mainly remembered for his analysis of inequality and deprivation among the working classes living in the 'abyss' and the indifference and corruption of the wealth-owning classes, given in his book *The Condition of England*, first published in 1909.[54] The same year, he was appointed Under-Secretary at the Home Office, becoming a close friend of David Lloyd George and working on the National Health Insurance Bill. When he entered the Cabinet early in 1914, a rule, later abolished, obliged him to seek re-election to Parliament. He lost two by-elections in quick succession and had to resign from the Cabinet in February 1915. Thereafter, he ran Wellington House without a position either in Cabinet or in Parliament.

Bone's appointment as official war artist was a matter of good timing, coinciding with a shortage of visual propaganda caused by GHQ's reluctance to allow photographers near the frontline, the imminence of conscription and the scarcity of interesting art in London which created a climate of opinion urging the use of artists in the war. The numbers employed expanded considerably from the beginning of 1917 and, like Bone, they found their way to Wellington House through recommendations and connections. For example, Francis Dodd was employed from February 1917, drawing Generals and later Admirals for a series of publications. Wellington House wanted Bone to do the portraits, needing the illustrations in order to interest neutral nations in personalities, but Bone preferred to draw munitions works and recommended Dodd, who was his brother-in-law.

In December 1916, Asquith resigned as Prime Minister and was replaced by Lloyd George, a turning point in the prosecution of the war. As a consequence of Lloyd George's enquiries into the functioning of the British propaganda effort, a new Department of Information was established in February 1917, headed by John Buchan. Although the Department took it over, Wellington House's status and independence hardly changed. The reorganisation of propaganda greatly facilitated relationships with the Treasury, enabling the numbers of artists employed steadily to increase. When the Commander-in-Chief in Egypt requested an official artist, Dodgson recommended James McBey, who was appointed in April. John Lavery and William

Orpen were championed by Lord Derby, Secretary of State for War; Lavery worked in Britain, Orpen went to France in April and was promoted to Major. C. R. W. Nevinson was helped by his father, the journalist Henry Nevinson, and supported by Bone. He arrived at the front in July 1917. Eric Kennington, endorsed by Dodgson, had made friends with Bone on an unofficial visit to France and had the support of Lavery. He replaced Nevinson at the front in August 1917. Nevinson assisted Paul Nash, who sent letters of recommendation from Eddie Marsh and William Rothenstein. He signed an agreement at the end of October and followed Kennington to the front. Dodgson secured the appointment of William Rothenstein, who was a friend of Kennington. During 1917, Wellington House also published a set of lithographs, *Britain's Efforts and Ideals*, by eighteen artists including Bone, Kennington, Nevinson and Rothenstein as well as Frank Brangwyn, George Clausen, Augustus John and William Nicholson.

There was no organised programme for employing artists. Although some artists who asked for an appointment were turned down,[55] in one sense, rather than Wellington House taking an active role, the artists selected themselves. Muirhead Bone, by applying himself so assiduously to finding an alternative to conscription, almost invented the idea of an official war artist. During 1917, Wellington House was regularly approached by artists, but not inundated, and there was no organised public campaign to expand recruitment. Obtaining Treasury sanction for the expenditure involved was sometimes an issue and artists like Nevinson, Nash, Kennington and Rothenstein worked without a salary. Like the organisation of propaganda as a whole, the appointment of war artists evolved in haphazard manner, in which opportunities were presented and rationalisation subsequently determined.

The state of the nation in 1916–17, absorbed in a total war effort, made the recruitment of official artists easy to assimilate. By the start of 1917, almost half a million British men had been killed in the war,[56] a scale of loss that might be redeemed only by acknowledging that the call to arms had generated a national debt to youth. Artists like Nevinson, Nash and Kennington, because they were young and had seen active service, exercised a special prerogative to depict the war and, by the time of their official employment, each had already exhibited war images in London. In the case of Nevinson in particular, art criticism had begun to argue for consensus and compromise reconciling avant-garde art with an audience learning to be tolerant of visual experimentation dedicated to depicting sights not only unprecedented, but ultimately only knowable to those who had actually participated. Younger artists, and especially avant-garde painters, had acquired a special authority to paint as they did. This climate of conciliation and tolerance predated the inauguration of the official employment of avant-garde artists. Nevinson, Nash and Kennington, together with Lavery, were all published by Wellington House and their employment, less so in the case of Nevinson, was crucial for their later careers as artists. At one level, although Wellington House was a propaganda organisation, employing artists might seem to be scarcely propagandist. Lucy Masterman, Masterman's widow and biographer, declared that the use of artists 'was one of the few pleasures in that grim time.'[57] Recruiting artists saved them from the firing line and, in so far as it is useful to speculate, it is possible to calculate the probability of Nash, Nevinson and Kennington surviving if they had returned to the front as soldiers.[58] When art histories detect a decline in the vigour of the British avant-garde and attribute this to official employment, it is tempting to ask whether it would have been preferable to have had no official artists at all. Rather than regretting the lack of a pure avant-garde, uncompromised by the fact of official employment, it is more fruitful, and much more revealing, to scrutinise how propaganda was construed at Wellington House and ask how the artists' work functioned within its activities.

BRITISH ARTISTS AT THE FRONT

PAUL NASH

PUBLISHED FROM THE OFFICES OF "COUNTRY LIFE," LTD.,
20, TAVISTOCK STREET, COVENT GARDEN, LONDON
AND
GEORGE NEWNES, LTD., 8-11, SOUTHAMPTON STREET, STRAND,
LONDON, W.C. 2

PRICE

5/-

13   Front cover of *British Artists at the Front, Part Three, Paul Nash*, 1918

one

Art, Propaganda and Persuasion at Wellington House

Liberalism and 'Englishness'

When C. F. G. Masterman was asked to establish a pro-paganda agency at Wellington House, he argued that propaganda had to be reasonable and accurate: 'We have determined . . . to present facts and general arguments based upon those facts.'[1] Wellington House pursued a policy of restraint, avoiding extremism and exaggerated rhetoric in favour of informed arguments and measured opinion, even going to the trouble to find material proving that indiscriminate propaganda was ineffective.[2] Its approach to propaganda was in tune with the moderating and conciliatory attitude towards modern art, and younger artists caught up in the maelstrom of war that prevailed in liberal newspapers like the *Manchester Guardian* in 1915. Wellington House commissioned distinguished authors to write pamphlets and books, discreetly circulated through a network of personal mailings and recommendations. When it began to employ war artists, their work was widely promoted, principally through collections of reproductions on a lavish scale. Over two hundred of Muirhead Bone's drawings were reproduced in a ten-part series titled *The Western Front* in 1916 and 1917 and a further series of four books in 1918 called *British Artists at the Front* reproduced work by Nevinson, Nash, Kennington and Lavery. These publications were printed in very large editions, for instance, 30,000 copies of each issue of *The Western Front*: 12,000 for

sale, 6,000 for distribution in the United States and 12,000 for propaganda, as well as numerous additional sets of plates and postcards.[3] The texts for *The Western Front* represented reasonableness and a lack of extremism as specifically English qualities rooted in an experience of English landscape.

In the early months of the war, Wellington House was mainly concerned with promoting British war aims in allied and neutral countries, particularly the U.S.A. During 1915, and coinciding with the publication in May of the Bryce Report into alleged German atrocities in Belgium, Wellington House became involved with disseminating the often salacious and lurid anti-German cartoons by the Dutch illustrator Louis Raemaekers. Published by the pro-war journal *Land and Water*, there were a number of foreign editions, organised and distributed through the Foreign Office. At the same time, Wellington House was beginning to produce its material through British publishers, in part to camouflage the official connection, but also because it was becoming increasingly useful to extend its work to the home front.[4] Although Raemaekers's cartoons were initially thought to be 'too strong meat for the British public', copies were distributed to the Bristol Trade Unions Conference in 1915.[5] An exhibition at the Fine Art Society attracted an astonishing 60,000 visitors in December 1915[6] but a further edition was rejected in November 1916 because it was said 'the later cartoons are such poor stuff both artistically and for propaganda.'[7] By then the need for visual material was being fulfilled by Muirhead Bone.

The propagandist intention of Raemaekers's cartoons is obvious and explicit, recently described as 'precisely the kind of writing that might be expected in wartime accounts of how enemy nations were depicted'.[8] Propaganda, however, was not a predetermined undertaking, but something more organic, at times haphazard and dysfunctional, and frequently ambivalent. As Daniel Pick has noted 'wartime propaganda was itself *active* and often unsettled, a continuing sometimes uneasy attempt to grasp and define national character'.[9] The recruitment of Bone and the publication of his work enabled a shift in the rhetoric of persuasion from the emotive and populist demagogy of Raemaekers to a more measured, seemingly factual representation of indigenous national values, more in tune with Masterman's desire, quite distinct from matters of efficacy, for reasonable and ethical propaganda. How this shift was effected visually can be seen by comparing the different ways Raemaekers's and Nash's works were marketed.

The front cover of Part One of the Land and Water edition of Louis Raemaekers's cartoons reproduces a drawing showing the moment after a rape and a murder (fig. 14). *Thrown to the Swine: The Martyred Nurse* depicts a herd of pigs, anthropomorphized as German officers, drooling over the bound and blood-soaked body of a woman. Rape and defilement are represented indirectly, displaced onto details such as the foreground rump of the pig decorated with an Iron Cross, the rearing boar in the background, the dripping saliva and especially the tongue of the bespectacled pig touching the woman and interrupting the contours of her legs and hips. Although not named, the martyred nurse is Edith Cavell, a British subject working in Belgium who was shot by the occupying Germans in October 1915 for assisting prisoners of war to escape. The drawing was reproduced twice, on the cover and in the book with an explanatory text by the Dean of St Paul's, W. R. Inge. The text alleged a German philosophical tradition for the subordination and abuse of women: 'Nietzsche recommends a whip.' Germany is revealed as a nation that has deserted and desecrated civilised standards, judged by chivalry towards women. Although there is no evidence that Cavell was raped before she was executed, the elabo-

ration of the 'Cavell' myth stressed condemnation of Germany and emphasised the 'otherness' of the enemy, what the accompanying text called the German's 'moral unlikeness to ourselves'.[10] The nation is often imagined as a 'mother country', or as a maternal body that nourishes, and the invasion of a country by an alien, enemy force is described as a violation.[11] Ruth Harris, in her study of the rape of French women in the areas occupied by the Germans, has noted that the First World War was obsessed with rape metaphors, inevitably focused on male anxieties and fantasies.[12] Here Cavell's martyrdom invokes the idea of national defence against a sexualised threat, emphasised by its framing on the bold, even vulgar, black and red cover of *Raemaekers Cartoons* with two medallions of Medusa's head, the primal image for male fear of the sexual power of women, the emblem *par excellence* of fascination with horror.

In contrast, the cover of Part Three of *British Artists at the Front* dedicated to the official art of Paul Nash, reproduces his *We Are Making a New World*, slightly cropped at its edges but in full colour (fig. 13). The picture is not reproduced elsewhere in the publication, nor is it given a title. The design is restrained, listing only Nash's name, the apparent publishers (Country Life and George Newnes) and the price. It was published in 1918 to coincide with an exhibition of Nash's work at the Leicester Galleries, advertised on the back cover together with shows by Eric Kennington, W. T. Wood and, at Agnew's, William Orpen ARA, and it is clearly addressed to an urban middle class. The imprint of Country Life, although not in fact the publishers, endorses its middle class credentials. The subject matter of Raemaekers's drawing and how it is framed in the publication look distasteful beside the discretion and discrimination implied in the design of Nash's book.

Nash's *We Are Making a New World* (fig. 15) is often read as a paradigmatic icon of the destruction and devastation of the First World War, the pictorial equivalent of the writings of the war poets. In this reading, it is the personal and independent vision of an artist expressing the desolation of Passchendaele. It is a transcendent image, uncircumscribed by the historical conditions of its production, that can embody a universal truth, not just about the Great War, but all war, including the unimaginable possibility of nuclear holocaust.[13] Accounts of Nash's work often fail to mention

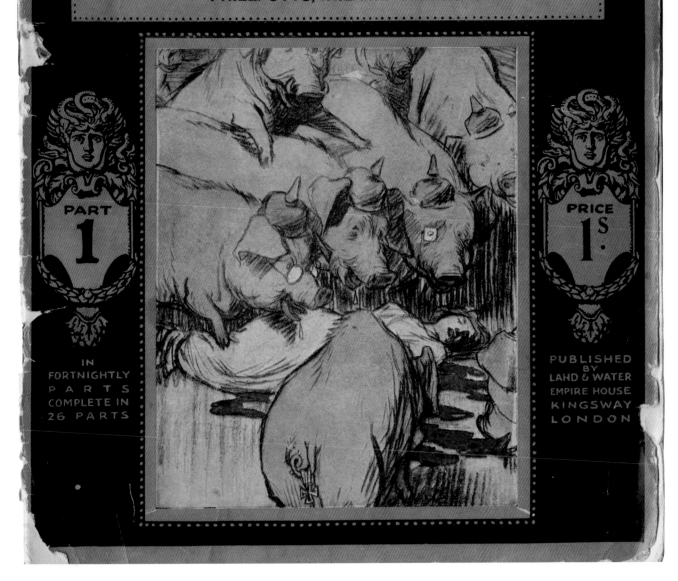

THE · LAND · & WATER · EDITION · OF

RAEMAEKERS CARTOONS

WITH · NOTES · BY

SIR HERBERT WARREN, K.C.V.O., G. K. CHESTERTON, THE
DEAN OF ST. PAUL'S, FATHER BERNARD VAUGHAN, EDEN
PHILLPOTTS, HILAIRE BELLOC

PART
1

IN
FORTNIGHTLY
PARTS
COMPLETE IN
26 PARTS

PRICE
1S.

PUBLISHED
BY
LAND & WATER
EMPIRE HOUSE
KINGSWAY
LONDON

14   Front cover of *The Land and Water Edition of Louis Raemaekers's Cartoons*, 1916

15   Paul Nash, *We Are Making a New World*, 1917–18, oil on canvas, 71.1 × 91.4, Imperial War Museum, London

that *We Are Making a New World* first appeared on the front cover of *British Artists at the Front* and its function in First World War propaganda in 1918 is rarely discussed.[14] In order to stand as an authentic image of war, the painting's use in Government rhetoric or political persuasion has been repressed or explicitly disavowed as something external to the image and outside the intentions and control of the artist. For example, it has been stated recently that 'Nash's despair [after his official visit to the front] was hardly likely to boost the war effort' and therefore his work failed as propaganda, but 'to its credit, the Department of Information provided firm support' for an attitude they were otherwise 'not . . . eager to promote'.[15]

While the situation is more complex than simply conjecturing an innocent Nash somehow pitted against the insensitive dictates of authorities who, except in a moment of uncharacteristic benevolence, were bound to constrain or compromise the artist, it will not do to argue that because Nash's work was produced to be used in propaganda, this must discredit it and implicate the artist. Margaret Nash wrote that Paul Nash suffered from the antipathy of Roger Fry, an antagonism 'centred on the fact that he had painted his war pictures in a spirit of propaganda, and therefore they were classed as journalistic and without aesthetic value'.[16] This cannot be dismissed as a case of Margaret Nash writing defensively about her husband, because she touches on an issue, especially critical for modern art and particularly acute for modern art in war: whether or not how a work of art gets made in the first place, and in what circumstances, determines all its subsequent histories, uses, readings and viewings. Roger Fry maintained that a painting is not an incentive to responsive action but a means to enlarge the imaginative life. It will not be topical nor will it instruct or proselytise. The viewer brings nothing to the encounter with the work of art, which is only what is present on the picture surface.[17] It was on similar grounds that Clement Greenberg, at a later time and another place, facing fascism, argued for avant-garde culture as resistance, not because it was critique but because it was too radically innocent, its inflexibility disabling it from being bent to propagandist use.[18] But all works of art get made to be used, indeed have work to do, and presuppose a response or a reading, including, for Fry and Greenberg, misreading and misuse. As T. J. Clark points out, 'a painting's public life [its being seen] is very far from being extrinsic to it', because its making anticipates context or reading, all the spaces it is meant to inhabit that 'enter and inform the work itself determining its idiom', meaning that some of its making will also be to do with striving to contain the work, attempting, however impossibly, to exclude certain kinds of uses, even audiences.[19]

Nash's work, together with paintings and drawings by other artists such as Bone, Nevinson and Kennington, was produced for a specific moment in which the negotiation of a particular sense of national identity was critical, a matter of life or death. It is a case neither of innocent artists and manipulative authorities nor of sullied practices contaminated by official employment. Instead, there was both a propaganda exercise, the specific instance of production, and there was an excess of meanings, capable of generating other kinds of readings. In a sense *We Are Making a New World* is both official propaganda and an anti-war image. While the issue is complicated by the fact that the success of British propaganda was based on the assumption that the artist functioned as a free agent, untrammelled by the demands of patriotic indoctrination, what counts is that the possibilities for contradictory, even contested meanings, were present from the moment of the work's inception. What is indeterminable, and unproductive to attempt, is stipulating that any particular reading is more authentic or 'truer'.

It is necessary to enquire more deeply into the wider framework of the liberal attitudes to the war and of liberalism in general, in part to get closer to what I meant when I wrote of Masterman's desire for an ethical propaganda, and in part to frame the discussion of Bone's work in *The Western Front* and the four issues of *British Artists at the Front*, especially the third devoted to Nash, which follows. Liberalism is used here not only in the sense of Liberal party politics and its factions but also in broader conceptions of the nature of the state, the relationship of individual rights to the power of the state and formations of nationalism. Liberal ideas about the state, the individual and the nation both informed the way Masterman construed the function and methods of propaganda and encompassed the culture put at stake in campaigns against Germany. The texts accompanying Raemaekers's drawings show something of the Liberal take on the First World War. In the preface to the first issue, the Liberal Prime Minister, Asquith, described the cartoons as giving 'form and colour to the menace which the Allies are averting from the liberty, the civilisation and the humanity of the future'. The editor of the series, Francis Stopford, wrote in the introduction: 'We must fight to the death. Either German philosophy is to be established, and freedom of body, mind, and soul crushed beneath the iron heel of Prussian Kultur or else, at whatever the cost, this fearful menace to the peace and liberty of nations and individuals has to be destroyed root and branch.'[20] Three points emerge very forcefully from this: first, the Liberals construed the First World War as a defensive fight against military aggression; second, it represented a conflict of cultural values; third, not only physical freedom was at stake, but an entire liberal heritage of freedom of thought and expression.

Wellington House's main activity was the production and dissemination of literature in which Government connections were suppressed,[21] because the indiscriminate and open broadcast of propaganda was said to characterise the methods of the Germans and to have damaged their cause. Staffed mainly by civil servants but including academics and MPs who volunteered their services, Wellington House drew on a network of writers, university teachers, literary agents and publishers representative of the intelligentsia. The literature was intended to appeal to educated readers, 'the principle being that it is better to influence those who can influence others than to attempt a direct appeal to the mass of the population.'[22] As a fraction of the dominant classes identified as opinion leaders and policy makers, such an educated audience was trained to make up its own mind on the basis of facts and reasoned arguments and would therefore respond only to a propaganda founded on principles of independent judgement. Defined by virtue of its forms of address, the conduct of propaganda could therefore aspire not to seem an unethical matter. So long as the war was construed as an obligation and a duty, British propaganda was a defensive activity involving only 'the interpretation, in theory and practice, of what German militarism stands for, and the emphasis of the ruin which would come upon all the free countries, if the Germanic powers and their allies should prove victorious'.[23] It was later stated that Masterman 'objected to . . . the demand that his department should lose all integrity or sense as a condition of the work they were doing'.[24]

There were, however, a number of ambivalences about the idea of liberalism, war and the state. There was a potential conflict of means and ends implied in arguments about the discharge of obligations to defenceless nations and the possibility that resistance to militarism might involve surrender to its methods. Similarly, the war involved restrictions on personal liberties, such as freedom of movement and information, central to the tradition of liberalism. At the heart of these contradictions was a more long-standing crisis in the ability of the liberal state to continue to represent social and political stability. In the years before the war, nineteenth-century liberal ideas about the laissez-faire state as a negative power, charged with overseeing and preserving the free play of the market and individual freedoms including the right to individual property, had begun to be displaced. Liberalism could no longer accommodate either the vastly expanded role of Britain as an Imperial power with worldwide obligations or the pressure for representation from newly urbanised masses, excluded from property, voicing different and alternative class interests. Liberal intellectuals began to call for the necessity for state intervention and collectivism in the management of capitalism, arguing that individualism could be preserved only within a concern for the welfare of the wider community. In other words, the exercise of individual liberty was seen to involve duties as well as rights and meant an egalitarian extension of civil enfranchisement in the interests of collective well-being.

This position was identified with the New Liberalism of academics and intellectuals such as Hobson and Hobhouse writing for *Nation* and including Masterman as well as writers such as Galsworthy, Bennett and Wells, all involved with Wellington House. In 1905, Masterman had called for a new, inclusive national spirit with 'a particular concern in the well being of England and the English people; a pride in its ancient history, its ancient tradition, the very language of its grey skies and rocky shores. . . . The assertion will be of a spiritual democracy, with a claim for every English man and woman and child to some share in the great inheritance which England has won.' It would be founded on a 'bedrock' of social reform.[25] New Liberalism would not negate 'the inherited ethos of liberalism. Its trajectory was evolutionary, its driving-force idealist and ethical.' Its policies were not socialist, however, because the New Liberals were opposed to analyses that privileged one set of class interests against the common good.[26]

The Liberal Government elected in 1906 introduced massive extensions to state power, not only through welfare provisions but also in the form of increasingly centralised control of manufacture and industry and the central management of information. Acts like the Official Secrets Act of 1911 and the Defence of the Realm Act (DORA), enacted as measures to preserve state security at the outbreak of the war, permitted the Government to manipulate access to and the dissemination of information. The interests of the state became increasingly identified with the state apparatus, its Government and Ministries, rather than with a democratically accountable Parliament.[27] Similarly, the First World War, as an occasion necessitating greatly increased state powers in the organisation and regulation of society, was also the point at which propaganda became an intrinsic rather than a subsidiary function in warfare. For example, Peter Chalmers Mitchell argued in his entry on 'Propaganda' for the *Encyclopaedia Britannica* in 1922 that modern nations could not hope to conduct a protracted war that drained national resources unless public opinion was favourable. The authority and stability of the state had to be maintained by persuasion not compulsion. In a summary that reiterates the main tenets of Wellington House's programme, Chalmers Mitchell, who was involved in War Office propaganda, set out the nature of the arguments the state needed to organise in order to present failure to support the war it was prosecuting as an act of bad faith contrary to the general welfare of all:

> It will not neglect the moral appeal. It will insist that the war is one of defence, or at least for an unselfish purpose; that victory will be for the good of the world, will be a permanent triumph of right over wrong. At the same time, . . . it will insist on . . . material benefits to be derived from victory, appalling consequences of defeat. The outrageous conduct of the enemy, his unnecessary cruelty, his breach of international law are all important.[28]

The Defence of the Realm Act curtailed access to information, at first as a defensive measure to prevent the circulation of information useful to an enemy. It was then extended to prohibit the dissemination of statements likely to cause disaffection or to prejudice recruitment. DORA regulations, as well as enabling a wide range of restrictions and controls on things like lighting and food, also provided a mechanism to censor and suppress dissenting views from early in the war. Furthermore a report in *The Times*, passed by the censor, that revealed demoralising details of the British retreat from Mons, led to the exclusion of journalists from the front and a dearth of news reporting mitigated only partially by the establishment of official correspondents at GHQ in 1915.[29] In the event, not only did the national press tend to be loyal and patriotic, but the only source of information available that might arbitrate between conflicting interpretations of the causes and events of the war was controlled by the Government. Masterman's policy of official veracity caused no conflict with the one ultimate vindication of war. The radical liberal conscience was appeased.[30]

The idea of self-defence, allied to a national mission to save the world, is an important component in promoting collectivism together with the fiction of a singular and united national identity. Marwick describes DORA as 'the very embodiment of the theory of national self-defence: it did not itself, in its original form, involve any solid collectivist experimentation with industry or society, but it was, as it were, the unsubstantial awning under which the bits and pieces of collectivist organization could be built up.'[31] In part, national identity could be defined by

naming the characteristics of its antithesis – the enemy. However, the circulation of exaggerated imagery, the stereotyping of other nationalities on racial and discriminatory grounds, ran counter to the policy at Wellington House to prepare propaganda representing reasoned and objective views. Instead, implied in the promotion of reasonable arguments for educated audiences, was a view of the moderateness of free-thinking Englishmen. It was a view of England and Englishness that originated in the anti-Imperialist politics of the New Liberals, sometimes termed 'Little Englanders', and which had coalesced around abhorrence at the jingoism of the Boer War and support for Irish Home Rule. The patriotism of the New Liberals has been described as an island *patria*, while their foreign *patria* 'was an oppressed national right.'[32]

'Englishness' could also be invested in a specific construction of an English landscape. The period from about 1880 to the 1920s has recently been extensively discussed as a time when 'Englishness' was created or rather remade and recast. A component in this forging of modern Englishness was the discovery of rural England and the reinvention of an image of the countryside.[33] Rural England was identified with 'South Country', the name of a book by Edward Thomas published in 1909 and a poem by Hilaire Belloc of 1910. 'South Country' was characterised by a domesticated and fertile garden landscape, small pockets of land enclosed by neat hedgerows and the village hamlet nestling in a rolling landscape with no extremes of height, flatness or extensiveness. It was not specific to southern England and could encompass Shropshire but exclude Cornwall. The rural image has an association with the conservative and anti-progressive, but, as Alex Potts has argued, images of countryside were pervasive in many European nations as well as England because they 'could accommodate a variety of different responses, not just celebratory notions of an ideal England purged of social and political tensions'.[34] For Masterman and others, the rural was a resource of hope under threat from neglect offering the potential of well-being in a cooperative rather than competitive community.[35]

On the one hand, countryside images could be mobilised in wartime to promote a nationalistic hatred of outsiders. On the other hand, a feeling for a countryside under threat could also motivate a sense of self-defence as self-love and self-sacrifice that transcended not only individual self-preservation but also the obvious incidental causes of war in favour of an abstracted essence of Englishness located in the country. Hence Edward Thomas could articulate his motivation for fighting in a poem called 'This is No Case of Petty Right or Wrong':

> But with the best and meanest Englishmen
> I am one in crying, God save England, lest
> We lose what never slaves and cattle blessed.
> The ages made her that made us from dust:
> She is all we know and live by, and we trust
> She is good and must endure, loving her so:
> And as we love ourselves we hate her foe.[36]

Or close his essay 'This England' with a thought 'that overpowered thought' that he had never loved England unless he was prepared to die for it: 'Something I had omitted. Something, I felt, had to be done before I could look again composedly at English landscape, at the elms and poplars about the houses, at the purple-headed wood-betony with two pairs of dark leaves on a stiff stem, who stood sentinel among the grasses or bracken by hedge-side or wood's-edge. What he stood sentinel for I did not know, any more than what I had got to do.'[37] Alex Potts states that mobilising images of rural England 'could sometimes backfire as a propaganda exercise. If the troops in the trenches during the First World War were supposed to be fighting for an ideal England of unspoiled countryside, this image could also become a vivid reproach to the ugly inhuman landscapes of death and desolation that the war was creating.'[38] This was not necessarily the case. What Potts's account obscures is how the more despoiling the impact of the war on the foreign territory of France was, the more urgent the necessity to evoke and defend an English sanctuary might become. What his account overlooks is how much this antithesis of war landscape and home country was animated within the drawings and paintings of official war artists with their accompanying texts. The ravaging and annihilating effect of war was represented not just by independent artists drawing their own conclusions but by artists as free agents functioning as part of the propaganda promoted by Wellington House.

★   ★   ★

The Western Front

Muirhead Bone arrived in France in August 1916. He returned home at the end of the year to make drawings of munition works, going back to France in April 1917 until the beginning of June, when he travelled to Glasgow to draw shipyards. He produced prodigious quantities of drawings and prints based on first-hand observation until exhaustion forced him to stop in October 1917.

Bone was unnerved by his first sight of battle, the Somme offensive that opened on 1 July 1916.[39] He did not serve as a soldier, however, and the forms of his drawings suggest the detachment of a travelogue composed by an uninvolved spectator. In *The Battle of the Somme* (fig. 16), he used a conventional topographical device – a dark foreground land mass rising to the the left of the picture against a broad light horizon and a large sky. The viewer surveys the prospect from a distance. Intersecting wedges of light and dark lead the eye into the recesses of the picture where the battle is represented by puffs and wisps of smoke on the horizon. The illustrations are drawn broadly in loose charcoal strokes and given body by sombre brown and grey washes. Bone himself later insisted that he drew only from observation which resulted in work that was 'limited' and 'prosaic'.[40]

In other drawings from his visits in 1916, Bone depicted war scenes, such as the ruins of Ypres, dugouts and officers' messes with the directness and appeal of sketchbook drawings. Sometimes a war context is supplied only by the title: *Distant View of Ypres*, for instance. Drawings from his trip in spring 1917, following the German retreat to the Hindenburg Line, are more confident and more finished than the work of 1916. Rather than quick sketches of the war in progress, he concentrated on setting down the havoc and destruction wrought in the now deserted Somme area. The drawings use a consistent compositional device of a single building, a ruined church or château acting as a focal point and set back in the pictorial space behind a foreground filled with wreckage and detritus. That Bone has witnessed what he depicts is affirmed by the way the drawings survey the sights, using the codes found in graphic art and photography of a topographical and antiquarian tradition for the depiction of ruins. The sites are specific and identified; figures are rare, appearing only as staffage to frame a

16   Muirhead Bone, *The Battle of the Somme*, 1916, Plate VI, *The Western Front*

prospect and provide scale: the evidence of destruction, for example in *The Great Crater, Athies* (fig. 17), is never exaggerated; lighting is clear and even; the viewer is placed in a position of surveillance and dominance. These drawings are not romantic invocations of the sublime. Ruins are also metaphors for transience, however, and Bone's drawings sometimes include signs of temporary graves, always of allied soldiers, and evoke remembrance. Ruined buildings are set amongst broken trees or wrecked gardens and the elements of architecture and nature are equally weighted. The drawings play on the permeability of culture and nature or how ruins symbolise transience at the same time as they also suggest decay arrested and immortalised. In this way, Bone's depictions of the Western front take on a permanence that is distanced in time

17   Muirhead Bone, *The Great Crater, Athies, May 1917*, charcoal on paper, 55.8 × 76.2, Imperial War Museum, London

while their documentary realism functions to create what Charles Merewether has termed 'a blind spot, obscuring the complicity of technologies of representation in technologies of destruction'.[41]

On the whole, Bone's drawings look like impartial records, carefully witnessed and meticulously detailed from sights seen at first hand: the legibility of the drawings places them firmly within established, orthodox practices; space is continuous and the compositions balanced; and the work is reasonable and factual. Bone was described as an artist who 'inclines to inform rather than suggest'.[42] The lack of finish in the sketches, however, is evidence of the artist's touch, evoking the immediacy of capturing a changeable landscape and emphasising that the work is unpretentious, genuine and personally observed, not fabricated. It was a kind of stylistic paraphrase for the moderateness of free thinking and rational Englishmen.

Bone's work had an authority in complete contrast to the emotive and dramatic character of Raemaekers's topical and violent imaginative cartoons. Where Raemaekers's drawings were published with lengthy texts by a varied collection of British writers, the homogeneity of Bone's output in *The Western Front* was substantiated by the introductions and notes to the plates supplied by C. E. Montague at GHQ.

It seems to have been Bone's idea that he and Montague might collaborate to produce illustrated texts on the basis of Montague's knowledge of the front line, and a rapport between them established after only two weeks at the front: 'we are thrown very much together'.[43] Montague was a leader writer and critic with the *Manchester Guardian*, married to the daughter of the editor, C. P. Scott. The son of an Irish Catholic ex-priest, Montague was a committed Liberal and a man of deep religious convictions. He was one of the most respected journalists of his day and right-hand man to Scott. Although the *Manchester Guardian* had argued initially against intervention, once war became inevitable both the paper and Montague professed the view that British entry was both righteous and essential for the defence of civilisation.[44] Although over age, Montague enlisted early. After a short career in the ranks, including three weeks in the trenches, he requested an Intelligence job. As a second lieutenant in the lower levels of Intelligence at GHQ, he was responsible for conducting visitors seeing the sights in France. He worked in close contact with the official press correspondents and became their censor in 1917. Montague's career and qualifications made him almost the archetypal New Liberal, an intellectual and moral complement at the front to Masterman in Wellington House.

In the introduction to the first part of *The Western Front*, Montague establishes for the reader how the French landscape occupied by the British front line resembles three regions of England. These are the area between the Somme and Arras, like Salisbury Plain, where 'journeys on foot seem long, as they do on our downs, because so much of the road before you is visible while you march'; north of Arras, a mining district, is compared with parts of Wigan; and near Ypres, a level sandy area is likened to Rye and Winchelsea.[45] English rural locations are evoked to give a sense of the place and the scale of the front line. The Somme battlefield is 'about as high as the Hog's Back in Surrey'.[46] The experience of the English countryside to any reader familiar with its representations sets the mood for understanding war as an interruption into the normality of rural reverie. Describing the hour before dawn on 9 April 1917 near Arras, he writes how night-time sounds such as the grumbling of guns and the 'short run of the woodpecker taps of a Lewis gun' had become so routine that the war seemed to be taking its rest 'as in quiet places in England you seem to hear the earth breathing in its sleep when the only sound at night is the bark of the distant fox, or an owl calling'. When battle began, it was like the breaking of a sudden storm.[47]

Pastoral references became a conventional antithesis to the destructiveness of war, pastoral images becoming sources of comfort and consistent motifs in writings by serving soldiers.[48] Twenty-three-year-old Stephen Hewett wrote one month before the opening of the Somme offensive, seven weeks before his own death:

We are taught laboriously to make sorrows for one another and to tear up and harass the earth, but after a single spring the traces of the past are overwhelmed by a riot of growth 'which labours not,' and in their place spring up the poppies of oblivion. The trenches which in February were grim and featureless tunnels of gloom, without colour or form, are already over-arched and embowered with green. You may walk from the ruins of a cottage, half hidden in springing green, and up to the Front line trenches through a labyrinth of Devonshire lanes.[49]

At once, a well-schooled Arcadian *memento mori* is set up as fatality and consolation, and relocated to a specified English countryside.

In Montague's writing, once the measure of northern French Englishness is established, the war intrudes to bring 'strange violences' and 'degrees of desolation' leading in an ascending scale to the front line, 'the ultimate desert where nothing but men and rats can live'.[50] War not only turns the rural into the urban,[51] it inverts the normal order of the world and infests the apparently reassuring with malignancy. In a note to accompany an otherwise unexceptional

18 Muirhead Bone, *Road Liable to be Shelled*, 1916, Plate XXVIIb, *The Western Front*

drawing, *Road Liable to be Shelled* (fig. 18), the reader is told that 'the whole drawing is remarkably instinct with the artist's sense of a malign invisible presence – a "terror that walketh by noonday" – infesting the sunny vacant length of the forbidden road.'[52]

Malignancy gives way to horror never overstated and almost possible to overlook. Deserted trenches contain the detritus of prolonged warfare, 'fragments of shell, displaced sand-bags, broken stretchers, boots not quite empty . . .'.[53] Even evidence of the industrial nature of war can be reworked into rural imagery to provide an image of obscenity by a parody of the rural. The contributions of women workers produce munitions that level tangled wire where once 'the corpses of whole platoons of our men were hung up to rot and look,

from far off, like washing put out to dry on thorned hedges'.[54]

The most evocative and extended discussion of the malignancy of war occurs in Montague's invocation of the Somme battlefield: 'No eloquence has yet conveyed the disquieting strangeness of the portent. You can enumerate many ugly and queer freaks of the destroying powers . . . But no piling up of sinister detail can express the sombre and malign quality of the battlefield landscape as a whole. "It makes a goblin of the sun." '[55] The quotation is from Rossetti's poem 'Jenny', a complex multilayered meditation by a young male narrator over the sleeping form of a prostitute. It appears in a comparison of a good and a fallen woman, metaphorical vessels both shaped by the potter from the same clay.[56] In a recent discussion of Rossetti's themes of fallen women, Linda Nochlin points out how 'Jenny' fades from view in the poem becoming 'a cipher' for man's lust and a riddle.[57] Montague's own use of this disturbing and disruptive line implies a metaphor for war as corruption and prostitution. The spirit of the war calling men to volunteer, or sometimes as an avenging figure, was nearly always a woman, Bellona or Minerva, but not Mars.[58] Nochlin observes in connection with Rossetti, the masculine 'fallen' means an honourable death in war, whereas a 'fallen' woman has participated in vice and unauthorised sexual activity. In Montague's prose, the suggestion that war corrupts like a prostitute is averted by the introduction of a further antithesis. The aberrant effects of war are mitigated: ' "It makes a goblin of the sun" – or it might if it were not peopled in every part with beings so reassuringly and engagingly human, sane and reconstructive as British soldiers.'[59]

The image of stoicism and decency, essentially English qualities, can be set against 'Germanness' to propose a contrast between wilful deliberation and inventive endurance of involuntary circumstances so that features of the front line reflect national landscape embedded in national character. Montague contrasts the trenches of the two sides, pointing out the regularity of the German defences, built as though by a single contractor with an overall design in mind. English trenches are altogether more organic affairs and the accumulation of individual improvisation in the making of personal niches more haphazard but more expressive. Montague describes them with images that recur in his writings. British Tommies in the trenches are 'good campers-out'. The trenches themselves echo English country lanes where 'each farmer has made gates and hedges to his own mind'.[60] Camping out in trenches, said Montague, was like a boyish outdoor adventure.[61] Although conscription had been introduced in 1916, until early 1917 the war was still being fought by a volunteer army. In his own account of being a soldier, Montague describes how enlistment meant the elimination of choices and responsibilities so that existence became immensely simple, remote from the complexities of civilian life. It was like a second boyhood.[62]

Furthermore, the Germans use means dishonourable by European standards. Montague tells the reader that there is a difference between the random effects of shell fire and the deliberate destruction of retreating Germans in the ruins of buildings, a difference difficult for the untutored eye to detect in Bone's descriptive scenes of demolition. Although told through the impartial authority of 'the staff' that the German destruction is a legitimate and objective tactic of organised retreat 'when you look into German demolitions between the Scarpe and Aisne, you feel that many things here were done not in cold blood but something worse.'[63]

Montague's texts interpret Bone's descriptive drawings. Through appellation and interpellation, the reader is recruited to the text as eye witness and as civilian soldier on active service: 'Soon you take it for granted that German shells miss, . . . you reflect on its cost to the German taxpayer.'[64] This is not a case, however, of Montague's texts alone turning the drawings into propaganda, as is sometimes argued.[65] Montague's writing is skilful and intelligent. It is allusive and literary, implying a high degree of personal integrity. But the text cannot stand alone and the drawings and the writing are not separable. The realism, uniformity and appeal to truthfulness of Bone's work legitimate the text. Montague's writing depends as much on the sketches to evoke the visuality of its imagery as the sketches depend on the writing to imprint their textuality, their telling of the sights they witness. Works of art are read and writing is seen.

When *The Western Front* was published in book form, the consumption of the prose and pictures became a solitary and private activity. Informed by the text, the reader addresses the sights through the eyes of Bone and Bone's pictures provide their own authority.

The drawings are both objective and rational and they are the first-hand sketches of a professional and experienced artist. The sketches draw on the stylistic codes of topography to assert their objectivity but unlike, for instance, photographs, they are also personal. The evidence of the practice of the craft is delineated in the sketchiness of the work evoking the sincerity of fine art to give the text credibility that underlines the personal appeal of Montague's words: 'when you look . . .'.

Montague's writings also reveal self-doubt and a sensitivity to anomaly that could be heightened to irony, characteristic of liberal attitudes to war. The war had created a dilemma for liberal opinion that Montague tried to resolve in the preface to the second volume of *The Western Front*, formulated in letters to his wife and written late in 1917. Titled 'War as it is', Montague addressed the question of whether Bone 'uses his art . . . for weaving some sort of web of beautiful untruth over your eyes, lest you should see and know "war as it is"'. Although, Montague argued, war was something first to be avoided, once it was inevitable it must be won 'by every honourable means', an obligation that had increased since 1914 with the escalating debt to those who had already given their lives. The function of art was an affirmation of the value and validity of the renewal of life that must follow the winter of death and sacrifice. The ultimate vindication would be the coming of the time when those who had made the most direct contribution would be summoned again to 'help . . . re-make the old world as eagerly as they have helped to save and clean it'.[66]

This was a reiteration of early cultural motivations for war as a purification. The boyhood adventure of life in the trenches for 'good campers-out' had its own reward in 'the re-discovery, every year, of the sun. Some day in March it is suddenly found to have a miraculous warmth, and everybody off duty comes out like the bees and stands about in the trench, sunning his head and shoulders in the tepid rays and adoring – quite inarticulately – and feeling that all's well with the world. A winter in the trenches revives, in us children of civilisation, a pre-Promethean rapture of love for the sun . . .'[67]

The promise of war is the rediscovery of innocence before experience. Spring sunshine, to those purged by the deprivations of war, comes as a benediction and, ultimately, the promise of resurrection and redemption.

The text of *The Western Front* assembled sets of antitheses within which to construct a rationale for the war and to articulate national war experience. War landscape was contrasted with home country, normality set against malignancy. Like English landscape, facets of English national character were represented as lacking extremism and as revealing a national personality that was undogmatic and sincere. The direct and unpretentious look of Bone's sketchbook drawings functioned with the text to make visible the decency of the English war effort. Whereas Montague was not named as the author of the text, dated and signed 'G.H.Q., France.', authorship of the drawings and therefore of *The Western Front* enterprise was attributed to Bone and the persona of the artist was represented as an unassuming presence underlining and guaranteeing the continuity of the publication and affirming the authenticity of image and text.

The literary density of Montague's writing, however, had moved beyond Bone's unpretentious drawings. The limitations of his work are obvious in his drawing *Road Liable to be Shelled* (fig. 18) which is comprehensible only because the inscription is on the drawing itself. Paul Nash, who depicted landscapes that had been shelled, made paintings that now symbolise the Great War as a national trauma. The publication and exhibition of his work in 1918 became the visual realisation of Montague's scholarly and principled texts.

British Artists at the Front

When Bone stopped producing drawings as a result of exhaustion, the pantheon of Generals and Admirals commissioned from Francis Dodd in January 1917 was already in the process of publication as collections of portraits with short biographical studies. What replaced *The Western Front*, however, was not Dodd's work but a new series *British Artists at the Front*, each edition featuring the work of a single artist.[68] The title itself signalled a shift in emphasis and augmented an appeal to the specialised and partial vision of individual artists implied but not stressed in *The Western Front*. Four artists, Nevinson, Lavery, Nash and Kennington, were published until the demise of Wellington House, following its incorporation into the Ministry of Information, halted the programme.

The format of *British Artists at the Front* followed that of *The Western Front* with a contextualising essay signed

19 Front Cover of *British Artists at the Front, Part One, C. R. W. Nevinson*, 1918

and dated from GHQ and a collection of plates with commentaries by Montague, now identified as the author on the title page. Biographical essays were also added, each headed by a picture of the artist, self-portraits by Nevinson and Kennington, a lithograph of Lavery by Flora Lion and a drawing of Nash by William Rothenstein. The biographies of Nevinson and Kennington were by Campbell Dodgson, who had selected the drawings for *The Western Front* and continued to be directly involved in the production of the new publication. Robert Ross was commissioned to write about Lavery and John Salis (Jan Gordon) on Nash. The essays established a set of credentials for each painter to confirm the credibility of what was depicted. In particular, the essays assembled the components of artistic personality. The format of *British Artists at the Front* (fig. 19) constructed a reading of the reproductions as self-evident truth about the war both because they expressed the integrated persona of the artist, based on a romantic cult of individualism, and because they visualised actualities confirmed in an independent written account authorised by GHQ.

Descriptions of each artist's training emphasised the inadequacy of conventional educational attainment for measuring individual artistic development. Accounts of origins, training and influences sustained a notion that each painter's evolution was both non-conforming and self-sufficient, an attribute guaranteeing an independent perspective, disinterested but not impersonal, uncommercial but not unsuccessful, to representations of war. Dodgson stated that Nevinson's training at the Slade was less valuable for the rigour of the school's instruction in draughtsmanship than the stimulus of mutual exchange with his contemporary students, described by Dodgson as 'gifted'.[69] The essay devoted most of its text to explicating Nevinson's avant-gardism while stressing his quest for intelligibility. Gordon described Nash's inadequacy in mathematics and his failure to enter a naval career (evidence frequently cited in subsequent literature on Nash and derived from Nash himself).[70] He then recounted the artist's 'discovery' in an evening class by William Rothenstein, who also supplied the portrait heading the article, in terms of a rescue from another alien and vulgar destiny. The brilliance of the Slade generation contemporaraneous with Nash and advice by William Richmond that directed Nash to landscape were mentioned, but Nash emerged in Gordon's account as a virtual autodidact.[71]

Lavery, unlike Nash, Nevinson and Kennington, was an older and more established artist, but Ross narrated the vicissitudes of Lavery's early career and his humble origins in Belfast and Glasgow as a series of struggles with adversity to be offset against the facility evident in Lavery's painting: 'Few modern painters have experienced a more romantic career . . .'.[72] Like Nash, academic failure, in particular in mathematics, was the special attribute of unworldly artists.[73] Lavery's commercial success was read as the coincidental consequence of talent and Ross played down Lavery's status and knighthood by presenting him as something of an outsider who, because he was only an ARA, still lacked recognition in England.

A further layer of qualification was indicated in accounts of the artists' war service. 'He played his part', said Dodgson of Nevinson's discharge with rheumatic fever, while Nash made his first independent war drawings 'partly in Hospital.'[74] Furthermore, all three of the younger artists were prequalified by virtue of producing a body of 'unofficial' war painting. The reader was to understand that it was the War Office that had accommodated the artists, not the artists who had accommodated themselves to official demands, and that their appointments were the result of popular acclaim over the veracity of their independent work. Kennington's *The Kensingtons at Laventie* (see fig. 12) of 1915 was described as autobiographical, witnessed and accurate because painted with 'a heart moved deeply by share and experience of suffering and hardship.' Furthermore, Kennington had returned voluntarily to the front to make drawings on a visit 'unofficial and hampered by many obstacles'.[75] Dodgson described Nevinson's 'enforced leisure' as an altruistic sacrifice leading to works that had been widely celebrated in London for their truthful rendering of war experience and their ability to incite the viewer to perform his war service.[76]

The biographical essays established a framework for viewing the reproductions through the specialised vision of artists. Montague contributed perspectives on the pictures from the point of view of the front line. Three of Montague's essays reworked ideas from *The Western Front*. 'Trench Housekeeping', written to introduce Kennington's drawings, elaborated the theme of improvisation and makeshift existence germane to the notion of trench warfare as 'camping-out' (fig. 20). 'The Front's Foundations' prefaced Lavery's paintings of the home front by setting up a contrast between the magnitude and extent of the industrialised home effort and the view of soldiers as an antithesis of city and country, centre and periphery. Trenches represented the 'finger-tips', aware only dimly of 'the power of the muscles of the heart', while 'a soldier coming to England on leave from the front sometimes feels rather insignificant and abashed, like a villager on his first day in a capital.'[77] Nevinson's collection provided the occasion for an essay titled 'War Aeroplanes' in which Montague represented flying officers as a new romantic element in the fighting forces, removed from ordinary soldiers by class difference and the unconventional and untraditional nature of flying itself, prefiguring film representations of the RAF in the Second World War.

When Montague came to write his essay on Nash's work, however, he changed tack to use his text to test

20 Eric Kennington, *Raider with a Cosh*, 1917, pastel on paper, 62.9 × 47, Tate, London, presented by the Contemporary Art Society, 1925

the veracity, taken for granted in the other essays, of Nash's representational means. Gordon's biographical introduction had classed Paul Nash in the category of prophetic artists, isolated individuals with an innate message to future generations many of whose insights never found an audience. Blake was cited as an obvious precursor. Nash was therefore established as an exemplar of the romantic tradition. Montague's essay was entitled 'Strange, But True', a reference to a verse from Byron's 'Don Juan', emphasising the construction of a romantic framework for reading Nash's work.[78]

Montague set out to answer his own opening statement: 'Some fault will be found with what Lieut. Paul Nash has done here.' About *Sunrise: Inverness Copse* (fig. 22), Montague informed the reader that 'If you examined the place, in comfort and at leisure, with the eye of a competent, literal land-surveyor, you would

find in it all sorts of forms, which have been left out or distorted in Mr Nash's harsh epitome.' Drawing on an analogy with Pilgrim's Progress, Montague related the 'bedevilled and macabre' vision conveyed by Nash to the nervous, internalised view that a soldier would experience during the duress of a night patrol or following lengthy sentry duty in the cold before dawn when the body was at its lowest ebb. The visions were the product of a heightened sensibility hallucinating under stress.[79] Montague referred again to Byron to state how 'life and art had changed places and life illustrated, as well as it could, the fantasies of a fanatic's allegory'.[80] Montague's unease continued in his qualifications about Nash's style, writing that 'other means perhaps might have gained the end better'. Commenting on *Crater Pools, Below Hill 60* (fig. 21) Montague saw Nash, 'Using the right of art to turn ugly things, as Ophelia did, "to fashion and to prettiness"',[81] implying that the coherence of stylistic means gained its own credibility, distinct from content, allowing escape from unpalatable truths in the refuge of intrinsic formal qualities.

An ambivalence also marks Nash's own views of the war with implications for his war drawings and paintings, and it may be, as John Rothenstein remarked, that Nash never settled on a consistent attitude towards the war.[82] *Sunrise: Inverness Copse* was a significant image for Nash and the basis of the painting *We are Making a New World* (see fig. 15). On the back of a photograph of the drawing sent for censorship, Nash wrote:

21 Paul Nash, *Crater Pools, Below Hill 60*, chalk and watercolour, 25.4 × 35.6, private collection

22   Paul Nash, *Sunrise: Inverness Copse*, 1918, pastel on brown paper, 25.76 × 36.2, Imperial War Museum, London

The most dreadful place I ever saw. The sun was just breaking white pale shafts of light. Against it stood gaunt broken trees they seemed to reel. The ground as far as the eye could see was churned & twisted, gouged and heaped in fearful shapes. My guides would not let me stay longer: no man lingers in this country, they move hurriedly up & down the duck-boards or leaping from mound to mound. as if they were hunted. Sometimes they sink in the mud and then it is most difficult to help them out. I heard of a man sunk in the mud up to his chin: they were feeding him there. [K]eeping him alive. [T]hey couldn't get him out.[83]

When Nash was posted to France he told his wife that he was happiest in the trenches discovering a zest for life and that beauty was more poignant.[84] He told

Rothenstein when he returned home with a broken rib that he had had a wonderful time in France.[85] After he was appointed as an official war artist, Nash developed a sense of messianic urgency. Evidence for this comes from a letter to his wife that is cited frequently:

Sunrise and sunset are blasphemous, they are mock-eries to men, only the black rain out of the bruised and swollen clouds all through the bitter black of night is fit atmosphere in such a land. . . . the shells never cease. They alone plunge overhead, . . . anni-hilating, maiming, maddening, they plunge into the grave which is this land; one huge grave, and cast upon it the poor dead. It is unspeakable, godless, hopeless. I am no longer an artist interested and curious, I am a messenger who will bring back word from the men who are fighting to those who want the war to go on for ever. Feeble, inarticulate, will be my message, but it will have a bitter truth, and may it burn their lousy souls–.[86]

This statement is the concluding paragraph of the last letter from a selection dating from 1917 that Margaret Nash published to fill out the details of Nash's unfinished autobiography *Outline*. The autobiography consists of chapters about the early part of Nash's life up to 1913 and notes for the period to 1936. The book was begun in 1936 or 1937 and Nash worked on it through 1941, probably adding little after this date. He died in 1946.[87] Margaret Nash and Herbert Read put together the book published in 1949. Read added a selection of Nash's published articles. The book, like all autobiographies, recounts past events from the distance and perspective of maturity but it is also a product of the late 1930s and the Second World War. As Andrew Causey points out, in his introduction to the reprint, it 'also speaks for the moment in the England . . . when instability and war gave rise to a mood of national introspection in the arts. Many artists and writers were searching for the roots of Englishness in landscape, which is a main preoccupation of *Outline*.' The autobiography, as Causey puts it, 'presents a world of stable values'.[88] Read's foreword to *Outline* also explained the incompleteness of the text as evidence of a closure on a lost stability: 'As he approached a second war, and finally became involved in it, Paul Nash felt an increasing reluctance to expend his energies in the resurrection of a past that might have no future.'[89]

Citing *Outline*, including the letters and texts, as reflecting direct, unmediated evidence for Nash in the First World War must therefore be undertaken with some circumspection. Rather, *Outline* represents at least a double perspective. It is a retrospective view of the period in England up to and including the First World War that is vividly recalled in private letters edited into a narrative that concludes tellingly with Nash's 'godless, hopeless' message. It is a reflection on the nature and meaning of the Second World War by a comparison with that earlier war, more clearly perceived as a national trauma with the benefit of hindsight. In particular, what is reinstated in the later period is a search for national identity especially through the character of English landscape. This was an element in the Great War, formulated in Montague's texts for the publica-

tions of artists' work and disseminated by Wellington House.

Nash titled his notes for a chapter in *Outline* on the First World War 'Making a New World'. As well as being reproduced on the cover of *British Artists at the Front*, the painting was exhibited with its full title *We are Making a New World* (see fig. 15) at Nash's exhibition at the Leicester Galleries in May 1918, held under the auspices of the Ministry of Information and coinciding with the publication of the book. By the time of the publication of his autobiography in 1949, the painting (and almost any First World War image by Nash could substitute for it) had come to symbolise the totality of Nash's war experience inseparable from the text of the autobiography. The text culminates with an extension of the narrative into the war letters ending in Nash's declaration of himself as prophet and messenger. All this had already been prefigured in the framing of the painting on the cover of *British Artists at the Front* together with the construction by Gordon of the artist as oracle and seer. *British Artists at the Front* was the first monograph to be published about Nash at a point when he came of age as an artist. At the moment of its unveiling for public consumption, Nash's war work was already embodied in an officially endorsed reading.

For Gordon, who was recommended to Wellington House to write the biography by Nash himself, Nash's representation of landscape was to be read as a transparent revelation of the artist which was a metaphor for humanity.[90] His landscapes were therefore a metaphor for human suffering that was literally unspeakable: 'It is not possible to paint truly how this war has swept man, because horror will not permit this truth to be told. It is possible to depict the devastation of Nature, because partly we cannot understand the full horror, and partly because through it we may come to a deeper realisation of what the catastrophe may mean to man.'[91] This is no different, although more eloquently written, than the transcendent reading of *We Are Making a New World* as expressing a universal truth about war, even nuclear annihilation, cited in the first part of this chapter.

The trope of landscape-as-body was also continually evoked in Montague's notes to the plates. *Hill 60, From the Cutting* (fig. 23), plate IX, was 'disembowelled . . . its entrails laid on its outside'; *The Caterpillar Crater* (fig. 24), plate XI, was 'eviscerated'; *Landscape, Year of Our*

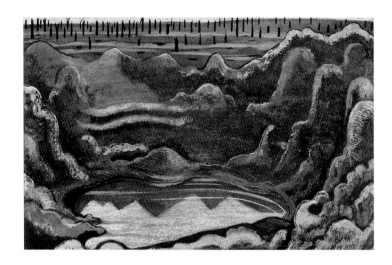

23 Paul Nash, *Hill 60, From the Cutting*, 1917, ink, pencil, chalk and watercolour, 41.3 × 48.3, private collection

24 Paul Nash, *The Caterpillar Crater*, 1917, ink, chalk and watercolour, 27.3 × 36.2, private collection

Lord, 1917 (see fig. 51), plate XIV, had 'pockmarks . . . as in severe cases of smallpox'; on *The Field of Passchendaele*, plate II, the ridge was 'a spine of raised gravel and sand'. Writing about *Sunrise: Inverness Copse*, plate I, the drawing to which Nash had attached notes about men trapped in the mud, Montague could no longer contain the metaphor of landscape as body nor sustain notions of enmity and national boundaries. The land literally embodied the decaying flesh of dead soldiers. He wrote, having explained the location to the reader: 'A quite appreciable proportion of its present surface soil has walked the earth in Germany, Great Britain or Australia.'[92] It is a rupture in rhetoric, as though the sheer material factuality of war had finally exceeded representation.

Nash's last 'godless, hopeless' war letter attempts to explain to his wife how the war cannot be represented in art or language. It is 'unspeakable', 'indescribable'. It is nearly invisible to sight, a reiterative blackness: 'black rain', 'bitter black of night', 'black dying trees'.[93] Sent back to the Front as an official artist, Nash declared that he was 'no longer an artist' but a messenger taking his revenge against 'those who want the war to go on for ever'.

Sunrise: Inverness Copse is a sparser, chillier image, markedly slighter than *We Are Making a New World*. Traces of ink and white chalk, some touches of brown pastel for shadows and shaded tree trunks map out the subject; in a kind of negative procedure, the reverse of a positive act of drawing on white paper, muddy earth, the cloud bank and the body of the image are the brown paper ground. Colour floods the painting where the churned-up soil is warmed by the rising sun touching the right quadrant of the canvas; trees standing like sentinels acquire long shadows fanning like serried ranks before the sun, always symbolised as masculine. The sky stained blood red suggests the possibility of new life or resurrection and redemption, prefiguring the iconography of war memorials, such as Kipling's *Lest We Forget*, and recalling Binyon's *For the Fallen* from 1914: 'At the going down of the sun and in the morning/We will remember them.' It is a repetition of Montague's purgative black winter of war giving way to spring sunshine in order to redeem the nation, a nation embodied in a land that is saturated with the bodies of the nation's dead.[94] *We Are Making a New World*, at least in this moment of its first and official unveiling and promotion, functions as a counterpart and an antithesis to Raemaekers's *Cavell* as the sexualised and violated mother country. Raemaekers's cartoon is too literal, too pornographic, too insistently propagandist but also possibly unstable through the inclusion of Medusa heads. The nation-state is feminised and a victim, potentially an emblem for masculine failure and impotence. Framed on the cover of *British Artists at the Front*, *We are Making a New World* resists this scenario of failure and lack because it figures the blood sacrifice of young men as re-fertilising the nation in order to guarantee its continuity through its re-masculinisation. Except that the guarantee that its meaning will finally be fathomed is undercut because Montague's battle-front graveyard knows no national frontiers, and in his letter Nash had declared 'sunrise and sunset are blasphemous'. *We Are Making a New World* is one of the most successful propaganda images of all time, because it takes the form of an art object speaking directly of an authentic, independent artistic vision. Geoffrey Grigson called it in 1948 'a masterpiece of English painting of this century . . . simply formed, rich, real and visionary'.[95]

two

Realism, Representation and Censorship

Lies have long legs: they are ahead of their time.
Adorno, *Minima Moralia*

War and Truth

Official war painting became the most talked about art in London in the first half of 1918, when Nevinson displayed *Paths of Glory* with a strip of brown paper labelled 'CENSORED' obscuring the dead bodies he was apparently not allowed to show (fig. 25). As a consequence of initiatives by Wellington House, a number of official artists held exhibitions in London between March and June, often timed to coincide with the publication of an issue of *British Artists at the Front*. For the moment, however, there were no artists at the front because all had been recalled when the Germans launched an offensive on 21 March. Visits did not resume until July. Most of the exhibitions took place at the Leicester Galleries, the leading avant-garde art dealers of the war years. Nevinson's second big exhibition of war work opened there at the beginning of March, Nash's, titled *Void of War*, in May and Kennington's in June. Orpen exhibited at Agnew's in May and Rothenstein at the Goupil Gallery in April. As well as the four issues of *British Artists at the Front*, catalogue introductions were commissioned from Robert Graves for Kennington and Arnold Bennett for Nash and Orpen. Nevinson also published a book, *The Great War: The Fourth Year*, which appeared in September 1918. Texts in all their forms, as aids to viewing in books and catalogues and as part of the critical recep-

tion of the pictures, focused on whether or not what artists had represented, inevitably partial and mediated, could none the less be described as 'truthful'. Crawford Flitch, introducing a selection of Nevinson's paintings, asked 'can the painter give us the truth?'[1] Bennett prefaced Orpen's official exhibition, held under the auspices of the Ministry of Information established in February 1918, with the startling statement: 'it demonstrates an untruth.'[2]

The visibility of official art circulating in the press, in books and London shows also made available for public debate an issue that had been simmering for a while – whose prerogative it was to tell the truth about the war, in whose interest and by what means. In May 1918, the *Graphic* launched an attack on the work of official war artists, singling out Nevinson and Nash in particular. It reproduced a spread of images headed *The Trench from Different Points of View: The Battle of the War Artists* (fig. 26) contrasting three modes of depiction. At the top, and privileged in the *Graphic*'s account were three official photographs of soldiers in trenches. Below these, across the middle of the page, was a reproduction of an academic painting by James Beadle, *Zero-Hour*, then titled *Dawn – Waiting to Go Over* (fig. 27). At the bottom, mirroring the photographs above, were two drawings. Nash's, untitled by the *Graphic*, was *Existence* (fig. 28); Nevinson's had been reproduced the previous year by the paper as *Looking at Battle from New*

OF GLORY (CENSORED).—This picture, 'ritish official artists, at the Leicester -hibited with the large brown p was 'n, bat I for t was

he shown by Mr. C. R. W. Nevinson, Green-street, Leicester-square. are above. The Exhibi' ["Dail'

25   *Paths of Glory (Censored), Daily Mail, 2 March 1918*

Points of View (fig. 29), which was meant in the double sense of both sighting a rifle through a periscope and Nevinson's modernist style, what the *Graphic* called 'idiosyncratic'.[3] The text complained about lack of access to the front and Government control of information and described the work of official artists as 'chosen from what may be called the esoteric schools, or at any rate, from the ranks of artists who appeal mainly to art connoisseurs. The idea seems to be to supply pictures which afford complete contrast to the highly detailed inventorying work of the camera.'[4] The article and spread set up a number of correspondences between different modes of visualisation and their capacity to provide evidence about the significant matter, for a home front readership, of the appearance and nature of trench life. It is not so much the disavowal of 'official art' that makes this page so interesting and relevant. Rather, it is the way that *Graphic* was evaluating what kinds of pictorial imagery could most authentically convey 'the truth about the war', an issue that also raised questions about the ways representations were addressed to and received by different audiences.

The shortage and poor quality of photographs from the frontline was a consistent problem for newspapers and there were frequent complaints. Partly in response to pressure from newspaper proprietors, Wellington

House established a Pictorial Propaganda Department in February 1916, run by Ivor Nicholson who was formerly employed in advertising at *The Times*. It was noted that 'the enormous circulation of pictorial papers reveals, as much as the crowds at the cinematographs, that there are millions of voters (who ultimately control the policy of Governments) in all countries who will not read the letter press, but from whom the demand for war pictures is unlimited'.[5] By late 1916, Wellington House was distributing 7,000 prints a week to the press, rapidly rising to 19,000 a week, and had established *The War Pictorial*, a monthly paper illustrated with photogravure that had a worldwide distribution of 700,000 copies. Official artists were appointed as part of the same drive to overcome a shortage of visual material but they were never part of Nicholson's Pictorial Propaganda Department. Masterman often took personal responsibility for liaison with them, assisted by Alfred Yockney, a journalist and art writer for *Art Journal* and the *Studio*, who was taken on at Wellington House in July 1916 and handled most of the day-to-day administration.[6] The work produced by official artists raised issues about the intended audiences for visual imagery, at odds with and sometimes in conflict with a policy for pictorial propaganda apparently aimed at a mass population.

When it was first mooted that Bone might be employed, there were contradictions in the speculation about the intended audiences for his work, and no coherent pattern about its reception emerges from the evidence. As far as the *Western Front* publications were concerned, his patrons were said to be representatives of 'cultivated opinion' and that *Country Life*, whose title endorsed *The Western Front*, was bought by the 'wealthy class'.[7] Yet when Masterman negotiated with GHQ on Bone's behalf, he argued that the needs of propaganda had changed with greater popular demand for details of actual military events. When he urged Bone to stress 'not only the artistic but the realistic side' and to include sketches of places known by name to the general public, he seemed to have a wide popular audience in mind.[8] In 1918, however, Yockney confirmed that the *Western Front* books were intended for working-class viewers and that these had failed in their objective: 'The Bone publications were produced at a popular price, in order that they should filter through to the homes of the workers. This effect has not been secured . . .'[9] These contradictions were echoed in the

THE TRENCH FROM DIFFERENT POINTS OF VIEW
THE BATTLE OF THE WAR ARTISTS

AS THE CAMERA ARTIST SEES IT — THREE PHOTOGRAPHIC EXAMPLES OF THE SOLDIER'S LIFE IN THE TRENCHES

AS THE ACADEMY ARTIST SEES IT — "DAWN — WAITING TO GO OVER." BY JAMES P. BEADLE
Exhibited at the Royal Academy. Copyright reserved for the artist by Walter Judd, Limited, publishers of the "Royal Academy Illustrated."

AS AN OFFICIAL ARTIST SEES IT
By Lieut. Paul Nash. (See page 584.)

While the present war has involved more people than any other war in history, the methods of letting us know what we are doing have been more restricted than in the case of any modern campaign. In consonance with the policy of Government doing everything, private enterprise in describing the war has been abolished in favour of official supply. Newspaper correspondents and pictorial artists are under Government control, each writer being attached to several journals, while the work of the photographers, who hold commissions, goes to anybody who will buy it. In the matter of pictorial artists, they have been "officially" chosen from what may be called the esoteric schools, or, at any rate, from the ranks of artists who appeal mainly to art connoisseurs. The idea seems to be to supply pictures which afford complete contrast to the highly detailed inventorying work of the camera. This page illustrates the different methods employed, more especially as applied to trench life. At the top we see the plain unvarnished tale of the photograph; in the middle a typical example of Royal Academy illustration—of which other specimens will be found in our pages devoted to the Academy. The two pictures at the bottom represent the work of the "official" artists, of whom Mr. Nevinson has so far distinguished himself most strikingly. In conclusion, it must be noted that a very large sum of money has been spent by the Government in reproducing in various forms the drawings of some of the "official" artists, notably those of Mr. Muirhead Bone.

THE METHODS OF ILLUSTRATING THE WAR
A little account of the variety of view points.

AS AN OFFICIAL ARTIST SEES IT
By Mr. C. R. W. Nevinson.

27 *left* James P. Beadle, *Zero-Hour*, or *Dawn — Waiting to Go Over*, 1918, oil on canvas, 107.9 × 185.4, Imperial War Museum, London

28 *bottom left* Paul Nash, *Existence*, 1917–18, black chalk and watercolour on paper, 48.3 × 32.4, Imperial War Museum, London

LOOKING AT BATTLE FROM NEW POINTS OF VIEW

This picture looks at the war from new points of view in a double sense, first via a periscope, and secondly via the highly idiosyncratic art of Mr. C. R. W. Nevinson, whose war pictures have aroused the greatest interest, partaking, as they do, of the character associated vaguely in the average man's mind with what is called "cubism" or its congeners. Mr. Nevinson, who is a son of the well-known war correspondent, Mr. Henry W. Nevinson, certainly brings out in a very striking way the dominating features of the present war, namely its awful mouotuuy and the terrible mechanical task of clearing up that mess.

conflicting successes of exhibitions of the artist's work held during 1917, but in this instance the largest audiences were achieved in working-class locations. A show at Colnaghi's in the West End drew only 386 visitors in one month, whereas 45,000, including numerous soldiers and school children, attended an exhibition at the Whitechapel Art Gallery in the same period.[10] A collection of Bone's drawings toured the provinces for the last six months of 1917; it attracted 25,000 visitors in one week at the Mapin Art Gallery in Sheffield, the highest number since the gallery's opening in 1887, whereas the same exhibition in Oxford attracted very few people, although 'only the better class' according to the gallery.[11]

During 1917, Wellington House initiated a portfolio of sixty-six lithographs by eighteen artists, including Bone, Nevinson and Kennington, called *Britain's Efforts and Ideals*. Described recently as 'by far the most ambitious print publication project in either world war', *Britain's Efforts and Ideals* was, perhaps surprisingly, a conspicuous failure, and the reasons are revealing.[12] How the series came about and for what purpose is obscure, because all the correspondence and files have been lost. The project was directed by Thomas Derrick and one of the contributors, Ernest Jackson, supervised the printing. It was evidently underway by February 1917 when Derrick wrote to Henry Tonks, asking him to contribute (he refused) and mentioning that George Clausen was already working.[13] There were a number of exhibitions, beginning in July 1917 at the Fine Art Society, a tour of provincial art galleries in Britain and shows in Paris, New York and Los Angeles. The series had a lot of publicity – it had some well-known artists such as Frank Brangwyn, Edmund Dulac, Augustus John and Charles Ricketts – and it was widely reviewed. Twelve of the prints were large colour lithographs illustrating various 'Ideals' such as specific diplomatic restitutions (fig. 34) – the restoration of Alsace-Lorraine (Maurice Greiffenhagen) or Serbia (Gerald Moira) or 'Italia Redenta' (Ricketts) (fig. 30) – or more abstract aims imagined as the reward for sacrifice – the triumph of democracy (Rothenstein), the rebirth of the arts (Charles Shannon) (fig. 32), the end of war (William Nicholson) or *The Dawn* (John) (fig. 31). Nine artists each produced a set of six black and white 'Efforts' thematically linked and illustrating home and war front actualities such as *Making Sailors* (Brangwyn), *Making Guns* (Clausen), *Women's Work*

(A. S. Hartrick), *Making Soldiers* (Kennington) (fig. 33) and *Making Aeroplanes* (Nevinson). The contemporary British print market was dominated by etching and intaglio; its leading artists were Bone, McBey and D. Y. Cameron. Unlike Germany, however, there was no particular emphasis on the print portfolio, and lithography was a relatively marginal medium, although the Senefelder Club established in 1908 by Joseph Pennell with Hartrick and Jackson was an attempt to promote it. One must suppose that Campbell

29 facing page, bottom right C. R. W. Nevinson, *Looking at Battle from New Points of View*, the *Graphic*, 5 May 1917

30 below Charles Ricketts, *Italia Redenta (Britain's Efforts and Ideals)*, 1917, colour lithograph, 68.6 × 42, Imperial War Museum, London

31 *left* Augustus John, *The Dawn (Britain's Efforts and Ideals)*, 1917, colour lithograph, 46 × 68.9, Imperial War Museum, London

32 *bottom left* Charles Shannon, *The Rebirth of the Arts (Britain's Efforts and Ideals)*, 1917, colour lithograph, 74.3 × 49.5, Imperial War Museum, London

33 *bottom* Eric Kennington, *Making Soldiers: In the Trenches (Britain's Efforts and Ideals)*, 1917, lithograph, 46.7 × 36, Imperial War Museum, London

Dodgson, given his connections and links to the print market, had something to do with the Wellington House project. In Germany, print portfolios offered narrative possibilities in thematic and sequential images, often pitched at a middle class, middle income intelligensia (das Bildungsbürgertum), for privatised seeing in intimate spaces, a market for subscription portfolios especially attractive to avant-garde artists, such as der Brücke.[14] Such marketing methods resembled those used to disseminate Bone's *Western Front*, a means consonant with Wellington House's, and Masterman's, preference for subtle methods of infiltration and indirect appeal. Print portfolios were popular in the war years in Germany and perhaps the 'Efforts' and 'Ideals', even the *Western Front* and *British Artists at the Front*, were some sort of response to this.

34   F. E. Jackson, *United Defence Against Aggression (England and France, 1914) (Britain's Efforts and Ideals)*, 1917, colour lithograph, 63.5 × 43.8, Imperial War Museum, London

It was the 'Ideals', the most prestigious element in the set, that were excoriated in the press, because they were seen as propaganda and rather too obvious an attempt to influence public opinion, and therefore not art. They were 'not spontaneous efforts on the part of the artists represented, but something they were asked to do', wrote Laurence Binyon.[15] P. G. Konody speculated whether 'several of the artists . . . [had] been working under restrictions which kept their imagination enchained'.[16] Charles Marriott got to the heart of it: 'The moral is that war, while claiming the artist as man, must leave him free as artist or prejudice his value.'[17] On this occasion, Wellington House miscalculated the medium and the message, misjudging and underestimating its audience. The 'Efforts' had a more positive reception – 'The superiority of the works illustrating 'efforts' to those attempting to express the 'ideals' must be evident to everybody' (Marriott) – because these were not imaginative portrayals of remote or abstract and ill-defined war aims but depictions of actualities exercising a claim to realism. These were more persuasive when produced by the artists who had served: Kennington and Nevinson. 'All the good work has been done by "plain" artists in active service,' wrote Marriott, and 'the best . . . by men who are at least touched by the newer movements in painting' because such artists are motivated by 'a wish for a more intense reality than is to be got by "realism".'[18]

What the clamour for war photographs, the reception of the 'Efforts and Ideals' and the promotion of official exhibitions and publications in 1918 all have in common is a call for immediacy, actuality and contemporaneity, all terms associated with any painting that intended to be modernist. The illustrative realism of Beadle's *Zero-Hour* (see fig. 27), a 'typical' 'specimen' according to the *Graphic*, looked unpersuasive; the real contest for truth-telling about the war was modern art versus photography and the stakes were very high. From the start Wellington House had insisted on the promotion of 'truthfulness' and the necessity for candour. The format of *The Western Front* was designed to assert its authenticity.[19] Bone's work was in many ways intended as reportage – Masterman asked for drawings to be sent speedily 'as we want to be up to date with the next issue and to get as many scenes of places still fresh in the public mind'.[20] It was a substitute and supplement for photographs, but at the same time the drawings functioned differently from photo-graphy. As soon as work by artists who had seen active war service was available, however, these displaced Bone's contribution, because such work gave testimony to something not just witnessed but also experienced, that pushed on the boundaries of convention in the desire for 'a more intense reality'. P. G. Konody stated that Nevinson's 'Efforts' were 'the least literal, and for that very reason the most truthful'.[21] Campbell Dodgson concluded his introduction to Kennington's work in *British Artists at the Front* with an open acknowledgement: 'Many of his drawings are unspeakably sad; how could they be otherwise . . . in this most terrible of wars?'[22] In Robert Graves's essay in the catalogue for Kennington's exhibition, the last vestige of any chivalric ideal of the British soldier, a blend of Galahad and Don Quixote, was dismissed and instead the reader was asked to note how 'the trench stinks, terrifies, is beastly, the shell jolts, crushes, blots out, . . . the face of the dying man is mottled purple or dead white, the face of the corpse is hideous yellow or green or black, and in the middle of horror, frozen, stunned, bleeding, tired nearly to death, choking with gas, the British soldier . . .'.[23]

The guarantee of authenticity of the official war artists' work was based on a warranty that the painter had also served. Graves told the reader that Kennington was 'not the embarrassed visitor in a strange drawing room nor the bewildered old lady at her first football match: he is a soldier, at home in trench and shell hole, knows what is happening, what to see, where and how to see it'.[24]

Brendan Prendeville has eloquently observed that for the real to count as modern in early twentieth-century painting its key ingredients are 'all that comprises the present, in its dimensions of subjectivity, corporeality and social existence'.[25] Subjectivity means the viewer is implicated in the representation, even complicit with it, and not provided with distance or a neutral, anonymous place for observation outside the viewing frame, as in classical academic painting. Corporeality, or the body, is what is most real to us and what we most have in common and also that about which we are most divided.[26] Social existence, in this period, means an emphasis on the city, work, the space and time of modernity, and especially social relations organised around consciousness of class and gender. If the most authentic, most real war images were by those most in the know, that is those with direct, real bodily

35 Eric Kennington, *The Cup Bearer*, 1917, pastel on paper, 63.5 × 43.8, Imperial War Museum, London

experience of being in it (and the British largely fought the Great War overseas with conscripted citizen armies and its civilian population was not directly exposed), then for those who had not served there was no way of really knowing. Dodgson called it unspeakable. Evidence from soldier–artists was irrefutable. You had to take it on trust. The viewer was recruited as a 'made-to-order witness', subpoenaed to testify to the authority of those presumed to know.[27] For war art, the 'made-to-order witness' includes those too old and too young or incapacitated, and whose masculinity is disabled, distrusted or otherwise incomplete, and women. The gaze of the 'made-to-order witness' is a feminine gaze, one that signifies lack. Graves's embarrassed and bewildered viewer possesses the blushing, disorientated glances of one who does not know where or how to look. Prendeville also notes an

intense concentration on the materiality of paint and surface in real modern painting and an emphasis on freshness, distinct from technical bravura, vigour and energy, all qualities that are absent from the tetchy, fidgety surface of Beadle's *Zero-Hour*, which, for all its striving to represent a pregnant moment, lacks any sense of immediacy and leaves the viewer safely unexposed. Prendeville does not say it, but vigour and energy are also the attributes of virility, a healthy manliness demonstrated in the very technical means at the artist's disposal, and in this period it was often named as such. What Dodgson meant when he said that Kennington's drawings (fig. 35) were unspeakably sad was 'how could they be otherwise being *manly* and serious portraits of men who also act and suffer'.[28]

Being realistic about war also meant giving testimony about its ugliness, brutality, squalor and sordidness. Soldier–artists had a licence and authority to tell it how it was, making breaches in propriety difficult to control. Nevinson's *Paths of Glory* was conspicuously censored. It was reproduced with its label, 'CENSORED', in the *Daily Mail*, the day before the show opened and the matter was discussed widely in the national Press. The ironic reference to Gray's 'Elegy' and the democratic impartiality of death, 'The paths of glory lead but to the grave', did not escape notice, exposing the subject matter of the painting. Everyone knew what it was they were not allowed to see. 'One can see barbed wire, the butt of a rifle, and a khaki cap', wrote *The Times*, 'and it only needs to recall the line from Gray's "Elegy" which gives the title to the picture to guess its subject'.[29] Censored dead bodies were an obvious and unconvincing untruth, easily discredited. It is not a question here, however, of exposing the 'truth' about censorship because acts of censorship also reveal anxieties. It is how testimonies of ugliness were used to preserve a regime of truth and contain a specific interpretation of the war, as well as the ways images sometimes escaped containment, that are revealing. Graves's grim and anti-heroic description of death in Kennington's work concluded with a stock image of endurance, 'the British soldier frowns and sweats and shows, with what majesty he can fight', just as Montague had mitigated the irredeemable Somme battlefield with a similar image of stoicism. Testimony had to be tempered with a sense of obligation that made continuance of the war a matter of necessity and national honour, and preserved a myth to coun-

36   C. R. W. Nevinson, *La Patrie*, 1916, oil on canvas, 60.8 × 91.5, Birmingham Museums and Art Gallery

teract other matters that threatened serious social disintegration.

Threats to the stability of the social order could be seen in organised and growing resistance to the prosecution of the war, including mutiny by troops, for instance at Étaples during 1917 and 1918. More covert and ultimately more repressive than ham-fisted and generally unsuccessful attempts to whitewash the horrors of war was a wide-spread, officially sponsored and escalating campaign throughout the war to counteract pacifism. In particular, attention was focused on the pacifism associated with organised labour and the Independent Labour Party, 'the one really formidable pacifist body in the country',[30] because such interpretations of the war included a call for the reconstruction of the social order. Socialism and pacifism were often conflated, and identified with unpatriotic interests, opposed to the national good. The export of those newspapers thought to be socialist was prohibited,

allegedly on the grounds that they could be used by the Germans.[31] *The New Age*, an avant-garde journal that published work by writers such as Ezra Pound, was banned from export late in 1916. Although the editor, Orage, protested that the paper was pro-war and anti-pacifist, it was alleged to have been cited by the Germans, was said to 'have a Socialistic hatred of Capitalists' and was described as 'an objectionable paper edited by an objectionable man'.[32] Part of the propaganda of MI7(b), a department of the War Office, included dropping leaflets over the German lines 'of an "inflammatory" and socialistic nature'.[33]

The most sustained campaign to identify socialism with anti-patriotic interests was the National War Aims Committee (NWAC), formed by MPs from the three main political parties in August 1917 to counter-act war weariness and defeat pacifism. With its basis in political parties and its organisation through constituencies, the NWAC appeared to emanate from

Parliament and not from Government. It was, however, the outcome of the Government's desire to augment the work of the Department of Information on the home front that its director, John Buchan, stated he lacked the resources to undertake.[34] The NWAC represented a shift from earlier propaganda, orientated towards a diplomatic perspective on the causes of the war and the threat to international freedoms said to be the aim of the Germans, to a concern for more parochial incentives and benefits from the conflict. The NWAC's objectives were stated as the strengthening and consolidation of morale and 'To counteract, and if possible, render nugatory the insidious and specious propaganda of pacifist publications.' Whereas Wellington House had pitched its efforts at a middle-class audience, the NWAC specifically targeted the working classes, referring to the need to 'inspire all war workers' and construing the war as a benefit to the living standards of labourers. By appealing to nationalistic motives, the NWAC intended 'To encourage unity and stifle party and class dissensions'.[35] Throughout 1917, general military surveillance of civilians had also increased. The work of MI5, responsible for counter espionage, the control of aliens and the civilian population during war, involved the assembling of 38,000 'dossiers' on people suspected of hostile acts, 'a series of black lists' and the investigation between June 1916 and October 1917 of '5,246 persons suspected of pacificism, anti-militarism etc.'.[36] Assertions of 'truthtelling' in the artists' work were linked to this general campaign of endurance and resistance to pacifism. It mattered who had access to what kinds of information and who was deemed competent to read evidence correctly, because there were sections of the population whose loyalties it was suspected could not be guaranteed, that mass audience who voted and ultimately controlled governments. The question of information and access was intimately linked with how art, especially modern art, and photography were assumed to function.

From the point of its first invention, photography was claimed to be an objective, mechanical transcription of reality and contrasted with what were held to be the more selective processes of art, the product of the sensibility and subjectivity of the artist. Consequently, photography had become privileged evidence in law, scientific enquiry and surveillance. The First World War enhanced the authority of photography, for example, when an existing role in military surveillance was combined with the use of the newly invented aeroplane in aerial reconnaissance. Information was collected and classified in representations that, as Alan Sekula points out, purported to be purely denotative. In reconnaissance photographs, meaning was yielded only by 'a rationalised act of "interpretation"' – "Is that a machine gun or a [tree] stump?"[37] In this period, photographs were made to function as direct and unmediated transcriptions of the real, as an effect of the real. Photographs were presumed to be radically innocent images, freed of being coded and constructed, and released from the contradictions of participation in a signifying system. Their power to convey authoritative information, their believability, depended on this innocence.[38] The censorship of photographs was handled mainly by curtailing access to sights, not because the photographer's loyalty was suspect but because the power of photography to reveal evidence depended on assuming its mechanical promiscuity, innocently revealing what other methods of representation could choose to leave out.

Photographs and war artists' paintings were frequently compared and exhibitions sometimes coincided. Nevinson's show at the Leicester Galleries in 1918 was opened by Lord Beaverbrook, newly appointed Minister of Information, three days before Field-Marshal Viscount French opened an exhibition of official photographs at the Grafton Galleries. For Jan Gordon, reviewing an exhibition of Canadian photographs at the Grafton Galleries in 1916, the fact of the artist's necessary selectivity made the matter of falsehood in photography a different moral issue from faking a work of art:

There is a picture of a trench with Germans lying in the abandon of death; we are moved, we know that they look exactly like that, we wonder who is waiting at home, in one breath we rejoice and weep . . . but in [sic] three days later we were told that these men had merely been posed in some artificial dugout on Hampstead Heath . . . Yet we know that the dead and dying, the agonised in Mr Nevinson's picture "La Patrie" never existed in fact. we[sic] know that the picture was painted after he reached England – no matter. We do not turn to this picture as if it were a document; the non-existence of *his* sufferers does not make it a forgery, for it is a synthesis. "This is war," cries the camera, "as I see it." "This is war," says Mr Nevinson, "as I understand it." And herein lies the difference [fig. 36].[39]

The 'untruthfulness' of Orpen's work for Bennett was the evidence of rich and varied subject matter in what everyone knew was the monotony and dullness of the war. It was the product of Orpen's individuality where his 'ingenuity in manipulating the material is simply endless, and yet he is never tempted to falsify the material.'[40] That manipulation could be exonerated as different from falsification was the basis for claiming that art was telling the truth and was therefore superior to photography. Because art was known to be selective and interpretative in a way denied photographers, art had both the power and the authority to tell it like it was. There was no question in press reviews of Bone's work in The Western Front that his drawings were anything other than interpretations. It was stated instead that the artist's unique role was to select and emphasise what the viewer might otherwise overlook, and thus to educate the viewer's perception.[41] Bennett described Nash's work as finding the essentials of the front. 'The convention he uses', said Bennett, 'is ruthlessly selective'. But this selectivity was authorised by temperament so that the works 'seem to me', he told the reader, 'to have been done in a kind of rational and dignified rage, in a restrained passion of resentment at the spectacle of what men suffer, in a fierce determination to transmit to the beholder the full true horror of war'.[42] To paint the 'true' picture, art had all the resources of emphasis such as tone, brushmark, colour, the articulation of space and line assumed to be missing from photographs. There was a contradiction, however, at the heart of Bennett's claims for 'non-falsifying manipulation'. The genuine work of art was knowable by the means at its disposal for depiction that guaranteed evidence of individual sensibility, but this was also the guarantee of the impartial objectivity of the artist. In statements that strain arguments about artistic licence and truth-telling to their limits, Bennett made claims about Nash's 'rational and dignified' rage and 'restrained' passion. Crawford Flitch stated that Nevinson's work was authentic because of its 'aesthetic disinterestedness', a term obviously indebted to the pre-war art criticism of Clive Bell and Roger Fry. The artist's emotional partiality and his selective emphasis were opposed to the 'inconsequential glance' of the camera. Instead his work was dictated by the aesthetic demands of the painting, the essence of truth-telling. Nevinson had:

> preserved his integrity as an artist. He has jealously guarded the impartiality of the eye. He has minded his own artistic business. Whatever his judgement upon war may be . . . he does not allow it to dictate to his vision. He is content to appear not as a judge or advocate but simply as an uncorrupted witness. He states without rhetoric what the eye sees. Or rather he sifts the evidence of the eye, selecting from its prolix and confusing report just that residuum of form which has vital significance.[43]

A special authority was therefore invested as much in the status of the artist as in the image itself. In the same way, the biographies for British Artists at the Front had established each artist as independent and nonconforming, a disinterested but not impersonal witness.

The First World War was the first major conflict to be accompanied by an extensive repertoire of photographs, and it was the first time photography was seen as essential armament in the campaign for managing public opinion. The British photographic record was almost entirely the product of official photographers and the total number of images was very small, only approximately 40,000 negatives, 28,000 from the Western front. Access to any of the various war fronts was highly restricted.[44] Until mid-1916, when two official photographers were appointed, there was none at all in France. What scant photographic evidence of the British in France exists from 1914–15 came from soldiers taking amateur photographs. By comparison, the French established a Section Photographique de l'Armée in April 1915, employing fifteen photographers with eight-six assistants and thirty laboratory technicians and mobile laboratories, that produced more than 150,000 plates. The Germans organised a Bild und Filmamtes (BUFA or Picture and Film bureau) in 1916 with seven mobile film units that claimed to have produced 200,000 slides and 30,000 negatives by 1917.[45] The shortage of usable photographs in Britain gave rise to complaints, and it was the lack of pictures that drew attention to the presence and intervention of official control. Artists were recruited at least in part to remedy the deficit in visual imagery but this also changed the nature of British propaganda. In order to carry conviction and have authority, in other words to be seen as art and not rhetoric, artists had to work free of constraint but this also made it impossible to predetermine or control all the meanings works of art when circulated might provoke. This was especially the case with younger artists, more likely to have served in the war and therefore the most compelling witnesses, but also the ones who had the most at stake establishing or maintaining reputations as modernists and independents.

Patronage and Censorship

Newspapers illustrated by photographs were aimed at the cheap, mass market, whereas weekly magazines, such as the long-established *Illustrated London News,* continued to use drawings and were marketed to more prosperous audiences.[46] Press photographers tended to be anonymous and were classed as craftsmen providing a service, rather than distinguished as individuals as artists were. This distinction was replicated in the mechanisms of official patronage. Although GHQ would only accept photographers who held a commission, insisting that those selected should have the necessary social standing, when Ivor Nicholson visited the front in October 1917, he complained to Masterman that the official photographers were not treated with the same respect as the correspondents, nor even as officers.[47] It has often been reiterated that the Army has a long history of distrust of the press.[48] The British press claimed to constitute the 'fourth estate', representative and guider of public opinion, independent of but influential upon politicians, and as a consequence relationships with GHQ were strained. By the period of the First World War, the press was intertwined inextricably with political institutions and it was sometimes claimed that it acted during the war as a forum for political debate and a substitute for Parliament.[49] When press correspondents were finally allowed to the front, a matching of social background between war correspondent and army officer guaranteed the loyalty of the reporter. All five English correspondents eventually authorised by GHQ were rewarded with knighthoods after the war.

Artists, once filtered through the agency of Wellington House, did not apparently represent problematic national institutions. Arguments put to the Foreign Office and the Treasury to approve their employment emphasised individual reputations at home and abroad, demonstrating the notion that British art itself had been mobilised in the British war effort, an idea underlined by the title of the publications, *British Artists at the Front.* Using artists fulfilled the needs of a propaganda designed 'to influence those who can influence others'.[50] The appeal to opinion leaders was 'an extension of the kind of personal diplomacy familiar to most members of the British foreign policy-making élite',[51] which was also the same art-buying audience that participated in the network of influential contacts and well-placed recommendations that serviced the art market as a whole and had brought artists to the attention of Wellington House. Official artists shared the same status as the official correspondents. Bone lived in their quarters; Nevinson and Kennington wore press correspondents' uniforms. Both found this uniform restricting and they were sometimes harassed until they had explained their position – Bone was arrested on at least one occasion.[52] War correspondents and war artists alike found themselves operating in circumscribed circumstances. Nash and Nevinson, their expectations raised by their experiences as combatant and medical orderly respectively, found it difficult, but not impossible, to gain access to those areas they wanted to see. Nash reported that GHQ was 'somewhat reluctant . . . to work on getting me up at least within gun-shot.'[53] Retrospectively, he wrote: 'I am expected to operate from G.H.Q. I am determined to operate around the Front Line trenches. I begin my campaign. Difficulties of an infantry subaltern behaving like a Staff Captain. I evolve a technique. Eventually I get where I want to be.'[54] That artists obtained drawings in difficult circumstances was sometimes specified. The Foreign Office asked Wellington House to obtain 'a photograph taken of Bone in uniform plastered in mud, if possible, and looking as if he had just been repulsing a Hun counter attack in Polygon Wood'.[55] GHQ refused permission arguing that there was a moratorium on officers advertising themselves, a proscription that did not apply to the less highly regarded photographers.[56]

Wellington House negotiated facilities for artists but did not stipulate what they should produce either in terms of subject matter or style and there was a consistent refusal to lay down any programme. In a letter headed 'confidential', Masterman wrote to Kennington, 'I am afraid I cannot give you any direc-

37   C. R. W. Nevinson, *Paths of Glory*, 1917, oil on canvas, 45.7 × 60.9, Imperial War Museum, London

tions as to what you should draw. I am quite content that you should go on drawing whatever you think best. I cannot pretend to direct or control artistic inspiration.'[57] When Hudson, the printer of the war artists' work, criticised Nevinson, Masterman wrote: 'Nevinson and Kennington have continually asked me for instructions as to what they should draw; but I have always taken the view that it is not for a Government Department to attempt to regulate artists in their work, art being so largely individual in expression.'[58] Derrick visited Nevinson's studio in October 1917 and even expressed some concern that Nevinson might have moderated his style in order to gain official approval.[59] When there was an attempt to ban some of Nevinson's work from publication, the artist protested

to Masterman, 'My only instructions from you were to paint exactly as I wanted' and added the important qualification 'as you knew my work would be value-less as an artist and propagandist otherwise'.[60]

Visits to the front brought artists within the author-ity of the military censor, Lieutenant-Colonel A. N. Lee at Intelligence, GHQ, who, for about a year, also censored all the official photographs alongside the artists' work.[61] The circumstances that led to the cen-sorship of *Paths of Glory* (fig. 37) reveal more than merely an ineffective attempt to suppress representa-tions of dead bodies. What emerged was an issue con-cerning matters of propriety in relation to different categories of pictorial representation. Censorship of representations, including paintings, photographs or

38   C. R. W. Nevinson, *A Group of Soldiers*, 1917, oil on canvas, 91.4 × 60.9, Imperial War Museum, London

films, was concerned with the regulation and permissibility of depictions – a policing of the limits and boundaries of what was allowed to be represented. The *Paths of Glory* incident began in November 1917 when Lee rejected one of Nevinson's paintings, *A Group of Soldiers* (fig. 38), later published in *British Artists at the Front*, exhibited in Nevinson's exhibition and purchased by the Imperial War Museum, on the grounds that 'the type of men represented is not worthy of the British army'.[62] Because this was not a case of the betrayal of military information, Masterman protested to Lee, 'We ought not to censor any "work of art" except for purely military reasons. If we judge of its ugliness or beauty as censors we are "in the soup" at once!!'[63] Although interventions by Yockney, Masterman and John Buchan relieved the ban on the picture, Lee continued to complain about the image as a detrimental portrayal of British soldiers and subsequently attempted to proscribe Orpen's drawings for similar reasons, including objecting to *Shell-shocked*, because mention of the term was forbidden.[64] At the end of November 1917, *Paths of Glory* was referred to the War Office, along with *A Group of Soldiers*, because Lee argued that both paintings raised matters of policy beyond the scope of the military censor. *Paths of Glory* was then banned because it was said that pictures of dead bodies undermined civilian morale. Neither painting raised any points about the revelation of military secrets. At one stage, Wellington House queried whether the War Office had any authority to prevent the exhibition of an artwork in a private gallery, arguing that censorship of artists' work could apply only to official publications. After Nevinson's display of the picture censored, he was summoned to the War Office and subsequently withdrew the painting from the exhibition.

The ensuing rumpus over *Paths of Glory* seems entirely predictable. Other Government agencies involved in censorship pursued a policy of covert rather than overt suppression. For example, in 1916–17 the Home Office resisted the introduction of a centralised system of cinema censorship through legislation because this implied making the matter open to public scrutiny and possible controversy. Instead, a more diffuse, less visible method of controlling film content through licensing arrangements with local authorities was preferred.[65] Matters of film censorship, in particular, were concerned with public morality and

propriety in what was to be viewed by the broad and often working-class audiences drawn to the cinema. The prohibition of *Paths of Glory* and the attempt to suppress *A Group of Soldiers* reveal censorship as an activity concerned with what were the proper or fit subjects for art. *A Group of Soldiers* was censored for its lack of 'fitness' whereas Nevinson made explicit reference to its basis in images of the working class, or perhaps a classless group, by insisting that the soldiers were portraits of men that 'I chose quite haphazard from the Tubes as they came from France on leave.'[66] The *Daily Express* maintained that, since soldiers were 'average commonplace citizens' they appeared as they should in Nevinson's painting: 'His soldiers are real, unidealised, and uncaricatured men.'[67] The *Saturday Review* was one of the few papers to pick up the inferences that were the source of Lee's anxiety about the image and draw the obvious conclusion, writing that Nevinson 'might be any Trotsky, spouting on about the Bourgeoisie while letting his job slide'. His soldiers were a threat to public order, 'A crew of hooligans', urban working class, adolescent and out of control.[68] When the painting was reproduced in *British Artists at the Front*, Montague wrote, 'From this "conversation piece" the spectator who cares to go beyond its artistic quality can extract any amount of inferences that he wishes as to trench life and its effects on men's faces and temperaments.'[69]

Aspects of how cinema censorship worked in this period, which Annette Kuhn argues are particularly revealing because the regulation of the cinema was in a state of flux before, during and after the First World War, were based on assumptions about the reading competencies of different constituencies of audiences. Because the cinema was a predominantly working-class entertainment, regulation of morality films about sexually transmitted diseases, itself an instance of moral panic about the health, wholeness and survival of the nation-race during the war, assumed the possibility of misreading and the consumption of films as entertainment not as education, as pornography not propaganda. Middle-class audiences, on the other hand, were deemed appropriately disposed to reading a film's moral, rather than its story-telling content.[70] GHQ viewed *A Group of Soldiers* as a transgressive picture both because it invoked fears of national racial degeneracy with its unromanticised subject-matter,[71] and because it raised the possibility of (mis)identification with its subject by a fraction of the population whose loyalty could not be guaranteed and whose class allegiances were suspect.

Press censorship within Britain was handled through a Press Bureau, established at the start of the war, and meant the abandonment of the voluntary system of press control that had been negotiated with newspaper proprietors in the years before the war. As a consequence, relationships between the military authorities and newspapers had deteriorated and improved only with the establishment of official correspondents at the front.[72] The War Office was slow to realise the ways in which censorship could also be a mechanism for propaganda and was often in conflict with organisations such as Wellington House and the Foreign Office for whom a flow of information in the form of news and pictures was vital to the construction of campaigns to influence public opinion. The War Office established a propaganda organisation in March 1916 with the formation of MI7(b) to complement MI7(a) in its responsibility for censorship. In a later history of War Office propaganda it was noted that 'the dividing line between news and propaganda was (and always will be) sometimes so indistinct that the relationship with M.I.7(a) – the military censorship machine – remained intimate throughout. Some of the activities of M.I.7(a) were, in fact, dominantly propaganda and some of the activities of M.I.7 (b) dominantly news; and vice versa.'[73]

It was even possible to use the fact of the existence of censorship, always construed as a matter of national interest to prevent the betrayal of military and defence information to the enemy, as a means to make an audience complicit with the necessity for military secrets. In 1917, Ivor Nicholson, assisting in the organisation of an exhibition of Admiralty photographs at the Royal Academy, replied to an Admiralty request for security in the exhibition with a suggestion to 'add a spice of excitement to the pictures, viz., that we should have a notice printed in the best official style threatening the most awful penalties of the Defence of the Realm Act for sketching any of these photographs that have never been shown to the public before'.[74]

For Nevinson's painting to be censored, it had to be censorable. In other words, in this period a return to a form of pictorial realism was a precondition for the work to be viewed as capable of conveying believable information. Nash escaped censorship because, Lee said, his 'funny pictures . . . cannot possibly give the enemy any information'. He described them as 'a huge joke'.[75] Nevinson's new work in 1918 was sometimes discussed as a return to sanity and commonsense. The journal *Ideas*, for example, wrote that Nevinson had 'now dropped the wildly fantastic, and his battle scenes and drawings of soldiers are noteworthy for sanity.'[76] A commonsensical view of pictorial realism understands a painting as a direct transcription of a single reality. Censorship then appears as a prohibitive instrument of power interfering in and distorting a 'faithful' transcription of a 'fixed' reality, and is defined habitually in negative terms as repression and prohibition. This definition, however, assumes that a fixed meaning is contained and replicated in a work of art, or a film or a photograph. Acts of censorship are acts of power that attempt to regulate and produce particular forms of knowledge or 'truths', but knowledges or meanings are produced in the way representations are circulated and read by different audiences in different times and places, and the regulation of representation is an active and provisional process of negotiation. Censorship is unable to cover all the readings generated because power is exercised rather than possessed and prohibitions also produce resistance. For example, the fact of its having once been censored caused some wartime and most post-war audiences to ascribe protest and anti-war sentiment to *Paths of Glory* as its intrinsic meaning, a meaning at odds with the intention of the censor, and at odds with the intention of the artist. When Nevinson protested to Masterman about the attempt to proscribe his work, he made it plain that his independence was the basis of his usefulness to Wellington House 'as you knew my work would be valueless as an artist and propagandist otherwise'.[77] Nevinson had the upper hand and he knew it.

Craig Owens has argued that to study (significantly he uses the term 'investigate') representational systems is not to show how such systems are appropriated for propaganda nor is it to unpick ideologies encoded in these systems. Rather, he states that representations need to be analysed for how they function 'as an integral part of social processes of differentiation, exclusion, incorporation and rule. . . . Representation . . . is an act – indeed, the founding act – of power in our culture.'[78] In the period of the First World War it was assumed that photographs, films and paintings were addressed to different publics divided along class lines. Censorship of cinema was severe and photographs limited and controlled because it could not be assumed that their mainly working-class audience possessed an induction into correct ways of reading the 'real', and this audience's loyalties were suspect. The prohibition of *Paths of Glory* gave rise to multiple and contradictory readings. It produced an excess of meaning which the act of prohibition was, by definition, unable to predict and control.

It was clearly nonsensical to censor *Paths of Glory* as though dead bodies were not a consequence of war. *Tatler* put it as 'that unending anxiety which eats like a canker at the heart of everyone *of us* with men out there these days',[79] a public acknowledgement of privately experienced grief. Nevinson himself wrote to Masterman noting a distinction between art and photography and the inappropriateness of attempting to suppress what was already public knowledge. He pointed out that the Canadians had an exhibition of photographs that included corpses, but he understood the need for a generalised prohibition designed to avoid offending relatives of the dead: 'My picture happened to be a work of art (but unlike the other, not actual portraits) therefore I cannot see how it comes into this photographic category, especially as civilians, at any rate, know that war causes casualties, even if soldiers do not.' He referred to the film of the Somme battle and the painting, *Mother, Mother*, at the Royal Academy as evidence of images of the dead circulating in the public domain.[80] At one stage in the negotiations over the prohibition, Nevinson suggested patriotically retitling *Paths of Glory*, *Shall the Sacrifice be in Vain?*[81] The incident was read as absurd, unwitting and innocent as well as publicity-seeking.[82] What was screened from public gaze remained obstinately open to full public scrutiny. 'Dead men evidently do tell tales', wrote the *Herald*, arguing that Nevinson senior, 'war correspondent and sturdy democrat', guaranteed Nevinson junior's independence, 'official' 'in name only, for he no more reflects the 'official' mind than permanent officials do the spirit of the nation'. This reading must not be mistaken for dissent, because the *Herald* construed the matter, alongside Nevinson's turn to realism, as an affirmation of the honour and justness of the British cause. Realism, or classical representation, was equated with a reassertion of the reasoned, an indigenous, national characteristic to be pitted against the invasion of a 'foreign' modernism: 'Nevinson has come out of the horrible vortex so foreign to his temperament with his art strengthened by its strife, . . . He has, as it were, stooped to conquer.'[83] *Nation*, on the other hand, produced what is now taken to be the single authentic construction of the matter as an attempt to contain criticism and curb dissidence by limiting representation.[84] Contradictory effects and disparate meanings were attributed to the same image.

The most extended comment about censorship appeared in *Outlook* as part of a discussion about propaganda. The journal directed most of its criticism against the Government and the censorship apparatus for distrusting the professional standards of journalism. A capacity for propaganda, it argued, reflected national characteristics, so that Germany excelled at the necessary deviousness and dishonour required to influence foreign opinion, while British insularity and reserve assured British ineffectiveness. Only 'Radicals' and 'sentimentalists', such as Norman Angell, Bertrand Russell, H. G. Wells and Arnold Bennett had gained a public platform in England, while censorship had underrated national characteristics one now tends to assume were invented only in the Second World War, 'that spirit of obstinate resistance which is inherent in our race'. This was no anti-war tract, for the paper argued for the relief of all censorship, except that bearing on information useful to an enemy, because the right of Britain to continue to press the war was self-evident: 'It was surely the limits of absurdity to censor one of Nevinson's pictures. . . . Truth is the best propaganda.'[85] The question that is raised is whose 'truth' is at stake here?

That acts of censorship can be publicised in ways that are sensationalist and opportunist did not escape Nevinson. The artist enhanced his standing as an avant-gardist by appearing to be persecuted and misunderstood. The credibility of his work was strengthened and censorship and the State apparatus for censorship were discredited. Attitudes to war art and the employment of war artists deployed arguments that maintained distinctions between art and journalism, between fine art and popular culture. There was an assumption that the interests and activities of artists enshrined a code of behaviour that guaranteed both the independence and the loyalty of the artist because the framework for the promotion and reception of works of art operated in a different sphere from the wider public domain of the popular press. In February 1991, John Keane, official

British war artist in the Gulf War, was prevented from publishing a 'war diary' in the *Guardian*, the newspaper that had sponsored his life insurance to get him to the Gulf and that would subsequently sponsor his exhibition at the Imperial War Museum, because the Ministry of Defence argued that he had been given facilities denied journalists,[86] presumably because his status assumed an artist's sense of discretion. While Nevinson had a discerning eye for the publicity opportunity, he was also the artist whose work most consistently blurred distinctions between fine art and popular culture and who self-consciously sought a broad audience and wide popular approval for his war paintings.

Images and Perceptions

Almost all the technologies deployed in 1914–18 were prefigured by the American Civil War and the Franco-Prussian War so that the Great War can be said to have been anticipated and represented before it was fought, although its scale and, as Daniel Pick argues, the heterogeneity of its forms of destruction were unprecedented.[87] The entire industrial apparatus of western Europe became tuned to the supply of armaments in a total war effort. Distant fire from artillery, mortar, machine-gun and sniper had long displaced hand-to-hand combat. Modern armies were complex organisms of specialised functions serviced by elaborate networks of communication. The colossal apparatus of industrialised technological war production, however, gave rise to a static, largely invisible battlefield of soldiers entrenched in opposing underground dug-outs, such as at Verdun, for years on end, separated by the empty space of no-man's-land.[88] The landscape appeared empty and yet it was saturated with men. Although the war appeared concealed, so that what Bone's drawing of the Somme battlefield reveals is how little could be seen, none the less, conduct of the war depended on a masquerade with perception, on seeing and not being seen. A high premium was placed on revelation, exposing what was hidden, through, for example, star-shells that briefly illuminated no-man's-land at night when raiding parties and burial details combed the terrain. Armies unseen by one another continuously trained their sights searching for unknown figures across the vacant field of no-

man's-land, what Apollinaire phrased as a sort of projection of desire.[89] In the compressed foreground space of Nevinson's drawing *Looking at Battle from New Points of View*, the spectator shares the hiding place of a British sniper sighting his target through a periscope.

Paul Virilio recounts how war-making recalls ancient magical rituals of spectacle. Modern technological war can never escape implicating magic because an essential component in its conduct is to manufacture spectacle and mystification. The purpose of war is not just to kill the enemy, 'not so much to capture as to 'captivate' him, to instil the fear of death before he actually dies.' Virilio continues:

> There is no war, then, without representation, no sophisticated weaponry without psychological mystification. Weapons are tools not just of destruction but also of perception – that is to say, stimulants that make themselves felt through chemical, neurological processes in the sense organs and the central nervous system, affecting human reactions and even the perceptual identification and differentiation of objects.[90]

Technologies of vision, of perception and representation, and technologies of war intersect. Colonel Gatling saw the possibilities for a cylindrical crank-driven machine-gun in 1861 while travelling on a paddle-steamer and watching its wheel. Janssen discerned in the multi-chambered Colt a means to invent a revolving unit to take a succession of photographs from which Etienne-Jules Marey developed his chromo-photographic rifle for aiming and shooting photographs of moving objects.[91]

Nevinson's exhibition in 1918 differed from his 1916 show because, as he explained in the catalogue, what he had attempted to depict was not the horror of war but the 'prodigious organisation' of the army.[92] The range of images emphasised the front as a workplace. Subjects can be grouped into categories such as soldiers, aspects of flying and front-line landscapes together with a few home front images. Jan Gordon saw *Nerves of an Army* (fig. 39) as symbolising the whole show and standing as a metaphor for the army as an organic organisation of colossal resources.[93] Nevinson's paintings stressed a commonplace, workman-like atmosphere. *The Roads of France* (figs 40–43), a series of four canvases purchased by the Canadians, reproduced in *British Artists at the Front* and in a separate booklet, narrates progress to the front

40   C. R. W. Nevinson, *The Roads of France*, 1917–18, oil on canvas, 63.5 × 170.2, Beaverbrook Collection of War Art, 8652, © Canadian War Museum

41   C. R. W. Nevinson, *The Roads of France*, 1917–18, oil on canvas, 63.5 × 170.2, Beaverbrook Collection of War Art, 8653, © Canadian War Museum

most tellingly in the way the rhythmic interval of leafy trees gradually disintegrates and breaks up. In particular, Nevinson's personalised, detailed and grimy subjects placed a new emphasis on the British working man and his destiny – the levelling, unpartisan effects of death. Crawford Flitch noted the slanting stretchers in *Roads of France* 'more poignant and impressive than regimental colours . . . carried like *memento mori* at the tail of the column'.[94] *Paths of Glory* is a claustrophobic painting. The two dead bodies occupy a shallow space close to the picture plane. At the same time they are trapped in the glazed paint surface which is scratched to reveal a livid green underpainting, marking the painting's aspiration to be read as modern and as real.

The exhibition also contained pictures of how new technologies of vision had produced new ways of seeing, such as Nevinson's images of aerial reconnaissance (fig. 44). Flitch wrote, 'when the painter has acquired the added experience of the airman he is impelled to adopt a new point of view'. In Nevinson's prints and drawings of aerial combat, the sky ceased to be a romantic symbol. For Flitch, it became instead a multi-dimensional space of 'volume, mass, density'[95] and a vehicle for representations that recreate in the spectator sensations of danger and visual mastery. Planes were highly visible from the trenches and Nevinson's pictures from aeroplanes suggest a commanding position from which to survey the Front in a way that is much richer and more suggestive than Bone's panoramic topographical records of the Somme. Virilio writes about air power in the First World War that:

> Airborne vision now escaped that Euclidean neutralization which was so acutely felt by ground troops in the trenches; it opened endoscopic tunnels

39   C. R. W. Nevinson, *Nerves of an Army*, 1918, oil on canvas, 90 × 56, Imperial War Museum, London

42 C. R. W. Nevinson, *The Roads of France*, 1917–18, oil on canvas, 63.5 × 170.2, Beaverbrook Collection of War Art, 8654, © Canadian War Museum

43 C. R. W. Nevinson, *The Roads of France*, 1917–18, oil on canvas, 63.5 × 170.2, Beaverbrook Collection of War Art, 8655, © Canadian War Museum

and even brought 'blind spots' within the most astounding topological field – vistas whose precursors could be found in the big wheels and other fairground attractions of the nineteenth century, and which were later developed in the roller-coasters and scenic railways of post-war funfairs.[96]

Trips in aeroplanes (civilian flights resumed in 1919), like venturing on fairground big wheels or paradigmatically scaling the Eiffel Tower, were essential aspects of the tourist spectacle at World Fairs and Great Exhibitions. These were not simply oppressive demonstrations of power but were a means to produce consent in mass populations to disciplinary instruments by offering a sight and a means, as Tony Bennett phrases it, of 'knowing power and what power knows.'[97] Pictures of soldiers in Nevinson's oeuvre represent the view on the ground; swept into the sky, Nevinson's aeroplane pictures re-enact for the spectator the frisson of power and compel an identification with the war machine reordered into a modern democratic hierarchy of working men overseen by airmen, recently promoted to the status of the new Gods. In the one, it is we, the viewers, who fight on the ground, and in the other, it is we, the spectators, who oversee and command the spectacle.

Nevinson's images offered not so much a panorama as a kind of schema for a panoptic sight of the total battle zone. The *Panopticon*, designed by Jeremy Bentham, was originally a prison, or other place of confinement, planned as a series of cells in a circular building with a high tower in the centre occupied by an observer monitoring the occupants of the cells. The Panopticon, as it is recast by Foucault, is a metaphor for a non-coercive disciplinary apparatus and the

regulation of the social body. It is an economic, almost invisible means for the hierarchical organisation of power and self-regulation.[98] Bennett argues that the spectacle of World Fairs and exhibitions, paralleling the development of new technologies of surveillance, was a means to transform 'the problem of order . . . into one of culture – a question of winning hearts and minds as well as the disciplining and training of bodies'. Spectacles or exhibitions 'through the provision of object lessons in power – the power to command and arrange things and bodies for public display – . . . sought to allow people and *en masse* rather than individually, to know rather than be known, to become the subjects rather than the objects of knowledge.'[99] World Fairs addressed a mass population transformed from an unruly populace that needed to be governed into a self-governing, ordered body of citizens. Fine art, painting and sculpture nearly always featured alongside displays of technological and economic achievement in international exhibitions of the late nineteenth and early twentieth century. But the marketing of modern and contemporary art in the same period was increasingly addressed to a discriminating and cultured elite distinct from mass spectatorship and self-differentiated by the assumption of specialist competence in the consumption of modern art.

Derrick's worries about Nevinson moderating his style may have had less to do with concern that Nevinson's work might appear compromised by official employment, that is, seen as conservative and restrained, and thus less valuable as art and as propaganda, and more with a feeling that Nevinson's was a transgressive practice that muddied the tenets and standards of liberal patronage. It is usual to see the turn

40A   C. R. W. Nevinson, *The Roads of France*, 1917–18, oil on canvas, 63.5 × 170.2, Beaverbrook Collection of War Art, 8652, ©
Canadian War Museum

41A   C. R. W. Nevinson, *The Roads of France*, 1917–18, oil on canvas, 63.5 × 170.2, Beaverbrook Collection of War Art, 8653, ©
Canadian War Museum

42A   C. R. W. Nevinson, *The Roads of France*, 1917–18, oil on canvas, 63.5 × 170.2, Beaverbrook Collection of War Art, 8654, ©
Canadian War Museum

43A   C. R. W. Nevinson, *The Roads of France*, 1917–18, oil on canvas, 63.5 × 170.2, Beaverbrook Collection of War Art, 8655, ©
Canadian War Museum

44 *left* C. R. W. Nevinson, *Banking at 4000 Feet (Britain's Efforts and Ideals)*, 1917, lithograph, 40.6 × 30.4, Imperial War Museum, London

45 *bottom left* C. R. W. Nevinson, *Throwing a Bomb*, 1918, present whereabouts unknown

in the form of Nevinson's work around 1917 to 1918 as a move outside the trajectory of modernism. Compared with the more consistent, and arguably more biddable, Paul Nash, whose work was stylistically secure from the threat of censorship, Nevinson's oeuvre exhibits all kinds of traits it ought not to. It was inconsistent – a factor that drew frequent comment, celebrated by commonsensical criticism and excoriated by informed connoisseurly opinion. P. G. Konody celebrated his courage in varying his technical means for different subjects as evidence of his independence and integrity, whereas Ezra Pound lampooned his quest for fashionability and *The Times* thought he was the victim of his own success.[100] *Throwing a Bomb*' (fig. 45) of 1918 is a kind of stylistic *volte-face* in the work of an artist supposedly becoming less avant-garde. His paintings were often visually impoverished. *Reliefs at Dawn* or *The Road from Arras to Bapaume, After a Push* (fig. 46) and also *Paths of Glory* (see fig. 37) are unattractive canvases with repellent paint surfaces that propose no kind of visual gratification for the informed spectator in search of an affirmation for their personal standards of good taste, pointing up a question about the price to be paid for 'good' or formally satisfying war paintings. The work was illustrative and topical, and it made acute references to modernity and the social relations of class and gender. *The Food Queue* (fig. 47) has a shallow frieze of masculinised working-class women, as though glimpsed from a vehicle passing in the road. One woman catches the spectator's eye and returns a confrontational stare. In February 1918, food shortages and rationing were giving rise to metropolitan anxieties about threats to public order.[101] In May the pastel was retitled *Squalor* and shown at the New English Art Club. *War Profiteers* (fig. 48) is richly painted in acidic colours but the two fashionably dressed women, probably prostitutes, seen on the street at night, have pallid green skins as though marked with necrosis. *A Group of Soldiers* occupies a shallow space but the paint is flatly handled and the men have mask-like faces. The *Saturday Review*'s objections to the image were not

46   C. R. W. Nevinson, *After a Push*, 1917, oil on canvas, 55 × 77, Imperial War Museum, London

just that the men were hooligans, symbolic of dis-order, but that they were 'dummy hooligans – they have no inward life'. But it is more than the figures that suggests racial degeneracy, the paint surface itself seems dead, lacking the vigour and energy that could act to make it read as a virile performance. All in all, Nevinson's practice was a deeply contradictory one from which it is possible to draw almost no consistent readings. It was as usable by left-wing journals and opponents to the war as it was by the fashionable and socially secure.[102] Nevinson's own pronouncements about his intentions and work were arrogant, hector-ing, anti-intellectual, sometimes irrational and border-ing on the paranoid.[103]

The 'showmanship' of Nevinson's work attracted criticism. He was accused of being 'journalistic' and the stigma provoked Konody into declaring that his protégé was 'emphatically not' journalistic.[104] The *Burlington Magazine* compared him with Daumier and stated that 'tried by the standards of those who find Van Gogh or Boccioni literary, and Marinetti a pro-nounced journalistic type, Mr. Nevinson must be found at least equally so.'[105] Nevinson was a problem-atic artist for Wellington House. Hudson, printer of Wellington House publications, complained that there was 'an approach to the pavement artist touch'[106] in some of his work. The Leicester Galleries tended to use its galleries to put on double one-person shows. Nevinson opened with Walter Bayes and Nevinson's delineation of the 'jangling conflict of industrialism and war' was compared with 'the rose-coloured world of Mr. Bayes'.[107] The two artists made playful references to each other's work in Bayes's *The Underworld* (fig. 49), shown later that year at the Royal Academy, and

47   C. R. W. Nevinson, *The Food Queue*, 1918, pastel on paper, 50.8 × 66, Imperial War Museum, London

Nevinson's *Food Queue*. Nash's show, on the other hand, opened together with a memorial exhibition to Gaudier-Brzeska, killed in 1915, which made the event altogether more specialised, more avant-garde. Nash's work was also impressed with the perceptual imperatives of sights at the front. *Very Lights* (fig. 50) is lit with Véry lights to induce, like Nevinson's picture, a similar visceral sense of danger. As the *Queen* put it 'the pictures themselves, in their suddenness and emphasis of the terrible jagged facts of battle, suggest the same kind of illumination'. They were also distractingly rich images (fig. 51). The article concluded 'One design, "Landscape, Year of Our Lord, 1917," looks at first like a pretty piece of lace work, until one sees that the subject is the mudheaps and reddened barbed wire in a setting of Flanders rain. It is an intensely interesting exhibition.'[108] Nash sometimes worked similar themes to Nevinson and his work also referred both to the caecal constrictions of trench warfare and the sensational fantasies of air combat. But Nash's vision was not that of the publicist or showman orchestrating a panoptic spectacle with verve and panache. Rather, Nash's pictures reworked late eighteenth- and early nineteenth-century ideas about landscape. He was a self-consciously poetic artist and an inheritor of that earlier romantic tradition.

John Barrell has argued that, in late eighteenth-century Britain, taste in landscape and landscape art

48   C. R. W. Nevinson, *War Profiteers*, 1917, oil on canvas, 91.5 × 71.11, Russell-Coates Art Gallery and Museum, Bournemouth

49   Walter Bayes, *The Underworld: Taking Cover in a Tube Station during a London Air Raid*, 1918, oil on canvas, 254 × 548.6, Imperial War Museum, London

50   Paul Nash, *Very or Verey Lights*, 1918, ink, chalk and water-colour on paper, 23.5 × 29.2, private collection

was a means to legitimate political authority. He compares two perspectives on the representation of landscape. The first, extensive prospects, was said to correspond to an ability to grasp abstract ideas and objects in relation to one another. In contrast, the other, occluded views, proposed secluded and private visions opposed to social interaction where details become objects of consumption and possession. The first is said to be the prerogative of a liberal man (and gender is emphatically important in this context) in the original sense of a free and sovereign subject, and the other to correspond to servile imitation. Barrell notes that, when Florentine republican theory was transplanted to Britain, the prototypical disinterested citizen with his ability to grasp the true interests of society was displaced to those owning landed property. Public man, disinterested citizen, freeholder and man of taste were synonymous. Illustrative topography was despised as something that detailed objects as things to be possessed for their use in commercial exchange. Landscape prospect and occluded view can be mapped over a number of oppositions; learned and ignorant, polite and vulgar, liberal and servile, civic duty and trade.[109] In this context, Nash's generalised, often schematic figures could be juxtaposed with Nevinson's particularised portrayals in *A Group of Soldiers* (see fig. 38), or perhaps Nash's more measured self-promotion – it was Nash who asked if Bennett could write for him[110] – versus Nevinson's posturing and self-advertisement.

Contrasts of public and private in late eighteenth-century landscape theory were also a kind of riddle because political authority could be appropriated and landscape art could be seen as a muted criticism or parody of how public civic life was conducted in the courts and cities.[111] (Dis)interested land proprietorship was a site for a struggle between landed aristocracy and a meritocratic bourgeoisie in early nineteenth-century Britain. In 1914 to 1918 the break-up of large estates was compounded by the decimation of aristocratic sons. Like many others of his class, Desborough, patron of Nevinson, lost two heirs in the war. They died within two months of each other in 1915.

Contemplation of the private and secluded also promises pleasure in escape from civic duty; and art as solace is often assumed to be its function. Nash was particularly successful as a pastoral landscape artist, that most innocent of landscape genres, and his war works were most frequently, and more persuasively, prospects drawn with uncensorable artlessness. Spectators of Nash's work are always observing from outside the scene. Although sometimes seen as a parody of the pastoral, Nash's work also offers a respite and a rest. The last image in Nash's volume of *British Artists at the Front* is *Ruin: Sunset* (fig. 52) annotated by C. E. Montague: 'The ruins are those of the Hospice, a large building in the open country, N.W. of Wytschaete. It was destroyed by bombardment in June, 1917. Its site was high ground and a good post for observation both eastward and westward; from it the King viewed the British front after the Battle of Messines.'[112] The text restates the prerogatives of the sovereign subject, or the sovereign self, to judge and affirm.

Nash received far fewer press notices than Nevinson and these tended to be by specialist writers such as Lawrence Binyon of the British Museum or the artist and critic Jan Gordon, who also contributed to his volume of *British Artists at the Front*. The artist was seen as a romantic ironist who had enriched the tradition of English landscape painting with images described as poetic and formally satisfying. *The Times* argued that he revealed 'the strange unaccountable beauty of the Front' with drawings that had 'an abstract music of their own',[113] and the *Westminster Gazette* stated that he had expressed his own vision of what the war meant to him 'with a beauty of colour and design, and with an innocence of perception'.[114] Nash's work satisfied the demands from art audiences emerging in

51 Paul Nash, *Landscape – Year of Our Lord, 1917*, 1918, pen and black ink and graphite with black and opaque white wash and coloured chalk on brown wove paper, laid down on mounting board, 25.9 × 35.9, National Gallery of Canada, Ottawa

1916 for new and authentic images of war that matched an English sensibility for poetic landscape painting.

In contrast, not only was Nevinson's practice transgressive, it also transgressed. His exhibitions and books were widely reported and his works often reproduced in the national, provincial and international press. It was frequently reiterated, particularly in popular newspapers, that his paintings affirmed what every serving soldier knew. The *Saturday Review*'s denigration of *A Group of Soldiers* was answered by a soldier writing: 'Show them to any fellow who has inhabited a dugout. Pass them round any Mess in France and Flanders. Ask the man next to you in hospital in Town what he thinks of them . . . You will hear 'Good Heavens! – he has got home there right enough. Oh!!! Absolutely It! Sight of it makes you feel queer' – as it does.'[115] While the *Connoisseur* described his work as having 'some of the merits and all of the defects of a heavily coloured photograph' and Ezra Pound, an avant-garde writer, found Nevinson wanting because he sought the approval of the public and not the judgement of the art critic, newspapers such as the *Daily Express* and the *Glasgow News* insisted that whatever was novel about Nevinson's images to the ordi-

nary public was not strange to the men at the front.[116] Sidney Dark wrote about *Bursting Shell*, 'I have stood for a whole afternoon watching similar scenes'. For Dark, Nevinson showed 'the stunning, aimless nightmare horror of the whole business' and that, in contrast to the falseness of recruitment posters, *A Group of Soldiers* depicted serving men as commonplace citizens 'real, unidealised and uncaricatured'. His work added up to an 'illustrated and annotated story of a fateful year',[117] a legibility that made the work unacceptable to connoisseurly opinion, whether academic or avant-garde, and uncomfortable for Wellington House to accommodate. Nevinson's formal means, a kind of visual 'greyness' and impoverishment, a wartime aesthetic that was appropriately modernised, and his tendency, within that aesthetic, to develop more literal or more legible modes of representation together with his subject matter, troops at the front engaged in work or views from aeroplanes, added up to a new aesthetic of reportage. This aesthetic obscured the boundaries between fine art and illustration or popular culture. The body of Nevinson's work as a whole by 1918 provided a view of the front as seen by the working soldier and proposed commanding sights from which

52   Paul Nash, *Ruin: Sunset*, 1917–18, pastel on brown paper, 25.4 × 35.65, Imperial War Museum, London

to master the spectacle, to know power and what power knows, exposing the operations of power and truth to questions and controversy about whose truth was being told. His work provoked anxieties about the coherence and the ordering of the social fabric and it was ineffectively, and revealingly, censored. Nash's work, for all that it suggested the devastation of the front line landscape and a renegotiation of romantic readings of landscape as admonitory and ironic rather than consoling, did not breech standards of decorum, affirming rather than disturbing his audience's aesthetic standards and taste.

Wellington House held contradictory notions about the audiences it imagined for the works of art it commissioned. It could accommodate liberal intellectuals with their self-doubts and unease about the war for which Nash's work was a richer, more persuasive alternative to Bone's. But there was also a political necessity to influence mass popular opinion or what one correspondent referring to the United States called 'a numerically large, half-educated (and hence apathetic) body of *voters*',[118] whose tastes were uneducated, even vulgar. If, by early 1918, Nevinson has successfully supplanted Raemaekers's demagogic cartoon, the readings it might give rise to were not necessarily any easier to control. As the war progressed, orthodox and traditional modes of depiction, such as academic battle pictures by Beadle or Détaille and De Neuville, and Wellington House's own 'Efforts and Ideals' lithographs, looked less and less persuasive. In the contestation of authenticity, Nash and Nevinson came to stand for different kinds of truth about the war. When more artists began to visit the Front on behalf of the British War Memorials Committee, part of the Ministry of Information, later in 1918, Nash and Nevinson had set a precedent but artists were to find that even when seen, it was scarcely believable.

three

Making History:
The British War Memorials Committee

Founding the Ministry of Information and Funding a War Memorial

In late December 1919, the writer Arnold Bennett published an article about what he called 'the miracle' of an exhibition of important modern war paintings at the Royal Academy and their acclamation by the press, connoisseurs and all artists, with the exception of Academicians. Bennett's article, 'Officialism and War Painting' was not a review of the work on show but a record of his own part on a small committee based at the Ministry of Information. It was a story of obstruction and hostility from the War Office and the Treasury, but also of an extraordinary combination of vision, talent and expertise that had succeeded in creating opportunities for artists. A unique collection of works of art was the result. Motivated only by the needs of connoisseurship and not partisanship, the committee had done its job without prejudice to any faction, considering itself 'a conspiracy in aid of good painting, and of good new painting in particular'. For the purposes of art, wrote Bennett, it had 'held itself . . . to be the nation. . . . [It] was *de facto* the Government'. The best of the period had been recruited including new, young and, most importantly, untried artists. Dedicated to the needs of art and acting only in the national interest, the committee, remarked Bennett, had 'never considered politics, even the politics of art'.[1]

The 'committee' was the British War Memorials Committee. It met for the first time on 6 March 1918, two days after the formal constitution of the Ministry of Information. The initiative was that of Lord Beaverbrook, in March 1918 newly appointed Minister and Chancellor of the Duchy of Lancaster, but he recruited Bennett and Masterman to do most of the work. Renamed the Pictorial Propaganda Committee in July 1918, it met for the last time two weeks after the end of the war. A project closely identified with Beaverbrook, it intended to assemble a significant contemporary collection representative of 'the greatest artistic expression of the day' by a wide range of young and modern artists as a memorial to the war.[2] Seventeen history paintings by artists such as Wyndham Lewis, C. R. W. Nevinson, Paul Nash, Stanley Spencer and John Singer Sargent; two large sculptural reliefs by C. S. Jagger and Gilbert Ledward; and twelve smaller canvases were produced by thirty-one artists either commissioned to make a single work or employed full-time for up to ten months (see appendix). The project was wound up by the new Imperial War Museum in 1919 which also acquired all the work.

The British War Memorials Committee was important and timely. It was the first twentieth-century incidence of British state patronage to commission modern history paintings, and in many ways it was the most ambitious. The Second World War official artists' schemes, for example, never envisaged anything comparable with the memorial canvases produced in the First. Much of the committee's time was taken up with reviewing lists of artists of all persuasions from the academic to the avant-garde. In this process, it established a canon of British art that remains cogent to the present. It was timely because its activities coincided with a major change in the status of the Tate Gallery at Millbank, established in 1897 under the National Gallery in Trafalgar Square as the National Gallery of British Art. In 1917 the Tate was given its own director and board of trustees, the outcome of an enquiry initiated under Lord Curzon in 1911. In the reorganisation, the Tate's responsibility for modern British art was emphasised. National prestige, and especially the standing of the nation's collections in relationship to other European countries, was at stake. Modern art from abroad was inadequately and unsystematically represented and the Curzon Report argued for the necessity to develop the national collection. When Joseph Duveen offered to endow an extension in 1916, it became the nation's Gallery of Modern Foreign Art.[3] There was an overlap of personnel between the Tate Board and the British War Memorials Committee and comparable priorities therefore informed the work of both. Robert Ross, an art critic, served on the Tate Board and was adviser to the committee and to the Imperial War Museum. Although he refused, Sargent, a major contributor to the memorials scheme, was invited to join the Board.[4] Muirhead Bone, adviser to the committee, subsequently joined the Trustees and the Tate wanted to appoint Alfred Yockney, secretary to the committee, as assistant to its director.[5] For a period after the war, key works from the memorial scheme were on loan to the Tate from the Imperial War Museum.[6]

There were simple reasons for the cessation of the memorials project. In part, the financial vicissitudes of the British War Memorials Committee and conflict with the Imperial War Museum over the anomaly of a Ministry of Information operating as a patron of a war memorial were to blame. The project ran out of time when the war came to an abrupt end in November 1918. The story of the financial circumstances in which Beaverbrook's project came unstuck and the quarrel with the Imperial War Museum can be summarised briefly.[7] Beaverbrook based his idea for a British scheme on the Canadian War Memorial Fund, which he, together with Lord Rothermere (brother of

Lord Northcliffe) and Captain Bertram Lima of the *Daily Mirror*, had set up in 1916. Throughout 1917, this scheme had been commissioning large canvases from British and Canadian artists. Beaverbrook intended to repeat and enlarge the enterprise in a British context. The Canadian project had been self-financing, but Beaverbrook had reckoned that a British scheme would have a legitimate call on public expenditure and had initially authorised £2,000 from the Ministry to cover the committee's expenses. Proposals to raise funds and make the project self-financing never materialised although moves were made to register the British War Memorials Committee as a war charity. At one point Beaverbrook and Rothermere personally guaranteed the Committee's expenditure up to £10,000 each. Early on in an expansionist phase of the venture, attempts were made to persuade the Imperial War Museum to desist from collecting works of art, and it was even proposed to take over the Museum's existing art collection. This complicated a dialogue that had been initiated between Wellington House and the Museum about the eventual destiny of the official artists' work. A meeting had been held at the War Museum in February 1918, shortly before the Ministry got going, involving Robert Ross, as adviser to the museum, Alfred Yockney of Wellington House and Campbell Dodgson, Keeper of Prints and Drawings at the British Museum and long standing consultant about war artists for Wellington House. To add heat to an already charged situation, early on the Ministry decided it was the proper recipient of William Orpen's proposed gift of all his war paintings to the nation. Orpen was fairly indiscriminate about the offers he made to both the Imperial War Museum and the Ministry but the matter was pre-empted when Beaverbrook made arrangements to appropriate the entire collection at the opening of Orpen's exhibition held at Agnew's in May 1918. Hostility from the museum, which was employing its own war artists, was guaranteed.

Alfred Mond, First Commissioner of Works and responsible for the Imperial War Museum, manoeuvred to discredit Beaverbrook and to question the propriety of a project to commission war memorial paintings as part of the brief of a Ministry of Information. The crisis in the affairs of the British War Memorials Committee occurred quickly in June 1918. All the advisers, Ross, Konody, Dodgson, Derrick and

Bone were sacked. At the same time, there was a scandalous libel action involving Oscar Wilde's reputation which implicated Ross, Wilde's executor. Financial irregularities in the work of the Ministry were also being discussed by a Select Committee on National Expenditure and Beaverbrook was involved in a protracted row with the Foreign Office. At one point, Beaverbrook invited Mond and Sir Martin Conway, Director General of the Museum, to join the committee but ensured they would be out-voted by recruiting Rothermere, Bertram Lima, Needham (a Ministry official) and Bennett, who was already a member. He also renamed it the Pictorial Propaganda Committee. Whereas Beaverbrook had often been absent from the discussions of the committee, meetings sometimes became extravagantly high-powered and were devoted to minuting such questionable notions as 'normally, bad art could not be good propaganda'.[8] When the Ministry set about legitimating the activities of the British War Memorials Committee by writing to the Treasury for retrospective approval of expenditure and commitments to artists, Mond arranged for questions to be asked in Parliament designed to ensure that any works of art acquired with public funds by the Ministry would go to the museum. He also wrote to the Treasury to quash any claims the Ministry might make for a special building to house its collections. Late in July 1918, Beaverbrook surrendered the enterprise to the Imperial War Museum and then resigned as Minister in October 1918. Towards the end of the war, the Treasury, which had questioned the whole idea of commissioning major works of art for the nation as a part of a propaganda campaign, sanctioned a severely curtailed budget and acceded to the works being transferred to the War Museum for permanent preservation. The paintings were unveiled at the Royal Academy in winter 1919/20, not in order to state the case for the memorial collection, but as part of the museum's art acquisitions under the title *The Nation's War Paintings*.

The development of the British War Memorials Committee is inconceivable without the appointment of Beaverbrook, whose emergence as a member of Government was itself a consequence of alterations in a sense of national mission that affected the organisation of official propaganda. Beaverbrook's appointment followed a series of crises about the British propaganda effort and a succession of enquiries criticising Wellington House and the Department of Information, which had absorbed Masterman's agency when it was established in February 1917. A policy of clandestine and reasoned propaganda directed at informed and educated audiences no longer seemed to fit perceptions of how the war ought to be conducted. Complaints about official propaganda identified a failure of coordination in the organisation of agencies, duplication and waste of resources and lack of evidence of success. Wellington House and the Department of Information were investigated by Robert Donald, editor of the *Daily Chronicle*, for the second time in October 1917.[9] Donald, along with Lord Northcliffe (eventually replaced by Lord Beaverbrook), and C. P. Scott of the *Manchester Guardian*, were members of an advisory committee to the Department of Information which Buchan had rarely convened. In March 1918, Wellington House was closed down.

By the end of 1917, the Department of Information's annual expenditure was running at £750,000 and it had estimated for a budget of £1.8 million in 1918.[10] Wellington House was the most expensive element in the operation.[11] When Wellington House was abolished, Beaverbrook cut the proposed budget for the Ministry to £1.2 million, although annual expenditure eventually ran to £1.3 million.[12] In the shake up of propaganda organisations, Buchan became Director of Intelligence, a department reduced by the transference of much of its work to the Foreign Office. The Wellington House organisation moved to the Howard Hotel, Norfolk Street, and became the Literature and Art Department under Masterman. Its output was drastically curtailed. Robert Donald became Director of Propaganda in Neutral Countries, thereby taking over Masterman's original appointment in August 1914. Donald resigned at the beginning of April 1918 because of the pressure of the work. Lord Northcliffe, appointed to the British Mission to the United States in May 1917, became Director of Propaganda in Enemy Countries with a separate organisation at Crewe House.

Wellington House and Masterman were sacrificed against the background of a difficult situation. The war blundered on draining men, money and national morale. Official propaganda was a convenient target for blame because it was by necessity and policy a secret undertaking. They could not easily estimate its success and could mount no public defence without compromising its activities. By closing Wellington House, a partial solution was offered. Propaganda attained ministerial status with access to the Cabinet and it was cheaper to run. For obvious reasons, it is difficult to estimate the extent of Wellington House's activities, although a note of its publications provides a gauge for the part played by the war artists employed at the agency. Its principal publication was *The War Pictorial*, a monthly magazine of which 750,000 copies, 110,000 in English, were printed each month.[13] Its average monthly dispatch of books and pamphlets in England was estimated at 2.5 million.[14] It circulated around 19,000 photographic prints each week.[15] There were four full-time artists – Muirhead Bone, Francis Dodd, James McBey and William Orpen – and four unpaid contributors – John Lavery, Eric Kennington, C. R. W. Nevinson and Paul Nash (six, if one includes marginal associates, Spencer-Pryse and William Rothenstein). In addition, there were early dealings with Louis Raemaekers and Joseph Pennell as well as fourteen further artists engaged on *Efforts and Ideals* – Frank Brangwyn, Edmund Dulac, Maurice Greiffenhagen, A. S. Hartrick, Augustus John, Ernest Jackson, Gerald Moira, William Nicholson, Charles Ricketts, Charles Shannon, Claude Shepperson, Edmund Sullivan, George Clausen and Charles Pears – a total of twenty-six artists. Incidental to changes in organisations during winter 1917/18, but part of the story of the employment of war artists, General Charteris was removed from control of Intelligence at GHQ and became Deputy Inspector of Transport. All the artists at the front were sent home after the Germans launched a major offensive in March 1918 and broke through the British lines, scoring a tactical success on a scale that had eluded Haig throughout 1917. By the time of the establishment of the Ministry, the prospects for employing war artists did not seem auspicious, but as it happened, rather than coming to an end opportunities were enormously increased.

Beaverbrook's appointment as Minister of Information signalled two related shifts in the propaganda campaign which also index alterations in the tenor and conduct of the war. First, propaganda became a more public undertaking, assuming the effectiveness of the propaganda of self-advertisement, already latent in Wellington House's activities and reflected in the change from *The Western Front* publication to the title and format of *British Artists at the*

Front. Second, propaganda organisations staffed by civil servants, government officials and academics, a kind of public service intelligentsia, were replaced by an association of newspaper ownership, business interests, the press and the Government. In other words, the state was to be marketed and the media were recruited to do this. Beaverbrook had a track record for participation in aspects of the British propaganda effort. He had been a member of the War Office Cinematograph Committee, replaced Northcliffe on Buchan's advisory committee and attended meetings of the War Cabinet Press Advisory Committee. Beaverbrook, as Sir Max Aitken, had also made himself Canadian Eye Witness early in the war, acquired the rank of lieutenant-colonel and established the Canadian War Records Office. He had been close to the 'palace revolt' that had brought down Asquith in 1916 and he was created a peer early in 1917. He acquired control of the *Daily Express* in 1916, a paper he had an interest in from before the war, when he supplied £40,000 as a first mortgage on condition that the paper inserted 'paragraphs about Sir Max Aitken, the rising young MP for Ashton-under-Lyne'.[16] Running a Ministry, however, meant he was barred from active management of a newspaper. There was widespread opposition to Beaverbrook's appointment, including a resolution passed by the Unionist War Committee to the effect that no member of Government should be a newspaper correspondent or control a newspaper. According to Beaverbrook even the King expressed reservations about his appointment to the Duchy of Lancaster and questions were raised in Parliament. Disquiet was voiced about the blurring of boundaries between Government and the press, resulting in the public exposure of an erosion both of the independence of the press and of the disinterested functioning of the Government as the expression of the state and the nation. Beaverbrook appointed business associates to the Ministry; neither they nor Beaverbrook himself accepted a salary. It seemed as if private wealth was being used to purchase immunity from criticism.[17]

It is clear that Beaverbrook used his appointment as a Cabinet minister as an opportunity to repeat and enlarge on the Canadian War Memorials project in a more prestigious context and the Canadian Fund suffered from the diversion of commitment, finance and artists.[18] The orchestration of the British War Memorials Committee was bound up with Beaverbrook's perception of the role of a prominent public figure and the congruity of his particular capacity as a publicist and promoter with his official position as a politician and minister of propaganda.[19] Two factors are useful to consider in connection with the intricacy of Beaverbrook's politics and methods. First, dating from the 1880s, British politics and liberal conceptions of the state underwent a series of crises and redefinitions. The Liberal alliance fractured over the issues of Irish Home Rule in 1886 and imperialism. The traditional division between the owners of manufacturing capital aligned with the Liberal party and the owners of agricultural wealth associated with the Conservatives became blurred. In addition the growing complexity of capital accumulation generated a new plutocracy for managing capital, such as bankers and stockbrokers, who achieved high social prestige. Taken together, these factors brought about a political recomposition of the capitalist class and gradually the Conservatives came to be the only political party representative of capital. Related to this was the growth of working-class pressure on politics and increasing recognition that the regeneration of Conservativism, following election failures from 1906 onwards, also needed a broad popular base. This created openings for political influence by Conservative newspaper magnates operating and controlling a mass circulation press.[20] Second, Beaverbrook was an outsider to British society and its established political institutions both by birth and by temperament. Although a life-long member of the Conservative Party, an MP and then member of the House of Lords, he was non-conforming, rarely attended either house, held government office only during periods of national crisis and coalition politics during both world wars and preferred less accountable methods of negotiation and political influence.[21] This was entirely consonant with the activities of newspaper ownership, which took an increasing amount of his attention after the war, and a perception of the press as representing an independent but influential organ of the free state.

These two factors, the changing political terrain and the sense of outsiderness, account for why Beaverbrook sought both to influence broad popular opinion through the persuasiveness of the mass media – he was also involved in cinema production – and to develop a national memorial through the more specialised and traditional appeal of art. Both the British and the Canadian War Memorials Committees were motivated by the recognition that art was prestigious and enduring. The schemes were an act of self-commemoration. Beaverbrook is said to have said to Masterman, 'Queer isn't it . . . to think of the people that will be looking at this when we are dead'.[22] On the one hand, the Memorial scheme was a private and personal project with Beaverbrook acting as a modern aristocratic patron and, on the other, it was a national state project, an extension of statesmanship assuming and acting in the national interest. This differentiates the War Memorials Committee project from pre-war enterprises such as Barnett's Whitechapel Art Gallery or Henry Tate's gift of a National Gallery of British Art on Millbank that linked cultural authority with a philanthropic mission.[23] It explains also how Beaverbrook could conceive the British project as part of his personal aggrandisement and delegate all the day to day running and important decisions to experts, particularly Bennett.

As the most active committee member, Arnold Bennett was keen to promote opportunities for younger avant-garde artists. P. G. Konody, recruited as an adviser because of his position advising the Canadian fund, was always an outsider to the deliberations, and his proposals were the least persuasive. When Beaverbrook dismissed the advisers at the point of crisis in the Committee's affairs, Bennett stated that he was never in favour of Konody's presence. His taste was said to be eclectic and unreliable and he lacked the status of Dodgson or Ross. Moreover, Konody was Hungarian and trained in Vienna. Bennett said 'he is not English, and his reputation is in various ways peculiar'.[24] Dodgson was present at many meetings, but he seems to have contributed little and the prime motivation for his involvement in Wellington House days, the benefit to the British Museum, was no longer an issue. His long and essentially conservative influence on the employment of war artists was eclipsed. In later years, Yockney wrote that the quality of the collection owed something to 'the early sieve of Masterman, Bennett, Ross and others'.[25] Masterman supplied administrative expertise but played an ever less active role in any decision-making. He made no interventions to avert the crisis in the Committee's financial status, considering the whole episode a romantic example of departmental defiance of Treasury objection. He clearly understood the spurious nature of the arguments employed: 'Its [the Treasury's] perpetual request to know how the painting of pictures which could only be exhibited after the war could be defined as British propaganda during hostilities provoked a series of replies which as State documents might serve as monuments of persuasive casuistry.'[26] Bennett functioned as an intermediary between the executive members and the expert advisers. He was a personal friend of Beaverbrook and shared Masterman's politics.[27] His standing in literary and artistic worlds was high. Bennett's influence, in combination with Bone's, was decisive in the formation of a distinctive body of work, for representing the spectrum of British art and for including original and risky practitioners and excluding the safe and second-rate.[28]

The particular form of the pictures, their size and the conception of 'monumental . . . historical paintings'[29] was determined by Ross, who set out the aesthetic character of the scheme. Ross was better connected in the art world and had greater authority than Konody through his position as trustee at the Tate and adviser to other bodies. When the advisers were excluded, Bennett, not understanding the politics of the situation, attributed Ross's dismissal to a connection with Oscar Wilde, and seeing it as a form of censorship threatened to resign. He wrote to Beaverbrook, having noted Konody's lack of credibility as an adviser:

> There can be only one reason for getting rid of Ross. His name was mentioned in the Billing trial; his friendly relations with Oscar Wilde are well known; and Alfred Douglas is his declared enemy. Ross is an entirely honest man. He stuck to Oscar when Oscar was ruined, and without reward of any kind he has put Oscar's family on its feet. He is not a sodomist, never was, and never defends sodomist doctrines. He merely has a weakness for looking after people in adversity. He is one of the foremost experts in the world, a trustee of the Tate Gallery, adviser to Colonial governments, and prominent in various art organisations. After one of the trials into which he was forced by Alfred Douglas he received a public testimonial from 200 of the most distinguished people in England, of all ranks and camps. His character will stand any investigation.

If Ross was sacked, he said, 'It could not fail in the end to prejudice the Committee.'[30]

The context of Bennett's letter was the libel action brought by the actress Maud Allan in May 1918 against the right-wing MP Pemberton Billing for an article in which Billing had alleged that Allan was sexually perverted on the evidence of a private performance in Wilde's *Salome* at the Independent Theatre Company. Billing had claimed that the Germans had assembled a 'Black Book' listing the sexual weaknesses of prominent English men and women and were using the information to blackmail individuals into taking up a pro-German position. This fantastic story, trading on war-weariness and Wilde's disgrace, won Billing wide public acclaim and he was acquitted of libel. Ross, as Wilde's executor and friend, was implicated. Bennett, some days before his note to Beaverbrook and coinciding with the Committee's crisis, had written an article in defence of Salome.[31] At the trial, a direct connection with the Ministry of Information and propaganda was made public.

J. T. Grein, who ran the Independent Theatre Society, was instrumental in bringing the prosecution of Billing. He had been invited by Robert Donald to become General Organiser of the Theatrical Propaganda Companies, and admitted his part in propaganda under cross-examination. He declared in the witness-box that he intended to produce *Salome* abroad in neutral countries because the play was 'a masterpiece and contains the finest piece of prose in modern English. It is cherished and honoured in every civilised country'. When asked about finance, Grein stated 'I render an account of everything to Lord Beaverbrook'.[32] Although Grein's role was very small, the Ministry issued a denial and disposed of Grein, who in turn denied the denial. In the process the Ministry incurred certain legal expenses that had come to the attention of the Treasury, at a point of great sensitivity in the financial arrangements of the British War Memorials Committee.[33]

The Billing case and Bennett's defence of Ross reveal also how avant-garde culture, related to a claim for aesthetic freedom, continued to be associated with the sexually libertarian. In the context of war, to assert social and cultural freedoms was to risk being termed disloyal, unpatriotic and subversive. Bennett disengaged Ross's status as an expert and his character from any connection with an illegal sexual act and attributed his public vilification to the selflessness of caring for 'people in adversity'. When homosexuality was treated as a public spectacle and became a cause of moral panic, it was linked in this period at one level with imperialist sentiment and a fear of racial decline and at another with fear of the corruption of the young and the crossing of class barriers, as exemplified in the trials of Oscar Wilde. During 1918, Ross was also harassed by the police and suspected of being a pacifist.[34] When Ross died at the age of forty-nine in October 1918, the Tate recorded its 'deep sense of its loss', but his death did not warrant a mention in the minutes of the Pictorial Propaganda Committee by then chaired by Mond.[35] Together with the other advisers, he had already been quietly dropped from the Imperial War Museum.

There was a challenge, as well as a denial, in Bennett's repetitive assertion of Ross's innocence. Those involved with the British War Memorials Committee were inclined to characterise their project as an act of defiance. Bennett declared in a letter to a friend that he had succeeded 'in turning down *all* the R.A. painters, except Clausen. Some feat, believe me!' In retrospect, Masterman described the Ministry's relationship to the Treasury as 'defiant departmental action', and Bone recalled Bennett's mock-seriousness over 'the owlish world of use and wont being highly surprised' by what amounted to 'a revolution in official patronage'.[36] The committee visualised itself as a highly original and transgressive enterprise. What was being transgressed was an imagined model of state patronage as hackneyed, mediocre, unenterprising and, therefore, inimical to artistic freedom and licence. Opposing such an imaginary model provided the Memorial Committee with its own sense of identity, and it attributed the characteristics of the opposing tendency towards conventionality to the duller and more prosaic War Museum, set up to collect records and not art, which had hastily convened an art committee in August 1918 to counteract Beaverbrook. Chaired by an MP, Ian Malcolm, with General Sir Baden-Powell (founder of the Boy Scouts), it included no experts in art.[37] Given the British War Memorials Committee's independence and originality, it was not anomalous for it to seek the release of Duncan Grant to paint war pictures even though he was registered as a conscientious objector. The effort failed despite Grant's willingness, Beaverbrook's appeal to Viscount Hambleden and an attempt to enlist the influence of Maynard Keynes.[38]

The British War Memorials Committee operated without official sanction. It could claim, on the one hand, that the pictures that would emerge were in the national interest because the authority of the State was represented by a peer of the realm and a Government minister. Although effectively a conservative process, on the other hand, it could claim liberal credentials because it was illegitimately formed and subsequently harassed. It could define itself almost as an avant-garde activity expressing the values of a cultural elite in twentieth-century art. In this way, the political nature of commissioning modern history paintings of an epochal event could be erased and public debate about how the war might be represented was postponed until the unveiling of a complete and conclusive representation. A memorial formed in such circumstances would not produce representations for open critical appraisal because it was predetermined in the national interest and could only be patriotic. It was in this sense that Bennett could claim that the committee's activities had nothing to do with politics.

Canons, Subjects, Money

The British War Memorials Committee changed the whole emphasis of official war art. Wellington House had employed artists primarily to meet the exigent needs of propaganda. Beaverbrook's committee was set up to create what it termed 'a legacy to posterity'.[39] First named the Imperial Permanent Memorials Committee, it was designed to serve the purposes of remembrance. The idea that the Great War was an epochal event that required immortalising in permanent memorials emerged as early as 1915 and became urgent once the War Office had banned the exhumation of bodies from France for reburial in Britain.[40] War memorials were planned to commemorate the citizen–soldiers of conscripted armies; their deaths were remembered as acts of self-sacrifice for the greater need of national survival. Because the war was construed as the war to end all wars, the magnitude of the conflict created a debt to be repaid in the lessons it had to teach the future. Sir Martin Conway wrote in 1915 that those who died in the fight for freedom would deserve the gratitude of generations.[41] The preoccupation with imagining how to commemorate a war when an Allied victory was far from guaranteed was a matter of capitalising on the moment while expressing the hope that there was a future. The basis for the British War Memorials Committee's first discussions was the Canadian War Memorials Fund article, published in 1917 for Canadian readers, in which clichéd platitudes masked anxieties about wasteful destruction. Art was imagined rising phoenix-like from Armageddon and surviving 'to teach posterity of the glorious past of the race, and to keep alive the flame of patriotism'. Works of art had to be made while there was still a war to witness because an urgent historic mission necessitated that these be 'based on personal experience . . . created from actual impressions . . . whilst emotions and passions and enthusiasm are at their highest'. It was argued that 'the colourless, academic reconstruction from descriptive material, which has brought the art of the battle-painter into discredit' had no value to the future. It was a logical consequence that a range of artists, rather than a single prominent individual, had to be employed in order to capture the diversity of experiences representing 'the whole vast significance of this war'.[42] Each artist had to evolve their work freely with 'the fullest liberty to do whatever may best suit his temperament' or the quality would suffer and its value would be compromised. But 'rather elastic restrictions' aimed at preserving a general decorative unity demonstrated the co-operative nature of the collective effort or, as the British War Memorials Committee put it, setting standard sizes for paintings guaranteed works of art 'epitomizing the war in as varied and conclusive a way as possible'.[43]

The Canadian scheme set the precedent for the British one, but it was the product of a distinctive national context and its purpose was different. The first canvas commissioned and completed, in 1917, was the Academician Richard Jack's twenty-foot epic *The Second Battle of Ypres, 22 April to 25 May 1915* (fig. 53). Although Jack received an honorary commission and visited the front to survey the terrain and interview participants, this was a conventional, illustrative battle-piece not a witnessed image. The painting, however, commemorated the first major action of Canadian troops at the front and like other subjects commissioned later, such as Jack's own *The Taking of Vimy Ridge*, Augustus John's *The Canadians Opposite Lens* (fig. 54), William Roberts's *The First German Gas Attack at Ypres* (see fig. 90), or David Bomberg's *Sappers at Work:*

A Canadian Tunnelling Company (see fig. 83), it served the purpose of recognising the Dominion's contribution to the Imperial cause but also enabling the visualisation of a nascent Canadian nationalism not dependent on colonial ties. By contrast, no painting in the British scheme illustrated a retrospective event and artists were not allocated topics. Potential subjects for paintings were considered by the British committee – Bone, J. H. Watkins (secretary to the Canadian War Memorials Fund) and Yockney wrote a paper assembling subjects suggested by the western front and Konody and Derrick prepared a similar one about the home front – but while both papers attached artists' names to specific topics they also argued for the necessity of consulting individuals in order to guarantee the best work.[44] When the two lists were amalgamated, fourteen names emerged, of whom only eight painted canvasses, and only two proposals, Henry Tonks the R.A.M.C. and Darsie Japp, Artillery, were actually painted. The exercise did not determine which artists were chosen to paint which subjects.[45] Artists were given considerable autonomy in choosing their own. John Nash, William Roberts and Randolph Schwabe were asked to suggest their titles. Nevinson wanted to paint a field casualty clearing station but because this was already being covered by Tonks, he was asked to consider an alternative.[46] The title he eventually chose, *The Harvest of Battle*, represented casualties of war. Artists were often interviewed by the committee's advisers when details of subjects and titles were negotiated and agreed.[47] Ross wrote to Yockney 'Nash and Nevinson have promised to write formal acceptance before Wednesday stating what subject they suggest'. Paul Nash's canvas was nominally set as *A Flanders Battlefield* and when he submitted three sketches, Yockney advised 'so long as you keep within the scope of the title it would be better for you to develop the theme you prefer'.[48] Henry Lamb was told he could represent France or Palestine as he wished.[49]

Memorial paintings by older artists such as Charles Sims and D. Y. Cameron who did not serve, still required those artists to see the sights of the front. Visits to France resumed in July 1918 but much of the character of the front, its staleness and stagnation, was changed. In early August, the German army began a rapid retreat and large numbers deserted or surrendered. The Armistice in November was unexpected. Given the rapid turn of events, many trips ended

53   Richard Jack, *The Second Battle of Ypres, 22 April to 25 May 1915*, 1917, oil on canvas, 371.5 × 589, Beaverbrook Collection of War Art, 8179, © Canadian War Museum

up taking place after the war, including Sims's and Cameron's for example. Consequently, these works often depict the aftermath and detritus of conflict, and appear like melancholic acts of remembrance. Other painters, such as Stanley Spencer and Henry Lamb, were not free to begin their commission until 1919. Younger soldier–artists, some of whom declined the opportunity to re-visit the front line, usually elected to paint major canvasses that summarised remembered experiences. These were highly specific and acutely tuned to a sense of time and place, not imaginative compositions or allegories. When Robert Ross wrote a paper for the British committee outlining the aesthetic questions involved in commissioning history

paintings, he warned about making a fetish of working from first-hand observation, noting that to produce a monumental work necessitated time for reflection and a process of synthesis 'so that in one sense while we must avoid popular misconceptions of events such as are seen in the illustrated papers, the panels must be *reconstructed* from sketches'.[50]

The Canadian memorial paintings self-consciously documented historic Canadian participation in the war effort and so some process of artists negotiating their choices from a list of topics was necessary; not at all the same as being told what to paint, however. William Roberts, for example, recollected an interview with Konody about his painting for the Canadians in which

54   Augustus John, *The Canadians opposite Lens*, 1919, charcoal on paper, 370 × 1230, National Gallery of Canada, Ottawa, Massey Foundation gift

he was told that all the subjects had been allocated except one, but he decided to take the one on offer.[51] The documentary nature of these works were in the tradition of ambitious nineteenth-century military painting such as that by Édouard Détaille and Alphonse de Neuville in France after the Franco-Prussian War which served to demonstrate the unity of army and nation (fig. 55).[52] The Canadian scheme was dominated by British artists, justified in January 1919 when the first set of pictures were shown at the Royal Academy as a determination to avoid parochialism. It is an obvious consequence that some stipulation about relevance to 'Canadianess' must have figured in the negotiations with these artists, a condition not applicable to the British scheme. The Canadian War Memorials Fund set out to collect what it termed 'a fair picture of the artistic conditions which prevailed at the most momentous epoch of the world's history', and its choice of artists was catholic and encyclopaedic rather than selective.[53] Early commissions went entirely to British artists but in autumn 1917, Eric Brown, curator of the National Gallery of Canada, Ottawa, and Sir Edmund Walker, chair of its Trustees, pressed for the inclusion of Canadians.[54] The National Gallery of Canada was founded in 1880 but did not have a board of trustees until 1913, received meagre funding and did not have its own building.[55] Brown, an Englishman, was its first full-time curator and was appointed in 1910. The gallery was closed from 1916 to 1921 when its rooms in the Victoria Museum were occupied by the Canadian Houses of Parliament after a fire in 1916. The War Memorials Fund was intended to build up the national collections and Beaverbrook used it to

acquire historic paintings relevant to Canadian patrimony for the national collection, most importantly George Romney's *Portrait of Joseph Brant (Thayendanegea), Sachem of the Mohawks* (fig. 56) of 1776, purchased at Christies' in March 1918, and Benjamin West's *The Death of General Wolfe* of 1770, donated by the Duke of Westminster in recognition of the Dominion's contribution to the war effort (fig. 57). Wolfe's victory over the French at the Battle of Québec in 1759 was decisive in securing Canada for the British Empire. A renewed cult of Wolfe, expressed for example in the draping with Canadian regimental colours of Wilton's Monument to Wolfe in Westminster Abbey during the war, emphasised the unity of Canada and England at a time when French Canadians were articulating a nationalism based on an independent federation of autonomous provinces in order to preserve the distinctive linguistic and cultural identity of the Québecquois.[56]

The British War Memorials Committee's primary emphasis was on selectivity and exclusiveness. Bennett wrote that 'if the collection of pictures as a whole is to have real weight and authority it must first of all reasonably satisfy the expert' and urged the employment of younger artists 'with ideas of their own opposed to traditional conventions'.[57] The most influential recommendations of artists to recruit came from Bone, who worked closely with Bennett and Ross; from the Slade teacher Henry Tonks, who was also a contributor; and from Walter Sickert, incidentally one of the few artists to decline to participate and the only one of any note to do so. In the selections, two institutions dominated, the Slade School of Art and the

New English Art Club, an artists' organisation established in 1886 to oppose the Royal Academy. The Academy itself had no influence over the scheme. The way the British War Memorials Committee operated consolidated initiatives, begun before the war and focused particularly on the Tate Gallery, to control key national institutions, to modernise their policies and to promote a progressive image of contemporary British art. The Tate's main source of acquisitions, apart from donations, was the Chantrey Bequest. This came into effect in 1877 under the terms of the sculptor Sir Francis Chantrey's will to purchase works of art produced in Britain though not necessarily by British artists. The bequest, an obvious and important source of contemporary patronage, was administered by the Royal Academy and purchases tended to be from Academy summer shows, such as Joseph Farquarson's *A Joyless Winter Day* of about 1883 and Lawrence Alma-Tadema's *A Favourite Custom* of 1909. The Tate was required to accept these as set out in a Treasury minute when the gallery was established. The critic D. S. MacColl, Keeper of the Tate 1906–11, campaigned against the Academy's control of the bequest, leading to an enquiry by a Select Committee of the House of Lords in 1904. When the Tate's Board of Trustees was established in 1917, the Academy sent a delegation to the Treasury demanding representation and complaining that the board had been taken over by 'a few self-constituted experts' (Poynter, President of the Royal Academy) and 'our active enemies . . . the parasites of the arts' (Blomfield). They received an unsympathetic hearing.[58]

In the period before the war, a close coterie of critics, art collectors and art administrators manoeuvred to take control of the Tate and its acquisitions policies at a crucial point in the formation of the modern collection. These circles of influence overlapped significantly with the British War Memorials Committee. One of the first activities of the Tate's new board was the appointment of a sub-committee consisting of MacColl, Ross, C. J. Holmes (director of the National Gallery and a contributor to the British War Memorials scheme), and R. C. Witt (who together with MacColl and Roger Fry had been instrumental in the establishment of the National Art Collections Fund (NACF) in 1903, designed to save major works of art for the nation). The purpose of the Tate's sub-committee was to draw up lists of artists who ought

55   Alphonse de Neuville, *Le Cimetière de Saint-Privat 18 Aout 1870*, 1881, oil on canvas, 23.5 × 34.1, Musée d'Orsay, Paris

56   George Romney, *Portrait of Joseph Brant (Thayendanegea), Sachem of the Mohawks*, 1776, oil on canvas, 127 × 101.6, National Gallery of Canada, Ottawa

57   Benjamin West, *The Death of General Wolfe*, 1770, oil on canvas, 152.6 × 214.5, National Gallery of Canada, Ottawa

to be represented at Millbank.[59] The NACF worked closely with the Contemporary Art Society (CAS), formed in 1909–10, to purchase through private initiative works by younger artists for public collections. Original members included MacColl, Holmes, Fry and Charles Aitken, then director of the Whitechapel Art Gallery who replaced MacColl at the Tate. They were joined by Ross, who along with Fry and MacColl made the first purchases. In 1917, the CAS presented Nevinson's *La Mitrailleuse* (see fig. 8) to the Tate.[60] In May 1918, the CAS was involved with the Ministry of Information's selection for an exhibition of pictures for Switzerland. Fry wrote to his mother 'it may interest you to know that an exhibition of English art is being organised in Switzerland (as propaganda!) and that I'm sending a good many things and also writing the

preface. The fact that not a single R.A. is invited to send shows how things have moved.'[61] When Ross came to advise the British War Memorials Committee he was already practised at identifying significant contemporary artists to form a canon of modern British art. When the question of housing the committee's collection was first broached, Ross suggested a special wing at the Tate, in effect integrating the works into the existing national collection of modern British art.[62]

It was Ross who argued that the committee's paintings should be uniform in dimension and scale, adding to their value as a series and making them easier to hang: 'They ought then to possess that monumental character essential to historical paintings.' If any special building were to be built he imagined it as modest and select, with architecture subordinated to works of art and something like the Scuole in Venice decorated by Carpaccio, Tintoretto and Tiepolo. Velasquez's *Surrender of Breda* (fig. 58), at ten by twelve feet, which was the size selected for the majority of the Canadian paintings, was one idea for scale, but Ross settled on six by ten feet, the dimensions of Uccello's *Battle of San Romano* (fig. 59) in the National Gallery, the only extant successful battle-painting.[63] A reduced 'Uccello' size, six by seven feet was also adopted. The Canadian paintings were bigger and the scheme itself much larger. Forty decorative or allegorical canvases were eventually produced, most twelve by ten feet, plus larger canvases by Jack and Sims (fig. 60) and a forty-foot epic panorama by Augustus John (see fig. 54) which he never completed. The National Gallery of Canada eventually received the entire collection in 1921, but in January 1919 plans for a war memorial building to house their collection were published. Designed by E. A. Rickards, a partner in the firm Lanchester, Stewart and Rickards, architects for Cardiff City Hall and the Wesleyan Central Convocation Hall, Westminster, the proposal was presented less as a definitive idea and more as a suggestion best developed by a Canadian architect. Rickard's drawings and plans showed a monumental neo-Baroque building, cruciform in plan and symmetrical in elevation capped with an octagonal dome. It deliberately evoked the Pantheon, Paris (fig. 61).[64] When the Canadian Houses of Parliament were rebuilt they were dedicated as a war memorial, including a Peace Tower and a Book of Remembrance. The neo-Gothic chapel-like Senate Chamber was hung with eight of the Canadian War Memorials canvases in 1922, all by British artists including Clausen, William Rothenstein and Clare Atwood (fig. 62). The idea of a separate memorial building for the Canadian War Memorial Fund pictures alone became irrelevant, although throughout the 1920s the existence of the collection was used in numerous campaigns to fund a permanent building for the National Gallery of Canada.

When the British scheme established standard sizes for commissioned canvasses, it was decided to include three 'super-sized' pictures, or twenty-foot 'double-Uccellos', by Sargent, John and Orpen, possibly depicting American and English, British and French, and Italian and British co-operation at the front respectively. Sargent was the only artist to make a twenty-foot painting and he selected his own subject, *Gassed* (see fig. 72); John and Orpen never started theirs (an eight-foot canvas, *Fraternity*, by John has been misidentified as a fragment of his planned work) (fig. 63).[65] Muirhead Bone took the initiative writing a paper about a 'Great Memorial Gallery' in response to Ross's proposals about 'monumental . . . historical paintings'. He imagined a modest but noble building with a small set of galleries and including sculpture, to be sited on Richmond Hill.[66] The costs of the paintings planned, three super-sized, twelve large canvases and twenty-one smaller works in three galleries, fewer and smaller works than the Canadian memorial paintings, were estimated at £29,267 4s (£29,267.20).[67] Yockney wrote to the architect Charles Holden asking if he would be interested in the architectural project, but no reply seems to have been received and Holden never made any designs.[68] The idea was ill-timed and disappeared when the British War Memorial Committee became the Pictorial Propaganda Committee, although a paper referring to a scheme for the works' ultimate exhibition rather than permanent installation was produced.[69] In the developing crisis over the finance and future of the Memorial Committee the issue of sculpture was also put in abeyance. While Bennett addressed a memorandum to Beaverbrook urging discussion because it was absurd to employ sculptors without knowing how the work was to be displayed, Needham, acting as administrative adviser, had discovered that it was virtually impossible to develop the sculptural aspects of the scheme. He pointed out that as a consequence of negotiations with

58   Diego Rodgriguez de Silva y Velasquez, *The Surrender of Breda (Las Lanzas)*, before 1635, oil on canvas, 307 × 367, Prado, Madrid

59 Paolo Uccello, *Niccolò Maruzi da Tolentino at the Battle of San Romano*, c.1438–40, egg tempera with walnut oil and linseed oil on poplar, 181.6 × 320, National Gallery, London

the Treasury, the Ministry found itself in a situation where its activities must demonstrably arise out of the war and where it could spend money only on propaganda. Sculpture could be commissioned if it was of transitory interest, but only work of more than transitory interest was appropriate. There was no future for sculpture: 'What you can do, you will not do, because it would be poor propaganda compared with other forms (having regard to cost and effect) of propaganda; and what you would like to do, you may not do.'[70] Because it was envisaged that a successful sculpture project must be both monumental and enduring, the issue of how to develop it was in a logical impasse. C. S. Jagger and Gilbert Ledward each executed an eight-foot plaster relief as samples of sculpture that might have been produced (fig. 64).

Several artists in the Canadian scheme, including Wyndham Lewis, William Roberts and David Bomberg, worked on a speculative basis with materials provided but no guarantee of acceptance. When it came to determining payments to artists in the British scheme, two principles were established. First, Ross proposed that these should be uniform, regardless of an artist's reputation. For artists commissioned to paint one major canvas, known as Scheme I, payment followed size: £300 for the large canvases and £150 for five-foot paintings, with expenses for materials, visits and studios paid. It was assumed that the artists would each take about six months to com-

plete a canvas. Related to the principle of uniform prices was the assumption that artists would work below their usual market rate. The idea that state employment involved an element of patriotic duty and democratised salaries and conditions had already applied in the salaries negotiated for Bone, McBey and Dodd under Wellington House where, for instance, Bone's salary of £500 per annum represented a substantial drop on his pre-war income. It was a consequence of large-scale enlistment that many civilians who volunteered also opted for uniform income and conditions of service and the idea of total war and national effort implied submission of individual status and lifestyle to collective endeavour. In practice, national service recreated social class divisions with an immense gulf between officers, whom these scales of payment represented, and other ranks. Yet virtually all the artists in Scheme I were receiving payments well below their usual rate. For instance, Sargent, who was an exceptionally well-paid artist, charged 1000 guineas (£1,050) for a full-length portrait and £500 to £800 for lesser pictures in the years before the war and raised £20,000 for the British Red Cross with two canvases during the war,[71] but was paid a double rate of £600 for his twenty-foot canvas. Artists who were employed full-time in what was known as Scheme 2, were offered salaries of £300 per annum plus army pay and expenses for materials and studios. However, it proved difficult to maintain army pay for artists who were

60   Charles Sims, *Sacrifice*, 1918, oil on canvas, 416 × 409, Beaverbrook Collection of War Art, 8802, © Canadian War Museum

61 E. A. Rickards, *Design for a Canadian National War Memorial Art Gallery, Ottawa, 1918*, © Canadian War Museum

62 Houses of Parliament, Canada: Canadian Senate Chamber

63 Augustus John, *Fraternity* (fragment of *The Canadians opposite Lens*, fig. 54), *c.*1918, oil on canvas, 237.5 × 145, Imperial War Museum, London

technically still serving soldiers, and a salary of £500 per annum was offered, reduced to £400 in November 1918 as a consequence of Treasury cuts to the Memorial project.[72] All the work of an artist during his period of employment was retained and conditions were strict. Yockney refused permission for Nash to work on tapestry designs for Sims, and Meninsky was required to work for a period without pay to make up a day a week teaching at the Central School of Art he had taken on during his employment.

Many of the Scheme 2 artists also made a major memorial canvas for which there was no additional payment. For some of the artists in the scheme, particularly young painters like Roberts and Meninsky, the salary was probably an improvement on more precarious pre-war circumstances and compared reasonably favourably with service pay. It was, however, adequate but only modest by middle-class standards (Yockney was appointed on a salary of £4 per week in 1916)[73] and was probably considerably less than the earnings of most reasonably successful and established artists.[74] In 1920, Yockney estimated the total cost of the Memorial Committee scheme at £10,569 15s 3d (£10,569.77)[75] about half the £20,000 that Beaverbrook had thought essential for the success of the project.

Commissioning History Paintings

Benjamin West, whose *Death of General Wolfe* (see fig. 57) was shown as part of the Canadian War Memorials exhibition at the Royal Academy in January 1919, was an apposite precedent for modern artists engaged in the reinvention of history painting. When it was shown at the Royal Academy in 1771, *The Death of General Wolfe* was said to have occasioned a revolution because a painting in the grand style showed its principal figures in contemporary dress. The 1919 catalogue reproduced the story, promoted in John Galt's biography of West which the artist himself largely controlled, that when Joshua Reynolds, first president of the Royal Academy, heard about West's intentions he declared that it would go against all traditions and result in a loss of grace and elegance. West is said to have answered 'What I lose in grace I shall gain in Simplicity.'[76] The idea that West was an independent but not irresponsible artist who drew his own conclusions and acted out of principle could then be transposed to the image of the modern avant-garde artist, officially employed by the state but untrammelled by convention or constraint. The reason for the success of West's *Death of General Wolfe* over earlier versions of the same subject by George Romney (now lost) or Edward Penny, in 1763, was that it was an invention painted in the epic style that also appeared compellingly truthful even though none of the figures depicted surrounding Wolfe was actually present at the moment of his death. The Reverend Bromley's eulogistic account of the work in 1793 declared that the invention was the basis of its authenticity:

> In every one of those circumstances there is a freedom, and a most legitimate, judicious, and masterly, though abundant, freedom of variation from the real circumstances of the case. As they stand before us, they are so natural that no-one would hardly expect them to be otherwise than they

64   C. S. Jagger, *The Battle of Ypres, 1914: The Worcesters at Gheluvelt*, 1918–19, plaster relief, 243.8 × 391, Imperial War Museum, London

appear; and they come so near to the truth of history, that they are almost true, and yet not one of them is true in fact. . . . Had he taken facts merely as they stood, in vain would he have tried to reach any one passion of the heart. But mark what a climax of most interesting concern now arises from the whole, gathering new feelings in it's [*sic*] gradations to consummate glory in the hero, and consummate admiration with distress combined in the beholder.[77]

West's epic painting was designed to provoke the viewer's empathetic identification with the death of the hero. In a similar way, the British scheme commissioned works of art that played on a relationship between reportage and invention when it sought monumental history paintings of witnessed events. The work would provide authentic testimony and it would serve the purposes of remembrance.

Earlier British state initiatives for national commissions were building on a spasmodic and not always successful tradition for national commissions in the nineteenth century. For example, between 1907 and 1910, decorations for the Palace of Westminster were extended to the East corridor, but these were by conservative and academic artists illustrating subjects from Tudor history, and criticised at the time for lacking contemporaneity and therefore real value as history paintings.[78] The British War Memorials Committee was a more radical initiative because, unlike the Canadian scheme, it deliberately rejected even the recent past of the Great War by refusing to commission retrospective battle pictures and insisting that artists undertake paintings of subjects they had witnessed. An existing tradition for nineteenth-century battle painting was viewed as inauthentic and populist, and lacking the credibility and authority needed in a project that sought to incorporate avant-garde artists.

The advent of the avant-garde in the mid-nineteenth century unsettled a prescribed hierarchy of genres that assigned decorums of scale and ambition to different types of subject matter. The great tradition of 'la peinture d'histoire' degenerated into a thriving practice of realist history painting, markedly so after the Franco-Prussian War of 1870–71 and with the growth of European Imperialism. It became banal because of its over-presence in civic, municipal and state buildings. Ernest Meissonier in France or Anton von Werner in Germany are taken to exemplify realist history painting, with perhaps an early twentieth-century British example being Frank Brangwyn, who was excluded from the British War Memorials Committee's selections.[79] Such work was said to be historical painting in the service of history and it was put into crisis by artists such as Courbet and Millet with their insistence on the contemporaneity of their work, both being and becoming history itself – 'L'ambition de cette peinture fut *d'être* de l'histoire et de *devenir* histoire'.[80]

In contrast to such widely accepted narratives about the eclipse of history painting, however, avant-garde artists did not signify their modernity by abandoning ambitions to tackle big programmatic pictures. On the contrary, the avant-garde continued to attempt to secure a place in art's most significant recent history by challenging its most prestigious genre, and it was also a crucial strategy in a contest for advanced status to undertake a large-scale canvas. Examples include Seurat's *La Grande Jatte*, Matisse's *Le Bonheur de Vivre*, Picasso's *Demoiselles d'Avignon* and Wyndham Lewis's nine-foot square now-lost *Kermesse* (fig. 65) of 1912 – all in some way worth thinking about as forms of modern history painting because they take on some of those concerns, such as being philosophically grounded and self-reflective, even political, or referenced to art-historical precedent, or ambitious for an audience and aiming to impress by more than simply scale. In Britain, the aspiration to make major canvases was fostered in art education by the curriculum of the Slade School of Art, which set termly compositions and themes for summer competitions for fourth-year students in which Memorial artists such as William Roberts and Stanley Spencer participated.[81] If producing works on the scale of great history painting was still a preoccupation for the pre-war avant-garde and subject painting was part of art-school training, the British War Memorials Committee was not necessarily putting pressure on young or avant-garde artists to do something very exceptional, even academic and anti-avant-garde, by commissioning major paintings on the subject of modern war. But this still leaves questions about the successes and failures of modern history painting and how to do it, and read it, for an event as self-consciously historical as the Great War.

The prime English text, and the most modern, on history painting and its value to the nation-state, was Reynolds's *Discourses*, first published in 1778 and reissued in a new edition edited by Roger Fry in 1905. An early and influential exponent of modernist and formalist protocols, Fry viewed his own life's work as an attempt to update Reynolds's work for the modern period while preserving the ambitions of his project.[82] The contemporary value of *Discourses* for Fry was its promotion of art as a serious intellectual activity

65 Wyndham Lewis, *Kermesse*, 1912, ink, wash and gouache, 35 × 35.1, Yale Center for British Art, New Haven

essential to civilised society which could be properly practised and appreciated only by an elite, free of commercial self-interest.[83] Fry set out the basis of his formalist aesthetics in his 'Essay on Aesthetics' published in 1909. The work of art was to be adapted to what he described as 'disinterested intensity of contemplation' in order to serve the imaginative life, distinguished from actual life 'by the absence of responsive action' or 'moral responsibility'. Contemplating art did not involve an ethical attitude and the viewer would not be prompted to act or judge. Instead, viewing art would stimulate the imaginative life of the spectator which was to be fully and freely experienced without constraint or persuasion.[84]

When Fry exemplified Reynolds's principles of unity in the grand style, by comparing Rubens's *St. Augustine Altarpiece* (1628) with van Eyck's *Adoration of the Lamb* (1432), to the detriment of Rubens, he was making a judgement that had become commonplace by the early twentieth century. High renaissance and baroque art had been almost completely eclipsed by admiration of early Renaissance artists, then usually termed 'primitive'.[85] The British War Memorials Committee could have drawn on two major Renaissance works in English collections – the Raphael cartoons and Mantegna's *Triumphs of Caesar* – as examples of an epic narrative series, although only the Mantegna corresponded to the aesthetics of the period.[86] The linearity, relative flatness and simplicity, particularly of early Italian art, not only fitted in with a modern aesthetic, it was also equated with sincerity, which was taken to mean directness and purity or naiveté. It was assumed such work could never moralise or dissimulate. Not only did Italian and Flemish painting before 1500 lack rhetorical pretension, it was also said to avoid narrative closure and resolution. It left matters open to the spectator's imaginative speculation. Mantegna was the subject of a major monograph by the Berlin art historian Paul Kristeller, published in English in 1901 in advance of the German edition. For Kristeller, Mantegna's relevance was his appeal to a modern desire to turn away 'from the rhetoric of Raphaelesque form-harmonies that sought to reconcile all contradictions'.[87] Fry said early Renaissance art moved the contemporary viewer because 'we love sincerity and intensity of feeling more than the artifices of a careful rhetoric.'[88] The crucial point is that advanced liberal thinking suspected all works of art that were appar-

ently overtly persuasive or prescriptive; as Wolfgang Kemp puts it in his study of transformations in history and narrative painting, the modern artist was called upon to arrange 'spaces and surfaces, which are open to the projective activity of the beholder' now summoned simply as witness, not judge or actor.[89]

Promoting openness, lack of prescription, reverie and imaginative activity, however, was not the same as admiring works of art that were contradictory, even confused, and open to misinterpretation. Ambiguous and perplexing images risked readmitting the moral imperative, making viewing once again an exercise in rhetorical exegesis. To be truly modern, the spectator's imagination had to be freely exercised, never coerced. Moreover, rather than the subjects selected, what really mattered was how forms and materials were disposed in works of art. What an artist could do with subjects was more proscribed than it was prescribed. The free exercise of imaginative faculties in modernist viewing would never amount to an incitement to rebellion, however, because only those already equipped for disinterested contemplation could ever form the public for modern art. For Reynolds, as John Barrell has shown, the proper use and disposition of form mattered more than exemplary subjects or rhetoric, and works of art were 'an instructive metaphor' for public citizenship rather than direct incitements to acts of public virtue,[90] a reading that is compatible with Fry's own use of Reynolds.

The point of all this is that not only did the cult of early Renaissance art offer stylistic possibilities, which makes some of the British War Memorials Committee's big pictures look as they do, but that choosing a certain sort of style could also be taken as an instruction to the viewer to read a work for evidence of the artist's open-handed sincerity about what he showed. For example, the flatness and linearity of Stanley Spencer's *Travoys Arriving with Wounded at a Dressing Station* (fig. 66) was modelled on quattrocento painting, and it would have conveyed to the contemporary viewer the authenticity of what Spencer had witnessed as though unmediated by visual rhetoric or aesthetic convention. Even more to the point than how pictorial style addresses audiences, however, is the fact that because the Committee, claiming to act on behalf of the national interest, aspired to create and address a cultured public by commissioning modern history paintings, it could not have dictated subjects to the

66 Stanley Spencer, *Travoys Arriving with Wounded at a Dressing Station at Smol, Macedonia, September 1916*, 1919, oil on canvas, 183 × 218.4, Imperial War Museum, London

artists it employed, and therein lies its radicalness and its modernity.

Konody published an article about works of art as war memorials in which he argued for a modern war art that was individualised and democratic. He cited Goya's partisan *Los Desastres de la Guerra* and the Russian Vereshchagin's *Apotheosis of War* (fig. 67) of 1871–2, as precedents for modern humanitarian and anti-heroic images. In his survey of western war art from Assyria and ancient Egypt to the modern period,

he identified two factors that had made heroic images and battle panoramas inappropriate for the modern period, whether the 'unutterably dull' Galerie des Batailles, Versailles, or decorative pageants, such as Uccello's *Battle of San Romano*, selected as the standard bearer for the British pictures. First, modern wars were now fought by camouflaged and drab armies, concealed within vast areas of terrain in trenches and dugouts, and hand to hand fighting was virtually unknown. Modern warfare was unvisual and unvisual-

67   Vasily Vereshchagin, *The Apotheosis of War*, 1871–2, oil on canvas, 127.0 × 197.0, Tretyakov Gallery, Moscow

isable. But second, and more important than military tactics, modern nations were characterised by a new democratic spirit and an emphasis on the sufferings and deprivations of the common soldier. He argued that modern war art would not celebrate militarism, but function as 'a plea for universal peace' as befitted the war fought 'to end all wars'.[91] The British War Memorials Committee, in seeking to maintain the contemporaneity of its public historical enterprise and aspiring to recruit individual modern artists, was therefore predicated on an almost impossible negotiation and a delicate balance between the individual and the collective.[92]

Konody's article was published in 1919 and consequently it is not so much a prospectus for as a reflec-

tion on the outcomes of both the British and Canadian projects. In many ways, the immediate aftermath of the First World War was a point of historical vacuum, and commissioned war artists were being called upon to fill that vacuum, reinventing war painting in response to a sense of historical urgency. Like the Memorials project, this historical mission in 1918 was founded on a play between the private and the public, because a particular investment was made in works by artists who had served and who could therefore, it was assumed, in some way provide an insider's personal perspective within the public form of history painting. British society during the war was subject to a marked increase in Government control of the dissemination and interpretation of information. One function of soliciting participant testimony from soldier–artists was in part to fill gaps in public knowledge of war in its aftermath through assumptions about the authenticity of soldiers' accounts. As shall be discussed in the next chapter, a cult of authentic testimony did not guarantee that the work produced would satisfy public use. These works of art were sometimes greeted with misapprehension in what Leila Kinney has termed 'broken transactions of looking'.[93] The British War Memorials Committee's project was a fractured undertaking, and this fracturing was most acutely experienced in the uncertain and socially unstable period when the work was produced and exhibited, the closing months and immediate aftermath of the First World War.

four

Modern Art, Modern War
and the Impossible Project of History Painting

Representing the Unrepresentable

The British War Memorials Committee set a number of conditions concerning the size and format of a major canvas to provide a framework for what artists would produce. Because the specific details and subject matter were to be realised in the practicalities of viewing sights and generating material, however, what was left to the artists was the business of inventing some sort of visual realisation of war. A small community developed at the front when artists employed on behalf of the Canadian War Memorials Fund began to arrive in France towards the end of 1917. William Orpen came across Alfred Munnings at the Canadian Cavalry HQ.[1] Augustus John, collecting material for his forty-foot decorative canvas and billeted near Arras, was in touch with William Rothenstein working for Wellington House in the Péronne area alongside Kennington. In January 1918, Wyndham Lewis joined John. D. Y. Cameron and Charles Sims visited on behalf of the Canadians. Artists were inducted into a seemingly insulated existence joining the circuit of what Lewis later called 'the charmed circle of the Staff'.[2] Beaverbrook's patronage involved cultivating a fellowship of masculine camaraderie and celebratory dinners. Orpen recalled meeting Beaverbrook 'gee! I remember that day I first set eyes on you at Bologne. How tight I got ='.[3] The increasing numbers was also a change of experience from the isolation of Welling-ton House artists earlier in 1917. Orpen told Henry Tonks that once the Canadian contingent arrived it was 'not quite the same as it was . . . I liked it all alone'.[4]

The older artists were non-combatants and needed official visits to gather material for paintings. They came to see themselves as marginal to the real war, almost unworthy of the privilege. Rothenstein described army life with its lack of complexity as 'a kind of simple state-Socialism; & an official artist a kind of official parasite'.[5] Orpen titled his book about being a war artist *An Onlooker in France* and reinforced the self-deprecation by telling the reader that he was 'a mere looker-on'.[6] Augustus John was cold and often bored, feeling 'like a fish out of water'.[7] He wrote about 'wondering who I am . . . When out at the front I admire things unreasonably – and conduct myself with that instinctive tact which is the mark of the moral traitor.'[8] The crisis broke when he assaulted an officer and was hastily bundled out of France by Beaverbrook.[9] The guilt induced by being an artist at a war front preying on the deprivations and sufferings of others generated self-imposed obligations, different from those that may have been owed an official patron. The search for subjects, which was the purpose of the visits, started to become a duty compounded with debt and remorse or anxiety about the morality of painting the war. Rothenstein called it a 'sacred task' dedicated to the soldier but also voiced a dilemma: 'Had I asked myself, would I rather there had been no war, and consequently no such strange, livid beauty, I should have been at a loss how to answer'.[10] Anxieties about decorum imposed limits on what it might be decent to represent, but there was also something so overwhelming about the sights of war that it escaped comprehension making it incommunicable. Rothenstein, when he left the front, wondered 'if the horrors I had left behind me were real'.[11] Orpen remembered 'an officer saying to me, "Paint the Somme? I could do it from memory – just a flat horizon-line and mudholes and water, with the stumps of a few battered trees", but one could not paint the smell'.[12] Artists were not sheltered from the appalling spectacle. Henry Tonks, visiting from July to September 1918 with Sargent, was free to come and go at will but found the work difficult, 'I don't quite know how one does see more unless you're fighting in it'.[13] Twenty years later Lewis still maintained the exclusiveness of first-hand experience in the land beyond civilisation, 'the lunar landscape, so often described in the war-novels and represented by dozens of painters and draughtsmen, myself among them, but the particular quality of which it is so difficult to convey'.[14]

War has been called 'an impossible subject, the subversive force in the account which seeks to master it'.[15] Annegret Jürgens-Kirchhoff, writing about the problem of the visual representation of all twentieth-century wars, quotes a speech made by the German art historian Richard Hamann in 1917 about the unde-pictability of modern war. Either artists showed humanly interesting episodes which were merely minute trifles, a fragment of the enormous events, and the more naturalistic they were the more petty they became; or an artist tried to survey the entire battle-field in its vastness, in which case the battle was no longer visible becoming devoid of humans and showing only open country, ruins, smoke, clouds, heaven. The more painterly the depiction the less worthy it was to the greatness of age, the artist seemed to be an aesthetic and connoisseur. 'We would rather appreciate the voices that cry out in condemnation, representations of the martyrdoms of the fighters and wounded, the captured and fugitive. The martyrdom, however, that those enlisted to stand by their posts in the heavy barrage, which no depiction can describe, and the mass, the quantity of grief which such a war has brought over the world, cannot once in passing be compressed in the narrow space of a picture.'[16] If war painting was to seem compelling to its contemporary audiences, it had to attempt to convey the incommensurability of the Great War. When it commissioned modern history paintings of modern war, the British War Memorials Committee set its artists a challenge. Artists with their major canvases were to attempt to redeem this incommensurability.

Public and Private in the Nation's War Paintings

The British War Memorials Committee did not dictate subjects or styles. In as much as the Committee had visualised what it had in mind when it set about commissioning these large works of art, two distinctive ideas figured. One was to appeal to a remote but dignified past in the form of the Italian renaissance, which implies some conception of art in the service of civic humanism and public discourse. 'Grand tradition' intentions were signified by selecting Uccello's *Battle of San Romano* (see fig. 59) as the standard bearer in more than just size. The second was that the work should be distinguished from the discredited traditions of nineteenth century battle painting by representing both a democratic emphasis on the human costs of war and the unique and private visions of artists. It was considered vital that the works be free of any evidence of constraint. 'Grand tradition' aspirations and an investment in personal testimony meant that the project was attempting to satisfy two contradictory purposes. It would serve a disinterested public function, imagined as a national need to give instantaneous form to remembering the 'war to end all war' or art in its public civic role. But it would fulfil this ambition through independent and unconstrained works by individual artists, chosen as the best and most representative practitioners of the state's contemporary artistic capital in all its diversity, doing something new.

To measure up to the ambitions of the scheme, the artists were under pressure to come up with some invention for representing the unprecedented, and to use convention to make it comprehensible as historic and epoch-making. A tension between the giving of personal testimony and the making of a significant statement sometimes appears both in the self-conscious construction of the compositions and their deployment of painterly repertoire, and in the feeling that the images do not always quite leap the disjunction from private to public. It is this disjunction, often more overt in the case of work by artists who had served, that makes the pictures so interesting and compelling, and impossible to dismiss as merely the constrained products of over-bearing public patronage.[17]

Unlike older artists, young painters usually made works of art based on experiences remembered from their own service. It was they who were active in the pre-war avant-garde and whose canvases tended to use more innovative forms, often reworking the languages of pre-war experimentation. This implies that the younger artists' work was somehow more genuine than that of the older painters, creating the idea of a gulf, even contest, between the generations that was replicated in the press reception of the pictures in 1919–20, when they were first exhibited at the Royal Academy as *The Nation's War Paintings*. Here, the 'veracity' of the younger artists' work was often acclaimed as a truth-telling that had vindicated pre-war avant-gardism by its fitness to represent the almost unknowable and unprecedented experience of the Great War.[18] It was said that the war had restored content to formal experimentation.[19] Modern art had finally discovered a public function, and, as a consequence, a 'new renaissance' had come about, based on a consensus eliminating the polarities and fractures in pre-war British art.[20] These themes also formed the agenda of Lloyd George's Coalition Government in the period 1918 to 1920. There was a sense of Government obligation, arising from wartime conditions, to apply the state apparatus that won the war, to the health and wealth of the nation at peace through benevolent and tolerant state guidance. A debt to a generation was to be extended across the barriers of class divisions to embrace the dominated and disadvantaged in a partnership of co-operation. Collectivism would guarantee the continuity of British values through the creation of a political and social consensus.

Arguments about collectivism and reconstruction, which anticipate the national planning consensus of post-1945, might indicate a visionary idealism, but more cynical motives informed Lloyd George's search for consensus as a basis for continuance in Government. When a general election was called the day after the Armistice, it was the first since 1910. Not only was

it long overdue, but the Coalition Cabinet was not the Government originally elected. In addition, there were millions of newly enfranchised electors, including young working-class men and, for the first time, women. The election is notorious for the 'coupon' arrangements, an alliance between Lloyd George Liberals and the Unionist party, which gave MPs regarded as loyal to the war-time Government a degree of immunity in the political contest. The alliance had been arranged because the war had needed the endurance of a National Government assured of popular support. The rapid collapse of Germany required Lloyd George to seek a vote of confidence; the Government that had won the war should also conclude the peace. A national spirit of wartime would endure to assure that peace was properly conducted through broad agreement and to present a united face to the spectre of revolution that threatened to engulf Europe. In the event the electorate voted for conservative interests, but the Lloyd George coalition acted as a moderating influence, maintaining an elasticity of approach to the strikes and disturbances that threatened alarming consequences in 1919.[21] When Charles Marriott claimed that in comparison to European art, English art was less prone to revolutionary upheaval because it reflected national stability of character and the flexibility of British traditional institutions, he was endorsing this politics of consensus.[22]

The press reception of *The Nation's War Paintings* orchestrated a notion that the avant-garde had been reintegrated into national art history and a reconciliation had taken place, healing simultaneously both the fissures in pre-war art and the disfigurement of national self-image inflicted by the war. The promotion of a 'new renaissance' and the discovery of a consensus or middle-ground functioned as a strategy of containment that inhibited more disturbing readings of the war and sutured avant-garde art into a discourse of heroic sacrifice for an honourable cause, with whatever implications for neutralising, even neutering, avant-garde disruption one wants to engender. But rather than fix this critical reception as some kind of hegemonic tactic of ideology, I want to undo any possibility of closure by taking two occurrences, within this body of art criticism in 1919–20, of discomfort and uncertainty about the work on view. Both are related to the notion of historical vacuum mentioned at the end of chapter three and the idea of broken contracts of looking.

68   William Roberts, *A Shell Dump, France*, 1918–19, oil on canvas, 183 × 317.5, Imperial War Museum, London

69 *facing page, top*   Wyndham Lewis, *A Battery Shelled*, 1918–19, oil on canvas, 183 × 317.5, Imperial War Museum, London

70 *facing page, bottom*   Paul Nash, *The Menin Road*, 1918–19, oil on canvas, 183 × 317.5, Imperial War Museum, London

The first occurrence raises the question of the terms of the address of history painting to its public, an issue that was clearly of concern in the particular historical conjuncture of the Great War and its immediate aftermath, for instance in declarations that war would give rise to a national renaissance in the arts. The second opens up questions about the function of art in relationship to war and social protest, perhaps a key issue for twentieth-century art, and one that was widely experienced as a dilemma for the first time in the First World War. These two cases relate to the two frameworks of public and private, historical and personal, that I am arguing underpin the British War Memorials Committee's project and the challenge it set to artists.

Like many others, R. H. Wilenski's short review in the *Athenaeum* authenticated the testimony of those he called 'tortured by the war' and in the know, and set them against the majority of other artists. Pictures by John and Paul Nash, Gilbert and Stanley Spencer, Lewis and Roberts exemplified individualised responses, characterised by Wilenski in appropriately modern bourgeois terms through such things as their intensity, emotion and expression.[23] But interestingly, Wilenski singled out Roberts's *Shell Dump* (fig. 68) and Lewis's *A Battery Shelled* (fig. 69) (and this is a measure of their importance) as unsuccessful pictures. The canvases, he said, failed to 'carry' in their overall compositional effect. The viewer could grasp them only in particular details and, stepping back, lost any sense of their significance. What one got from the pictures when one leaned forward to read them closely was lost on an audience positioned in the more public and social spaces at the centre of the gallery. Robert's *Shell Dump* was a confused picture perhaps deliberately so, Wilenski speculated. *A Battery Shelled* lacked structural

94

coherence; its central focus was missing, displaced onto the three detached observers to the left of the canvas. Both these works were commissioned Uccello-sized memorial project pictures. On the basis of the argument that history painting's form of rhetorical address was intended to persuade its audience to subordinate private interest in favour of public good, then it would amount to a substantial failure of its project were a picture's composition to disintegrate into particularised details, to fail as a generalised, and generisable, whole, and thereby apparently to privilege private consumption over public appraisal. Lack of compositional coherence, however, in Lewis's and Roberts's work might simply indicate the pictures' modernity. But when Wilenski's discomfort is juxtaposed with his desire for evidence from those 'tortured by war', another issue about what is being represented and for whom comes into focus.

My second example of critical uncertainty is provided by J. Middleton Murry. His review hinged on a dilemma about art as a practice and the demands of the moment as history and event, and it opened up a question about war and representation. Like many other critics, Murry also divided the exhibition into what counted and what had missed the point, but he did not accept that significant work was solely the prerogative of one generation. Because he grouped Nash, Nevinson, Sargent and Orpen as artists who had registered the war as an event that happened to the minds of men as much as it was a phenomenon with an impact on the material world, his review suggests reading the war pictures in ways other than terms derived from the procedures of art history and aesthetics.

Like Wilenski, Murry was uncertain about the pictures, describing Nash's *Menin Road* (fig. 70) as a failure because it had not quite mastered the subject nor marshalled the image to a singular effect. It was 'desolate, phantasmagorical and mad'. But the failure of the canvas was also its virtue. Somehow the subject had exceeded Nash's aesthetic skill and disrupted the artist's attempt to submit a vision of war to pictorial representation. Similarly, Nevinson's means, a kind of modernist realism in works such as *The Harvest of Battle* (fig. 71), were a form of journalism that, because it was journalism and therefore in some way not art, was

71   C. R. W. Nevinson, *The Harvest of Battle*, 1919, oil on canvas, 183 × 317.5, Imperial War Museum, London

72   J. S. Sargent, *Gassed*, 1918–19, oil on canvas, 229 × 610, Imperial War Museum, London

73 *below right*   William Orpen, *Blown-Up*, c.1919, pencil and watercolour on paper, 58.4 × 43.2, Imperial War Museum, London

quite wilfully and deliberately, said Murry, 'insensitive to the particular problems of his medium'. It was not the work of mere recorders of war who, he claimed, 'never saw any dead men', rather, Murry read Nevinson's work into a tradition of socialist protest by describing Nevinson's conscience and courage as comparable with Henri Barbusse's. The same adjectives applied to Sargent's *Gassed* (fig. 72), which was also unaesthetic, but here Murry named the issue as one of a disjunction between experience and the representation of that experience. Where *Gassed* had been denounced as melodramatic, Murry asked what else was 'a man with half his face shot away' but 'just such another piece of melodrama'. By voicing this, he was also saying that some things about the war were unspeakable.

His longest comments were reserved for Orpen as a unique instance, whose vision was like that of a child, wise in the midst of human folly and wicked in mocking human failure. Orpen's work added up to a series of unstable and paradoxical inversions. He found beauty in the shambles and filth of war and folly on the faces of great men. He had stripped the racial and sexual identity of a shell-shocked soldier in *Blown-Up* (fig. 73), simultaneously disarming and unmanning him 'as a lovely Chinese girl playing a guitar'. But hints of insanity in Orpen's work ultimately touched on some universal of the human condition and this made him impotent in the specific context of the Great War.

Orpen's madness averted the mind from the necessity to redress war crimes and reconstruct devastation by hanging bad generals and rebuilding destroyed cities. There was a fundamental contradiction. 'Art', wrote Murry, 'is not a protest; but the art that deals with war must be a protest'. War was crime and this meant registering its melodrama and madness and, in conscience, redressing its wrongs by political action. But art was faced with an impossible paradox. It could not provoke action and still be art.[24]

Murry's review opens up a set of questions about war and about representing the unrepresentable which problematise the general issue of modern history painting raised by Wilenski and makes the matter of the British War Memorials Committee's pictures more than a contest of the ancients and the moderns. In particular, what appears in Murry's review as a spectre stalking the production and reception of these pictures is death and disfigurement. His review is hardly a call for revolution, although it borders on becoming one. The time-frame for the production and reception of the pictures was a moment of threatened and real social instability in Britain and Europe – for example, the revolutions in Russia, Czechoslovakia and Hungary, as well as the failed uprising in Germany. In January 1919, there were mutinies by soldiers at several army bases in Britain. At Calais, 2,000 ordnance corps and infantry established a 'Soviet'.[25] There were industrial strikes too throughout the period, including the railway strike in September 1919 that brought the country to a standstill. In 1920, the government enacted the Emergency Powers Act to enable it to seize and control food, essential services and transport, and do whatever necessary for the defence of the community. Meanwhile, until about March 1919, the Committee's artists went on visiting the now silent battlefields, while at the same time the War Graves Commission was quietly clearing up bodies. In 1920, some 128,577 corpses, assumed to be British, were reburied; in 1921, 204,650. By 1938, 38,000 more had come to light.[26]

This social history is germane to the works' production and reception. Gassed and wounded soldiers, prisoners of war, shell-shocked and unmanned figures, mutilated landscapes, disordered and unsatisfactory compositions, or questions of art and not-art were produced in works of art by both artists themselves and by critics reviewing the works. Arguments were also mounted that attempted to neutralise disruptive or disturbing readings, a measure also of the extent to which such readings were possible in 1919–20.

Veterans and Soldier–Artists

To talk about artists who served in the war or 'soldier–artists' in the Committee's project is actually to refer to veterans, survivors whose memories might also be peopled with other ghosts haunting whatever it is that must be recalled to mind to picture the war, including the presence of dead comrades. The First World War privileged veterans as uniquely qualified witnesses, a notion that still persists, for instance in the cult of the war poets, and one that is also, and not incidentally, distinctly androcentric. E. J. Leed describes the veteran as an initiated man who has directly experienced the knowledge of his own material and human fragility. He is a liminal figure, who has journeyed to the limits of civilisation and beyond, crossing the border of two 'disjunctive . . . worlds, from peace to war, and back' and like other figures inhabiting the margins, is feared by those within the border who desire the power of the veteran. Leed says that veterans were sometimes romanticised as natural socialists or 'comrades', or, because they were initiates into violence and death, understood as dangerous 'primitives' who needed to be reintegrated, recultured and re-educated.[27] Both desires, to embrace in a spirit of community, and to tame in the interests of normality, are projected in the way *The Nation's War Paintings* was acclaimed as a 'new renaissance' in which the nation is imagined as reinvigorated, but also restored and reintegrated.

Leed argues that soldiers' 'comradeship' was a defensive mechanism against both the murderous dictates of authority and the death-threat of technology. He points out that it was not so much a kind of natural socialism that led veterans to go on strike, because they were also involved in violence against pacifists and socialists, but rather they were motivated by a sense of victimisation and felt like superfluous men who had been used up and betrayed. Front-line comradeship hardly ever translated itself into any form of social understanding that could give rise to constructive political action, hence the presence of veteran associations in the early phases of German fascism.[28] Daniel Sherman also maintains that the homo-social bonds formed in military service, which included loyalties to dead and missing comrades, could 'pose just as serious a threat to the stability of the social order as the independence of women'.[29] During 1919 and continuing into 1920, the components of national remembrance ritual were put into place, most conspicuously by the adoption of Lutyens' Cenotaph, first made as a temporary memorial for the Victory Parade, July 1919. Sherman argues that remembrance imagery in war memorials, and in the numerous speeches and invocations that accompanied unveilings and commemorative ceremonies, attempted to contain 'the subversive potential of this all-male world' and to channel militant, disruptive masculinity into socially useful roles.[30] Victory Day parades on 19 July were broken up by soldiers in Glasgow, Coventry, Epsom and Luton.[31] At the conclusion of the war, Britain had a conscripted army of approximately 6.5 million men, the largest army it had ever raised; effective demobilisation began only in the first half of 1919, but by December 1919, 2 million men were still enlisted.[32] Demobilisation was slow because after the Armistice and until autumn 1919, Britain sent troops to support White Russians against the Soviet Union, and even an official war artist, Henry Tonks, until public opinion and the suspicion that attempting to defeat Bolshevism might strengthen its prospects in Britain caused troops to be withdrawn.[33] The issue was how to represent adjusted masculine ideals and accommodate a damaged generation, resocialising the veteran in the process.

An asocial, even anti-social, vision, characteristic of the veteran, could be exemplified in how the soldiers in Roberts's work seem sightless, or how the actors in Lewis's theatrical *A Battery Shelled* refuse the gaze of the viewer. Wilenski's unease about how to read these two paintings was a non-combatant's perplexity about where to look. By contrast, the paintings by older artists do not present the same visual conundrum to the viewer. For example, the foreground space of Sargent's *Gassed* is filled with figures cut by the frame so as to suggest that pictorial space is coextensive with the spectator's space, and therefore inclusive. There is also the way the eye can traverse the seamless, rational continuity of Cameron's *The Battlefield of Ypres* (fig. 74) whereas before the eye can engage with the column of soldiers going home in Nevinson's realist and literal *The Harvest of Battle*, an alienation of the viewer is staged, because the foreground interposes a quagmire strewn with bodies. This is not a matter of having uncovered some sort of 'truth' about the soldier–artists' work, which merely romanticises the veteran and endorses the fiction that participant testimony is more authentic, but it does complicate the question of just who is being imagined in these works as the audience for modern history paintings of war. It also opens up the question of testimony, not as one about 'who is telling the truth' but as one that is much more concerned with how evidence is used and to what purposes.

74 D. Y. Cameron, *The Battlefield of Ypres*, 1919, oil on canvas, 183 × 317.5, Imperial War Museum, London

75   John Nash, *Oppy Wood*, 1918–19, oil on canvas, 183 × 218.4, Imperial War Museum, London

The Forms of the Pictures

The look of the principle war memorial canvases depended on the play of convention and invention, or the pictorial repertoires available to artists at the time and the visuality of the war itself. It was a question of how to make something from the resources to hand out of what could be seen. This is more than stating the obvious, because it is also an example of what Ronald Paulson says of representation or imagery, when discussing the French Revolution, in which the historical referent, the war, is privileged to an unusual degree.[34] For example, many of the Memorial canvases showed large expanses of skies, simply because the scheme had selected landscape-format. But the skies were more emphatically painted and more significant in the work of the younger painters who had served than in paintings by older artists. In pictures by John and Paul Nash and Nevinson, for instance, the sky draws attention to dawn and dusk in a way that it does

not in Cameron's painting. Any soldier who had served on the western front would know about the significance of the twice daily ritual of stand-to, in the morning and in the evening. The sunset behind the British lines silhouetted British emplacements for the unseen Germans; the reverse occurring in the morning. Some critics in 1919 noted that the sky in John Nash's *Oppy Wood* (fig. 75) would resound for many who had been in France.[35] The symbolic resonance of dawn and dusk had already entered the public imagery of the war in lines from 'For the Fallen' by Laurence Binyon, published in September 1914. These were often invoked to symbolise a way of maintaining respectful remembrance at a distant point in time, and were subsequently incorporated into remembrance ritual: 'They shall grow not old, as we that are left grow old:/ Age shall not weary them, nor the years condemn./ At the going down of the sun and in the morning/ We will remember them.'[36] The sky and what you can do with it in a work of art is obviously already culturally loaded in other ways as well. No English artist in this period could be unconscious of the precedence of Turner and Constable. In this sense, the war was not knowable outside the means available to represent it, or, as Paulson puts it, one can assimilate the unknown only by analogy with areas of experience previously encountered. But what is unknown and unprecedented also pushes on the boundaries of what is familiar.

The sky is conspicuously denoted in Nevinson's *The Harvest of Battle* (see fig. 71) and Nash's *Menin Road* (see fig. 70), and, in both canvases, it is reflected in numerous water-filled crater holes. Both landscapes refer to the Passchendaele battlefield in 1917. In Nevinson's canvas the sky reflected in water multiplies the dawn light, heightening the livid, stagnant quality of the land. The sky in Nash's and Nevinson's pictures functions at several different levels. It is evidence remembered by those who had direct experience and it was an element of established cultural symbolism, which made the recognition of the significance of skies from the trenches possible and provided a language within which to articulate experience. This could then be worked back into public discourse with new meanings arising from the new circumstances created by the war.

In *Menin Road*, the atmospheric sky with its rays of sunshine breaking through thundery clouds shows a storm clearing. Nevinson's column of troops, wounded soldiers and prisoners of war trudges, right to left, from the dark flames of the front towards a cold light dawning over charred ruins where the fire has passed. Both suggest some fairly commonplace ideas about war's end giving way to new hope. But the drama of Nash's sky invokes also the sublime or the awesome terrifying power of nature. To make something heroic out of natural occurrences is one way to raise landscape to the level of history painting. In both *Menin Road* and *The Harvest of Battle*, explosions and gun fire are equated with the elements of nature, implying that war itself is a natural force outside human agency.

In Nash's painting, however, any indication of the sublime is ultimately mastered. The terrifying potency of war can be envisioned as a threat that is controllable and useable as a source of renewal. In *Menin Road*, the horizon runs right to left from a bald hill with some graves implied, through a denuded copse to a vacant blue and gold centre and on to some ruins

suffused in glowing sunlight. When reflected in the foreground pool, trees become smooth and the sky is blue; plants are beginning to grow. The painting, Nash's first major canvas, is also artfully stylised. It is not only composed in the grand manner, but is decorative in the modern style. Its répoussoir concrete blocks are decorously cubified; the curves of rusted corrugated iron sheets are repeated across the surface like arabesques. Decorative landscape was revived in France and England in the years before 1914 and was associated with mural painting and Puvis de Chavannes, often with a sense of the fitting and the inviting, designed for contemplation and reverie.[37] Nash made a drawing in 1917 called *Chaos Decoratif* (fig. 76), a loosely ironic evocation, with its play of arabesque, to the Fauves' 'paysage decoratif'. There is something reassuringly bourgeois in the way that Nash thrills the spectator with the violent potential of nature but does not disturb his or her decorum. This leads one to spec-

76 Paul Nash, *Chaos Decoratif*, 1917, ink and watercolour on paper, 25.3 × 20, Manchester City Art Gallery

ulate whether the canvas would be much more ambivalent as war art without its little figures.[38]

The best one can make of Nevinson's sky is something rather hackneyed, and yet it can be argued that his crude and anti-style *Harvest* implies something more like 'épater le bourgeois'. Nevinson described the subject matter of *The Harvest of Battle* as a typical scene after an offensive at dawn showing an area passed through by the infantry advancing behind a creeping barrage and leaving behind the dead. Former infantry positions had been re-occupied by the artillery, which was subjecting the enemy to further bombardment. The enemy were sending up SOS signals.[39] The column is made of captured German prisoners of war and wounded soldiers assisted by British infantry, the only figures carrying weapons. Although the image is unheroic, it is not straightforwardly a protest painting. The three dead soldiers lie on the surface and none is mutilated. There is a problem, however, with the placing of the nearest cadaver in the chronological order of the scene – rigor mortis has set in and it is partly decomposed, implying that this is not a recently dead soldier.

The painting is abject, not only in the obvious, literal cadaver, its face inverted towards the spectator, but also in all the ways it strips itself of artfulness. It is distasteful, uncomposed and incomplete. It uses illusionistic sources in photography and panoramas in pursuit of disillusion. It both fascinates and it repels. It ought to be a telling indictment of war, but so long as the officer with the loud-hailer can marshal the batteries, the guns go on firing and the Tommies have rifles, it never quite adds up to a protest painting, and

yet there is something defeated about it, which its title, *The Harvest of Battle*, suggests.

The pictorial space is strange and disconcerting.[40] The column in the middle plane describes a wide ellipse beneath a flat horizon and behind a deep foreground. These qualities, augmented by the literalness and crudeness of the painting, almost certainly derive from William Rider-Rider's panoramic photographs taken at Passchendaele in 1917, where he was an official photographer for the Canadians. These have titles such as *Boche prisoners and wounded Canadians coming through the mud* or *Hun prisoners and wounded captured by the Canadians* (fig. 77). Although he revisited the front in September 1918 to refresh his memory, Nevinson always referred to the *Harvest* as his Passchendaele picture. Like Nevinson's, all the figures in Rider-Rider's photographs advance right to left. They were taken with a Kodak Panoram camera, introduced in 1900 for both the amateur and professional market, which has a pivoting lens describing a 142-degree arc and produces large celluloid negatives (3.5 × 12 inches or 8.9 × 30.5 cm).[41] The unusual elliptical space in Rider-Rider's photographs and Nevinson's painting is characteristic of this camera's effects. In some of Rider-Rider's pictures, the column is silhouetted dramatically against the skyline, in others it is beneath the horizon. A motif that recurs in the photographs is the stretcher bearers, which Nevinson repeats in his canvas.

The Harvest of Battle is quite deliberately not constructed on the principles of fine art composition in the grand manner, and Nevinson's use of panorama here plays on all the connotations of popularity,

77 William Rider-Rider, *Hun prisoners and wounded captured by Canadians*, 1917, photograph, Imperial War Museum, London

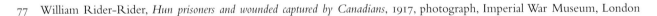

vulgarity and spectacle associated with panoramas. Painted panoramas had been revived as a popular spectacle at places like Crystal Palace, Sydenham, and Alexander Palace in the 1880s and were almost always battle scenes, especially Franco-Prussian War subjects. Sometimes researched through photographs, battle panoramas were meant to be illusionistic and theatrical and, although sometimes said to be educational, they offered the spectator the now customary thrills of comprehensibility, control and domination.[42] Panoramic painters, as skilful showmen and illusionists, were not highly rated as artists.

Panoramas were usually displayed on the inner surface of a cylinder, and, if they were less than 360 degrees, figures at the edge would be enlarged so that the spectacle would seem to envelop the spectator. The opposite effect is created in both Rider-Rider's photographs and Nevinson's painting. The elliptical space curves away from the viewer and figures diminish in scale towards the edge, making the image self-contained and elusive, almost as if it is impenetrable to the eye. This is more marked in Nevinson's painting because it is unfinished at the bottom corners, particularly the right. From the early stages of the project Nevinson was adamant about using oil paint and rejected tempera and matt surfaces. He wanted to work up chiaroscuro in the manner of Rembrandt, Velasquez and Goya because, he said, war was dramatic, not decorative.[43] Although the colour scheme in *Harvest* is subdued and dark greyish-green, the oil paint is richly and densely applied. But Nevinson has represented the rain in ruled lines, sometimes scratched through the surface down to the canvas, and touched in the piquets and barbed wire with swift arabesques of red paint that lie on the surface. While its painterliness invokes the artist's touch and an appeal to high art, the arabesques are cursorily and superficially applied and the ruled lines imply a surface that has been vandalised.

Nevinson was refused permission to send *The Harvest of Battle* to the Royal Academy Summer Exhibition in 1919, where Sargent was showing *Gassed* (see fig. 72), apparently as a foretaste for *The Nation's War Paintings* then in planning.[44] Nevinson worked a publicity stunt, organising a private viewing of his canvas for the press in his studio. He got a few days' worth of notices under headings such as 'Forbidden War Picture' or 'Academy Closed to Grim Flankers Scene'.[45] With a vulgar and anti-style painting,

Nevinson used the strategies of the showman to draw the crowds and address a larger public. The *Daily Express* published a lengthy description (a reproduction was disallowed) which used interestingly anaesthetic and abject terms such as 'desolation', 'misery' and 'squalor'. The newspaper wrote that the figures were ghostly shades so well done that one could feel the effort it took to struggle through the mud. It showed a purgatory that somehow exceeded every possible 'combination of the Deluge, the Last Day, Dante's Inferno and the "Sea Giving up its Dead."' It was, said the *Express*, 'fascinating and dreadful'. Nevinson had got 'the dismal soul of the real thing'.

That Nevinson's picture is abject suggests an order of excess that is something more than merely a challenge, in bad taste, to the decorums of *The Nation's War Paintings*. There are a number of ways in which, because it does not cohere, the picture threatens representational order. There is its insistent decaying cadaver, which is mismatched to the chronology of the scene; the image's meaning is unfixed and unfixable; it is not an obviously didactic anti-war image, but it is not reassuringly heroic either; it is photographic and literal, and yet not convincingly so; its surface is damaged with scratches and dabbed with bloody marks, as though it is the image itself which is wounded. In Kristeva's well known analysis, *Powers of Horror: An Essay on Abjection*, the abject is a borderline, something expelled from the body and yet still of the body, like faeces, urine, blood and vomit. The corpse is abject because more than the wastes that fall from the body and permit life, the cadaver is the utter dereliction of the body, fallen entirely into waste and something we will all become.[46] Kristeva identifies the abject with the demonical potential of the feminine, particularly the mother, and she cites the powerful prohibitions and taboos associated with the female body and menstrual blood. The abject, which has to be expelled to make the symbolic order, or law and culture, possible, also threatens the identity of that order and exposes its frailty. Abjection has to be constantly and ritualistically warded off and purified. The problem is that the abjection that *The Harvest of Battle* threatens might tend towards psychosis and dysfunction, not constructive political, cultural or social action. If it is possible to imagine this image giving rise to political effect, it would be impossible to predict what its effects might be. In some ways it is akin to the violence and lawlessness of the veteran complex outlined by Leed and cited above. When Middleton Murry gives the picture a conscience by comparing Nevinson with Henri Barbusse, he is intervening to attempt to divert it from being read otherwise.

Nevinson complained endlessly that *The Harvest of Battle* was hidden away at *The Nation's War Paintings* because it was not shown in the prestigious main gallery of the Royal Academy where twelve of the Memorial canvases were hung to frame Sargent's *Gassed*, the one extant centrepiece to the Memorial scheme.[47] Nevinson's painting was extensively noticed in reviews, and the siting of his work is therefore possibly not all that significant. But it is arguable that *The Harvest of Battle* was shown outside the main collection because it unsettled and disrupted the aspirations of the War Memorials' project. The painting is particularly troublesome when juxtaposed with Sargent's *Gassed*: both canvases share the subject matter of the aftermath of battle and war causalities.

Lewis's *A Battery Shelled* (see fig. 69) was also exhibited alongside Nevinson's painting outside the main gallery at *The Nation's War Paintings*. The form of Lewis's painting has presented problems to art historians, as it did for Wilenski in 1919. In particular, the three detached figures to the left have been misidentified as officers or artists. Sources for these have been found, for example, in Piero della Francesca's *The Flagellation*, and it has been said that they are stylistically inconsistent with the remainder of the canvas, and even that the work is 'schizophrenic'. A more complex, reflective reading has seen the figures as sardonic commentators, standing for evidence of a form of psychological damage in their emotional implacability, characteristic of soldiers over-exposed to sights of death and mutilation.[48]

All of these readings of *A Battery Shelled* attempt to test the evidence of the painting, either its form or content, as the basis for uncovering a 'truth' about war experience that the image is assumed to be telling. The sheer physical factuality of the Great War and its toll on human lives produced an urgency, intensified by all subsequent twentieth-century wars, to voice its truths and call up experiences that resisted, indeed exceeded, representation. Lewis made numerous statements about his war service and the work he made in letters, pamphlets and catalogues, as well as in his autobiography, *Blasting and Bombardiering*, first published in 1937. The

texts are just as knowingly crafted as his art. None offers an explication of the work. Rather, texts and images function together to promote an anti-romantic, satirical view of war as an artifice and a spectacle, and deliberately refute the idea that any consoling myths of redemption or meaning can be gained from the catastrophe.[49] One way to understand why Lewis's painting so perplexes those who have attempted to analyse it with the benefit of historical perspective, is that it draws attention to the desire to close the gap between extreme events and their representation, and the impossibility of ever being able to do so.

The picture is cleverly composed, the three figures and the machinery behind them setting up a répoussoir element linked to the dark swirling forms of the tracery of a shell in the sky and counterbalanced by three abstract forms, possibly blasted trees, on the right side. Although all the figures are generic, they are recognisably British soldiers engaged in identifiable actions such as pitching into a dugout, fleeing the bombardment or lifting a dead or wounded comrade. *A Battery Shelled* is quite different from the knowing naiveté of stylised decoration with which the canvases by Nash and Spencer demand to be regarded as sincere, and the painting is clearly a challenge to the logical coherence of work by artists such as Sargent and Cameron, because it is every bit as competent in its deployment of established compositional codes and reference. If one dismisses the alleged stylistic 'schizophrenia' of the work as simply inadequately thought out and note general art-historical citations as further evidence for the work's complexity, one is still left with a carefully constructed but puzzling composition: for all the deployment of *répoussoir* or framing to the central recessionary space, the picture does not complete its classical composition because it has no foreground. A landscape prospect is staged for the surveying eye of a sovereign subject, but it lacks the one element that guarantees the spectator's secure command of the scene. In this respect, it is unlike Lewis's earlier canvas for the Canadian War Memorial scheme and at odds with work by painters such as Nash. By lacking a foreground, it has something in common with Lamb's *Irish Troops Surprised by a Turkish Bombardment* (fig. 78), the viewpoint for which seems obviously more a matter of displaying out the scene so that the viewer observes the spectacle from above, and therefore figuring the notion that one is at some

78 Henry Lamb, *Irish Troops in the Judean Hills surprised by a Turkish Bombardment*, 1919,
oil on canvas, 183 × 218.4,
Imperial War Museum, London

remove from the danger. In *A Battery Shelled*, the middle distance, being uncontained by a foreground, spills off the bottom of the canvas and the figures in the near and middle distance are all cut by the frame at a point just beneath the torsos of the bodies. There is an open empty shape in the ground, at the middle lower edge, approximately equivalent to the grave in Courbet's *Burial at Ornans* (though I am not suggesting this as a source). The viewer is not invited to identify with the detached figures and is left literally not knowing where they stand. It is perhaps the lack of a foreground that disconcerted Wilenski and caused him to write, rather absurdly, that the picture was 'obviously unfinished'.[50] Where Nevinson marks out a foreground to contain an apotropaic corpse seemingly designed to repulse the viewer, Lewis simply leaves one out altogether.

When classical compositions use a tripartite schema of foreground, middleground and distance, these can be used to signify three domains of meaning, what Christopher Prendergast, in his study of Gros's

La Bataille d'Eylau (fig. 79), has recently termed stock, as in painterly repertoire, and code, for producing meaning. The three domains might be foreground, sufferers and sinners; middle ground, redeemer; and distance, heaven and salvation.[51] Although Prendergast argues that the signs of tradition can never run smoothly into modern and secular scenes of war,[52] Sargent's *Gassed* lays out a war picture in an affirmation of traditional values, as if this is the natural order of things. The foreground displays the war's victims, all legible to the viewer as whole and unmutilated bodies, unlike, for example, the disarrayed dead and wounded in Gros's 1808 painting. In the middle distance there is a frieze of soldiers, guided by orderlies, arriving at the casualty clearing station tent, and all processing towards a point of narrative resolution just beyond the edge of the frame. In the background, the football match and the encampment, all suffused in the warm glow of sunset, completes the myth of redemption.[53] Nevinson's picture can be analysed in the same way, but it goes against the grain by approximating

79 Antoine-Jean Gros, *Napoléon sur le champ de bataille d'Eylau le 9 février 1807*, 1807, oil on canvas, 521 × 784, Louvre, Paris

something rather more like apocalypse than heavenly salvation. When the bottom appears to drop out of Lewis's painting, the viewer is left with no purchase on the scene, floundering in an attempt to attribute meaning. It might read like a masquerade of war, a theatre set peopled with what Lewis termed 'those titanic casts of dying and shell-shocked actors, who charged this stage with a romantic electricity'[54] but even this is not guaranteed, because the audience is displaced from taking up the role of chorus or Everyman by the three observers who do not admit identification.

The Critical Response

When the British War Memorials Committee first began to meet in March 1918, it had spent its time establishing the ambitions of its scheme, envisaging large history paintings and sculpture and even drawing up lists of significant subjects. In the course of its work, however, the emphasis had shifted from imagining great works of art and topics for paintings to selecting names from lists of artists. It had become less a case of determining the sort of work that ought to be produced and much more one of getting the right kinds of names signed up for the project. In effect, the Committee was drawing up a canon of significant artists who collectively would demonstrate the scope and depth of British art at a particular point in its history, which was also a point of momentous importance in

the history of the British nation itself. For example, it was of no consequence to the project whether Sargent ever actually came up with a canvas to show British and American co-operation at the front, the subject suggested to him. It did matter to the ambitions of the scheme that he produced something commensurate with its grandeur and relevant to the war, but subject and style were ultimately up to the artist.[55] It was this condition that made it possible for disruptive works to be made. The task of art criticism when the pictures were viewed was also an urgent one, as productive of the moment as the work itself. The dominant mood in critical responses to the exhibition in 1919–20 was one of an insistence on reading the exhibition as a whole, in terms of its consequences for the future of British art. *The Nation's War Paintings* were to be judged for evidence of the wealth of visual responses to the war as though these were an index of the political health of the nation itself.

There was dissent from two camps to the dominant mood of acclamation. Reginald Grundy and the *Graphic* represented conservative interests and were outsiders to the main arena of British art.[56] The second, more radical attack was launched from a section of critical opinion central to the formation of modernism in Britain, the Bloomsbury Group. In January, an editorial appeared in the *Athenaeum* called 'A False Dawn', which argued that the stress of war had amplified the national habit of self-deception. There was growing awareness that the promised millennium was not imminent but emerging disillusion had merely transferred its aspirations to art and literature. Only through the corrective of disinterested criticism, said the paper, could any intellectual or aesthetic renaissance be brought into being. The 'new movement' had been inaugurated in 1912, a reference to Roger Fry's second post-impressionism exhibition, but it had now disintegrated and was greeted only as an 'arrival' because its proponents were showing in Burlington House.[57] In March 1920, *Athenaeum* published Clive Bell's notorious philippic 'Wilcoxism', in which Bell particularly deprecated the war pictures because the painters had been motivated not by visual stimulus but 'moral conviction'. The artists were 'not expressing what they feel for something that has moved them as artists, but, rather, what they think about something that has horrified them as men.' It was 'mere "arty" anecdote' that had guaranteed the pictures' popular reception.[58] It was implied that the paintings failed because, lacking neutrality of subject matter, the works expressed emotions only at the level of the topical or banal. In dismissing the nation's war pictures, Bell was asserting a continuity with his pre-war ideas for a formalist aesthetic.[59] Bell was a close associate of Roger Fry.

Reviewers of *The Nation's War Paintings* at the time said the war had remedied a deficit in modern art, supplying artists with a subject matter of epochal importance. As a consequence, form and content had been reunified in avant-garde art and formal experimentation justified, or vindicated, by its fitness to represent the subject. Modern art had at last found a purpose. But the same arguments about the topicality and relevance of the war paintings to a nation at peace were used by writers such as Bell to reject the work precisely on the grounds that it was motivated by subject matter and not aesthetics. War pictures did not qualify as art. However persuasive and cogent representing the war was for its era, the official paintings could not serve both the needs of their own epoch and the purpose of art. Bell was saying that painting war was not part of the history of modern art.

From opposing positions, both Bell and Middleton Murry had found in *The Nation's War Paintings* the means to articulate one of the central problems for modern art in the twentieth century, that is how to make a critical contribution to representing the major events of the twentieth century and yet still be art. What was at stake was the opportunity for art to regain the high status of great history painting and find a place as an essential component in the armament of the nation. But guaranteeing the benevolence and continuity of the contemporary state meant abandoning any pretence to an independent critical position, in effect to return impossibly and irrelevantly to a past before the advent of the avant-garde. One solution was simply to accept this situation and give up making art in a dadaistic gesture of negation. Bell's answer was to exclude the war or indeed any subject matter, but such a disavowal meant to survive but be rendered impotent. The paintings by Nevinson and Lewis cannot be accommodated in any of these positions. They were not quite art and not quite politics, not quite acquiescence and not quite protest. These two works had to be reconciled with the agendas of *The Nation's War Paintings* at the same time as they also had to be set to one side.

I have argued that the large canvases in *The Nation's War Paintings* are self-consciously styled in ways that draw on a range of painterly repertoires and codes, which are rooted in older traditions for making major works of art. This complicates the question of reading the works simply for evidence of artists' direct and unmediated responses to the sights of the Great War. In the process of production, artists imagined a public. Lewis's and Nevinson's work was so compelling, and awkward to accommodate into the British War Memorials Committee's project as it was realised at the Royal Academy in 1919, because it refused to satisfy that public.

five

Post-War Modernisms: William Roberts, David Bomberg, Wyndham Lewis and C. R. W. Nevinson

Modernism and War

The artists who are the focus of this chapter – Bomberg, Roberts, Lewis and Nevinson – were key players in the most avant-garde art of the pre-war period.[1] They each enlisted for active service on the western front, Nevinson as a voluntary ambulance driver, the others as soldiers. Subsequently, all became official artists and made major history paintings, Bomberg for the Canadians only, although there are two versions of his canvas. These four also produced a body of war art either independently or, in the case of Roberts, as part of official employment. It has sometimes been argued that official employment was a determining factor in how the avant-garde in Britain changed after 1918, but this combination of avant-garde activism, war service and official employment applied only to these four artists.[2] No other prominent avant-garde artist who was a veteran had been taken up so extensively as an official artist. For example, Wadsworth worked in naval camouflage in Britain and made one canvas based on this experience for the Canadians; the British War Memorials Committee's attempts to commission Epstein were fruitless and he never arrived at a frontline as a soldier. Gaudier-Brzeska had been killed in 1915; Harold Gilman of the Camden Town Group died in the influenza epidemic of winter 1919; several members of the Bloomsbury group, for instance Duncan Grant, were conscientious objectors and

others, such as Mark Gertler, were registered unfit to serve. Nor were these artists employed as official artists, though both Grant and Gertler were approached and Grant at least was willing to contribute. Although there were some limited employment schemes in Germany and France, no other European nation recruited avant-garde artists on behalf of its war effort or to make history paintings as part of its war memorials. By taking a closer look at the work of Bomberg, Roberts, Lewis and Nevinson in the aftermath of the Great War, I want to suggest that the trauma of war had volatile and unpredictable consequences that are more complex than a simple question of influence and response. I will begin by asking about the implications these artists' expectations of war service had for how they reworked experience at the front into new careers as post-war artists.

Virility and aggression, amounting to a cult of violence, were the hallmark of the most radical pre-war avant-gardes including Lewis and Nevinson. The outbreak of war caused no particular crisis of conscience for these artists who were not pacifists. They had no connections with anti-war protests, such as those found in the circles of the Independent Labour Party for example. They were not conscripts but volunteers in the war effort, although none was motivated by narrow patriotic sentiment. Nevinson had declared that, without glorifying war for its own sake, exposure to death and violence was an essential test of virility in art.[3] Lewis seemed to see war service as inevitable but also something of an opportunity.[4] Bomberg and Roberts, economically and socially less secure than Nevinson and Lewis, volunteered because the contraction of the art market in 1915 was making it difficult to survive as an artist. These artists did not enter the war with high ideals and their profiles as veterans do not trace the trajectory of innocence turned to disillusion, bitterness and protest that is commonly described in literature about culture and the First World War.[5] Possibly as a consequence of not having unrealistic expectations about war service, Lewis, Roberts, Bomberg and Nevinson did not subscribe to the fiction of sacrifice and redemption that was germane to liberal thinking about the war and the starting point for reappraising the war work of artists such as Nash and Spencer whose practices are rooted in English pastoral traditions and late romanticism. Leo Bersani has suggested that ideas about culture as redemption make art redeem 'the catastrophe of history. To play this role, art must preserve what might be called a moral monumentality – a requirement that explains, I believe, much of the mistrust in the modern period of precisely those modern works that have more or less violently rejected any edifying or petrifying functions.'[6] Mistrust or uncertainty about what a work of art adds up to might explain why Nevinson's and Lewis's big pictures for the British War Memorials scheme were difficult to accommodate in 1919, given high audience expectations that such prestigious works must have been intended to supply an answer to the meaning of war. Anti-liberalism, or the rejection of the notion that art has any redemptive function, leaves a vacuum, however, and it is a factor in the formation of what has been termed 'reactionary modernism'. Michael Long has referred to how 'an intriguing, and sometimes exasperating problem of English Modernist literature is its connection with the politics of the extreme right', which would include Wyndham Lewis.[7]

Official art of the First World War had high status in the 1930s when economic crisis and the rise of fascism put the possibility of another war back on the agenda, demonstrated by the publication of such works as John Rothenstein's monograph in 1931, *British Artists and the War* and Francis Klingender 'Content and Form in Art', which cited English war paintings by Nevinson, Nash and Lewis as exemplifying radical activism.[8] Lewis, Bomberg, Roberts and Nevinson were not, however, key participants in any of the forums for anti-fascist and anti-war struggles in the 1930s, unlike, for example, Nash, Eric Gill and even John. Far from being part of the significant art practices of the late 1920s and '30s, all four were relatively isolated, even neglected artists, in this period. Lewis worked primarily as a novelist and essayist; Bomberg spent lengthy periods abroad, first in Palestine and then Spain; Roberts had a secure if unexciting career as a painter; and although Nevinson was a society celebrity his work was not highly rated. In 1935 the *Daily Express* called him 'a good second-rater'.[9] Nevinson's practice through the '20s and '30s does, however, reveal a nihilistic impulse that might be called a paradigm for war as a destructive resource for art and even demonstrates that there is a kind of inverted value in the anti-aestheticism or 'badness' of Nevinson's work. This evaluation is an antithesis to the decorums of modernism with its emphasis on affirmation and its disavowal of the non-aesthetic.

Modernist decorum is exemplified by the art criticism of Roger Fry, established as a critical orthodoxy by the end of the 1920s.[10] Modernist protocols have insisted on a radical separation between art and history or politics. At the end of the war, Fry wrote to Charles Vildrac in France about the social role of art, making a statement that is uncannily prescient of Walter Benjamin's famous declaration about fascism rendering politics aesthetic, in his 1936 essay 'The Work of Art in the Age of Mechanical Reproduction'. Fry wrote: 'no art is useful to morals or to politics. Useful yes, above all, but its real use is a direct result of its detachment from any actual goal. It is there that we must drink our fill of the absolute and not in matters concerning society . . . It is as dangerous to be political in art as it is to be artistic in politics.'[11]

Fry's collection of essays, *Vision and Design*, published in late 1920, was one of the most widely read and influential art books of the '20s, rapidly establishing itself as a canonical modernist text. By 1940, well in excess of 75,000 copies had been printed.[12] Reviewing the book in 1920 for the *Burlington Magazine*, C. J. Holmes, Director of the National Gallery, referred to Fry as 'modernist'.[13] A measure of Fry's influence and evidence of the institutionalisation of his version of modernism is his impact on Samuel Courtauld, who donated £50,000 to the Tate in 1923 specifically for the purchase of post-impressionist French art, corresponding to the canon of modern art promoted by Fry.[14] Although more than half the essays in *Vision and Design* were first published between 1917 and 1919 and in that sense were a product of the war, Fry's fundamental premise was that war was irrelevant to aesthetics and not a legitimate motivation for art. The opening essay, 'Art and Life', assembled from notes for a lecture to the Fabian Society in 1917, argued that although art was sometimes open to social influence it was 'in the main self-contained', its changes 'determined much more by its own internal forces'. For Fry, this was conclusively demonstrated by the way the revolution in modern art, by which he meant Manet and the post-impressionists, had not been matched by any social revolution. He ended by declaring that modern art was becoming 'more and more remote from . . . the ordinary man. In proportion as art becomes purer the number of people to whom it appeals gets less.'[15] All of this anticipates Clement Greenberg's well known essays 'Avant-garde and Kitsch' of 1939 and 'Towards a Newer Laocoon' of 1940. It is not just a matter of Fry's influence on Greenberg, however, because both critics were similarly motivated and it is not incidental that periods of historical urgency and catastrophe have given an impetus to assertions about the autonomy of the aesthetic realm. Klingender was challenging Fry's dominance in 'Content and Form in Art', arguing that the progressive energies of artists had been fettered by service to the decaying class of the bourgeoisie and had found refuge instead in the revolutionary transformation of form, with the consequence of rendering art politically impotent.[16]

Fry's aesthetic is a product of its social context. Even its disavowal of the war can be counted as a factor in its success amongst audiences anxious to forget. It is also germane to the social history of the period that his emphasis on audiences equipped with specialised competences in the appraisal of modern art corresponded with the rise of expertise and the growth of the professions in bourgeois societies from the late nineteenth century onwards. Moreover, Fry's Francophile preferences were useful to the war and served popular anti-German sentiment that was greatly bolstered by Germany's defeat. D. S. MacColl, in an article linked these ideas in a spurious argument about national characteristics. The question was whether to develop a gallery of selective acquisitions or a museum with a comprehensive collection. A museum, however,

was 'a scientific (shall we say a German?) ideal', whereas a choice gallery of modern foreign art, such as that proposed for the Tate, would serve at the conclusion of peace as 'a monument to the genius of France'.[17] Fry's rise to dominance as a critic in the 1920s, and the hold his version of modernism continued to exercise in the Second World War, was a consequence of its capacity to serve as reparation for traumatic experiences, in other words it fulfilled that redemptive function absent from the work of artists such as Lewis, Nevinson, Bomberg and Roberts.

That Fry's writing could be seen as redemptive is linked to the way his emergence into a wide public domain paralleled the establishment of psychoanalysis in Britain. At the time that Fry was assembling the essays for *Vision and Design*, he was also reading Ernest Jones's monumental introduction to the work of Freud, *Papers on Psycho-Analysis*, newly reissued in a revised edition in 1918. He wrote to Vanessa Bell, 'It would amuse you by it's [*sic*] extreme indecency'.[18] In February 1919, Jones, Edward Glover and others established the British Psycho-Analytic Society in London, which quickly developed close links with members of Fry's Bloomsbury Group. Authoritative translations of Freud's work were published through its Hogarth Press. At this point, just after the war, Jones recalled that Freud was a household name in Britain and a cult figure in intellectual circles, but also subject to misrepresentation and a source of scandal. Intent on securing the scientific respectability of psychoanalysis, through recognition by the British Medical Association, for example, Jones writes that the vogue for Freud amongst intellectuals was not entirely welcome.[19] Psychoanalysis and modernism were seeking institutional legitimation simultaneously and there were strong associations between Bloomsbury modernism and the psychoanalytic establishment.

As is clear from his pamphlet 'The Artist and Psychoanalysis' of 1924, Fry was an exception in Bloomsbury circles because he was no sympathiser, rather a resistor to the propositions of psychoanalysis. Much of his text is concerned with keeping what he calls 'pure' art, with its detachment and disinterestedness, free of contamination from 'impure' art rooted in the impulses of wish fulfilment and the clamour of the libido. Fry was responding to Freud's war-time *Introductory Lectures*, first translated into English in 1920. In Lecture 23, 'The Paths to the Formation of Symptoms',

Freud writes how art provides consolation and reparation. Despite his antipathy, however, Fry's aesthetics mount a similar argument. Out of the chaos and debased emotions of everyday life, art was a means of access to a higher and truer emotion, or an act of reparation, making whole and unified what was ordinarily experienced in fragments and shocks. Or as Hanna Segal, writing in Kleinian terms about readers' (or viewers') identifications with works of art and their authors, puts it:

> The author has, in his hatred, destroyed all his loved objects just as I [the viewer] have done, and like me he felt death and desolation inside him. Yet he can face it and he can make me face it, and despite the ruin and devastation we and the world around us survive. What is more, his objects, which have become evil and were destroyed, have been made alive again and have become immortal by his art. Out of all the chaos and destruction he has created a world which is whole, complete and unified.[20]

According to Segal, what Fry missed in his insistence on form and his denial of subject matter was that far from guaranteeing art's purity and disinterestedness, pure form embodied the unconscious even more insistently than content because it was only on this basis that it could be characterised as significant and give rise to meaningful aesthetic emotion. Aesthetics is the sublimation of impulses that are sadistic and destructive because art allows us 'to avow our own sadism'; it is the means 'to contain and redeem what history could not'.[21] Segal was writing just after the Second World War, but the image of introjected ruin and desolation applies equally to 1918–19. In his letter to Vildrac about the new prospects for his aesthetic project, Fry stated how 'we are . . . beginning to awaken from the nightmare', meaning the war.[22] Lyndsey Stonebridge, in her excellent study of British modernism and psychoanalysis, writes that Fry eventually 'arrives at a position where his theory begins to sound like a form of psychoanalysis . . . aesthetic experience is superior to everyday experience, not because of the intrinsic value of purely formal relations, but because it brings to light what culture would have us repress. A far cry from Fry's attempt to immunize art from history, . . . aesthetic significance is a way of asking what contemporary history means in psychic terms'.[23]

Reading against the grain of Fry's writings uncovers if not the realisation of reparation, then the fantasy of its possibility, and suggests that the persuasiveness of his texts in the 1920s lies in the mourning work they accomplish in the aftermath of the First World War.[24] Fry's modernism, however, has also supplied the paradigm for histories of the period that argue that the post-war period marks an interruption amounting to a void in the story of modernism in Britain, when conditions in the art world were inhospitable to innovation and no new avant-gardes appeared. Charles Harrison, for example, in his book *English Art and Modernism*, called his chapter dealing with this era 'Hiatus 1919–1924'. David Peters Corbett's more recent *The Modernity of English Art', 1914–30* gives a more nuanced account but arrives at similar conclusions.[25] The idea that the 1920s was a quiescent decade, sometimes termed a return to order or a new sobriety, is widespread in histories of European art as a whole.[26] Characterising the period in this way, however, means leaving a great deal out of the account, including omitting the avant-garde's right-wing as well as its left-wing variants. If the period is a hiatus, Dada in Germany and elsewhere must be discounted. It would involve overlooking Lajos Kassak's journal *MA* (Today) published in Budapest and then Vienna from 1916 to 1925 or *De Stijl* in Holland or the flourishing avant-garde in post-Revolution Russia (one of T. J. Clark's 'limit cases' in his *Farewell to an Idea: Episodes from a History of Modernism*, 1999), and the exchanges between these groups and English artists. Wyndham Lewis was in touch with both Theo van Doesburg of *De Stijl* and Herwarth Walden, owner of Der Sturm in Berlin, and he met Ivan Puni from Russia.[27] Nevinson described Dada as the only really interesting movement after the war. Although in the interview he gave to a newspaper in 1921 he stated that he did not approve, he characterised it as 'an explosive scepticism, a devastating cynicism, such as has never existed before, which could not exist before the war. . . . What it really says is that nothing is worth while, . . . It is a gigantic spiritual nihilism.'[28] Bomberg had contacts with *De Stijl*, to which Sacheverell Sitwell, brother of Osbert who collected work by Roberts, Nevinson and others in the 1920s, contributed a 'London Letter' in 1921. John Rodker, poet, publisher of Joyce's *Ulysses* in 1922, translator of the cult surrealist texts of the Comte de Lautréamont in 1924 and a conscientious objector who had been imprisoned during the war, replaced Ezra Pound as the London correspondent on the New York *Little Review* and wrote about the Dada poet Baroness Else von Freytag-Loringhoven as well as setting up the Ovid Press, which published anthologies of drawings by Gaudier-Brzeska and Wadsworth. He was part of the pre-war group of Jewish activists and intellectuals who grew up around Whitechapel, including Bomberg from whom he had commissioned a book jacket in 1914. Poet and artist Sidney Hunt printed phonic poems by Schwitters and van Doesburg, as well as Malevich's *Black Square*, in his journal *Ray* in 1927.[29] Elsewhere, in 1923, Sylvia Pankhurst published reproductions of George Grosz's drawings and commissioned work from the Cologne Progressive Heinrich Hoerle for her *Workers' Dreadnought*.[30] There was even a proposal, circulating in 1919–20, for a Proletcult movement in Britain modelled on the Soviet Union and discussion about proletarian culture in English journals.[31] All of this mobility and exchange between English artists and wider European and American avant-gardes tends to belie what Harrison says was the 'historically uncontroversial' nature of 1920s art-making.[32]

Artists were eventually to conceive the war itself, rather than its aftermath, as a hiatus. Bomberg, Lewis and Roberts were each to repudiate their pre-war work and attribute a change of heart to the Great War, Bomberg in unpublished notes written in the last years of his life, Lewis in *Rude Assignment* in 1951 and Roberts in his autobiography published in 1974. Nevinson did so during the war itself. Looking back in 1937, Lewis described the Great War as 'such a tremendous landmark that locally it imposes itself upon our computation of time like the birth of Christ'.[33] Because the war period is always bracketed as 1914–18, in retrospect it has seemed to have clear-cut boundaries. Experience, however, was a different matter. When war broke out, in common with many, artists and the art world as a whole assumed it would be a specialised professional affair swiftly concluded. As the war became all consuming of men and resources, 'normal' civilian life was less easy to sustain, the art market contracted and most younger artists drifted into war service, almost all during 1915. As a consequence of the British and Canadian schemes, many artists serving in the military were transferred, but not demobilised, in order to make official pictures. This raises the interesting question of whether these commissions

were perceived as part of an individual's war service or as part of their careers as artists. There is a sense, however, in which the circumstances and nature of this war make this question irrelevant. Joining up was a rite of passage involving both the donning of a uniform and the subscription to uniform circumstances. Not only was access to materials, space and time an issue so that many made no art for a couple of years or more, but joining the army meant a temporary suspension of the self. Spencer, who volunteered for the Royal Army Medical Corps in 1915, reflected on his posting to Beaufort Hospital, Bristol that 'the problem was in most respects the same as most young artists at the time, the question of still continuing to be artists'.[34] Epstein described his enforced enlistment in 1917 as 'my decease as an active artist'.[35] Moreover, because enlistment meant volunteering to expose oneself to the risk of death or injury and being a witness to the death and mutilation of others, newly identified by force of circumstance as comrades, artists returning from war came back as changed individuals, as veterans or those liminal figures discussed in the last chapter, who were also entering an altered world. Daniel Pick has recently addressed the problem of the boundaries of the Great War, arguing that in retrospect it comes to be perceived both as impermeable barrier to the past and as a 'porous membrane through which something trickles back, 1914–18 reshaping the historical reality of the pre-war world'. War experience was subject to repeated acts of recollection, an activity in which its meanings were endlessly remade and reshaped, so that remembering comes to involve 'the reconceptualising of time, the recognition of ruptures and the subtle retracing of the immanence of the future in the past'.[36] This process began in 1919 with attempts amongst artists returning from war to reforge broken connections and remake careers in the light of radically altered circumstances. It was carried out with particular intensity by Bomberg, Roberts, Nevinson and Lewis, artists with high profiles in the pre-war avant-garde, who had a great deal at stake re-establishing what it meant to be an artist after the war.

★ ★ ★

The Ethics of Art-Making: Bomberg and Roberts

Following active service at the front in 1916 and 1917, both William Roberts and David Bomberg undertook large canvases for the Canadian War Memorials Committee in 1918. When Bomberg delivered his *Sappers at Work: A Canadian Tunnelling Company, Hill 60, St. Eloi* (figs 82 and 83) to the Royal Academy for the Canadian War Memorials exhibition opening in January 1919, P. G. Konody, organiser of the exhibition, refused to hang it. Bomberg painted a new canvas that was completed around July 1919. The rejection of the first version, which was not destroyed and is now in the Tate, is an important and problematic issue in the war artists' schemes.[37] In the surviving records, only one other artist, Anna Airy, working for the British War Memorials Committee, is known to have had her work rejected, but she contributed a major canvas to the Canadian scheme and was commissioned by the Imperial War Museum to make four large paintings.[38] The incident over Bomberg's work is said to have destroyed the artist's confidence and the story is a crucial component in the posthumous construction of Bomberg as an unjustly neglected artist.[39] Furthermore, the matter has discredited the Canadian scheme, fuelling a belief in later literature that all official employment undermined artists and compromised their independence. In 1919, the Bomberg controversy was well known and it augmented the British schemes' sense of itself as the more prestigious project. Bone wrote to Yockney when the exhibition of the British paintings was in planning, 'The Canadian pictures . . . are not very impressive. We ought to have a far better show! I hear Konody would not hang Bomberg's picture!'[40]

The narrative is made additionally murky and complicated because Konody, the villain in the Bomberg rejection story, was himself fairly badly treated. He was omitted from the catalogue for the Canadian show and left off the platform at the opening ceremony because the Academy protested that he should not be prominently associated with the exhibition, even though he did most of the work.[41] Despite the fact that he was an adviser to the British scheme, his suggestions were the least influential and his name was always left out of the accounts Yockney later gave. Konody was Jewish and Viennese. Anti-German feeling was at its height in the closing months and immediate aftermath of the war, and anti-Semitic sentiment greatly augmented, after the Balfour Declaration and the Russian Revolution, and Konody was the victim of this.[42]

As is so often the case, the surviving evidence about the circumstances of the rejection is fragmentary and inconclusive. The primary source for the argument that the incident seriously undermined Bomberg as an artist is the typescript of recollections dated 1972 and now in the archives of the Tate Gallery by Alice Mayes, Bomberg's first wife. Both William Roberts and Bomberg were asked to paint canvases on a speculative basis and were guaranteed a refund for materials in the case of refusal – presumably in this case, they would have been free to dispose of the paintings independently.[43] It is not known if this was an exceptional condition or if it applied to other artists. Roberts was released from active service in April 1918 to work on his painting, but Bomberg arrived home only shortly before the Armistice, meaning that his large canvas was planned and executed in scarcely two months. Many years later, in 1957, Bomberg wrote about 'The large panel I dispatched too quickly'.[44] The timing of the Canadian exhibition, unlike the British show held the following winter, was very tight and complications about artists on active service were common in both schemes. Stanley Spencer, for instance, did not arrive home from the Balkans until December 1918, many months after he received the invitation from the British War Memorials Committee. A number of significant paintings for the Canadian scheme were shipped for exhibition in Toronto and Montreal during 1920, sometimes without a showing in England or shown unfinished, including works by Eric Kennington, William Rothenstein, Paul Nash, D. Y. Cameron, George Clausen, J. A. Turnbull and Frederick Etchells, as well as Bomberg's second canvas. All were illustrated in the catalogue *Canadian War Memorials Paintings Exhibition 1920 New Series The Last Phase.*

Richard Cork, author of the most extensive and considered studies of Bomberg's work, has written 'of the British government's refusal to consider him for an official war artist's post'.[45] It is not so much that the British scheme refused to consider him, rather his name never cropped up. In March 1918, Harold Watkins, administrator of the Canadian scheme, prepared a list of artists employed by Canada for the British Committee, partly as a test of availability. Neither Bomberg nor Roberts were listed (nor were

80 *right* David Bomberg,
Russian Ballet, *c.*1914–19,
lithograph,
76 × 159, Tate, London

81 *below* Stanley Spencer,
Swan Upping at Cookham,
1915–19, oil on canvas,
148 × 116.2, Tate, London

Etchells or Wadsworth), although Lewis and Nevinson were. Roberts first appears as a potential artist for the British at the second meeting of the memorials committee, 14 March 1918. Both Wadsworth and Bomberg later wrote to Yockney seeking a commission, and both applied too late, when the British War Memorials Committee was already in crisis in the case of Wadsworth in November 1918, or after the transfer of the whole project to the Imperial War Museum in the case of Bomberg in February 1920. Yockney sent Bomberg a friendly and apologetic letter.[46]

Some aspects of the Bomberg/Konody affair seem more a matter of misunderstanding and bad timing than any sort of conspiracy to compromise the artist. He cannot have been completely cowed by the experience if he entertained the notion of applying to the British scheme. The last quarter of 1918 and 1919 were highly productive months for Bomberg, as they were for others returning from active service such as Lewis and Roberts. This intense phase of work is marked by several interwoven, sometimes competing imperatives. Bomberg had much in common with other artists in that, unlike say Nash or Nevinson, he did not have a public profile as an official artist in 1917 to 1918 and had been totally absent from the London art scene. It was a matter of picking up the threads and re-establishing a practice after a gap of three years. Bomberg's Russian Ballet lithographs of 1919, timed to appear when Diaghilev's ballet performed in London with sets by Larionov and Picasso, relate to work on the theme of dancers done in connection with a dust-jacket design for John Rodker's poems in 1914

(fig. 80). A similar strategy of starting from where one left off was pursued by others, literally by Stanley Spencer who finished *Swan Upping at Cookham* (fig. 81) in 1919, left incomplete when he volunteered in 1915, or with more strategic self-consciousness by Wyndham Lewis.

82   David Bomberg, *Study for 'Sappers at Work: A Canadian Tunnelling Company, Hill 60, St Eloi'* 1918–19, oil on canvas, 304.2 × 243.8, Tate, London

83   David Bomberg, *Sappers at Work: A Canadian Tunnelling Company*, 1919, oil on canvas, 304.8 × 243.8, National Gallery of Canada, Ottawa

84 David Bomberg, *Study for a Memorial to T. E. Hulme 1917*, 1918, ink and pencil on paper, 22.4 × 15.5, Imperial War Museum, London

This process of reconnection was also marked by the fact that witnessing war suggested new subjects and new obligations. Bomberg lost crucial professional colleagues to the war, notably T. E. Hulme in 1917 and Isaac Rosenberg in 1918, and some of the work, such as a collection of war poems written from August to October 1918 and a sketch for a war memorial to Hulme (fig. 84), were a means of paying tribute. As well as numerous sketches for the Canadian commission, he produced a set of over one hundred richly inventive drawings, what his first biographer called a 'frieze of life', organised as twelve thematic portfolios with titles such as *The Visitor*, *The Square Floor*, *Bargees*, and *Lock-up*, and exhibited at Frank Rutter's Adelphi Gallery in October 1919 (figs 86–9).[47] The drawings pick up themes from the pre-war work but also reflect on the sights of war. They were reviewed by Herbert

Read, who referred to their 'high standard of formal beauty', and by *Jewish World*, which discussed them as poetic memory pictures, 'that delicate half-seen vision which floats through our minds when we think upon the subject, or when the subject is conjured up for us by the words of a poet'.[48] The following month he showed canvases at the London Group. He was also approached by Robert van t'Hoff, Dutch architect of Augustus John's London studio, to join de Stijl but declined because, as he wrote in 1953, he felt it 'could only lead again to the Blank Page'.[49]

Both Richard Cork and Lisa Tickner have compellingly demonstrated that even the most abstract of Bomberg's pre-war works, such as *Mud Bath* of 1914 and *In the Hold* (fig. 85) of 1913–14 are embedded in social subjects, specifically modern life in the Yiddish community of the East End, but Tickner also writes about how *In the Hold*, the master work with which Bomberg intended to stake a claim as the leading avant-garde artist in 1914, separates form and content, abstraction and figuration and holds these elements in tension.[50] She discusses it as an allegory of modernity, in which diasporic experience is central. A similar set of preoccupations is at work in the 'frieze of life' drawings, about which Bomberg wrote that they were intended 'to prove that form plays one part, content another. Both can operate within one another, but

85 David Bomberg, *In the Hold*, 1913–14, oil on canvas, 196.2 × 231.1, Tate, London

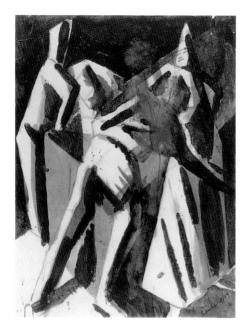

86 David Bomberg, *Players*, 1919, pencil, ink and watercolour on paper, 26 × 19.7 Tate, London, Presented by Mrs Lilian Bomberg 1976

87 David Bomberg, *Figure*, 1919, pen, ink and pencil on paper, 26 × 20, private collection

88 David Bomberg, *Figures*, 1919, blue chalk, pen and blue wash on paper, 26.4 × 19.9, University College London, Slade Collection

89 David Bomberg, *Stairway: Drawing no. 3*, 1919, ink and wash on paper, 26 × 19.5, James Hyman Fine Art

[remain] basically unrelated'.[51] In 1935, a few weeks before the birth of his daughter and while he was painting in Spain, Bomberg wrote to his sister Kitty: 'before I went to Palestine [in 1923] I had a more characteristic manner of expressing myself . . . These paintings of mine [experimental canvases made in Ronda] may be better or worse sellers than the more detailed representational ones but I enjoyed doing this more, and am beginning to feel myself again – something like before the war + immediately after it'.[52]

Sappers at Work represents a Canadian Tunnelling Company of Russian Canadian, Canadian and Yorkshire miners digging under German fortifications at St. Eloi, an elaborate operation that took six months and resulted in a massive explosion in March 1916 that blotted out the landscape and two German front-line companies.[53] The subject matter of the labouring figures in cramped space is comparable with the subject of dockers unloading a ship in *In the Hold* or the communal baths of *The Mud Bath*, and a highly abstracted and geometric study in bright colours is closely related in form to these paintings and their preparatory works. There is also a more descriptive but less highly finished pencil and ink drawing, where the handling of line is fluid, almost nervous, as it is in the final canvas of the first version. Both these studies are landscape format and the original invitation referred to a picture '12 feet wide'.[54] In the finished first version, about one third of the right-hand and a smaller strip from the left were cut and worked out in a pencil drawing squared up for transfer in which all the final elements are present but which does not anticipate the handling of paint. The composition became vertical in format, bringing the focus in more closely to the massive, twisting, self-absorbed figures. The final painting is a new departure in Bomberg's work, and, with its flamboyant colours and splintered discontinuous surfaces from small areas of fractured triangles to loose patches of colour with uneven boundaries, unlike any other war painting. Tickner writes about *In the Hold*, a more dramatic, more inventive work, that 'it seems *sui generis*. . . . There was nothing like it in Europe at the time.' But while this painting may be said 'to look back to Futurism and forward to Op-Art',[55] *Sappers at Work* cannot be pinned down in any sort of trajectory. The first version may owe something to a viewing of William Roberts's *The First German Gas Attack at Ypres* (fig. 90) for the Canadians, which is also a high-keyed,

90   William Roberts, *The First German Gas Attack at Ypres*, 1918–19, oil on canvas, 304.8 × 365.8, National Gallery of Canada, Ottawa

colourful and evenly toned canvas of wild gesticulating figures being routed through a siege battery.[56] Yet Bomberg's painting is not completely assured in the sense that form and content, or abstraction versus figuration, are unresolved rather than held in tension, and if we set on one side the story of its rejection, we might think it a work Bomberg had not quite pulled off. In the second accepted version, the figures are smaller, set further back in the recesses of pictorial space, and there are more of them, twelve as opposed to seven, more overtly engaged in constructive tasks. It is more tightly, less fleshily painted, with more emphasis on describing the geometry of the tunnel, making it legible as a space working men can occupy and taking over from the figures as the main motivation for the painting. It appears more realistic, more photographic in reproduction than it is, because it has a painterly surface and the flesh and clothing of the men are not so much described as built up from solid, block-like forms anticipated in the Tate version. It has been shown only once in England, at the Tate's Bomberg retrospective in 1967. Compared with the first canvas, the second is a darker, more strongly contrasted painting where light and shadow dramatise the architecture.

Ten years after the war, Konody, who evidently believed that the artist had failed to rise to the occasion, wrote that the rejected canvas was 'a huge canvas of patchwork in pretty, gay colours, in which the rigid lines of props and rafters, which gave him an ideal opportunity for geometricisation, were twisted into snake-like writhing forms that conveyed no meaning'.[57] In 1957, Bomberg wrote that he was so excited about the commission that he did not take part in the Armistice celebrations and that the aim of the painting 'was to extinguish the phase of war – I had had enough of that – but [and?] wanted the relief – and the sublimation of creating the forms of war – not in the dark, death-smelling underground mine – like a coal pit – but in the open-air, bathed *in* sunlight'.[58] It does not follow, however, that one is a more authentic picture, somehow more true to the artist's intentions. Nor did he necessarily disown the second version. The letter ends 'what is wanted to eliminate in my sunlight version of the Sappers under "hill 60" was uncompromisingly rendered in the accepted work'. At some date unknown he sent a photograph of the final version to Eddie Marsh, a well-known supporter of young artists. He also sent a reproduction to the Tate for the 1939 exhibition of photographs 'Mural Painting in Great Britain 1919–1939', where it was duly shown.[59] Since it is obvious that Bomberg ordered a new canvas when he started on the second version, rather than painting over the first, the survival of the two in what seems to be a spontaneous, immediate and private response and a public, more deliberated, more negotiated version, is extraordinarily interesting and revealing of an artist who did not or could not fuse public and private in one work. Much later, Bomberg stated that during the war 'I had contemplated the problem of survival for life and for art – I had found that my life was too deeply interwoven with my art to conceive art as a profession.'[60] This was a disavowal and refusal of Bell's separation of human and aesthetic motivation in the review 'Wilcoxism' he wrote of the 1919 *Nation's War Paintings* exhibition, an article Bomberg knew and kept in his papers, even referring to it in a letter he wrote to Roberts in 1957.[61]

Both Roberts, the son of a carpenter, and Bomberg, the son of a Jewish immigrant and leather-worker, were from working-class backgrounds. Roberts went to the Slade on a London County Council scholarship and Bomberg on a grant from the Jewish Education Aid Society.[62] Their war experience was not that of the quintessential First World War subaltern-volunteer, whose upper middle-class and public school origins gave rise to fantasies of self-sacrifice and self-immolation that war experience recast as a 'militarized proletarianization'. Here the bourgeois individual experienced the banal, repetitive, work-world of war not as a vocation, a process for shaping self-identity and creating values, but as an alienating and dangerous necessity and an insight into the ordinary day-to-day life of his social inferiors: 'the men'.[63] If scholarship opportunities provided Bomberg and Roberts with a means to aspire to upward social mobility, enlistment was a reversal, a set-back to that aspiration. Roberts became a gunner in the Royal Field Artillery, having failed to enter either the Artists' Rifles or the Welch Regiment.[64] In his description of his war experiences, however, he seemed always to feel slightly detached from his comrades, the 'Tommies', discovering by chance, and preferring, a retreat away from them for time off from the barracks. The inn he found was reserved for officers and Roberts, encouraged by other soldiers, applied for and failed to get a commission. He lacked the courage, however, to introduce himself to Colin Gill and Leon Underwood in order to seek their influence for a transfer to camouflage. He found leave in London at the Tour Eiffel 'a novel experience . . . having for a year or more taken orders from sergeant-majors, sergeants, corporals, bombardiers, not forgetting gunners, to find myself associating with majors, captains, lieutenants, actors and art critics.'[65]

The war drawings that Roberts undertook as part of his official employment as a war artist for the British are amongst the most acerbic and cynical produced by any official artist and represent perhaps the only body of work by an English artist that approaches the social realism of German artists like Grosz and Dix. He seems to have done most of this work in the first half of 1918 while painting his Canadian picture. When he came to the British as a salaried artist paid for his total output, he did little additional work besides his large memorial painting.[66] In January 1919, however, Roberts decided to cease paid employment and to continue

91 William Roberts, *On the Wire – Inspired by 'With a Machine Gun to Cambrai'*, *c*.1974, pencil, charcoal and water-colour on paper, 46.9 × 36.8, Imperial War Museum, London

to work on his large canvas at his own expense, although he was entitled to a further month's salary. Like Bomberg, he was chronically short of money throughout 1919.[67]

The exact circumstances under which Roberts carried out his terms of employment as a war artist and the level of his commitment to the enterprise remain enigmatic. His autobiography, *Memories of the War to End War*, is a simple unemotional narrative. In contrast to the literary aspirations of Nash's unfinished autobiography, *Outline*, Robert's account, written in 1975 when he was a Royal Academician, mimics the simple, unembellished narratives and diaries of

working-class writers, such as George Coppard's *With a Machine Gun to Cambrai* (fig. 91) of 1969. Coppard's is based on his war-time diary; Roberts's is authenticated by the inclusion of contemporary letters to his future wife, Sarah. In these, he reveals an intense dislike of the war and a longing for it to end, so that he can be released from an obligation to serve. He even contemplates the possibility of a fortuitous illness as an honourable discharge from war service: 'If only I could get ill: trench feet, a fever of some kind, and thus get back to England, I should be happy.'[68] The letters are marked with an awareness that it was a determinant of experience as a soldier at the front that the complexities of modern urban life were eliminated and that survival at its most basic level was the dominant way of life. It was monotonous and simple; excitement was provided only by the rediscovery of the instinct for self-preservation. In his letters, Roberts expresses a characteristic disjunction between his own ordered, restricted living and the complex, contradictory life style from which he was severed, recalled only through his relationship with Sarah. He wrote:

> The difficulty is our two ways of living and environment are so different that my judgement, for you, can have very little point. One whose existence is so absolutely monotonous, repetition always, every day lived to order; the only excitement being to dodge and duck for your bloody miserable life; finds it almost impossible to transport his imagination into the intricasies and complexities of town living. Simplicty is the keynote here, and too, a complete rest for the brain.[69]

E. J. Leed argues that voluntary enlistment in the First World War represented an escape from society to community that 'could be welcomed as a cure, a release, or a liberation from the pathologies of experience, human interaction, and psychic disequilibrium that were seen to be increasingly endemic to life in modern technological society'. Motivation to go to war was founded on a 'bifurcation of values' that was in turn based on the 'polarization of peace and war', and expectations were inevitably bound to turn to disillusion. Illusions, however, were not discarded in the face of reality but were suppressed and internalised:

> experience provides the material in which cultural polarities are resuscitated and redefined. At the front the antithesis of society and community becomes an antithesis of "home" and "front". The antithesis of a technological and human world is mapped upon the landscape of war to define the tension between the "external" world of physical, threatening forces and an "internal" world of mechanical solidarity and fantasy.[70]

Roberts had to abandon himself and his new status as an artist when he joined up and wished for a way to be free of the war. When Konody offered him, if not liberation from the war, a semblance of his pre-war practice that, although defined and delineated, was at least an escape from the front, he was keen to accept

and anxious to be accepted.[71] Wyndham Lewis stated that he undertook the work with bitterness.[72] As it was an escape, but not freedom, I would argue that Roberts took with him the tensions and internalised contradictions that had underpinned his military service. Consequently, although he worked initially with enthusiasm, his actions were qualified by obedience and he could not sustain his commitment. His war service did not finish, and therefore could not be reflected upon and given form, until he had finally achieved liberation through demobilisation in October 1919. When demobilisation came, however, the opportunity had passed. He concluded his recollection of the war: 'With the war ended and no more war paintings to be done, it was now time to give up my uniform and regimental number.'[73]

In Roberts's war sketches, 'the tension between the "external" world of physical, threatening forces and an "internal" world of mechanical solidarity and fantasy' is manifest. Soldiers don gas masks and resemble blind insects; signallers, trampling on a fallen man, yell wordless orders and make empty gestures against a backdrop sepia like dried blood; gunners stumble out of dugouts in a single jumbled body with multiple arms and legs; actions take place in compressed spaces; when Tommies fill water bottles with rain from a shell hole, comrades exchange sightless glances; a group of British Generals is a single insensitive body oblivious to the saluting soldier beneath their feet, a figure that almost distorts into an inchoate faceless spectre, its arms raised in despair. The finished drawings have a nervous quality: broken patches of wash are applied to uniforms and figures etched in jutting angry lines, the landscape is delineated in coherent, less yielding blocks of colour. In slighter sketches, forms are more diffuse. Where signallers lay wire Rosières Valley is poxed with shell holes, a dead horse rots, the signallers move like dummies. When Germans shell an infantry duck-board track, a single isolated figure dissolves going west 'overland to kit and kat', his companions recoil in horror. In Roberts's drawing the apocalyptic madness of the front is unrelenting (figs 92–101). For his war drawings, 'Cubist work' was unacceptable because it was inappropriate, but Roberts's war pictures, while they rendered the war as farcical, do not articulate protest. When Roberts was finally released from war service, the moment and potentiality for dissent and disobedience had been neutralised and disarmed.

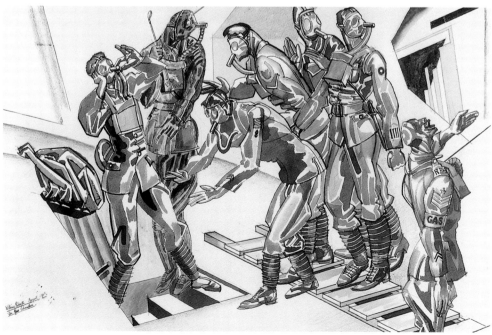

92 *top* William Roberts, *Rosières Valley*, 1918, pen, watercolour on paper, 16 × 25.4, Imperial War Museum, London

93 *right* William Roberts, *The Gas Chamber*, 1918–19, ink and watercolour on paper, 31.7 × 50.8, Imperial War Museum, London

94   William Roberts, *During a Battle*, 1918, pencil and watercolour on paper, 15.8 × 25.4, Imperial War Museum, London

95   William Roberts, *Brigade Headquarters: Signallers and Linesmen*, 1918, ink and wash on paper, 15.2 × 25.4, Imperial War Museum, London

96   William Roberts, *Gunners: Turning Out for an SOS Battery Action at Night*, 1918, pencil and watercolour on paper, 32.3 × 32.3, Imperial War Museum, London

97 *facing page* William Roberts, *Infantry Duck-board Track being Shelled by the Germans*, 1918, pencil and watercolour on paper, 36.8 × 29.8, Imperial War Museum, London

98 *right* William Roberts, *A Group of British Generals*, 1918–19, pencil and watercolour on paper, 13.3 × 10.1, Imperial War Museum, London

99 *below* William Roberts, *Signallers*, 1918, ink, pencil and watercolour on paper, 31.1 × 49.5, Imperial War Museum, London

101   William Roberts, *Died of Wounds*, 1919, private collection

100 *facing page*   William Roberts, *Tommies Filling their Water Bottles with Rain from a Shell Hole*, 1918, ink, pencil, chalk and water-colour on paper, 50.8 × 38.1, Imperial War Museum, London

Roberts made other works on social themes, for example *The Cinema* (fig. 102), or working-class street scenes and entertainments such as boxing. Only one known drawing makes any overt political statement, however: *Taking the Oath* (fig. 103) of 1920. Here a group of middle-aged and middle-class civilians are portrayed as complacent and oafish while being sworn into the Royal Ulster Constabulary beneath a map of Ireland, transmogrified into a grinning face labelled 'BRITISH POSSESSIONS MARKED RED'. They are the 'Black and Tans', recruited from unemployed veterans during 1920 to suppress the Irish rebellion, nicknamed after their improvised uniforms of khaki and black and described by Churchill as 'selected from a great press of applicants on account of their characters and their record in the war'. Roberts cynical characterisation records the alternative view of British action in Ireland as excessive and oppressive.[74]

In one sense, official employment rescued Roberts from the front and it could not have come too quickly. In another sense, the opportunity also returned him to

103   William Roberts, *Taking the Oath*, 1920, pen, ink, pencil and sepia wash on paper, 24 × 23.9, Victoria and Albert Museum, London

102   William Roberts, *The Cinema*, 1920, oil on canvas, 91.4 × 76.2, Tate, London

art and imposed obligations too soon for him to have resolved both the rich possibilities and the dilemmas involved in giving form to ideas such as acknowledging solidarity with soldier companions, some of whom did not come back, and re-establishing himself in a culture altered by the war. Similar dilemmas affected other artists, including Stanley Spencer, who also resigned from his employment. Spencer admired Roberts's work and it was not only Roberts's style that Spencer learned from but also a kind of ethics of war-painting. Spencer, unlike Roberts, was eventually to find a way of making a major work, independent of but informed by both the war and the official schemes, at Burghclere Chapel in the late 1920s.

The Politics of Art: Lewis and Nevinson

When Wyndham Lewis's *A Canadian Gun Pit* (fig. 104) was shown as part of the Canadian War Memorials exhibition at the Royal Academy, in January 1919, its catalogue entry was annotated rather strangely: 'It is an experiment of the painter's in a kind of painting not his own.'[75] The same comment, with its reference to

104   Wyndham Lewis, *A Canadian Gun Pit*, 1918, oil on canvas, 304.8 × 363.2, National Gallery of Canada, Ottawa

Lewis experimenting in means belonging to someone else, was repeated in the publication of plates *Art and War*, which accompanied the exhibition, and it may have been written by P. G. Konody.[76] It makes the intriguing assumption that there was elsewhere a form of authentic Wyndham Lewis painting, and one that is at odds with Lewis's own refusal of a singular self, for example his Art Vortex, *Be Thyself* of 1915.[77] Lewis told Herbert Read in December 1918 when he was working on the canvas that 'I came to the conclusion that Konody had succeeded in making me paint one

of the dullest good pictures on earth. I have just done another painting in an afternoon which is at least 17 times as alive. What a nightmare this wicked war has been!'[78] *A Canadian Gun Pit*, depicting a camouflaged howitzer being laid in, was worked up from material Lewis collected on a visit organised by the Canadians that he made to Vimy Ridge, December 1917. It was a quiet sector and, in contrast to the canvas Lewis painted for the British scheme the following year, *A Battery Shelled* (see fig. 69), the painting reveals no battle action. *A Canadian Gun Pit* is also arguably less ambitious than the later work in the sense that its forms are played out across its surface in varied, more dispersed ways, and its subject-matter is deployed as a series of anecdotal and disparate vignettes. Lewis maintained in his autobiography that he chose his own subject for the Canadian canvas whereas Roberts and Bomberg were allocated theirs, but his comments to Read none the less suggest that he himself was not satisfied with the work.[79] Unlike Roberts, who was employed full-time for the British, Lewis carried out his two major canvases as one-off commissions, but like Roberts he also produced a body of war drawings, which he organised as an independent exhibition titled *Guns* at the Goupil Gallery, February 1919, timed to capitalise on the Canadian exhibition.

In his foreword to the catalogue for *Guns* Lewis wrote that the public might be surprised to find that the artist had 'abandoned those vexing diagrams by which he puzzled and annoyed'. It was not, he argued, a consequence of a change of heart, merely the product of a different task necessitating a new approach.[80] At the same time he told a newspaper 'In the years before the war I was thinking less about the subject than of the treatment. The war made me think more of the subject matter. The war was a great human event and human methods had to be adopted in dealing with it if it were to be registered in art at all.'[81] Writing to John Quinn, the American collector, in order to interest him in some purchases, Lewis described the work in *Guns* as having 'a subject matter postulated, & therefore necessitates a more representative treatment'.[82] Although this motif of content and form (or, put another way, more figurative with more explicit subject matter, if not greater verisimilitude, versus abstraction) recurs in Lewis's own writing and his work as it had in the work and more private speculations of Bomberg and Roberts in this period, Lewis's reappraisal, as well as being more public and more knowing, was also more complex than theirs. In the foreword to *Guns* and an article published in the *Daily Express* in February 1919, 'The Men Who Will Paint Hell', he was joining a public debate about war art that the Canadian show had triggered and securing publicity for his own exhibition as well as pursuing strategies for reclaiming leadership of a regrouped post-war avant-garde. He was a scholarly commentator citing Goya and Uccello as standing for alternative visions, biting and satiric compared to dispassionate and decorative, a

humanist compared to an inhuman vision. But he also pointed out that what he had done were personal, immediate responses to a tragic event. Real understanding and interpretation of war could be undertaken only in the fullness of time.

In his work, Lewis seems to seek to retain something of the sharpness and invigoration of his war service experienced as purgative, dangerous and exciting. He wrote to Ezra Pound 'I am both glad and ashamed to say that I rather enjoy it'.[83] Although Lewis began to be anxious to work his way out of the Artillery, he could describe the sights in letters to Pound with a certain callous cynicism or perhaps bravado: 'You meet plenty of dead men. I stumbled into one (of two) with his head blown off so that his neck[,] level with the collar of his tunic, reminded you of sheep in butchers' shops, or a French Salon painting of a Moroccan headsman . . . So you see –. The O.P. [Observation Post] amuses me'.[84] Above all, Lewis was aware that modern war was an artifice, and a manufactured spectacle: 'Ypres and Vimy . . . were deliberately invented scenes, daily improved on and worked at by up-to-date machines, to stage war', he wrote in 1919.[85] *Blasting and Bombardiering*, first published in 1937, is a consciously theatrical and comic text where anecdotes are selected and worked up as vignettes of war, as farce and entertainment, for example, the often quoted story that Augustus John, with whom he shared a car while working for the Canadians, looked like the king and startled sentries.[86] Robert Graves also confessed that he had concocted *Goodbye to all that*, first published in 1929, with 'the obligatory "ingredients" of a popular memoir',[87] and Lewis announced that *Blasting and Bombardiering* was a '"good-bye to all that" sort of a book', although its purpose was different.[88] Lewis is not simply calculating and opportunist because he was also conscious of how ephemeral the war atmosphere was, writing in 1919: 'The eight-mile-wide belt of desert across France will be a green, methodic countryside in five years' time. The harsh dream that the soldier has dreamed – the barbaric nightmare – will be effaced by some sort of cosy sun tinting the edges of decorous lives.'[89] Lewis was resisting romanticised readings of war, however much such readings had been renegotiated in the light of the reception given to artists such as Nash in 1918.

The *Guns* drawings were highly stylised views of siege batteries as places of work such as *Action or*

105 *right*   Wyndham Lewis, *Action or Artillery*, 1918, water-colour and ink, 35.2 × 50.9, Cooper Art Gallery, Barnsley

106 *below*   Wyndham Lewis, *Battery Salvo: A Canadian Gun Pit*, 1918, pen and brown ink, graphite and watercolour on paper, 35.4 × 50.9, National Gallery of Canada, Ottawa

107 *right* Wyndham Lewis, *Drag Ropes*, 1918, pencil, pen, ink and watercolour on paper, 35.5 × 41.5, Manchester City Art Gallery

108 *top, facing page* Wyndham Lewis, *Drawing of The Great War No. 1 (The Menin Road)*, 1918, watercolour on paper, 29.8 × 46.6, Southampton City Art Gallery

110 *below* Wyndham Lewis, *Great War Drawing No. 2*, 1918, watercolour, 38.1 × 54.2, Southampton City Art Gallery

109 *bottom* Wyndham Lewis, *Shell Humping or Howitzers*, 1918, chalk, ink and watercolour on paper, 31.5 × 47.3, Norwich Castle Museum

Artillery (fig. 105), *Laying* or *Battery Pulling-in (II)*. Figures are schematised like automatons or insects. Some drawings celebrate muscular, collective exertion, for instance, *Drag Ropes* (fig. 107). Lewis's gunnery is a relentlessly masculine world. The motif of detached observers, like the ones in *A Battery Shelled*, recurs in *Battery Salvo: A Canadian Gun Pit* (fig. 106) or sometimes as off-duty soldiers relaxing as in *The Menin Road* (fig. 108). These figures act as metaphors for the ruthless theatricality of the front. In July 1917, when recuperating from trench fever in a French hospital, Lewis wrote to Pound 'Life as you know is only justifiable as spectacle: the moment at which it becomes harrowing

and stale, no aesthetic purpose is any longer served, War would be better exchanged for Diplomacy, Intelligence! – or something else.'[90] Other drawings, however, reveal a sense of apprehension at the threat of annihilation, as in *Study for 'To Wipe-Out'* (fig. 113), where shell bursts become solid three-dimensional dervishes that pock-mark the landscape and obliterate men. In the drawings, where the land is revealed, churned up mud resembles a solidified sea, pleats and folds of heavy cloth or shapeless scabrous skin (figs 105 and 106). The scribbled pen strokes and pale watercolour washes delineating land in the drawings contrast the purposive muscular geometry of the

111   Fred Varley, *For What?*, c.1918, oil on canvas, 147.2 × 182.8, Beaverbrook Collection of War Art, 8911, © Canadian War Museum

automatons operating on its surfaces. Unlike the organic vitalism of Otto Dix's battlefront landscapes-cum-flesh, which Lewis would not have known, or the commingling of putrifying bodies and livid land in Frederick Varley's aftermath paintings such as *For What?* (fig. 111), which Lewis would have seen at the Academy in January 1919, Lewis's formless, almost colourless mudscapes appear barren and their mortified fleshiness does not engulf the man-machines operating within their boundaries. The mechanised impersonal soldiers appear armoured with indifference to its flux. One view would read the figure/ground opposition in these drawings as mirroring a feminine/masculine binary, where the land is a passive canvas, the backdrop for a virile performance. Hal Foster argues that post-

113 Wyndham Lewis, *Study for 'To Wipe-Out'*, 1918, black chalk, pen, ink and watercolour on paper, 34 × 50, Courtesy of Ivor Braka Ltd., London

112 Wyndham Lewis, *Officers and Signallers*, 1919, ink, water-colour and gouache on paper, 25.4 × 35.6, Imperial War Museum, London

war machinic modernism such as Lewis's, with its cult of geometries and automatism, was a reaction to the mass dismemberment of bodies on the battlefront and the basis for a new corporeal order in which the body is already dead, 'deader than dead'. He describes Lewis's celebration of deadness but argues that aggression enlivens this, particularly in his depiction of eyes.[91] In the war works, the drawings and the two major canvases, however, active working humanoids almost always appear sightless (fig. 112). Only in the Canadian painting does one figure meet the spectator's gaze with a confrontational stare – close to the centre of the canvas, beneath the camouflaged canopy in the group

of four soldiers checking shells. The *Guns* series of drawings was one of the most accomplished body of war works produced by a British artist. Yet they enact no redemptive, or as Bersani puts it no edifying function, because they simply described a gunner's life at the front, and the catalogue entries in 1919 mimicked the descriptive texts in the Canadian Royal Academy catalogue, in a deadpan and pitiless way. As a series, culminating in 1919 with Lewis's British memorial painting, they act out what Walter Benjamin wrote much later in 1930 about Ernst Jünger's writings: 'Without going too deeply into the significance of the economic causes of war, one might say that the harshest, most disastrous aspects of imperialistic war are in part the result of the gaping discrepancy between the gigantic means of technology and the minuscule moral illumination its affords.'[92] Lewis does not mediate a Goyaesque satire and a Uccello-type pageant so much as his war work oscillates between these two poles of humanitarian identification and heartless exploitation. The narrative enunciated and enacted in the works produces no narrative closure, no cosy sunsets to tinge Hell with comforting portents of hope.

At the same time, in 1919 to 1920, Lewis was involved in attempts to re-establish a continuity with his pre-war activities. He tried and failed to bring out another volume of *Blast* but succeeded in organising an exhibition for Group X, in March 1920, including some pre-war Vorticists.[93] In the foreword to the catalogue for this and an essay 'What Art Now?', written

114   Wyndham Lewis, *L'Ingenue*, 1919, black crayon and water-colour, 51 × 35, Manchester City Art Gallery

115   Wyndham Lewis, *A Reading of Ovid (Tyros)*, 1921, oil on canvas, 165.2 × 90.2, Scottish National Gallery of Modern Art, Edinburgh

in April 1919, Lewis argued for the consolidation of pre-war experimentation. He was also making studies from the model and portrait drawings that emphasise linearity and cool clarity comparable with the revived classicism in post-war French art, such as the Ingrist drawings Picasso began to exhibit in Paris during 1919 (fig. 114). Although he exhibited portraits at Group x, he did not abandon abstraction, experimenting with small inventive papiers collés such as *Abstract Composition* of 1921. Group x was timed to pre-empt the London Group exhibition by then dominated by Roger Fry.[94] Many of Lewis's writings in the period satirised Fry's aesthetics, arguing for art as energy and power in contact with and enriched by life and constantly articulating a version of the primitivist impulse distinct from Fry's etiolated and effete espousal of

'primitive art'.[95] In 1921, he metamorphosed Fry's promotion of child art and played it back as the Tyros (fig. 115) with which to threaten and terrorise Fry's tasteful, Francophile modernism, seeing his pursuit of the pure as 'only a graceful dilettantism', a form of art for art's sake, 'always liable . . . to degenerate into a cultivated and snobbish game. My Tyros may help to frighten away this local bogey.'[96] In 'The Children of the New Epoch' published in his new review *The Tyro*, established in 1921, Lewis identified the war as an impenetrable barrier that allowed 'no passage back' to the past. He did not repudiate nor did he renounce the avant-garde activism of pre-1914. Nor was it the case, as had been recently argued, that war in 1914 'induced a revulsion against the attraction of the new art . . . that persisted throughout . . . and did not disappear in 1918'.[97] Rather, as already noted, the mass slaughter of young men, symbolised for modern art in the death of Gaudier-Brzeska, had fostered the promotion of a new tolerance for avant-garde experimentation and gave rise in 1919, at the time of *The Nation's War Paintings*, to a critical consensus seeking to integrate modern art into the life of the nation, healing the fissures and disfigurements inflicted by the war on art and the nation alike. Instead of either renouncing experimentation or yielding to assimilation, Lewis resisted the neutralisation of innovative art implied by such a critical consensus, calling instead for 'a constant and perpetually renewed effort'. It was Lewis's refusal to derive any redemptive value from war that makes his position so compelling and distinctive.

Nevinson volunteered as an ambulance driver for the Red Cross in France and Belgium, then transferred to the RAMC and the 3rd London General Hospital until his discharge in 1915. Unlike Bomberg, Roberts and Lewis, not only was his practice as an artist not disrupted by war service, he had established himself as *the* British war artist, showing at every significant London exhibition from 1915 and becoming an official artist from 1917 onwards. His output included two major solo exhibitions at the Leicester Galleries; three monographs were written about his war work – the one by P. G. Konody and one by Crawford Flitch – and an issue of the Wellington House publication *British Artists at the Front* was dedicated to him. His *La Mitrailleuse* (see fig. 8) in the Tate was purchased and presented by the Contemporary Art Society. He enjoyed considerable popularity and fame from his war paintings and began to make a virtue out of a refusal to maintain loyalty to formal integrity, asserting in the preface to the catalogue of his 1919 *Peace Show* pictures his right to select method solely according to subject matter.[98] It was not particularly welcomed. Michael Sadler called the show 'an anthropological parody of the last thirty years of Western European art'

and many reviewers found the variety overwhelming and unconvincing.[99] By the early 1920s, Nevinson had begun to lose the support of serious critics including Claude Phillips and even P. G. Konody who saw his work, now that it no longer concerned war subjects, as coarse, sentimental, vulgar and in poor taste.[100] As Gerald Cumberland put it in 1920, 'Bohemia has been conquered by the Philistines.'[101]

Although Nevinson had little serious critical support, he exhibited regularly and sold widely in the boom years of the art market from its revival in the latter part of the war until the beginning of the slump in the mid-1920s and the crash in 1929.[102] He exploited the expanded market for printmaking, working in the favoured media of drypoint and lithography. He also occasionally worked in mezzotint but, except for some early experiments, not in the more decorous medium of woodengraving. Nevinson continued to be a consummate self-publicist, joining populist and self-righteous causes such as 'The Brighter London Society' in 1922 and 'The National Spring Cleaning Movement' in 1923. He was ready to supply a trenchant pithy opinion for the press on anything from women's fashions to the benefits of paganism and lived the life of a raconteur and bon viveur. As Ian Jeffrey puts it, he had 'discovered a peace-time society beyond hope of redemption'.[103] He was a sort of archetype of the 1920s media personality and star, a kind of clown figure, with whom he sometimes identified. 'The artist's position, as it seems to me . . . is perfectly hopeless. He is dying – as the circus clown is dying' he said in 1925.[104] In the 1920s, he sometimes parodied Mussolini 'earning a new notoriety as a black shirt. Not the Fascismo variety, but a strictly all-British brand of one.'[105]

Early in 1919, Nevinson declared that *The Harvest of Battle* (see fig. 71) would be his last war picture and that he was turning his attention to modern industrialism and portrayals of human activity.[106] The *Peace Show* collection at the Leicester Galleries was a disparate medley of miscellaneous subjects. It included urban images, particularly his first New York pictures based on his trip there earlier in the year, as well as suburban themes such as *When Father Mows the Lawn*. *The Ploughshare*, a Quaker pacifist journal, reproduced three paintings from this show in an article subtitled 'Preparing the Class War', Nevinson's work could be read as revealing evidence of social unrest in winter

1919. The large and dramatic lithograph *The Workers* (fig. 116), exhibited in 1919, is said to be based on the mass meetings held at Tower Hill during the nine-day rail strike in September to October 1919.[107] A cloth-capped crowd seethes before a platform of hectoring speakers and trade union banners. Dwarfing the scene, a darkened and menacing warehouse blocks the light. The sombre image evokes a sense of working-class solidarity. Some works combine general social observation with specific contemporary reference. In *Lilies of the Café* (fig. 117) of 1919, the commonplace social interaction of an ordinary youth turning to chat to a girl seated at an adjacent table and drinking with her female companion reflects new freedoms in women's behaviour in public, changes accelerated by the war. Discarded in the foreground of the picture lies a copy

116   C. R. W. Nevinson, *The Workers*, 1919, lithograph, 51.5 × 35.3, Manchester City Art Gallery

117   C. R. W. Nevinson, *The Lilies of the Café*, 1919, pencil and watercolour on paper, present whereabouts unknown

of the *Star* newspaper, a radical working-class paper run by T. P. O'Connor, that blazons the headline 'STRIKERS' for the casual appraisal of the viewer.

Like the reception given to *Paths of Glory*, Nevinson's work could be interpreted in contradictory ways and an appeal to the artist's intentions does not clarify matters. In 1924, when a picture by Nevinson was apparently reproduced by a student Labour Party magazine without his authority, he wrote 'They obviously use my name as a sympathiser with this particular party, though by bitter experience I have found Socialists even greater rogues than Conservatives, and even greater canting humbugs than Liberals.'[108] *The Workers* was reproduced by *The Tatler* as well as by socialist papers.[109] From 1929, Nevinson began to write regular newspaper columns for the popular press. In an article, immodestly titled 'ME: by C. R. W. Nevinson,

A number of British artists made the trip across the Atlantic in 1919, often inspired by Joseph Pennell's work. In Nevinson's case the metropolis is revealed as multifaceted, busy and alienating. *The Soul of a Soulless City* (fig. 118), reproduced by the *Star* in 1925 as *The Son of a Soul-less City*, is an empty rail track cut through overcrowded tenements and skyscrapers. More desolate than his war landscapes, human beings are shut out while the pinkish beige tones of smog and skyscrapers work in a way that mocks the vacuum of the central space, a combination of enchanted palaces and comfortless urban desert. Nevinson later used an elevated viewpoint in *Amongst the Nerves of the World* (fig. 119), a view down Fleet Street towards St Paul's where light and space become a three-dimensional metaphor for the ether filled with information crackling on

118   C. R. W. Nevinson, *The Soul of the Soulless City ('New York – an Abstraction')*, 1920, oil on canvas, 91.5 × 60.8, Tate, London

119   C. R. W. Nevinson, *Amongst the Nerves of the World (London with St. Paul's)*, 1928–30, oil on canvas, 75.3 × 50, Museum of London

'The Famous Painter' for the *Daily Express*, Nevinson sounded off about the burden of being a compulsive rebel by genetic inheritance from rebellious parents, both Fabian Socialists. His mother was a suffragette and campaigner on socialist issues. He blasted even-handedly the rich who were 'thieves' and the poor who were poor because of 'their incapacity for getting rich'.[110] He offered his solution to the national crisis of mid-1930 by calling for a strong national leader whose 'appeal will have to take the form of an intense nationalism, in reaction to the internationalism of our present-day Socialists'.[111]

Nevinson's pictures of New York (about which he was also inconsistent deploring the Americanization of culture[112]) like his war work, demonstrate his ability to extract telling images from topical subject matter.

telegraphs and telephones while buildings and people are dematerialised by texts: 'PAPERS', 'NEWS', 'NEWS'.

Newsworthiness was Nevinson's forte and in 1924 he was at it again with a triptych called *Glittering Prizes* (fig. 120) included in his show at the Leicester Galleries that opened in March.

The central picture of the triptych is a landscape format canvas that reproduces *The Harvest of Battle* but compresses it both horizontally and vertically so that there is less foreground. Although the bodies remain, the one nearest to the spectator is reorientated and most of the background is suppressed. The two smaller canvases show two men in a street singing and holding out their hats, usually understood as ex-Service men, and the other, an elderly theatre-goer and his overdressed partner, framed by two crudely drawn caryatids. It was widely reported in the press in the two days before the opening of the show that the title was based on Lord Birkenhead's well-known speech made earlier in the same year, in which he said 'The world continues to offer glittering prizes to those who have stout arms and sharp swords'. The main picture, which was extensively reproduced, has a mock coat of arms in the top centre consisting of a glass of champagne above a crossed pair of smoking cigars. The painting was subtitled *A peace memorial to our heroic (after-dinner) speakers from a few unknown soldiers*. The flanking images were called *Yes, and they still have their hats off* and

Success. When the show opened, Nevinson had painted out the symbolic crest, replacing it with white paint said to represent a very light exploding, and retitled the series *Peace*. The centre panel was now called *A memorial to our heroic Speakers, from a few unknown soldiers*; the other two remained unchanged. No evidence for the original titles appeared in the catalogue and the Gallery issued a disclaimer that neither they nor the artist had any political intentions. The 'censorship', if that is what it should be called, arose because Lord Birkenhead had apparently objected and the artist had complied. The incident has all the trademarks of a well-organised publicity stunt and it was sometimes read as such: 'Mr Nevinson . . . knows that an artist sells more pictures by furnishing subjects for dinner-table talk than by beautiful painting.'[113] Although some reviewers saw the paintings as shallow, exploitative, populist and cynical,[114] others also found the incident amusing[115] or the pictures timely reminders of matters best never forgotten.[116] The rest of the work in the exhibition was viewed as journalistic and unconvincing. The portrait of his wife was titled *Portrait of a Pretty Girl* (and he really did design a chocolate box in 1933, but so did Paul Nash and Mark Gertler)[117] and the subject of one portrait, the Bohemian notoriety called Dolores who also modelled for Epstein, was reported in July as *Poisoned By Food: Crab Sandwiches Suspected*.[118] But such breeches of good taste and decorum were noted by the *Observer*[119] as necessary and opportune while the *Morning Post* produced the conservative argument that the work was 'a condemnation of Nevinson's lack of respect for dead and living heroes in associating them with *banal* ideas illustrated'.[120] Nevinson was compared with Epstein, three of whose works were left over in the Gallery from a previous exhibition: 'Are the two . . . preparing to form a great picture-and-sculpture combine of the future *pour épater* all of us mere *bourgeois*?'[121] Epstein and Nevinson, together with Augustus John, were sometimes described as the leaders of 'Bohemia' monopolising the Café Royal. When the Imperial War Museum was relocated in November to the Imperial Institute, South Kensington, the publicity came in useful, for here, prominently displayed, was *The Harvest of Battle* of 1919, 'considered too painful to be shown during the war',[122] when, of course, the painting itself had not actually been begun.

There was an extravagance of 'Nevinson' the artist: he was almost an anti-artist, if not a Duchampian nihilist then a kind of proto-Warhol for his time, an artist in the modern tradition of transgression, resistance and negation. If this seems over-claimed, then it is substantiated by the fact that Nevinson was also a peripheral artist, sometimes marginalised by his peers, who looked upon him as not very good. He plagiarised his own work flagrantly, recycling his imagery in his paintings, which were often redone as prints. He did not maintain the proper distance between high art and mass culture, crossing the boundaries into popular culture by writing columns for low-brow newspapers and judging beauty contests. In 1930, he did the backdrops for the first televised drama. He satirised the film industry as a thinly disguised vehicle for soft pornography in 'Comment on Vulgarity; or, World Definition of Beauty and Grace'. His work could debunk the status conferred on art by parodying, quite literally, the framing devices used to secure the aura of a work of art: 'It is rather refreshing to hear . . . that Nevinson has chosen carved frames of Renaissance pattern for his pictures. The famous Dolores portrait, which he painted in seven hours, is to have a particularly attractive one.'[123] He courted publicity, fabricated controversy, manipulated the press and was an inexhaustible supply of good copy. The work produced was populist, tasteless and shallow. The critic of the *Sphere* mocked the whole business of art criticism by comparing

Nevinson's work to food: 'To those sated with the roast beef of the Academy, the mushrooms on toast of the Lefevre Galleries, . . . where Nevinson is now holding a one-man show, [this] will come as a welcome *bonne bouche.*' There were his 'condiments of artistic seasoning', some 'cayenne pepper' but less 'cardamons of Cubism' derived from when he was 'the toast of *les jeunes*'.[124] Nevinson's work did not fetch high prices.[125]

Nevinson died in 1946, four years after a stroke that blinded him in one eye and paralysed his arm (his last pictures shown at the Royal Academy were finished with his left hand). The stroke, it was reported, was the consequence of his disregard for his own health in assisting casualties during the Blitz. Like Warhol, he knew the value to the market of a 'personality':

the *persona* is always a construct, a product, an artifact, functioning in a complex arena of conflicting social and economic values and relations. Warhol's work demonstrates more profoundly than any other artist that the art market is no different from any other market. The artist creates demand. The buyer purchases an identity. The artist who can manipulate this greed for contingent celebrity becomes, by contingency, a Star.[126]

It was said at his death that Nevinson 'never found another subject so suited to his genius as war'.[127] In vacuous and ill-nourished post-war allegories, Nevinson went bankrupt on the strength of his reputation as a war artist.

War Artists and the 1930s

Raymond Williams has pointed out that radical militant avant-gardes who denounced the bourgeois social order before 1914 did so from markedly different political positions 'which would lead eventually, both theoretically and under the pressure of actual political crisis, not only to different but to directly opposed kinds of politics: to Fascism or to Communism; to social democracy or to conservatism and the cult of excellence'. Where the avant-garde was mobile, diverse and competitive before 1914, the political crises of the First World War, and particularly the Russian Revolution, dramatically altered this dynamic so that 'the relation between politics and art was no longer a matter of manifesto but of difficult and often dangerous practice'.[128] Williams's examples are the Russian avant-garde after 1917, the Italian Futurists with the emergence of fascism and the bifurcation in Germany between radical intellectuals of the revolutionary left and the fascist right. In Britain, Wyndham Lewis identified with right-wing politics, which Williams describes as idiosyncratic and Fredric Jameson in his 1979 study, *Fables of Aggression: Wyndham Lewis, the Modernist as Fascist*, has termed proto-fascist, by which he means Lewis never became an official apologist for Fascism. By contrast, David Bomberg visited the Soviet Union in 1933, wrote extensively on socialism and art, although he never published the material, and was for a time a member of the Communist Party.

That there were connections between fascism and some aspects of modernism became impossible to conceive after 1945, following the depolitization of the avant-garde in the Cold War of the 1950s, one consequence of the labelling of all modern art as degenerate by the National Socialists in Germany.[129] In contrast to numerous commentators who have seen fascism as anti-modern, both Jameson and more recently Mark Neocleous have argued the case for acknowledging right-wing modernisms. Jameson's proto-fascism is characterised as 'a shifting strategy of class alliances', at first populist and anti-capitalist, defined against Marxism and communism which are both construed as a threat and a taboo. Proto-fascism also discredits middle-class ideologies, such as liberalism, conservatism or social democracy, and repudiates the parliamentary systems in which they are represented. It eventually finds 'practical embodiment in a mass ideological party which can also stand as a figure for the new collectivity at the same time that it serves as the vehicle for the seizure of state power'.[130] Neocleous uses the term 'reactionary modernism' to describe fascism's role 'as the culmination of conservative revolution'. In his discussion of the modernist avant-garde amongst writers such as Ernst Jünger, Gottfried Benn, Marinetti, Ezra Pound and Wyndham Lewis, it is characterised by a commitment to the freeing of the creative spirit, to the triumph of will over reason, and a reaction against the stifling normalising world of the bourgeois, alongside a fascination with violence and horror and an engagement in a quest for an authentic self.[131] Lewis's right-wing politics and his anti-Semitism are highly problematic issues in the very large literature on the artist. He did publish

an endorsement of National Socialism in 1931 that he subsequently refuted. He was antipathetic to Jews but so was Roger Fry, something that is much less well known.[132] Recent literature on Lewis has seen the war as the turning point in his career, when he experienced a collapse of agency that makes his subsequent work constantly oscillate between being 'an instrument of history' or standing outside with 'the traumatic awareness that one cannot master history'.[133] Paul Edwards is overstating the case when he writes that 'Lewis' is the only 'adequate' response to the Great War, both in its comprehensiveness and in its sheer extremity and disproportion', but he does have a point when he argues that Lewis's rebellion makes him 'the creator of cruel and distasteful displays that are simply an affront to the humanity and sensibility that it is supposedly the function of art to cultivate'.[134] It is one consequence of a refusal to derive any comforting narratives of redemption out of the First World War. The issue is that accounts of modernism have to reckon with its reactionary variants. The trajectory that Wyndham Lewis's career traces also undermines Charles Harrison's claim that the period after the war was 'historically uncontroversial' and British art quiescent.[135]

Bomberg's socialist leanings appear more sympathetic and are certainly less embarrassing to modernist histories than Lewis's politics. But like Lewis, he was an isolated artist throughout the 1920s and, 1930s, writing to his sister in 1939 about going to Mark Gertler's funeral, an artist he had lost touch with after 1920, that the war and his subsequent trip to Palestine 1923–7 'may perhaps have been a reason why I felt disinclined to take up life where I had left it and reunite with the colleagues of my youth'.[136] His writings on art and revolution, composed around 1933 when he visited the Soviet Union, were conventionally Marxist, but he also identified an issue about the politics of modern art and the relationship of form and content that he was unable to resolve. Bomberg argued that the marketability of work by artists such as Matisse, Derain, Picasso and Braque was a consequence of its tendency to 'flatter the social relations of the period' and that revolutionary technique in form represented 'an advance in capitalist forms of production'. Abstract art, because of its lack of subject matter, obscured 'the class nature of the struggle'. Soviet art, dedicated to proletarian consciousness, however, had fallen back on classicism and lacked vigour. Only in a classless society

121 C. R. W. Nevinson, *The Twentieth Century*, 1932, oil on canvas, 183.7 × 122.5, Laing Art Gallery Newcastle

122 *Let's Mobilise Art*, 1 November 1939, *The Bystander*

under socialism would subject matter lose all significance.[137] In 1914, at his first solo exhibition at the Chenil Gallery, Bomberg had written 'My object is the *construction of Pure Form*. I reject everything in painting that is not Pure Form.'[138] In his rethinking in the 1930s, Bomberg appears to argue that the pursuit of such an aim was possible only under the utopian conditions of a socialism that did not yet exist. He worked in Spain from 1934 to 1935 and was a strong supporter of the Republican cause in the civil war that erupted in 1936. What is so perplexing about Bomberg in the 1930s is that, unlike other First World War artists such as Nash, Bone and John, he never deployed his polit-

ical commitments in any of the forums for radical politics and art such as the Artists International Association (AIA). He was rebuked by Bone for failing to support its 1939 Whitechapel Gallery exhibition *Unity of Artists for Peace, Democracy and Cultural Development*.[139]

The AIA was established in 1934 in response to the threat of fascism and became a broad left-wing organisation involving a wide range of artists in campaigns against totalitarian dictatorships and war. During the 1930s, Nevinson produced admonitory canvases prophesying mass civilian bombings as well as a novel, *Exodus A.D.: A Warning to Civilians*, in 1934 about a coming Armageddon. The best-known of his prophetic paint-

ings is *The Twentieth Century*, subtitled *A cartoon for a Mural Decoration of a Public Building or Seat of Learning, suggested by the Clash between Thought, Mechanical Invention, Race Idolatry and the Regimentation of Youth*, (fig. 121) of about 1935. It uses a badly drawn version of Rodin's *Thinker* as its centrepiece surrounded by Great War soldiers marching open-mouthed with teeth bared amidst revolutionary crowds waving red flags, a Union Jack and a swastika.[140] There were numerous cultural productions in the 1930s voicing anxieties about the threat of war, for example, Alexander Korda's and H. G. Wells's epic film *Things to Come* of 1935 about how the bombing of an English provincial city, Everytown, inaugurates a century of devastation. Nevinson sent *The Twentieth Century* to the international anti-fascist exhibition *de olympiade onder dictatuur* or *D.O.O.D.* (death), organised in Amsterdam in 1936 as a protest against the Nazi-organised Berlin Olympics.[141] In the same year he contributed an essay, 'The Arts within This Bellicose Civilization', to a collection titled *The Seven Pillars of Fire* which was written by prominent academics and religious teachers to diagnose and offer remedies to a contemporary crisis of values attributed to the rise of totalitarianism. In his essay, Nevinson repudiated Mussolini and Futurism's post-war turn to fascism as 'the enemy of tolerant culture, independent intellectual thought, free speech', but although he condemned war, the piece does not add up to a coherent aesthetic position.[142] Nevinson's *The Twentieth Century* has no possibility of exemplifying what Bersani terms the 'moral monumentality' of redemptive works of art. The best one could make of this vacuous allegory is a satire of the pretensions of history painting or any possibility that art could instruct an audience in acts of public virtue. In 1939, the artist was photographed 'at home', leaning on the mantlepiece over which hung the canvas. 'Let's Mobilise Art . . . so says C. R. W. Nevinson,' ran the headline (fig. 122).[143] What could not have been known in 1914, but which was much more widely understood in 1939, was the futility of ever attempting to do so.

State patronage of war artists in the Great War was always more haphazard than rationalised, more often a consequence of chance and coincidence than foresight and planning. It was mostly a provisional negotiated activity, but it was also motivated by a historic mission about the destiny of national culture and the possibility that the catastrophe could none the less leave a creative legacy to the future. Its ambitions meant it was compelled to incorporate modern avant-garde artists. Official employment was the primary means by which almost every significant artist in Britain gave form to their war experiences and it gave modern artists unprecedented scope to address their work to the needs of the nation state and to create new audiences for their work. Employing avant-garde artists was obviously going to carry a risk, and their incorporation was always guaranteed to be incomplete.

It is no longer sensible to argue that either official employment or the war put an end to the avant-garde in Britain. The avant-garde before 1914 was not unified and nor was it a unidirectional and simple matter of progress. It was instead a shifting, dynamic and volatile process within and across cultural fields. After 1918, avant-garde art was played out in highly charged circumstances and its politics became dangerous. That was a consequence of the war. In Britain, that meant that some of our most significant avant-garde artists sometimes identified with fascism. Writing this history necessitates reckoning with how this discomforts the story of British modernism, and unsettles what it means to be British.

six

Redeeming the War: 'Englishness' and Remembrance

> The past carries with it a temporal index by which it is referred to redemption
> . . . Like every generation that preceded us, we have been endowed with a *weak*
> Messianic power, a power to which the past has a claim. That claim cannot be
> settled cheaply.
>
> Walter Benjamin, 1940.[1]

Remembering the Great War

British losses in the First World War were estimated at one million dead. Early on in the war the exhumation of bodies for reburial at home was banned and the Imperial War Graves Commission was established to record graves and tidy the battlefields. The dead were not repatriated from where they had fallen at various fronts, the exact circumstances of an individual's death were often unknown and conventional rites of funeral and burial were not available to families and communities. Making memorials to the absent dead was a constant preoccupation in every locality in the British Isles throughout the 1920s and '30s, focusing local and personal grief and bereavement. The last major memorial in France was unveiled in 1938 at Villers-Brettoneaux. The Second World War did not give rise to a similar scale of activity and the names of the dead of 1939–45 were often simply added to First World War memorials.

In the early post-war years, rituals of remembrance were established. Between 1919 when the Cenotaph designed by Lutyens was unveiled in Whitehall, at first as a temporary structure, and 1925 when the Albert Hall became the site for a Festival of Remembrance on 11 November, the major features of commemoration ritual were put in place (fig. 123).[2] Annual ceremonies, including the two minute silence at 11am on 11 November, marked private moments of grief and contemplation in a shared public context. Armistice Day was sometimes a focus of dissent and protest by the unemployed, and in 1920 the date was also designated Obligation Day when employers were asked to give special thought to finding jobs for ex-servicemen.[3] The sale of poppies by the British Legion reinforced this sense of continuing obligation to those who had served and survived. Although there was organised protest against Remembrance ceremonies and in the inter-war years white peace poppies began to be sold in opposition to red poppies, the effect of public rituals and local memorials was, as Bob Bushaway has shown, to curb dissent and contain criticism so that: 'Through the annual act of remembrance the demons of discontent and disorder were purged and the mass of British society was denied access to a political critique of the war by Kipling's motto "lest we forget". The rituals of remembrance defined what was to be remembered in post-war Britain.'[4]

National remembrance was focused on the Cenotaph, a vacant tomb, and the Tomb of the Unknown

being ever"'.[6] The iconography and liturgy of memorial derived from the Christian Church, especially the Anglican Church, but religious references were made deliberately diffuse in order to avoid offending or excluding those whose religious allegiances lay elsewhere. The war gave a momentum to the ecumenical movement and an emerging redefinition of the Church of England as a pastoral ministry.[7]

The dominant motif for local war memorials was a cross on a public site in the community rather than in a church.[8] The Cenotaph contained in its empty tomb the promise of resurrection. The cross symbolised sacrifice and resurrection rather than death and served as a reminder of redemption. Graves in France and elsewhere were often marked by simple wooden crosses but these were replaced by headstones which were more stable and durable. Each cemetery had a Cross of Sacrifice designed by Reginald Blomfield and a Stone of Remembrance designed by Lutyens. In debates in 1920 about the design of cemeteries, there

124   *The Coffin of the Unknown Warrior in Westminster Abbey on 7 November 1920*, photograph, Imperial War Museum, London

123   *Peace Day Celebrations, 19 July 1919. 'To Our Glorious Dead'. The Cenotaph, Whitehall*, photograph, Imperial War Museum, London

Warrior in Westminster, an occupied grave (fig. 124). The unknown soldier, a corpse selected in an elaborate ritual at St Pol near Arras and returned to England for reburial, symbolised the average, ordinary citizen who died in the war and individual remembering. The Cenotaph stood for the totality of the men who had died in the war and national grief and memory.[5] National ceremony and liturgy became a matter of giving equal and impartial commemoration to all who had fallen in the war without reference to rank and class. D. S. MacColl suggested a rewriting of the inscription on the Westminster tomb so that it might 'sum . . . up the association of sacrifice and communion that have gathered about the celebration, rendering it a mystic rite; not life only lost, but identity, so that one who may have been the humblest or most heroic, the most timorous or most fearless of fighters, has become No-man or Everyman, "in the ecstasy of

were objections to replacing the crosses, which had a powerful hold on popular imagination. One witness stated 'I only wish we could preserve what we have there today, those beautiful simple white crosses.'[9]

Local war memorials almost always stood for sacred and religious values and were clearly distinguished from civic monuments.[10] The symbol of the cross equated the soldier's death with Christ's sacrifice. Although this idea was theologically controversial, conceiving of the death of a soldier in these terms represented the losses of the war not as duty and service but as sacrifices made in the sense of something sacred. Rather than victory, the idea of universal comradeship, peace and redemption could be asserted. Death as sacrifice suggested 'the instant redemption of the war dead' so that to die in battle was to expiate sin. It implied that the dead had died in a state of grace and that their deaths could redeem the living. War memorials offered a palliative and solace to sanctify or to literally make sacred mass slaughter.[11] In effect, criticism of the conduct of the war came to seem a dishonouring of the dead.

The landscape art of Nash to about 1925 and Spencer's war paintings, including Burghclere Chapel which he finished in 1932, can be framed within postwar questions about memory and remembrance and how these hinged on Christian notions of redemption, resurrection and renewal. Spencer is well-known as a religious artist but Nash also shared a similar inheritance formed in English Protestant traditions. Nash's personal beliefs, as with so many other matters, including his attitude to the war, is more elusive, less obviously stipulated by reference to fact or event. Both artists shared a strong commitment to places and especially the countryside and communities of southern England. Each was identified with an 'English' sensibility including English subjects and literary traditions. Neither had been active in a pre-war avant-garde. Nash, in particular, came of age as a war artist. Official employment brought him widely noticed and reviewed exhibitions and publications that established him on the London art scene. This was less true of Spencer, who in any case was not available for employment until the war ended. Before 1914, however, he had attracted the support of well-connected figures in the art world who fostered his prospects. It would later seem to Spencer that 1918 was a matter of starting again.

Spencer and Nash did not confront the dilemmas that faced participants in avant-garde art and the politics of international artistic exchange. Wartime nationalist rhetoric, as pervasive in France, Germany and elsewhere as in Britain, was at odds with being a cosmopolitan avant-garde. By putting national loyalties to the test, the war threatened avant-garde ambitions with the spectre of parochialism. When the war ended, many parameters had changed, including the political geography of Europe and the conception of international cultural community. In 1918 to 1919, Lewis, Nevinson, Bomberg and Roberts found out what they already suspected – there could be no return to a pre-war state of affairs.

War made nationality a critical matter and it focused attention on the components of national identity. A conception of 'Englishness' rooted in liberal constructions of culture, including the particularity of southern England, informed the work of Wellington House, which had first employed Nash. This was a consequence of the way Masterman, liberal politician and the organisation's director, construed the task of promoting Britain's cause, through which he also created opportunities for artists. The writing that C. E. Montague, a former *Manchester Guardian* journalist serving at the front, produced for the war artists' publications then orchestrated this sense of English national identity. Like Spencer, both Masterman and Montague were men of active Christian religious sensibility, which was indebted to a feeling for English community.

Winning a war was not synonymous with successfully concluding a peace. A feeling for England was not necessarily a matter of endorsing narrow nationalist sentiment because the intractibility of the war also raised questions about the cost of national defence and whether the means justified the ends. The more catastrophic the Great War, the more potent the appeal of an image of pre-war England as an Edenic state of prelapsarian innocence became. But innocence was increasingly difficult to sustain. In different ways, after 1918 Spencer and Nash each renegotiated a mythic sense of Englishness and attempted to discover a path to redemption out of the debt that the dead had charged to the living. It was a matter of keeping in tension an obligation to never forget without becoming fixed in an illusory past at odds with the facts of events that could not be changed.

Arcadia and Paul Nash

In *Outline* Nash called his chapter about the post-war years 'Old World Revisited'. It followed one about the war years called 'Making a New World'. The 'Old World' chapter, in the cryptic notes of the unfinished manuscript, begins: 'Struggles of a war artist without a war'. Further down the page he wrote: 'New life in a different world'.[12] After the war Nash worked mainly as a landscape painter of English scenes, although he also illustrated books, designed for the theatre and wrote art criticism. He was interested in the possibilities of a reformulated avant-garde, but Bloomsbury critics increasingly dominated the art scene and he found no access to the field. In 1921, his health broke down. He painted one further war canvas for the Canadian scheme, *A Night Bombardment* in 1919–20, and illustrated Richard Aldington's book of poems, *Images of War* in 1919, but otherwise obvious war themes disappeared from his oeuvre. His work after 1918 can be grouped into landscapes from the Chilterns, often involving images of journeys, such as *The Field Path* of 1918 and *The Paths* of 1919; woodcuts for the book *Places*, published in 1923 but dating from 1920–22 and developed from work produced in 1915–17, his *Dark Lake* of 1917 for example; landscape drawings, paintings and prints of Dymchurch, which Nash considered a distinctive series in their own right; and the plates to illustrate an edition of 'Genesis', the first book of the Bible, in 1924.[13] His major painting from the period was *The Lake* of 1923, later amended and retitled *Chestnut Waters*.

By the statement 'Struggles of a war artist without a war', Nash might have been implying both a need to find a new market in an altered economy and the necessity for a new subject in order to find a new direction. Writers such as John Rothenstein, however, have stated that the intensity of what Nash had witnessed on the Western front gave him an altered view of landscape and nature that outlasted his war painting and 'transformed his . . . way of seeing'.[14] In retrospect, Nash himself registered a sense of changed direction, which he dated from 1917 and attributed not to his war service but to his appointment as an official artist. The statement appeared in a conclusion to the preface to *Outline*, later deleted when it was published posthumously. He wrote that after 1917, 'with [the] last phase of the war and my participation in it as an official artist

on the Western Front, a change began to take place. Thenceforth the whole savour of living, and the nature of my work seemed direly affected. I was launched into a turbulent sea where the dramatic adventures of life and art were breaking anew.'[15]

Nash's work is never without a subject matter, specifically a sense of place or 'genius loci' and an interest in natural forms as metaphors for human life, but his imagery tends to be evocative, elusive and poetic rather than obviously iconographic. For example, the watercolour *White Cross* (fig. 125) of 1920 is a view of Whiteleaf Cross in the Chilterns and includes a couple walking as though on a pilgrimage towards the ancient crucifix carved into the hillside.[16] It was a subject that Nash painted on several occasions. Given that there was debate about the design of war cemeteries, the 1920 watercolour might relate to contemporary proposals to replace the crosses on war graves or it could be part of more private themes in Nash's oeuvre as a whole. Evidence for Nash's continuing preoccupation with war has to be sought from indeterminate and ambiguous allusions in his work.

The literature on Nash has it that after the war he returned to his roots in the English landscape and rediscovered a sense of England. The familiar and reassuring contrasted the alienation and 'foreignness' of the Western front.[17] Nash's landscape painting is said to be paradigmatically 'English' but the idea of English landscape altered in the post-war period, in part through the way its images were reworked by artists like Nash. Consciousness of the threat and the terror of the Great War surfaced often in literature and art during the 1920s and '30s and dominated living memories. Ian Jeffrey writes how in retrospect, the Great War could be thought of 'elegiacally', as a time of coming to 'consciousness of the earth's beauties'.[18] The visioning of Flanders, for example in Bone's work, as an immeasurable flattened horizon stripped of reference points and sights but contaminated with malignancy and fear was counterposed to an imaginary landscape of closed wooded valleys or Arcadian sanctuaries. Memories of war might also be imbued with remembered human companionship and anxieties about impersonality, industrialisation and modernisation also found expression in sanctuary images. The other dark area of foreboding was abroad – 'a boundless, anarchic terra incognita'.[19] Taking a longer perspective and considering more complex formations of land, nation and economy, writers such as Alex Potts have also argued that the idea of the rural as a retreat or a sanctuary to be viewed with detachment from the outside became a generalised perspective on the countryside only in the inter-war years. The Victorian and Edwardian countryside was seen as an epicentre and part of the social fabric of English life that needed to be sustained and reformed, whereas in the 1920s the countryside was thought about nostalgically, as fixed in form, and sometimes associated with premonitions of death and decay.[20] This engendered a mythic sense of its completeness and identity that had to be recreated imaginatively, making it a metaphor for the lost multitudes of the war dead.[21]

The immediate effect of the war was a restructuring of landownership and social, economic and political power passed from an aristocracy to farm owners. After 1921, countryside depression reinforced the economic marginalisation of the agricultural industry. At the same time, suburban expansion, improved public transport and growing car ownership further eroded the distinctiveness and separateness of country living.[22] By the 1930s, consensus politics produced a myth of the countryside as 'Englandism', or of the landscape itself as expressing national character, a concept that was developed further with neo-Romanticism in the late 1930s and '40s. Herbert Read began to promote Nash's work as standing for the embodiment of 'Englishness' from the 1930s. The idea that the forms of landscape, selectively viewed, embody the essence of nationhood, had already been enunciated in Montague's texts for *The Western Front* when English landscape was set up to articulate an antithesis to German character.

Clare Colvin describes Nash's book of prose poems and wood engravings, *Places*, as 'a very private book'.[23] The text and images meditate on the peace of secluded woodlands, which are also imbued with remembrances of war landscape and escape from death. Beech trees are 'steel' while 'bushes and grass seem black and rusty wire. A pallid gleam falls across metal spheres' and winter woods where 'the wet mould is fragrant' are compared to cathedrals in which 'the faint stink of tombs has tinged the air'.[24] The poems and prints include images of water as well as female figures together with symbols for passage and pilgrimage such as paths and gates. Text is subordinate to image. The location of each of the seven plates is identified and

125   Paul Nash, *White Cross*, 1920, ink, pencil and watercolour on paper, 35.7 × 27.3, private collection

depicts the deciduous woodlands particular to southern England. Iden and Wittersham were close to Dymchurch, Hampden and Whiteleaf were in the Chilterns, and Iver Heath was his family home.[25] The first four show a woman in woodlands beside a lake. She is naked in three and clothed in one. The frontispiece, *Meeting Place, Buntingford* (fig. 126) of 1922, was near the home of a friend, Claude Lovat Fraser, and Nash visited it in 1922, a year after Lovat Fraser's death as a consequence of his war wounds. In *Meeting Place* a thin, naked man isolated within a bower of tree anxiously approaches a recumbent woman who threatens to seduce and overwhelm him. The first four plates, *Meeting Place, Black Poplar Pond, Iden* of 1921, *Garden Pond, Wittersham* (fig. 127) also of 1921 and *Dark Lake, Iver Heath* of 1920, reveal a luxuriant and fertile wood enclosing still, sombre waters with isolated, self-

126 Paul Nash, *Meeting Place, Buntingford*, 1922, wood engraving, 11.4 × 15.3, from *Places*, 1922

absorbed figures. Andrew Causey calls these plates 'strongly erotic'.[26] In the next four images in *Places*, the lake disappears and paths, gates and fences appear in the forest. The figure, absent from the fifth plate, *Winter Hampden* of 1921, re-emerges clothed and with an air of mystery, meditating on a choice of paths in *Paths into the Wood, Whiteleaf* (fig. 129) of 1921 and walking away from the viewer in both *Winter Wood, Hampden* of 1922 (fig. 128) and *Tailpiece, Iden* (fig. 130) of 1922.

127 Paul Nash, *Garden Pond, Wittersham*, 1921, wood engraving, 10.3 × 12.8, from *Places*, 1922

The sequence suggests meditation, fertility and replenishment in secluded sanctuaries leading to choices, journeys and, in the tailpiece, resolution in a passage from wood to sunlight guided by two birds. In the last image, however, the viewer is barred from accompanying the woman as she passes through the gap in a gateway to a bright horizon, by the foreground fence and prevented by the gate from glimpsing what is

128 Paul Nash, *Winter Wood, Hampden*, 1921, wood engraving, 13.9 × 11.1, from *Places*, 1922

beyond the woods.[27] The images suggest danger and melancholy as well as secrecy and sexuality. Nash's poems described the woods and lakes as metaphors for human beings. The trees were likened to the naves of cathedrals and churches. For Nash, trees had human associations suggesting the passage from earth to heaven and, 'by embodying time and charting the seasons, . . . the brevity of man's life span'.[28] The female figure in *Places* is almost certainly his wife, Margaret Nash, and in 1917, Nash wrote to

156

John Rothenstein, that shows a drunken, fleshy nymph, sprawling in a woodland bower and dominating a guitar-playing Pierrot who resembles a figure of death. It more emphatically recalls 'memento mori' by being titled *Atque in Arcadia Ego*.[30] Lisa Tickner, discussing John's *Lyric Fantasy* (fig. 131), begun in 1909 but left unfinished in 1915 and titled only in 1940, notes how much John's work is 'bound up with idealisation and reparation' in the Kleinian sense of the infant's attempts to make good the harm it fantasises it has inflicted in the maternal body.[31] Depictions of the pastoral are sometimes viewed as reactionary or as an evasion repressing or obscuring the social and economic factuality of the countryside. But the use of the pastoral can also be a form of oblique criticism, as well as a way of contemplating melancholy and rejection.

Memories of childhood as a formative experience

129 *right*   Paul Nash, *Paths into the Wood, Whiteleaf*, 1921, wood engraving, 12.7 × 10.2, from *Places*, 1922

130 *below*   Paul Nash, *Tailpiece, Iden*, 1922, wood engraving, 9.8 × 7.7, from *Places*, 1922

Bottomley 'It is a great joy to live with a woman and be able to see new beauty every day in lines and forms & colours dwelling in her and growing out of her.'[29]

Ideas about arcadia and sanctuary were widespread in English painting in this period including Nash's work. Arcadia, a pastoral idyll, is associated with a longing for a permanent, secure and stable Golden Age now lost. It is a countryside peopled with shepherds and shepherdesses to whom nature gives sustenance without the necessity for organised labour. Panofsky, in his paper 'Et in Arcadia Ego' published in 1936, argued that it was Virgil, the 'discoverer' of evening, who shifted the resonance of the pastoral and the arcadian from a moralising mode where death and frustrated love coexisted in the presence of paradise to an elegiac mood that projected death into either the future or, and preferably, the past, from a sense of menace to one of remembrance. He noted that in England, unlike the Continent, an insular tradition retained the notion of 'memento mori', the correct translation, as 'Even in Arcadia there I [Death] am'. He cited the persistence of this English reading into the twentieth century, quoting a drawing by Augustus John, reproduced by informed much of Nash's work. *Outline* opens with an extended evocation of his childhood and especially the discovery of the enchantment of a sense of place. The war, for Nash, was a passage from innocence to experience, as it was also the period of the first years of his marriage. Margaret Nash recollected his 'boyish pride in the whole heroic adventure of the war' and the 'extraordinary childlike trust' of his acceptance of life in the army 'banishing from his mind as much as possible resentment against our separation and our loss'.[32] The work done at Dymchurch and in *Places* refer, in part, to the re-establishment of his marriage with Margaret after the estrangement of the war. Post-war neo-Classicism emphasised an arcadian paradise in landscape forms and fleshy depictions of women as passive and fertile bodies as well as images of women nurturing children. These motifs were not invented by the war and are found before 1914, for example in the work of Matisse and the Fauves where ideas of Arcadia were envisioned in paintings of women set in nature and closely linked to the idea of a French national heritage.[33] After the war such notions were more widespread, being associated sometimes with French pro-natalist policies. Works by Maillol and Matisse were exhibited at the Leicester Galleries in 1919. Renoir died in 1919, and his late canvases of large, fleshy nudes in landscapes were well known, for example amongst Bloomsbury artists such as Duncan Grant. Mark Gertler painted a Renoiresque *The Queen of Sheba* (fig. 132) in 1922. Bernard Meninsky published a book of drawings on the theme of mother and child in 1920. During the war, Bottomley had urged Nash to return to figure drawing but Nash resisted, describing landscape drawing in terms of an act of seduction: 'I know how secret & reserved Nature really is and what devotion and homage must be paid to her before she will yield her mysteries. Sometimes I am desperate at my impotence.'[34]

Nash had transcribed autobiographical accounts of war experience into landscape or pastoral sanctuaries. These images raise issues about gender. As a prophetic war artist, Nash had mediated his message from soldiers to a heterogeneous home audience. It was male experience as soldier and artist that was worked out over a body of landscape art, and separation from and desire for reconciliation to not just home and childhood but also women were undercurrents of Nash's and other artists' works. William Roberts had written

to Sarah Kramer about his separation from her and the implications this had for finding a form in order to represent war experience. Although Spencer did not meet Hilda Carline until just after the war, the Burghclere predella *Bedmaking* included images from the early years of his marriage. In Nash's Dymchurch paintings and the prints that relate to them, solitary figures are always female while couples are usually male and female.[35] Nash later remembered the first time he embraced Margaret just before the war: 'we became one only to become three – each other and ourselves. It was the only sum I ever understood'.[36]

Nash is thought of as a quintessentially English artist, and ideas of nation and gender are closely bound together. Benedict Anderson's influential discussion of nationalism, *Imagined Communities*, argues that the concept of 'nation' is both limited and imagined. It is limited because it is finite and it is imagined because although we can never know all of the people who are members of our own nation state, we picture ourselves as part of a kinship or community. A nation, Anderson writes, should be understood as a community because 'regardless of the actual inequality and exploitation that may prevail in each, the nation is always conceived as a deep, horizontal comradeship. Ultimately it is this fraternity that makes it possible, over the past two centuries, for so many millions of people not so much to kill, as willingly to die for such limited imaginings.'[37] It is obvious in the terms Anderson uses that the call of national community, dying for one's country, which he defines as 'comradeship' and 'fraternity', is a masculine calling. Being a soldier, risking death, is a test, not of people in general, but specifically of manhood. War, it has been said, makes men of boys as childbirth makes a woman of a girl.[38]

Anderson contrasts the universality of nationality in that everyone has a nationality, just as she or he has a gender, to the uniqueness of each nation.[39] The terms 'gender' and 'nation' suggest that the world is divided along seemingly natural lines. The editors of a recent collection of papers, *Nationalisms and Sexualities*, note, however, that neither 'nation' nor 'gender' is a stable, essential category. Rather nation, like gender, is 'a relational term' that derives its identity from what it is amongst others. Identities depend not on intrinsic properties but on difference so that 'nations are forever haunted by their [differential] others'. Because there is no essential attribute of nationhood, a nation has an 'insatiable need for representational labor to supplement its founding ambivalence, the lack of self presence at its origins or in its essence'.[40] A sense of national identity is formed by telling stories, inventing fictions and manufacturing traditions in a way that is invariably selective.[41]

The intersection of nation and gender reveals how the national terrain, the land, could be considered as a female body. The anthropomorphism of the representation of landscape, however, is not only worked out in images of women but also over the male form, Great Britain, for example, can be personified as both Britannia and John Bull. In C. E. Montague's texts for *The Western Front*, landscape was said to reveal aspects of national character. War landscape was also contrasted with home country, normality set against malignancy. The war was measured by its effect on the land and Nash's landscapes in *British Artists at the Front* were described as metaphors for the effect of the war on men, as the horror of war, too horrifying to be portrayed except obliquely. In letters to Margaret, Nash also described the distortion of nature by war as 'a terrific creation of some malign fiend working a crooked will on the innocent countryside'.[42] War was not only a malignancy but also a prostitution of the natural, a deviancy. Images of war's effect on landscape sometimes stood as a metaphor for the corruption of the healthy male body, as when Montague referred to landscapes depicted by Nash as 'disembowelled', 'eviscerated' or diseased and pockmarked. In *Disenchantment*, published in 1922 as a refutation of the conduct of the war and the loss of ideals it represented, Montague wrote about a pressman arriving in Cologne after the collapse of Germany: 'He seemed to be one of the male Vestals who have it for their trade to feed the eternal flame of hatred between nations, instead of cleaning out stables or doing some other work fit for a male.'[43] Montague also discussed the childlike innocence of the 1914 volunteers, the New Army, who pledged a commitment to the war's cause by abstinence, including sexual abstinence. Later with disillusion, he writes about how Bellona, the Roman goddess of war, sister of Mars 'has not the mystical charm, as of grapes out of reach, . . . All that veiled-mistress business is off. . . . They have seen trenches full of gassed men, and the queue of their friends at the brothel-door in Bethune. At the heart of the magical rose was seated an earwig.' The tedium and exhaustion of war produced the irrecoverable loss of hope, 'that deflowered virginity of faith'.[44] Roses stood for a sense of England and Englishness, and for sacrificial love. Montague evokes an image of virgin soldiers seduced into pursuing war and reveals anxieties about masculinity and desire that are more complex than Paul Fussell allows when citing this passage about roses as 'very English, indeed Blakean'.[45] Victory was also a woman who, when conquered, was found to be spoiled: 'The bride that our feckless wooing had sought and not won in the generous youth of the war had come to us now: an old woman, or dead, she no longer refused us.'[46] Post-war England, itself, is morally bankrupt and revealed as a stricken land rotting with venereal disease.[47]

Duncan Grant was a non-combatant and his *Venus and Adonis* (fig. 133) of about 1919 might stand as Grant's own personal memorial to the war years, although he stated later that it was not an illustration of the story of Venus and Adonis but an exploration of the rhythm of the figure.[48] It was included in his first one-person show in 1920. *Venus and Adonis*, linked to other works on classical themes that appeared in Grant's work at this time, has been described as figuring 'the passion and the transience of sexual pleasure' and the idea of 'impossible desire, and loss'.[49] The white jug is one of Grant's characteristic autograph devices.[50] The painting is also a preposterous revelation of a terrorised, diminutive Adonis, condemned to serve both Venus and Persephone, in which the luridly painted figure of Venus is both bodyscape and landscape. The myth of Adonis, born of a myrrh tree, refers to vegetation and to metaphors of summer and winter, heaven and hell. Festivals to Adonis involved mourning by women and celebration at his rebirth. Rituals of mourning in post-war Britain were centred on women, who also symbolised the nation's grief. At the funeral of the Unknown Warrior in 1920, widows and bereaved mothers were given priority for a seat in Westminster Abbey, but not fathers.[51] Paul Nash's most significant landscape painting, a 1923 depiction of a woman lying recumbent before a lake, Causey argues was possibly influenced by Grant's canvas and may refer either to Adonis or to Leda.[52] It is sometimes said that love and war came from Leda's eggs. The canvas, then titled *The Lake* (fig. 134), was the major work in Nash's 1924 exhibition and he specifically cited it in the 'Old

131   Augustus John, *Lyric Fantasy*, *c*.1913–14,
oil and pencil on canvas, 238 × 472, Tate, London

132   Mark Gertler, *The Queen of Sheba*, 1922,
oil on canvas, 94 × 107.3, Tate, London

133   Duncan Grant, *Venus and Adonis*, *c*.1919,
oil on canvas, 63.5 × 94, Tate, London

World Revisited' chapter of *Outline*. The figure was later painted out and the picture retitled *Chestnut Waters* (fig. 135). Roger Cardinal notes that Nash's landscapes were often an analogy for the female body without necessarily implying that Nash's work might be reduced to this or that it does not also set up other resonances.[53] I have argued here that the way that Nash's work was often framed in the period, particularly in association with C. E. Montague's writing, becomes a literal engendering of terms like war, landscape and nation that is certainly more complex than that Nash's landscapes sometimes veil female forms. Recently, the dealer Bernard Jacobson said in connection with an exhibition of English landscape painting he had organised: 'I . . . find the words . . . very emotive. Pastoral, nature, landscape. They have an almost sexual connotation.'[54] Once *Chestnut Waters* had lost its uncomfortable nude and its mythic associations, Nash's stifling and strange painting became a more disturbing image in which the sexualised chestnut flowers

134 *above*   Paul Nash, *The Lake*, 1923–4, photograph of earlier state of Fig. 135

135 *below*   Paul Nash, *Chestnut Waters*, 1923–38, oil on canvas, 102.5 × 153.2, National Gallery of Canada, Ottawa

fill the sky and menace the confined waters below. In later work, Nash would repeat the motif of aerial flowers that, by the time of the Second World War, had come to stand for bombing or for invasion. He writes, in 1945, of scouring the skies at the outbreak of the Second World War with a sense of unease searching for white flowers, the rose of death, a name given in the Spanish Civil War to the parachute and goes on to explore the idea of flying. The essay, reprinted in *Outline*, concludes: 'it is death I have been writing about all this time . . . Death, about which we are all thinking, death I believe, is the only solution to this problem of how to be able to fly. Personally I feel if death can give us that, death will be good.'[55]

Andrew Causey states that Nash had an early interest in Rossetti and the association of love and death in late nineteenth-century ideas of the *femme fatale*. Later, the earth takes over from women as nurturer, as 'an inspiration and creative force' in Nash's work.[56] The antinomies of love and war or, put otherwise, Eros and Thanatos or sexuality and death are archetypal themes. Paul Fussell titles one of section of his book on the First World War, 'Mars and Eros', noting the close association of war and sexuality in a study of homoerotic themes.[57] Elizabeth Bronfen has analysed the connections between sexuality and death. She notes how the satisfaction of repetition formulated by Freud's death drive, in *Beyond the Pleasure Principle* of 1920, fulfils several desires, including desire for pleasure through fantasies of wholeness, for the recuperation from separation and loss at birth of the maternal body and a desire for 'the fiction of the whole body' represented in fantasies about the maternal body and the substitution of 'surrogate love-objects'. It is a convention or a cultural myth that a woman's 'gift of birth is also the gift of death' and that embracing a loved one, or sexual union, 'signifies . . . dissolution of the self. Woman functions as privileged trope for the uncanniness of unity and loss, of independent identity and self-dissolution, of the pleasure of the body and its decay.'[58] Nash attempted to redeem war with images of replenishment in post-war landscapes. An image like *Meeting Place, Buntingford* associated with *Chestnut Waters* suggests a sense of both self-dissolution and restoration of wholeness through a return to the maternal body.

As well as a motherland, the nation is also a fatherland. In 'The Parable of the Old Man and the Young', Wilfred Owen writes how the angel of the Lord stayed the hand of Abraham about to sacrifice his first-born son Isaac: 'But the old man would not so, but slew his son, / And half the seed of Europe, one by one.' To talk figuratively of a lost generation in the First World War, an estimated one million dead, is also to speak of the loss of the procreative capacity of that generation, to refer to the unborn children of those sons and fathers, and the loss to women who would not bear these children, a double massacre of innocents. Images of replenishment were motivated by a knowledge of that loss and how to give voice to it.

Stanley Spencer and Burghclere

In 1924, R. H. Wilenski wrote how Spencer's *Unveiling Cookham War Memorial* (fig. 136) combined a sense of the specific and the general. Elements of the painting made explicit where and for what purpose people had gathered: 'The Cross speaks to us of a particular faith, the Union Jack of a particular land, and the cottages and landscape of a particular riverside village.' For all its specificity, however, the painting also suggested a subject 'without limits or bounds. The ceremony is but a momentary focus for a group of human beings who symbolize no particular point in time or space because they symbolize eternity and the universe.' These antithetical qualities, the particular and reality-based versus the general or imaginative, were not to be seen as ambiguities in Spencer's work but were to be held in tension. No interpretation, he said, could determine Spencer's work one way or another: 'the two elements are so merged and dove-tailed that there is no critics' formula which can describe this moving work or suggest the deep impression of mingled joy and sadness it conveys'.[59] In other words, Wilenski was suggesting that while there was an insistent particularity in Spencer's narrative composition that engaged the viewer in reading the image for identification, properly understood, the work itself resisted resolution into a singular definitive meaning.

Spencer is often considered an eccentric and provincial artist whose vision corresponds to the innocent or childlike. His motivation was said to be painting 'to perpetuate a childhood vision of people and places', and that he liked boyish, youthful images and cultivated a boyish appearance.[60] His work often includes children as participants and onlookers, and it was

136 Stanley Spencer, *Unveiling Cookham War Memorial*, 1922, oil on canvas, 155 × 147.4, private collection

claimed that he sometimes painted as though from a child's point of view: 'His is an art of close-up in which objects stand out emphatically, and it looks like the vision of a child for whom the world lies within arm's length, as close to touch as it is to sight.'[61] He was said to have found it important to emphasise the near foreground, 'something he could reach down and touch . . . "I have always wanted to have everything within my reach, where I can lay my hand on them"'.[62] Recent literature such as Carolyn Leder's essay 'Influences on the Early Work of Stanley Spencer' of 1976, and Andrew Causey's 'Stanley Spencer and the Art of his Time' of 1980, have revised views of Spencer as a naive artist with no obvious sources in the history of art or the avant-garde as though Spencer produced his painting on a tabula rasa like a child.[63] But rather than replace an innocent Spencer with a knowledgeable one, I want to argue here that Spencer's work is both knowing and innocent.

In retrospect, Spencer described his experiences in the First World War as disrupting his development as an artist and as standing for the loss of 'a kind of earthly paradise'.[64] He recollected that in 1915, after he had enlisted in the RAMC and while travelling to Beaufort Hospital, Bristol where he had been posted, he saw a children's home from the bus: 'I tried to picture a child but failed, I felt as if the whole order of childhood had suddenly become extinct'.[65] The war interrupted this childlike or prelapsarian perception of the world. Spencer's war paintings, begun first with an official commission originally from the Ministry of Information and painted in 1919 and culminating in the Burghclere Chapel series completed in 1932, were attempts to discover redemptive possibilities in the suffering and horror of war. Not only were the images to illustrate redemption, the act of painting was itself said to be a means to redemption. The Burghclere cycle was an 'attempt to express the very happy imaginative feelings I had in that hospital revealed through my different performances & leading to a kind of redemption of the atmospheres & feelings that the place & circumstances gave me'.[66] Painting war pictures of experience would be a means to recover a lost innocence.

It has been said that Spencer's own art was not in conflict with the demands of patrons and official commissions.[67] He painted *Travoys Arriving with Wounded at a Dressing Station at Smol* (see fig. 66) as a full-time offi-cial artist in 1919 and was to have made further compositions for the war museum. Two small oil panels, *Scrubbing Clothes* and *Making a Red Cross* may have been preliminary studies for these.[68] But like William Roberts, Spencer resigned his employment, claiming to have 'lost the thread of my "Balkanish" feelings'. He told Yockney, in an assertion of artistic independence: 'The thing is . . . as artists we can do just what we like (that sounds very nice) BUT WE MUST NOT DO WOT WE DONT LIKE, woe unto us if we break this law.'[69] Unsatisfactory experiences with other patrons followed. His work was rejected from a scheme organised by William Rothenstein to decorate Leeds Town Hall. *Unveiling Cookham War Memorial* was commissioned by Michael Sadler and then turned down. A plan by Muirhead Bone for him to decorate the Village Hall at Bone's home in Steep led to Spencer living with Bone and his wife, but it did not work out. In the Second World War, Spencer was employed by the War Artists Advisory Committee to paint shipbuilding on the Clyde, but he lost interest in this project, preferring an independent vision – *The Port Glasgow Resurrection Series*.

Walter Benjamin, in an essay called 'The Storyteller' written in 1936, noted that soldiers returning from the front were almost without the ability to communicate or convey their experiences in a shared public cultural form. In the late 1920s, after a gap of a decade, war books and memoirs by soldiers began to appear in large numbers. The inexpressibility and unrepresentability of the Western front had been cited by artists sent to depict it or working from remembered experience. Benjamin wrote:

> never has experience been contradicted more thoroughly than strategic experience by tactical warfare, economic experience by inflation, bodily experience by mechanical warfare, moral experience by those in power. A generation that had gone to school on a horse-drawn streetcar now stood under the open sky in a countryside in which nothing remained unchanged but the clouds, and beneath these clouds, in a field of force of destructive torrents and explosions, was the tiny, fragile human body.[70]

Like other artists and writers who had served, Spencer was preoccupied with giving form to his war experiences. The Burghclere Chapel series was painted in the late 1920s, the era of the war memoir. His official employment gave him an opportunity to re-establish himself as an artist. When he joined up in 1915, he stated to Henry Lamb that he felt he had to suspend his sense of self until after the war.[71] When he returned to Cookham in December 1918, he completed the canvas he had left unfinished in 1915, *Swan Upping at Cookham* (see fig. 81)[72] and began work on his official picture. He had written to Henry Lamb in 1917 that war experience had motivated him far to excel the quality of his pre-war painting: 'I am a thousand times more determined to do something a thousand times greater than anything I have ever done before . . . & am storing up energy all the time,' and he was able to re-establish almost immediately a continuity with his pre-war work.[73] *Swan Upping* shares a similar viewpoint and tonal distribution to the large *Travoys* canvas worked on in 1919. In *Travoys*, the operating theatre forms an area of light emanating from the background of the canvas; in *Swan Upping*, the sun strikes the river and creates a similar expanse of bright light to the rear of the picture space. But Spencer later expressed dissatisfaction with *Swan Upping*, believing that the painting bore evidence of having been begun and finished after a gap of some years. The persistence of war themes in his work was, in part, an attempt to recover a continuity and a sense of purpose lost, and yet not lost, in the war. Referring to landscape painting, Spencer later wrote of 'Being so easily blown away and blowable away from what I prior to it ['the vast 1914–18 war experience'] had purposed and felt convinced was my job, and the starting again needed a recovery of that confidence'.[74] In order finally to work out what the war meant for him, Spencer, like others, needed a degree of independence and time for reflection.

He explained to Yockney when he resigned from the Ministry commission that if the employment had been for several years, he would not have turned it down. Burghclere, said Duncan Robinson, is the apogee of Spencer's response to the war.[75] In many ways, the chapel is also the apogee of the war artists' schemes. It is based on Giotto's Arena Chapel frescoes (which Spencer knew only in reproduction), but the series is informed also by seeing *The Nation's War Paintings* at the Royal Academy in 1919–20. It is Spencer's own version of the British War Memorials Committee's memorial gallery that was never built and, like that failed project, fuelled by a belief that the war was a

cultural event that demanded to be represented in a monumental cultural form. Burghclere Chapel features many of the themes of redemption and renewal that had underpinned the way that Masterman and Montague at Wellington House framed the commissioning and promotion of war paintings. Burghclere is inconceivable without the employment of official artists as put in hand by Masterman and, later, the British War Memorials Committee. If Raemaekers's cartoons, with their obvious polemical sentiment, had set the tone for visual rhetoric, and not Muirhead Bone's more decorous topography of the Western front, then artists like Nash and Nevinson would not have followed him nor set a precedent for witnessed, autobiographical war painting.

There are other ways in which the decorations at Burghclere re-state, summarise and reflect on themes that have recurred in this book, making it appropriate to finish the text with a discussion of the chapel. In *Travoys*, Spencer arranged the row of wounded before the brightly lit opening of an old Greek church that was serving as an operating theatre, and attempted to create 'not a scene of horror but a scene of redemption'.[76] Spencer conjured a sense of atonement through his invocation of the adoration in *Travoys*, where mules face not the stable, but the opening to the church, now turned operating theatre with its radiating light.[77] It was a view of the war as a source of renewal and promise following purification and cleansing that underlay the liberal belief in the honourable necessity of a war fought to end all wars and informed a post-war interest in the child and the childlike. But Spencer's work refers to both the general and the particular, and figures both innocence and experience. In the bible, the Adoration is the prolepsis of the Crucifixion and Resurrection of Christ. It prefigures the Second Coming and the Last Judgement. Although *Travoys* represents an adoration, Spencer thought of the wounded men as belonging to another world like 'so many crucified Jesus Christs'. They were to be venerated and treated 'not as conveying suffering but . . . a happy atmosphere of peace'.[78]

Allegories of Remembrance

The decorations for the Oratory of All Souls, Burghclere were completed between 1927 and 1932. The designs were first made in 1923.[79] The idea of the chapel was Spencer's own initiative and mostly designed by him. Lionel Pearson, a partner in Charles Holden's architectural practice, followed Spencer's detailed instructions closely when the Behrend family offered finance and a motive to complete it.[80] The decorations consist of eight arched panels, each with a matching predella arranged either side of a simple space leading to an end wall with a massive *Resurrection of the Soldiers* (fig. 138). The paintings show images and memories of Spencer's war service, starting with work as a ward orderly at Beaufort Hospital and then overseas in Macedonia, followed by active service in the Royal Berkshire Regiment in the Balkans. There are continuities between the predella panels and the larger arched canvases above. The gates of Beaufort Hospital in the first panel, *Convoy Arriving with Wounded* (fig. 137), like *Gates of Hell*, separate the rich wealth of flowering bushes and open onto the confines of hospital corridors shown in *Scrubbing the Floor* (fig. 140) beneath. This theme connects to *Ablutions*, which in turn is echoed by *Moving Kitbags*. *Kit Inspection* is balanced by a hospital scene, *Sorting the Laundry*. *Dug Out*, a Salonica scene also titled *Stand-to*, together with its predella, *Filling Tea Urns* (figs. 139 and 141) leads to the Resurrection and then to *Reveille* (fig. 142) and *Frostbite*. *Filling Water-Bottles* matches *Tea in the Hospital Ward*; *Map-reading* is above *Bedmaking* and adjacent to *Firebelt* and *Washing Lockers* (fig. 144), the last two pictures. Above the side walls are two large panoramas, *Camp at Karasuli* and *Riverbed at Todorova* (figs. 145–8). To a certain extent, pictures and predella panels were once interchangeable. In the first studies, made in 1923, different combinations were sometimes proposed. For instance, *Washing Lockers* was matched with *Filling Water-Bottles*. Some compositions were already virtually in their final form but others were revised substantially.

The paintings progress in a logical narrative that is not immediately obvious,[81] from the arrival to ablutions to sorting kit, through to resurrection. These scenes are flanked by *Dug-Out* and *Reveille*, which are thematically linked to the centrepiece, and which lead to images of refreshment and rest. Finally, *Firebelt* and *Washing Lockers* both evoke the idea of a protective sanctuary. In *Firebelt*, the undergrowth encircling an evening camp is burnt. *Washing Lockers* shows the reassuring forms of the bathtubs with the spaces between which Spencer recollected hiding for peace: to draw

137   Stanley Spencer, *Convoy of Wounded Soldiers arriving at Beaufort Hospital Gates*, 1927, oil on canvas, 213.5 × 185.5, The Sandham Memorial Chapel, Burghclere

and write, the memory of which always made him feel inspired.[82]

The whole cycle was to be put together like a sonata. The predella panels would stand in relation to the main paintings as in a prelude to a fugue or in a sequence of prelude, fugue and codetta.[83] The predella is also traditionally that part of the altarpiece that is intended to be read at close quarters by the kneeling worshipper.[84] The scenes Spencer inserted here derived from his experiences at Beaufort Hospital, with one from a hospital in Salonica. They are even more closely autobiographical than the other images and often involve activities that take place on the floor. The predella panels and paintings are compositionally counterpoised. *Dug-Out* is divided vertically into two trenches; in *Filling Tea Urns* beneath it, the horizontal counter divides the image and shows two parts of the hospital that, as an asylum, was divided into male and female wings with separate counters at points of common supply such as the kitchens and the stores. Spencer recollected the strangeness looking across the

138 *facing page*   Stanley Spencer, *The Resurrection of Soldiers*, 1928–29, oil on canvas, The Sandham Memorial Chapel, Burghclere

139 (*left*) Stanley Spencer, *Dug-out* or *Stand-to*, 1928, oil on canvas, 213.5 × 185.5, The Sandham Memorial Chapel, Burghclere

140 (*below*) Stanley Spencer, *Scrubbing the Floor*, 1927, oil on canvas, 105.5 × 185.5, The Sandham Memorial Chapel, Burghclere

hospital counters and seeing men who would be his off-duty companions: 'they looked like some separet [*sic*] people belonging to another world, like Oddyseus [*sic*] seeing Achilles in Hades'.[85]

Spencer saw himself as 'by no means a casual onlooker; sort of war artist sent to this hospital to do pictures of the life there'.[86] The paintings were instead an act of homage to that part of his life and an attempt to confirm the potential discovered there that, even in the midst of uncomfortable circumstances, the possibility of artistic and spiritual fulfilment and salvation remained. The paintings were also a means to discover, affirm and celebrate a sense of self and personal identity.

Stanley Spencer made a number of paintings of Resurrection scenes throughout his life and the *Resurrection of the Soldiers* on the end wall at Burghclere was preceded by the large *The Resurrection, Cookham* (fig. 143) exhibited in 1927. The idea of resurrection, connected to redemption, is complex in Spencer's work.[87] It did not necessarily refer to a future, or an otherworldly apocalyptic event. Rather resurrection was a key to understanding the present. For Spencer, life and resurrection were reciprocal:

This life being a key to the next, tells me something of the next life and causes the resurrected life to tell me more of what the resurrection in this life is like. This intercourse brings out the meaning I see in this world.

. . . The contemplation of the Resurrection throws back into this life a light which picks on this life's perfection and its special meanings that I so much love and seek.[88]

Dug-Out was meant as a cross between an armistice and a resurrection, in which Spencer imagined that soldiers emerging at 'stand-to' would suddenly find peace had been declared.[89] *Reveille* was also a resurrection scene, a moment of peace. Although some of the soldiers emerge from graves, *The Resurrection of the Soldiers* was not necessarily to mean the resurrection of the dead.[90] Although the Cookham resurrection takes place in a graveyard, it includes portraits of himself, his family and his friends. Resurrection for Spencer was possibly 'the transition from several states of imperfection . . . to one state of perfection'.[91]

Burghclere can be read simply and directly as a Christian symbol promising rebirth and resurrection

168

narrated through Spencer's experiences in the war. The Chapel paintings would therefore function as a programme setting out a justification for the First World War as purification, an idea often articulated, for example in Montague's texts for Muirhead Bone's drawings. The purgative experience of war promises the rediscovery of pre-Promethean or prelapsarian

of closure and resolution. But Spencer's chapel paintings are not obviously judgemental. The series does not glorify or justify the war nor does it protest against it. At first sight it lacks any disturbing subject matter and the pictures appear to be simple and unmediated descriptions of commonplace, banal, wartime events. Wilenski, writing soon after the Burghclere pictures

innocence and thence benediction, resurrection and redemption. In such a reading of the chapel, Spencer would fulfil expectations that he is a childlike artist who produced innocent, autobiographical and specific pictures.

The Resurrection of the Dead in christian theology is part of eschatology or the study of four last things occurring at the end of time: death, judgment, heaven and hell. A resurrection scene implies the idea

144 Stanley Spencer, *Washing Lockers*, 1929, oil on canvas, 105.5 × 185.5, The Sandham Memorial Chapel, Burghclere

were unveiled, said the work was 'neither in the nature of romantic propaganda in defence of war, nor in the nature of a moralist's protest against it'.[92]

If Wilenski had indicated that *Unveiling Cookham War Memorial* might need to be read in a way that is open-ended, then what I am suggesting is that, despite the notion of closure implied by a Resurrection, a sim-ilar suspension of judgement is also required if we are to begin to comprehend Burghclere as a series that res-onates a number of themes about British cultural und-erstanding in the First World War. By including a resurrection, it figures the desire to bring First World War experience to a resolution, but it also makes that desire problematic. The paintings read as undermining any sense that the meaning of the war might yield to a singular effect. By their simplicity the Burghclere Chapel paintings resist being understood as a summation closing the war as an event, or as belonging firmly in the past with no implications for the present and the future.

Spencer was an artist who worked principally through storytelling and narrative. His most completely realised story sequence is Burghclere. Walter Benjamin, who had written about the difficulty of forming mem-ories of war into memoirs, saw storytelling as a social act, a means of passing memory from generation to generation and a way of re-enacting experience and integrating it with the personal experiences of listen-ers, who, in the process of memorising the tale, make the story their own. It survived in childhood fable and fairytales, the earliest source of 'good counsel', and was designed to blend the recounting and sharing of experiences with political desire, as a source of both pleasure and useful information:[93] 'the lesson, the moral, the allegory'.[94]

In 1976, Duncan Robinson said that Stanley Spen-cer's work had suffered from neglect because Roger Fry's influence dominated art criticism. Fry's emphasis on visual form led to a view of Spencer as provincial, isolated and illustrative.[95] When Spencer's Cookham Resurrection was exhibited in 1927, it was damned with faint praise by Roger Fry. He called him 'a liter-ary painter [who] works by imagery' that was often

145 Stanley Spencer, *The Camp at Karasuli (south wall panorama)*, with *Convoy of Wounded Soldiers arriving at Beaufort Hospital Gates* and *Ablutions*, 1930, oil on canvas, The Sandham Memorial Chapel, Burghclere

146 Stanley Spencer, *The Camp at Karasuli (south wall panorama)*, with *Kit Inspection* and *Dug-out* or *Stand-to*, 1930, oil on canvas, The Sandham Memorial Chapel, Burghclere

147   Stanley Spencer, *Riverbed at Todorova (north wall panorama)*, with *Reveille* and *Convoy of Wounded Men Filling Water Bottles at a Stream*, 1930–31, oil on canvas, The Sandham Memorial Chapel, Burghclere

'dull and inexpressive'. But in the Resurrection Spencer had found a mode, said Fry, that was 'no perfunctory sentimental piece of story-telling'.[96] Giotto's Arena Chapel frescoes informed the genesis of Spencer's Burghclere paintings and, interestingly, Fry had described the Arena Chapel as a series of separate compositions that lacked any overarching conception. What Fry celebrated in Giotto's work was his grasp of formal relationships, although in this early essay of Fry's written in 1901, an essentially pictorial conception was also a vehicle for humanist identification with emotion, an idea he later qualified.[97] Fry detected in Giotto's work a fusion of form and content, not just the representation of experience but experience itself, so that a formal aesthetic language is assumed to have direct access to a singular truth understood as total and universal.[98] 'He has in some [the allegorical figures of virtues and vices]' wrote Fry, 'succeeded in giving not merely a person under the influence of a given passion,

but the abstract passion itself, not merely an angry woman, but anger'.[99] That form and content are synonymous and aesthetic contemplation is the disinterested apprehension of form characterises modernist criticism. A formalist aesthetic, together with the rejection of any view that meaning may be conveyed through narrative, disabled Fry's criticism when it had to deal with an artist as insistently committed to narrative as Spencer and provided Fry with no means to consider the extraneous implications of a moral and historical event like war for the formation of art. It was a consequence of the logic of Fry's thought that he should maintain that there should be a distinction between what motivates people as people and what motivates artists as artists. Spencer said in 1923: 'The thing that interests me and has always done is the way that ordinary experiences or happenings in life are continually developing and bringing to light all sorts of artistic discoveries. There seems to me nothing that

148   Stanley Spencer, *Riverbed at Todorova (north wall panorama)*, with *Map Reading* and *Making a Fire Belt*, 1930–31, oil on canvas, The Sandham Memorial Chapel, Burghclere

ever happens to me where I would have to say to myself: "This has nothing to do with art." '[100]

Ruskin wrote an explanatory text to accompany woodcuts of the Arena Chapel pictures published by the Arundel Society which was one of Spencer's sources for the study of the cycle. In contrast to Fry, Ruskin viewed the pictures as a connected series of great subtlety capable of making meaning through a narrative, even an allegory, embedded in religious, moral and human exchange: 'the walls of the chapel are covered with a continuous meditative poem on the mystery of the Incarnation, the acts of Redemption, the vices and virtues of mankind as proceeding from their scorn or acceptance of that Redemption, and their final judgement'.[101]

Audiences for works of art are not simply human subjects equipped with sensory perception and stripped of all preconception as Fry's aesthetic presupposes, but also knowing viewers with variable experiences form-

ed in diverse times and places, differentiated social beings who bring resources to their viewing. Works of art are visual and complex texts that enter into a dialogical relationship with audiences and demand to be read. In a sense, a work of art is nothing other than its use in the possibilities of making and sharing meaning. Lecturing in the 1920s, Spencer spoke about being absorbed when reading a book and said 'This same absorption is possible in pictures and is a legitimate and proper thing for a painter to aim at . . . and expect the spectator to enter into . . . I wish people would 'read' my pictures'.[102] Allegorical texts, in particular, demand a knowledgeable audience to engage with a text's less obvious meanings. Allegories are narratives that make coherent sense at a literal or primary level but that also signify a second level of interpretation read through or behind the first meaning. Sometimes, allegory is deployed in order to disguise a controversial purpose in circumstances of censorship so that an audience becomes an accomplice in the sharing of a hidden meaning without ever being quite certain where the boundary between authorial intention and interpretation lies.[103] This raises the possibility that there is no one universal truth, no absolute idea, no closure on meaning and meaning-making as though meaning in art and culture is given once and for all time.[104] In effect, there may be no definitive conclusion to draw about the First World War and culture, just as the contemplation and use of works of art is never simply disinterested.

The years for completing Burghclere were years of wide public acclaim for Spencer – the Cookham Resurrection was presented to the Tate in 1927 and in 1932 he was elected to the Royal Academy. The Burghclere Chapel paintings are said to have been followed by popular success accompanied by a decline in quality and are sometimes viewed as pivotal works in Stanley Spencer's career. They are seen as a watershed between innocence and experience, between the wondering child and sexually awakened adult or as the point when the influence of early Italian painting is replaced by an interest in the grotesque, where carnival and orgy displace the notion of paradise on earth.[105] After Burghclere, sexual themes are made explicit in Spencer's work, part of his life-long 'Church House' project, along with parody and the profane. Spencer himself wrote of the existence of two kinds of joy, the innocent and religious on the one hand and the joy of change through sexual experience on the other. These were joys that seemed irreconcilable but were to be ultimately unified.[106]

Burghclere, with its relationship to early Italian renaissance literature – Spencer reported that he had begun to read Dante during the war and saw his war service not as 'a period of degeneration, but as a period of being in the "Refiner's fire" '[107] – might be more productively interpreted allegorically, as opposed to being viewed as the culminating achievement of an innocent Spencer. It can also be seen as belonging to a tradition of apocalyptic texts and narratives. Allegorical reading and interpretation may be motivated by a sense of estrangement from tradition, of a gap bet-ween the present and the past, that must be recuperated allegorically, or as Craig Owens writes, from 'a conviction of the remoteness of the past, and a desire to redeem it for the present'.[108]

Craig Owens states that allegories involve two or more 'clearly defined but mutually incompatible readings . . . engaged in blind confrontation in such a way that it is impossible to choose between them'. For instance, one image may figure both virtue and vice. In allegorical readings, reading activity is problematised and forever 'suspended in its own uncertainty'.[109] Moreover, doubled readings not only coexist but actively engage one another in confrontation. The Burghclere series narrates concurrently time past, time present (in the *Bedmaking* predella there are references to Hilda Carline and one of his daughters who was born in 1930) and time future. The obvious narrative structure of the series impels the activity of reading for meaning. Wilenski wrote that the pictures 'must be read from corner to corner, almost inch by inch'.[110] Yet its narrative elements confound and frustrate that reading. The series is not only biblical and sacred but also biographical and profane. It is mundane and realist but also metaphysical and universal. Burghclere is not as simple as it looks but it is also direct and accessible. It is a mute statement of innocence, benediction and redemption as well as a testimonial to death, suffering and experience.

Spencer wrote to Henry Lamb in 1915 about returning to Beaufort from leave and finding that a friend who was an orderly had died:

> He particularly told me a week ago that he did not want to end up in the Asylum mortuary. I could not help feeling what a damnable world this was when I was having my tea yesterday. I imagine a vast, & very melancholy dinning [sic] hall & me alone in the room having tea & 4 degraded lunatics, one sweeping the floor with an agravating [sic] sleepy sort of movement. What bloody concoction has God got that he should keep these miserable; (for they are miserable their life is a nightmare to them) men alive.[111]

As an allegory, the Burghclere paintings are immediate images, explicitly, even naively depicted in a form that is both richly painted and almost literally illustrative. None the less, for all its directness, without interpretative exegesis – visitors to the Chapel nearly always have in hand a text detailing the subjects in narrative sequence – or some knowledge of Spencer's biography, the exact meaning of the subjects and their interrelationship is difficult to decipher from the pictures themselves. There is, for instance, something almost wilfully obscure, even absurd, about *Scrubbing the Floor* and *Washing Lockers*, the first and last of the predella series. There is a sense in which, in the explicitness of the style of painting and literalness of the subjects, the work both proffers a promise of meaning and defers its fulfilment, that it both solicits and frustrates our desire that the images reveal themselves as transparent to their signification, that they make themselves clear to us.[112]

Spencer's paintings are highly specific and particular to time and place; he has an almost obsessive preoccupation with the banal and mundane, as in *Sorting the Laundry* or scraping feet in *Frostbite*. Yet almost all the images suggest a doubled reading in which mundanities take on religious and spiritual significance and references to biblical events, particularly the life of Christ, seem to be diffused throughout the series. Loaves of bread recur in the trays carried by hurrying orderlies in the subterranean corridors of the hospital, in the breakfasting and distribution of loaves amongst the bivouacs on the north wall panorama, in the packages carried by the unburdened mules in the extreme left of the Resurrection and in *Tea in the Hospital Ward*. The centrality and frontality of the east wall Resurrection scene emphasises that spiritual resonances are to be sought throughout the series. Only very occasionally, and then rather obliquely, do the paintings seem to illustrate any specific biblical text. *Filling Water-Bottles* and *Map Reading* might evoke Revelation 22: 1–2.

> And he shewed me a pure river of water of life, clear as crystal, proceeding out of the throne of God and of the Lamb.
>
> In the midst of the street of it, and on either side of the river, was there the tree of life, which bare twelve manner of fruits, and yielded her fruit every month: and the leaves of the tree were for the healing of the nations.

The south wall panorama, *Riverbed at Todorova*, is also a post-Resurrection pastoral and paradise including the clearing of a water course, collecting stones, washing clothes, playing 'Housey Housey' and making a red cross as a sign of sanctuary for an aviator while mules carry hay and an orchard is laid out with ploughed land beneath it. The north wall panorama, *Camp at Karasuli*, echoes some of these ideas but it includes a figure, said to be Spencer himself, skewering discarded issues of *The Balkan News*, and a scavenging dog, sol-

diers burdened with tomb-like stones and almost obscured, abutting the Resurrection, a figure muffling the sound of driving in a stake.

The Burghclere Chapel series stands a comparison with Picasso's *Guernica* of 1937. Both works were intended for architectural settings, both include elements of reportage – in Picasso's case an event he neither participated in nor witnessed. Picasso's painting, although it has given rise to volumes of critical interpretation and had a life as a media event toured and promoted in international exhibitions, has never yielded a consistent, singular reading. Furthermore, Picasso, a more public artist than Spencer, refused to supply one, insisting that the onus of interpretation rested with the viewer. Like *Guernica*, there is no definitive reading to Burghclere. Allegory places a particular emphasis on the business of interpretation, on the reading and reception of the allegorical work: 'The reader must proceed independently along a sometimes parallel and participatory course to arrive at his or her own ideas, experiences and responses.'[113] In his later notes about Burghclere, Spencer wrote: 'I don't like this cautious business in this search for truth & I don't think there is sufficient inspiration in the ideal to produce the urge to bring one to the point of its discovery. When you approach truth you are approaching not just one single intellectual point; you are approaching an intellectual realm.'[114] *Guernica* was a protest painting but Spencer rejected the depiction of horror in any of his war works. A scene of an operating theatre was left out of the chapel because Spencer thought it was too traumatic.[115]

The Resurrection of the Soldiers is a resurrection of the innocents to innocence, Christlike figures who bear the sins of the world so that the world might be redeemed. Unlike Spencer's other Resurrections, including the *Port Glasgow Resurrection Series*, which stands in relationship to Spencer's Second World War experiences as Burghclere does to the First and where men, women and children rise after death, Burghclere includes only male figures. This painting might be the Resurrection of the one hundred and forty four thousand:

> These are they which were not defiled with women; for they are virgins. These are they which follow the Lamb whithersoever he goeth. These were redeemed from among men, being the firstfruits unto God and to the Lamb.

And in their mouth was found no guile; for they are without fault before the throne of God (Revelation 14: 4–5).

Spencer was brought up in both the Church of England and the local Wesleyan Methodist chapel. During the war he corresponded with Desmond Chute, a Catholic and later a priest. As a generalisation, the crucifix is remembered in the Catholic Church and the cross in the Church of England and the Wesleyan Methodist Church, in one the path to redemption through sacrifice, in the other the after-life and the resurrection.

Burghclere is emphatically autobiographical. It does not narrate the war service of Lieutenant Henry Willoughby Sandham the dedicatee of the Oratory. A subsidiary plaque records: 'These paintings by Stanley Spencer and this oratory are the fulfilment of a design which he conceived whilst on active service 1914–18'. Spencer wrote that the bus in 'Convoy arriving with wounded' was 'full of thoughts – & ideas that I am going to paint'.[116] The paintings might also be an allegory of the path to self discovery and identity. The loss and regaining of innocence might refer both to the passage to carnal knowledge and the experience of loss of innocence as a soldier through witnessing and participating in death and suffering.[117] Aspects of the narrative often refer to the body and to a sense of touch – painting on iodine in *Ablutions* or treating frost-bitten feet – where the skin and surface of the body might function as a metaphor for the interrelationship of the self with the outside world. In a letter to Chute, written in 1926 when he had just begun to paint panels for transfer to the chapel, Spencer wrote about the self-doubts he had had as an artist since the war, linked with a need to paint landscapes to make a living: 'I feel so "lonely" when I draw from nature, but it is because no sort of spiritual activity comes into the business at all. Its this identity business: there are certain things where I can see & recognise clearly this spiritual identity in something but if I am drawing & dont see this clearly its all up.'[118]

The Burghclere series, as well as other paintings by Spencer in the period such as *Double Nude Portrait: The Artist and His Second Wife* of 1936 is also a complex meditation about gendered identities and the fixing and unfixing of roles assigned to men and to women.[119] *Double Nude Portrait* has been read as refer-

ring to the sanctity of human love, as a reference to the Communion or as signalling a crisis of faith in conventional ideas of masculinity.[120] The Burghclere paintings celebrate soldiery as an ecumenical, Christian fraternity. Women appear infrequently and always as distant figures. Images at Burghclere also contest or disrupt the stabilising of behaviours and attitudes as specifically masculine or feminine. The scarce female figures are often implied as functioning in a supervisory role. Spencer's own enlistment as a medical orderly suggested a form of feminising of the masculine, becoming a carer and a healer of others or undertaking intimate acts of service towards other human beings. Spencer subsequently volunteered for overseas service and then for active service as a soldier in Salonica, a kind of progressive rehearsal of female and male roles and a sort of testing of the self. As Caroline Walker Bynum points out in a discussion of the fluidity and mixing of genders in medieval art and theology, an 'emphasis on reversal . . . lay at the heart of the Christian tradition. According to Christ and to Paul, the first shall be the last and the meek shall inherit the earth.' Female images, or a feminised self, could 'attribute an inferiority that would – exactly because it was inferior – be made superior by God'.[121] War, it has been said, 'must be understood as a gendering activity, one that ritually marks the gender of all members of a society', whether one is called upon to fight, or not.[122]

In addition, the paintings refer back to a renaissance tradition for chapel decorations, but again in ways that are oblique and indirect. For example, the figure washing underpants in the central spandrel of the south wall has been read as a pastiche of Michelangelo's prophets in the Sistine Chapel. Duncan Robinson sees this as Spencer substituting 'his own kind of hero, without the slightest hint of irony', as an innocent and guileless act.[123] But this figure could also be read as deflating pretentiousness or as representing penance or the washing away of sin. The series, not without a sense of the ludicrous or feelings of apprehension of horrors barely held at bay, proposes that innocence is precariously and incongruously sustained.

Although Burghclere includes no scene of Armageddon, the Resurrection together with its narrative framework functions as an apocalyptic text. An apocalyptic narrative, part of Jewish literature and the form of the Revelation of St John, requires the revelation, usually of an eschatological vision, through the uncovering or disclosure of something hidden or unknown that is made clear to believers and disguised from non-believers. The Burghclere series implies the possibility of one narrative for participant soldiers and another for onlookers. Apocalyptic narratives, like Burghclere, have both a horizontal time dimension and a vertical, terrestrial–celestial axis. The narrative must be interpreted and often works with obscure material and literal imagery that does not illuminate the obscure. It may include secret signs or codes. The narrative may also be an allegory of the history of a community or a nation, or of contemporary events or of the struggles and tribulations of an individual. It may offer a universalised allegory of the human condition. Burghclere brings to rebirth, resurrection and immortality the event of the First World War and it was produced in a period of economic crisis and the rise of fascism in Europe, 1927 to 1932. Apocalyptic literature is said to be a literature of crisis and to accompany periods of persecution. It had a revival during the period of the English Reformation when Apocalyptic ideas informed English Protestantism, the English civil war and a sense of English national identity as a chosen people. In the Reformation and Protestant tradition, the Antichrist of Revelations is identified with the papacy. Apocalyptic premonition sometimes fuels social unrest and demands for social reform.[124] Spencer's vision was a pantheistic and socialist one. In September 1918 he wrote to Chute:

> I quite agree with you in thinking that everybody is becoming concious [sic] of a desire for Truth, but I feel that the poorer classes . . . are not being given a proper chance to live. . . . they will be heavily hampered, and their progress seriously impeded towards attaining a really high understanding of truth, purely through the fault of unnecessary, petty material inconveniences.
>
> . . . There is no such thing as 'individuality', 'personality', 'originality'. Every man has the same Name. His Name is the Resurrection & the Life. . . . There ought to be an equal distribution of Labour. If anyman is ignorant or a fool, or a knave, you and I are largely responsible.[125]

Spencer's Burghclere fraternity is an English brotherhood of boys resurrected as the chosen. There is no image of a reunion of nations and there is only one officer portrayed, in *Mapreading*. Spencer had a patriotic view of the war, writing to his sister in October 1918, 'Oh the deadly rambling stuntifying effect has everywhere been the result of German power & influence.'[126]

As allegory and apocalypse, the Oratory of All Souls cannot be seen simply as a personal provincial vision by an English romantic eccentric that is uncomplicated by irony or paradox. Spencer's 'childlikeness' is neither artless nor utopic. While his war work fulfils liberal expectations of redemption through the purgatory of war, it does so in a way that is troubled by allegorical melancholy and memento mori – by the sheer surplus of white crosses that the soldiers of the resurrection discard and pile up.

Postscript

The Great War was a complex event and its boundaries were permeable. It cannot be reduced to 1914–18. A case in point would be Stanley Spencer's monumental series at Sandham Memorial Chapel, Burghclere. It is one of the most resonant works to come out of the war, and both indebted to the imaginings of the British War Memorials Committee and yet radically different from anything it could have implemented. The power of Burghclere hinges on how the paintings narrate the paradox that the scale of slaughter in the First World War is irredeemable while the facts of its injustice insist that it is referred for redemption. As Benjamin puts it, they tell of a past that has a claim on the future and cannot be settled cheaply. The Great War has almost entirely passed out of living memory, but its hold on the present continues as its legacies are played out, its meanings re-shaped and its narratives endlessly retold.

appendix one

British War Memorials Committee Paintings and Sculpture, Artists Commissioned and Employed

ABBREVIATIONS FOR APPENDICES

AAA	Allied Artists Association
ARA	Associate of the Royal Academy
ASC	Army Supply Corps
Hon.	Honorary
I Division GHQ	Intelligence Division, General Head Quarters
IWM	Imperial War Museum
Lt	Lieutenant
NEAC	New English Art Club
Pte	Private
RA	Royal Academy
RAMC	Royal Army Medical Corps
RCA	Royal College of Art
RFA	Royal Field Artillery

SCHEME 1: ARTISTS COMMISSIONED TO PRODUCE A MAJOR CANVAS

Supersized Pictures: £600

Artist	Age in 1918	Title	Size (inches)	Payment[1]
J. S. Sargent (1856–1925) RA 1897.	62	*Gassed*	90 × 240	£600
Augustus John (1878–1961) ARA 1921, RA 1928.	40	*Anglo-French Co-operation* Never begun.		
William Orpen (1878–1931) ARA 1910, RA 1919.	40	*Anglo-Italian Co-operation* Never begun.		

'Uccello'-sized pictures: £300 + expenses

Walter Bayes (1869–1956) London Group 1913	49	*Landing Survivors from a Torpedoed Ship*	72 × 125	£341 8s 11d (£341.45)
D. Y. Cameron (1865–1925)	53	*The Battlefield of Ypres*	72 × 125	£324 1s 8d (£324.08)
George Clausen (1852–1944) ARA 1908, RA 1920	66	*In the Gun Factory at Woolwich Arsenal, 1918*	72 × 125	£312 6s 6d (£312.32)
Darsie Japp (1883–1973) Slade	35	*The Royal Field Artillery in Macedonia*	72 × 125	£308 8s 7d (£308.43)
Wyndham Lewis (1882–1957) Slade, London Group 1913	36	*A Battery Shelled*	72 × 125	£312 13s 9d (£312.69)

Ambrose McEvoy (1878) 1927 ARA 1924	40	*Night Flying* (unfinished)	72 × 125	presented by widow 1937
C. R. W. Nevinson (1889–1946) Slade, London Group 1913 (Transferred from Scheme 2)	29	*The Harvest of Battle*	72 × 125	£309 1s 6d (£309.07)
Charles Sims (1873–1928) RA 1915	45	*The Old German Front Line, Arras, 1916*	72 × 125	£322 11s 0d (£322.55)

Reduced 'Uccello-sized' pictures: £300 + expenses

| Henry Lamb (1883–1960) | 35 | *Irish Troops in the Judean Hills Surprised by a Turkish Bombardment* | 72 × 86 | £309 15s 0d (£309.75) |
| Henry Tonks (1862–1937) | 56 | *An Advanced Dressing Station in France, 1918* | 72 × 86 | £338 0s 0d (£388) |

Smaller canvases

| C. J. Holmes (1868–1936) NEAC, member 1905. Director, National Gallery | 48 | *A Two-Year-Old Steel Works, 1918* | 42 × 60 | £158 18s 7d (£158.93) |
| P. W. Steer (1860–1942) NEAC founder member 1886, Slade teacher | 58 | *Dover Harbour, 1918* | 42 × 60 | £242 7s 0d (£242.35) |

SCHEME 2: FULL-TIME SALARIED ARTISTS, £500 PER ANNUM, REDUCED TO £400 PER ANNUM + EXPENSES, TOTAL OUTPUT ACQUIRED

'Uccello-sized' or reduced 'Uccello-sized' pictures

Artist	Age in 1918	Title	Size (inches)	Dates of employment and payment.[2]
Colin Gill (1892–1940) Slade, NEAC	26	*Heavy Artillery*	72 × 125	?May/July 1918–March 1919. £407 18s 0d (£407.90)
John Nash (1892–1978) NEAC, member 1919, London Group	26	*Oppy Wood, 1917*	72 × 84	May 1918–?Feb 1919. £420 14s 1d (£420.70)
Paul Nash (1889–1946) Slade, NEAC	29	*The Menin Road*	72 × 125	1917–15 June 1918–Feb 1919. £318 10s 3d (£318.51)
William Roberts (1895–1982) Slade, NEAC, member 1919, London Group	23	*A Shell Dump, France*	72 × 125	from March–?May/June 1918 half time, Nov 1918–Feb 1919. £237 14s 2d (£237.71)
Stanley Spencer (1891–1959) Slade, NEAC, member 1919	27	*Travoys Arriving with Wounded at a Dressing Station at Smol, Macedonia, September 1916*	72 × 86	Feb 1919–July 1919. £213 12s 10d (£213.64)

Smaller canvas to standard dimensions

Bernard Adeney (1878–1966) Slade, London Group, President 1918–1932	40	*The Experimental Depot for Tanks, Dollis Hill, London, NW*	24 × 36	?July/Sept 1918–Jan 1919. £174 10s 9d (£174.54)
Thomas Derrick (1895–1954)	33	*American Troops at Southampton Embarking for France.*	28 × 36	Oct 1918–Jan 1919. £149 16s 10d (£149.84)
Alfred Hayward (1875–1971) Slade, NEAC, member 1910	43	*The Staff Train at Charing Cross Station, 1918*	42 × 60	Sept 1918–?March 1919. £296 13s 4d (£296.67)

James McBey (1883–1959)	35	*The Allies Entering Jerusalem, 11 December 1917*	42 × 60	1917–(?15 June/22 July 1918)–April 1919. £601 1s 0d (£601.05)
Bernard Meninsky (1891–1950) Slade, NEAC	27	*The Arrival of a Leave Train, Victoria Station, 1918*	42 × 60	Sept 1918–Jan 1919 + 1 month unpaid. £181 9s 4d (£181.47)
Henry Rushbury (1889–1968) Slade, NEAC, member 1917	29	*The War Refugees' Camp, Earls Court, 1918*	42 × 60	?July/Aug 1918–?May/June 1919. £421 15s 8d (£421.78)
Randolph Schwabe (1885–1948) Slade, NEAC, member 1917	33	*Voluntary Land Workers in a Flax-Field, Podington, Northamptonshire*	42 × 60	Sept 1918–March 1919. £266 14s 1d (£266.70)
John Wheatley (1892–1955) Slade, NEAC, member 1917, Slade teacher 1920	26	*Divers at Work repairing a Torpedoed Ship*	42 × 60	17 May/?15 June 1918–Jan 1919. £402 7s 0d (£402.35)
W. T. Wood (1877–1958)	41	*The Doiran Front*	42 × 60	May 1918–Dec 1918. £255 8s 1d (£255.40)

Sculpture, scheme never realised

C. S. Jagger (1885–1934)	33	plaster relief for The Battle of Ypres, 1914	96 × 154	Sept 1918–?March 1919. £296 13s 4d (£296.67)
Gilbert Ledward (1888–1960)	30	plaster relief design for a historical relief: The Germans violate the neutrality of Belgium		July 1918–April 1919. £442 3s 2d (£442.16)

Scheme 2 artist

Muirhead Bone (1876–1953), member NEAC 1902	42	–	–	1916–(?April/May 1918)–?March 1919. £566 18s 11d (£566.95)

WORK ADDED AFTER THE CLOSURE OF THE SCHEME

Artist	Age in 1918	Title	Size (inches)	Source and date of acquisition
John Dodgson (1890–1969) Slade, NEAC	28	*Motor Transport Troops and German Prisoners. Chaulnes: Autumn, 1918*	72 × 86	Bone Fund 1923
Gilbert Spencer (1892–1979) Slade, NEAC, member 1919	26	*New Arrivals*	72 × 86	IWM funds, £200, March 1919
Ian Strang (1886–1952) Slade	32	*The Outskirts of Lens*	72 × 125	IWM Funds, £300 + visit to front, Feb 1919
Elliott Seabrooke (1886–1950) Slade, NEAC, London Group 1920	32	*The Bombardment of Gorizia, 21 August 1917*	42 × 60	Bone Fund 1919
Leon Underwood (1890–1975) Slade	28	*Erecting a Camouflage Tree*	42 × 60	IWM Funds, £100, Feb–Sept 1919.
H. S. Williamson (1892–1978) NEAC	26	*A German Attack on a Wet Morning, April, 1918*	42 × 60	IWM Funds, £100, July 1919

Notes

1 Information contained in a memorandum from Yockney to Conway, 25 October 1919, (IWM, 324/7: 'Finance File'). Orpen was not listed as a Ministry artist in Yockney's calculations of expenditure on Ministry commissioned works of art. The Treasury had authorised £11,000 expenditure. £4875 14s 10d (£4875.74) was paid from Ministry funds by 1 January 1919, £5074 0s 5d (£5074.02) from IWM funds after 1 January 1919. Memorandum from Yockney to ffoulkes, 6 February 1920.

2 Artists did not sign contracts and it is sometimes difficult to determine the precise date of an artist's period of employment. Dates are worked out from letters in the artists' files, correspondence with the Treasury or extrapolated from Yockney's statements of payments and sometimes the information is contradictory.

appendix two

Lists of Artists Involved in War Artists Schemes During the First World War

★ Salaried artist

1 Artists who were employed or received facilities from Wellington House prior to the formation of the Ministry of Information in March 1918

Artist	Dates	Age at outbreak of war	Biography	Details of Involvement
Muirhead Bone★ (BWMC★)	1876–1953	38	b. Glasgow, member of NEAC 1902, trustee of National Gallery, Tate Gallery and Imperial War Museum, knighted in 1937.	From 1 June 1916 employed by Wellington House at £500 per annum. Hon. 2nd Lt General Staff, special employment, attached to I Div GHQ France. Contributed Efforts to *Efforts and Ideals*. Work was published in ten issues of *The Western Front*. Became a Scheme 2 artist for BWMC employed full-time. Adviser to BWMC. April 1919 donated all his war work to the Nation, divided between British Museum, IWM and other museums. Established the Bone Fund on the proceeds of his lithographs to purchase work for the IWM. Served on the Hanging Committee for *The Nation's War Paintings* at RA 1919–1920.
Francis Dodd★	1874–1949	40	b. Anglesey, trained Glasgow, Bone's brother-in-law, member NEAC 1904, ARA 1927, Trustee of Tate 1928–35. RA 1935.	February 1917–February 1918 employed full-time by Wellington House at £42 per month and until March 1918 at Ministry of Information. Work published as a series of books of portraits of *Admirals and Generals*. 2nd Lt I Div GHQ. April–May 1918 and July–December 1918 employed by IWM at £2.10 per day, as Major Royal Marines or RNVR on special employment.
Eric Kennington	1888–1960	26	b. Chelsea, son of a painter, ARA 1951, RA 1959.	Pte London Regiment, invalided home Jan 1915. December 1916 made a private visit to France assisted by Bone. From August 1917 given facilities to make work in France (unpaid). Contributed 'Efforts' to *Efforts and Ideals*. Work published in *British Artists at the Front*. Work purchased by

				IWM and made donations. Work exhibited in June/July 1918. Resigned from BWMC scheme and worked for the Canadians, visiting the Rhine with Canadian troops.
John Lavery	1856–1941	58	Irish, moved to Scotland, ARA 1911, knighted 1918, RA 1921.	Around May 1917 offered facilities by Wellington House. Intended to visit France but worked on the home front. Work was published in *British Artists at the Front*. Considered for BWMC. Offered his work to IWM at half his usual rates and was given facilities to visit naval dockyards. November 1918, donated all his war pictures to the nation (IWM). A number of pictures were purchased from him by IWM.
James McBey★ (★BWMC)	1883–1959	31	b. Newburgh, self taught, mainly a printmaker.	Lt Army Postal and Stationary Service. April 1917 employed full-time on £500 per annum, sent to Egypt. Became a BWMC Scheme 2 artist and then paid by IWM until about April 1919.
Paul Nash (★BWMC)	1889–1946	25	b. London, Slade 1910–1911, member of London Group.	Pte Artists Rifles, 2nd Lt Hampshire Regiment, served in France, February 1917, invalided home May 1917. July 1917 sought facilities from Wellington House. October 1917, agreement from Wellington House, end of October–early December visited France, paid allowances and expenses. Work published in *British Artists at the Front*. Work purchased from him for IWM. March–May 1918 paid a detention [*sic*] allowance. Held an exhibition of war work in May 1918. From June 1918, paid as a Scheme 2 artist by BWMC for his total output, IWM took over liability for his pay until around January or February 1919. Worked for the Canadians.
C. R. W. Nevinson (BWMC)	1889–1946	25	Studied at Slade 1908–1912, exhibited at AAA, London Group and with the Vorticists, ARA 1939.	Attached to Red Cross and then RAMC until about 1916, discharged unfit. Approached Wellington House in May 1917 and was offered facilities, signed an agreement June 1917 and visited France in July 1917. Contributed *Efforts* to *Efforts and Ideals* and work was published in *British Artists at the Front*. Work exhibited March 1918. Work purchased by IWM and made donations. Employed by BWMC as a Scheme 1 artist for a major canvas. September 1918, visited France. Worked for the Canadians.
William Orpen★ (★BWMC)	1878–1931	36	b. Dublin, trained at Slade and exhibited with NEAC, ARA 1910, knighted 1918, RA 1919.	Known as a 'Special Case'. From around April 1917 employed by Wellington House, who paid his salary and expenses, and then by Ministry of Information. Made his own arrangements to tour France. Commissioned by IWM to make Peace Conference pictures. Worked for the Canadians. Donated all his work to the nation in 1918. Lt and Major ASC.

| William Rothenstein | 1872–1945 | 42 | Studied at Slade, 1894 member of NEAC, 1920–1935, Principal of RCA, 1927–1933, Trustee of Tate Gallery, knighted 1931. | Contributed to *Efforts and Ideals*. Visited France, December 1917–March 1918. Considered by BWMC, offered Scheme 3 and given a sketching permit. Worked for the Canadians, visited France January–July 1919. Work purchased through Bone Fund. |
| G. Spencer-Pryse | 1881–1956 | 33 | Studied in London and Paris | Given facilities and a sketching pass by Wellington House in 1917 when posted to France. September 1918 given 2 months leave to work for Ministry of Information. Worked for the Canadians. |

Also associated with Wellington House:

| Louis Raemaekers | 1869–1956 | 45 | Dutch, illustrator. | 1915–16, in contact with Foreign Office and Wellington House who promoted his work, dropped in favour of Bone. Considered by BWMC, no outcome. |
| Ministry of Munitions artist: Joseph Pennell | 1858–1926 | 56 | American, printmaker. | Given facilities to visit munitions factories by Ministry of Munitions 1917. |

2 Artists who contributed to *Efforts and Ideals*

Artist	Dates	Age at outbreak of war	Biography	Details of Involvement
Muirhead Bone				(see above, Table 1)
Frank Brangwyn	1867–1956	47	b. Bruges, ARA 1904, RA 1919, knighted 1941.	Contributed an Ideal and a series of Efforts. Works acquired by the Canadians. Rejected by BWMC.
George Clausen				(see below, Table 3)
Edmund Dulac	1882–1953	41	b. Toulouse	July 1917 classed C3 (unfit). Contributed an Ideal. Rejected by BWMC May 1918. From around January 1918, Ministry of Information sought exemption for him for 6 months for work in pictorial propaganda, not employed full-time.
Maurice Greiffenhagen	1862–1931	51	b. London, member NEAC 1886, ARA 1916, RA 1922.	Contributed an Ideal.
A. S. Hartrick	1864–1950	49	Trained at the Slade 1884–5, member NEAC 1893.	Made Efforts. Worked for Underground Railway Company. Approached IWM in May 1918 and was rejected. February 1919 was approached by IWM Women's Work Section.
Ernest Jackson	1872–1945	41	1902–1921 taught at Central School of Art. ARA 1944.	Contributed an Ideal and organised the technical aspects of the series.
Augustus John				(see below, Table 3)
Eric Kennington				(see above, Table 1)
Gerald Moira	1867–1959	47	b. London, professor of decorative painting at RCA.	Contributed an Ideal. Rejected by Wellington House and BWMC.
C. R. W. Nevinson				(see above, Table 1)

William Nicholson	1872–1949	42	Knighted 1936.	Contributed an Ideal. Suggested for BWMC by Bennett but wished to do own work concurrently. Commissioned to paint a picture by Women's Work Committee of IWM, not finished. Portrait for IWM. Worked for the Canadians.
Charles Pears★	1873–1958	41	b. Pontefract, exhibited RA and NEAC.	Made Efforts. October 1917 approached by IWM and salaried January–November 1918 (see below Table 9a).
Charles Ricketts	1866–1931	47	Editor of *The Dial* and ran The Vale Press, ARA 1922, RA 1928.	Contributed an Ideal.
William Rothenstein				(see above, Table 1)
Charles Shannon	1863–1937	51	Editor of *The Dial* and ran The Vale Press with Ricketts, ARA 1911, RA 1920.	Contributed an Ideal. Approached by BWMC. Approached March 1920 by IWM to make portraits which he declined. Worked for the Canadians.
Claude Shepperson	1867–1921	46	ARA 1919.	Made Efforts.
Edmund Sullivan	1869–1933	44	Illustrator.	Contributed an Ideal. Work purchased by IWM, November 1917.

3 Artists who were commissioned by British War Memorials Committee under Scheme 1 (a major canvas)

Artist	Dates	Age at outbreak of war	Biography	Details of Involvement
Walter Bayes	1869–1956	45	Involved with Camden Town Group and the London Group.	June 1918, Scheme 1 £300. Work purchased through Bone Fund and by IWM in May 1918.
David Y. Cameron	1865–1945	49	b. Glasgow, ARA 1911/1916, RA 1920. Trustee of the National Gallery, Tate Gallery, knighted 1924.	BWMC Scheme 1 £300. Visited France January 1919 and delivered painting November 1919. Worked for the Canadians, Major, Canadian army.
George Clausen	1852–1944	62	b. London, ARA 1895, RA 1908, knighted 1927.	Contributed an Ideal and Efforts to *Efforts and Ideals*. BWMC Scheme 1, worked on picture August 1918–July 1919. Worked for the Canadians.
C. J. Holmes	1868–1936	46	b. Preston, 1905 member of NEAC, 1903–1909 editor of *Burlington Magazine*, 1909–16 director of National Portrait Gallery, 1916–28 director of National Gallery, knighted 1921.	BWMC Scheme 1 £150, completed December 1918, commissioned by IWM. Served on the Hanging Committee for exhibition at RA 1919–20.
Darsie Japp	1883–1973	31	b. Liverpool, studied at Slade 1908–9, member NEAC 1919.	Major RFA served in France and Salonica, awarded MC. January 1919 back in England. BWMC Scheme 1 £300.
Augustus John	1878–1961	36	Studied at Slade 1894–8, ARA 1921, RA 1928.	Contributed an Ideal. BWMC Scheme 1 but work never begun. Worked for the Canadians and visited France, unfinished cartoon. Commissioned by IWM to do Peace Conference picture which did not materialise. Drawings purchased by IWM. Hon. Major Canadian Army.

Henry Lamb	1883–1960	31	Studied medicine. ARA 1940, RA 1949.	Captain RAMC as a doctor. BWMC Scheme 1 £300.
Wyndham Lewis	1882–1957	32	Slade 1898–1901, Camden Town group, London group and Vorticists.	Lt RGA. BWMC Scheme 1 £300. Worked for the Canadians. Work also acquired through Bone fund.
Ambrose McEvoy	1878–1927	36	Trained at Slade 1893–6, ARA 1924.	October 1917 approached by IWM and completed portrait commissions. BWMC Scheme 1, canvas never finished. Visited France for IWM August/September 1918. Worked for the Canadians, Major RM for special employment.
C. R. W. Nevinson				(see above, Table 1) Transferred from Scheme 2.
J. S. Sargent	1856–1925	58	b. Florence of US parents, ARA 1894, RA 1897.	BWMC Scheme 1 £600, visited France with Tonks, July–November 1918. Work acquired through Bone Fund.
Charles Sims	1873–1928	41	b. London, ARA 1908, RA 1916, 1920–26 Keeper of RA.	BWMC Scheme 1, £300, visited France for picture, November 1918. Work purchased by IWM, worked for the Canadians and visited France for them in 1917/18.
Gilbert Spencer	1892–1979	22	b. Cookham, brother of Stanley Spencer, studied at Slade 1913–15 and 1919, member of NEAC 1920, ARA 1950, RA 1959–60.	Pte London Regiment. BWMC Scheme 1 paid for by IWM, March 1919, £200. Works acquired through Bone Fund.
P. Wilson Steer	1860–1942	54	Founder member NEAC 1886, assistant professor, Slade 1893–1930, OM 1931.	BWMC Scheme 1, £150. Worked acquired through Bone Fund.
Henry Tonks	1862–1937	52	Trained as a surgeon, Member NEAC 1895, assistant at Slade 1892, 1917/18–1930 Slade professor.	Lt RAMC, resigned commission 1916. February 1917 approached by Wellington House to help with *Efforts and Ideals* but declined. BWMC Scheme 1, £300. Visited France with Sargent July–September 1918. June 1919 went to Russia to make pictures for IWM. Declined to work for Women's Work committee at IWM, work acquired through Bone Fund.

4 Artists employed under Scheme 2 by the British War Memorials Committee, total output of artist acquired

Artist	Dates	Age at outbreak of war	Biography	Details of Involvement
Bernard Adeney★	1878–1966	36	b. London, Slade 1912, exhibited with the Vorticists, member of London Group 1913, president of London Group 1918–23.	Gunner Tanks Corps. February 1918 asked for work at Wellington House and was rejected. End of September 1918, BWMC Scheme 2 artist until January 1919.
Muirhead Bone★				(see above, Table 1)
Thomas Derrick★	1885–1954	29	b. Bristol, taught at RCA, lectured at the London Day Training College.	BWMC Scheme 2 from the end October 1918 until about January 1919. Was employed at Wellington House and served as an adviser on BWMC.

Colin Gill★	1892–1940	22	Trained at Slade, won Rome Scholarship 1913, member of NEAC 1926, exhibited at RA from 1924. Many public commissions for decorative murals and paintings.	Lt RE, Sept 1915–March 1918 attached to RE Camouflage Table. BWMC Scheme 2 July 1918–March 1919. Worked for the Canadians. Commissioned by IWM for a portrait.
Alfred Hayward★	1875–1971	39	b. London, Slade 1895–7, member of NEAC 1918.	2nd Lt RGA in anti-aircraft. February 1918, contacted Ross about war pictures. BWMC Scheme 2 July 1918–c.February 1919. Painted portraits for IWM.
C. S. Jagger★	1885–1934	29	Won Prix de Rome, sculpture 1914, ARA 1926.	Pte Artists Rifles, Lt Worcestershire Regiment, served Gallipoli, France, wounded and awarded MC April 1918. Contacted Ministry July 1918 with support from Sargent and W. T. Wood. BWMC Scheme 2 September 1918 until around April or May 1919.
Gilbert Ledward★	1888–1960	26	b. London, professor of Sculpture RCA, made a number of war memorials ARA 1932, RA 1937.	Lt RGA, served in Italy. BWMC Scheme 2 July 1918–April 1919.
James McBey★				(see above, Table 1)
Bernard Meninsky★	1891–1950	23	b. Ukraine, Slade 1912–13, member London Group 1919, member NEAC, 1923.	Pte Royal Fusiliers. BWMC Scheme 2, September 1918–c.February or March 1919.
John Nash★	1893–1977	21	Founder member London Group, ARA 1940, RA 1951.	Pte/Corp Artists Rifles, served in France. Applied to Wellington House January 1918. BWMC Scheme 2 end April 1918 to around February 1919.
Paul Nash★				(See above, Table 1)
William Orpen★				"Special case" (See above, Table 1)
William Roberts★	1895–1980	19	Slade 1910–13, exhibited with London Group, Vorticists and Group X. ARA 1958, RA 1966.	Gunner RFA. BWMC Scheme 2, from June 1918 but on loan to Canadians and paid part-time until November 1918, resigned January 1919. Worked for the Canadians in 1918. Work acquired through Bone Fund.
Henry Rushbury★	1889–1968	25	Studied Birmingham and Slade, member NEAC 1917, ARA 1927, RA 1936, knighted 1964.	Serg. RAF. BWMC Scheme 2 July 1918 until about June 1919. Commissioned by IWM.
Randolph Schwabe★	1885–1948	29	Slade 1900–05, London Group 1915, NEAC 1917, from 1930 professor of Slade.	Exempt, disabled. BWMC Scheme 2 September 1918 until about March 1919.
Stanley Spencer★	1891–1959	23	Slade 1908–1912, 1919–27 member NEAC, ARA 1932 (resigned 1935), RA 1950, knighted 1958.	RAMC, Pte Royal Berkshire Regiment. December 1918 returned from Salonica. February 1919–July 1919 Scheme 2 artist, paid by IWM, resigned appointment.
John Wheatley★	1892–1955	22	Slade 1912–13, member NEAC 1917, assistant teacher Slade 1920–25, Director Sheffield City Art Gallery, ARA 1945.	Sergeant Artists Rifles discharged March 1918. BWMC Scheme 2, May 1918–c. January 1919. Commissioned by IWM for portraits.

| W. T. Wood★ | 1877–1958 | 37 | Art teacher Regent St Polytechnic. | Cpl RAF, observer in kite balloons. November 1917 exhibited in Salonica, worked in Salonica on own initiative, on leave January 1918 to prepare exhibition, contacted by IWM. February 1918 suggested to Wellington House. Sold work to IWM. Exhibition June 1918 of war work. BWMC Scheme 2 May–December 1918. |

5 Artist who was offered facilities in exchange for first refusal of a canvas

Artist	Dates	Age at outbreak of war	Biography	Details of Involvement
Herbert Hughes-Stanton	1870–1937	44	ARA 1913, RA 1920, knighted 1923.	Approached by Ministry, November 1918 proposed visit to France. December 1918 in France, presented a canvas to IWM. Also worked for the Canadians. May 1919, work purchased by the IWM.

6 Artists who were considered by BWMC and from whom work was acquired through the IWM

Artist	Dates	Age at outbreak of war	Biography	Details of Involvement
Anna Airy (Mrs Pocock)	1882–1964	32	b. London, Slade 1899–1903, exhibited at the RA from 1905.	September 1918 BWMC Scheme 1, picture rejected January 1919. June 1918 commissioned by IWM for four paintings. Worked for the Canadians.
Clare Atwood	1886–1962	38	b. Richmond, studied at the Slade, member of NEAC 1912.	Approached by BWMC for Scheme 1 without outcome. February 1919 commissioned by Women's Work Section of the IWM. Worked for the Canadians.
Frank Dobson	1888–1963	26	b. London, showed with Group X, ARA 1942, RA 1953.	Capt RFC, invalided home 1917. Approached BWMC and work rejected, proposed for Scheme 3. Taken up by IWM September 1918 and picture commissioned and received July 1919.
A. Neville Lewis	1895–1972	18	b. Cape Town, studied Slade 1914–16.	Gunner RFA served in France. Work acquired through Bone Fund. Offered BWMC Scheme 2, suggested by Tonks for Mesopotamia, never begun. Release refused August 1918. Commissioned for portraits by IWM 1919.
Glyn Philpot	1884–1937	30	b. London, ARA 1915, RA 1923.	2nd Lt ASC, invalided 1917. October 1917, approached by IWM. Considered for BWMC Scheme 1. Commissioned portraits for IWM and donation to Women's Work section.
Walter Russell	1867–1949	47	Associated with Slade as a teacher 1925–7, member NEAC 1895, ARA 1920, RA 1926, Keeper of RA 1927–42, knighted 1935.	Lt RE. Approached by Ministry of Information. Offered Scheme 3 and sketching leave. Proposed to IWM by Lavery and commissioned to paint a portrait 1919.

Ian Strang	1886–1949	28	Slade 1902–6, exhibited NEAC and RA.	Capt RE. Approached by BWMC, no outcome. Commissioned by IWM for a painting that matched BWMC dimensions, given facilities in France.
A. Stuart-Hill	fl. c.1920–1950		Exhibited at RA.	Services sought by Ministry and was drawing in Dorset August 1918. Commissioned to make an Admiralty portrait for IWM in 1920.
Leon Underwood	1890–1975	24	b. London, Slade 1919–20, member of 7&5 Society.	Capt Camouflage in France. Considered at BWMC late in Schemes. Commissioned by IWM November/December 1918 for a painting that matched BWMC dimensions. Commissioned by IWM for a portrait 1919.
Harold Sandys Williamson	1892–1978	22	b. Leeds, RA schools 1914–15 and Turner Gold medal, headmaster Chelsea School of Art 1930–58.	Cp King's Royal Rifle Corps discharged November/December 1918. Recommended to BWMC and asked to do a painting. Sold drawings to IWM and a painting that matched the dimensions of BWMC canvases in 1919.
John Wright	1857–1933	57	Printmaker.	Approached by BWMC, given a sketching pass in England to depict air raid ruins April 1918. Work was censored and presented later to Ministry/IWM, December 1918.

7 Artists whose work was acquired through Bone Fund

Artist	Dates	Age at outbreak of war	Biography	Details of Involvement
Walter Bayes				(see above, Table 3)
David Bomberg	1890–1957	24	Studied at Slade 1911–13, exhibited with London Group and guest section of Vorticists.	Sapper, RE, released November 1918. Worked for the Canadians. Wrote to Yockney seeking work in February 1920 but no funds available. Work purchased through Bone Fund.
Dorothy Coke				(see below, Table 8a)
Alfred Egerton Cooper	1883–1943	31		Capt RAF. Pictures purchased by IWM, given facilities at Vickers in exchange for replicas of pictures. 1919 sought a commission. Work purchased through Bone Fund.
Tony Cyriax (Mrs Almgren)	fl. 1914–1920			Drawings commissioned by Bone in 1919.
John Dodgson	1890–1969	24	Nephew of Campbell Dodgson, Slade 1913–15, London Group member 1947, President of London Group 1950–51.	Work purchased through Bone Fund 1923, canvas matched BWMC dimensions.
Jacob Epstein	1880–1959	34	Exhibited with London Group, knighted 1954.	Called up 1918, August 1918 invalided out of army. 1917 suggested to IWM, also sought by BWMC as Scheme 1 artist, War Office refused his release. Commissioned by Bone March/April 1919 for a *Moeuvres Epic* relief. Two works bought through Bone Fund, 1919 and work also purchased by IWM.

Rupert Lee	1887–1959	27	Studied at Slade, member London Group 1920, President of London Group 1926–36, Chair of First International Surrealist Exhibition 1936.	Work purchased through Bone Fund.
A. Neville Lewis				(see above, Table 6)
Wyndham Lewis				(see above, Table 3)
D. S. MacColl	1859–1948	55	Art critic, member NEAC 1896, taught at Slade 1903–9, Keeper at Tate 1906–11, Keeper at Wallace Collection 1911–24, Trustee Tate Gallery 1917.	Drawing purchased by Bone.
Donald MacLaren	1886–1917	28	Nephew of D. S. MacColl, Slade 1903–8, showed with NEAC.	Lt army, killed in action 1917, drawings presented by Bone.
William Roberts				(see above, Table 4)
William Rothenstein				(see above, Table 1)
J. S. Sargent				(see above, Table 3)
Elliott Seabrooke	1886–1950	28	Slade 1906–11, showed with NEAC 1909–20, member London group 1920, President of London Group, 1943–8.	Recommended to BWMC by Tonks. Work purchased by Bone which matched dimensions of other BWMC canvases. Attached to British Red Cross Society.
Gilbert Spencer				(see above, Table 3)
P. W. Steer				(see above, Table 3)
Henry Tonks				(see above, Table 3)
Francis S. Unwin	1885–1925	29	Slade 1902–5.	Approached by BWMC without outcome. Work commissioned and presented by Bone 1919.

8a Artists who were considered for the BWMC but from whom there was no outcome

Artist	Dates	Age at outbreak of war	Biography	Details of Involvement
Dorothy Coke	1897–1979	17	Slade 1914–18, member NEAC 1920.	Offered Scheme 1 commission, sketches were rejected in July/August 1918 and later purchased through Bone Fund.
John Duncan Fergusson	1874–1961	40	b. Scotland.	BWMC Scheme 3 and visited Portsmouth, no work was acquired.
John Everett	1876–1949	27	Studied at Slade and with Orpen.	In April 1918, given a Scheme 3 arrangement and a sketching permit to paint river scenes. IWM were interested in acquiring his work, without outcome. Later donated all his work to National Maritime Museum, Greenwich.
Harold Harvey	1874–1941	40	Lived in Newlyn, exhibited RA 1898–1941.	Approached by BWMC and offered a loose Scheme 3 arrangement. Ill from July 1918 and abandoned work.
Flora Lion	1876–1958	37		Contributed portrait of Lavery to *British Artists at the Front*. Approached by Ministry and given a Scheme 3 arrangement, visited munitions factories, finished work October 1918, but not purchased, later donated to IWM. Worked for the Canadians.

Alfred Munnings	1878–1959	35	RA 1925, knighted 1944, PRA 1944–9.	Suggested to Wellington House and IWM. Worked for the Canadians and visited France, 1917–18. July 1918 was offered Scheme 2 and requested a horse not a car. Injured in October 1918 and did not take up work. Work was sought from him in 1919 but a canvas he offered was rejected.
Charles Oppenheimer	1875–1961	38	Father German, naturalised in 1894, studied in Manchester under Walter Crane.	Gunner RGA from 1916, served in France. Sought the position of official artist in Italy from Ministry of Information. October 1918, given leave to make specimen work for Ministry, November 1918 released for 6 months. Ill in January 1919 and gave up.
Ernest Proctor	1886–1935	28	Studied with Stanhope Forbes, NEAC member 1929, ARA 1932.	In France with Friends Ambulance Unit. Offered a Scheme 3 agreement and sent a permit to sketch in France in November 1918.
Harold Squire	b. 1881	33	Studied at Slade and under Stanhope Forbes.	In May 1918 considered as a Scheme 2 artist in Palestine but war ended before he could go.
John Turnbull	b. 1887	27	Showed with Group x 1920.	RFC, served at Gallipoli and in France, in London with air service. June 1918 unfit and classed C2 November 1918. Considered as a Scheme 2 artist but never began work. Worked for the Canadians.

8b   Other artists considered by Wellington House or Ministry of Information who were rejected or from whom there was no outcome

Artist	Outcome	Artist	Outcome
Henry Bateman, 1887–1970	Approached by Ministry, no outcome.	B. Roberts Bechtel, trained in France.	Recommended to Ministry by Canadians, rejected.
Henry Becker, 1865–1928	Approached by Ministry, no outcome.	Alfred Bentley, b. 1923	Approached by Ministry, no outcome. Worked as an illustrator of Information Department, War Office.
Robert Bevan, 1865–1925	Approached by Ministry, no outcome.	Gerald Brockhurst, 1890–1978, exhibited at RA from 1915.	Approached by Ministry, no outcome.
Gregory Brown, 1887–1941	Offered services to Konody and was rejected.	Ernest Cole, b. 1890, Professor of sculpture RCA 1924–6.	Approached by Ministry, but refused release by War Office, declined offer by Women's Work Committee IWM. Worked on Kitchener Memorial St Paul's.
J. Collard	Contacted Ministry and rejected.	Creelock	Considered by Foreign Office, May 1916.
Hanslip Fletcher, 1874–1955	Approached Ministry on advice of Bone, but graded Class 1 and Ministry could not apply for him.	Robert Fowler, 1853–1926	Work rejected by IWM, given facilities by Ministry but no outcome.
Douglas Fox-Pitt, 1864–1922	Approached by Ministry, no outcome.	Richard Garbe, 1876–1957	Approached by Ministry, no outcome.
C. Geoffroy-Dechaume, 1877–1944	Passed to IWM by Wellington House December 1917 and work purchased.	Mark Gertler, 1892–1939	Considered for Scheme 1, approached by Ministry, without outcome.

Robert Gibbings	Approached Ministry, October 1918, no work. (see also Table 9a).	G. D. Giles, 1857–1923, war correspondent.	Rejected by Ministry.
Eric Gill, 1882–1940	Approached by Ministry but called up August 1918, no outcome.	Duncan Grant, 1885–1978	Considered by BWMC but attempts to get him released from non-combatant service failed.
Leonard Gregory	Approached Ministry, rejected.	Alvaro Guevara, 1894–1951	Suggested to BWMC by Bone.
Arthur Hacker, 1858–1919, ARA 1894, RA 1910	Illustrated London News requested facilities for him from Foreign Office, June 1916, rejected.	Roderick Hill	Approached by Ministry, refused to do work.
William Hill	Offered work to BWMC, rejected.	David Jagger, d.1958	BWMC sought his 'Bolshevik', privately purchased by Beaverbrook.
Alexander Jamieson, 1873–1937	Recommended to BWMC 1918 by McEvoy and IWM 1919 by Bone and Mond and again in 1920 without outcome.	J. Kerr-Lawson, 1865–1939	Approached by Ministry, no outcome.
Laura Knight, 1877–1970, D.B.E. 1929	Approached by Ministry, no outcome, and by IWM, Women's Work, no outcome. Worked for Canadians.	Jacob Kramer, 1892–1962	Repeatedly approached Wellington House, IWM and Ministry, rejected.
E. H. Lacey, b. 1892	Approached by Ministry, rejected.	Thomas Lowinsky, 1892–1947, Slade 1912–14	Recommended to BWMC by McEvoy and rejected.
E. S. Lumsden, b. 1883	Recommended by Dodgson for Mesopotamia, December 1917.	Edward McKnight Kauffer, 1890–1954	Suggested to BWMC by Bone.
James Innes Meo	Sought by BWMC but turned out to be POW. BWMC proposed to send him materials, no outcome. Work acquired by Canadians.	William Monk, 1864–1937	Approached by Ministry, no outcome.
J. W. Morrice, 1865–1924	Considered for BWMC Scheme 1, worked for the Canadians.	Carey Morris	Rejected by BWMC.
Henry Payne, c.1888–1940	Sought work from BWMC September 1918.	C. Maresco Pearce, b. c.1878	Approached by Ministry, no outcome.
Lucien Pissarro, 1863–1944	Suggested to BWMC by Bone.	Henry Poole, 1872–1928	Approached by Ministry, no outcome.
James Pryde, 1866–1941	Approached by Ministry, no outcome.	Stephen Reid, 1873–1948	Approached BWMC but no work.
Albert Rutherston, 1881–1953	Approached by BWMC but no work.	Lester Sacre	Suggested to Wellington House by Foreign Office but not needed.
Frank Salisbury, 1874–1962	Approaches made to BWMC on his behalf but no work acquired.	Walter Sickert, 1860–1942	Refused to work for BWMC although he recommended some artists.
Charles Simpson, b. 1885	Offered his services to BWMC, no outcome.	Adam Slade, b. 1875	Considered for Scheme 3, BWMC.
Matthew Smith, 1879–1959, Slade, France, knighted 1954	Recommended by Konody to Yockney August 1918 but no work available.	Harold Speed, 1872–1957	No work available at Ministry.

Douglas Strachan, 1875–1950	Considered for BWMC.	William Strang, 1859–1921	Approached by Ministry, no outcome.
Annie Swynnerton, 1844–1933, ARA 1922	Approached by Ministry, no outcome.	Algernon Talmage, 1871–1939 RA	Approached by Ministry, no outcome. Worked for the Canadians.
J. Harvard Thomas, 1854–1921	Approached by Ministry, no outcome.	J. Alfonso Toft d.1964	Approached by BWMC, no outcome.
John Tweed, 1868–1933	Recommended by Wellington House to IWM as a joint artist, December 1917, without outcome. Approached by Ministry, no outcome.	Edward Wadsworth, 1889–1949	Sought work at Ministry too late and tried IWM, December 1918, worked for the Canadians.
Margaret Lindsay Williams	Approached Ministry, rejected.	Alfred Withers, 1865–1932	Suggested to Wellington House by Lavery in 1917 and rejected.
William Walcot, b. 1874	Sought work from IWM and BWMC.	Lawson Wood, 1878–1957	Recommended to Ministry by Colonel Lee and given a sketching permit, rejected.

9a Artists employed or commissioned by Imperial War Museum

Artist	Dates	Employer	Dates of Employment/Commission
Anna Airy			(see above, Table 6)
Cecil Aldin	1870–1935	Women's Work	1919
Geoffrey Allfree★	1889–1918,	Admiralty artist	December 1917–April 1918 part-time.
Norman Arnold		RAF	Purchases and donation, worked when off duty.
Clare Atwood			(see above, Table 6)
Geneste Beeton	b. 1880	Women's Work	1920
A. J. C. Bryce	1868–1940	Women's Work	1919
Richard Carline★	b. 1895	RAF	From late April 1918 on service pay.
Sidney Carline★	1889–1929	RAF	Attached to IWM from July 1918 on service pay.
Isabel Codrington	1874–1943	Women's Work	1919
Philip Connard★	1875–1958	Admiralty	Applied to Wellington House, supported by Dodgson, Sept 1917. Attached to IWM from January 1918, full pay from IWM late June 1918 until March 1919. Sent to Salonica/Mesopotamia. Portrait commissioned, unfinished.
Montague Dawson	1895–1973	?Admiralty	December 1918 lent to Naval publicity department, worked in Gibraltar until February 1919.
Nelson Dawson★	1859–1941	Admiralty	January–April 1918
G. Horace Davis	b. 1881	RAF	1919
Cowan Dobson	b. 1893	RAF	VC portraits 1919
Frank Dobson			(see above, Table 6)
Francis Dodd★			(see above, Table 1)
Sholto Douglas	1872–1958	Admiralty	1918–1919
T. C. Dugdale	1880–1952		Commissioned for Mesopotamia subjects 1919.
Reginald Eves	1876–1941		portrait 1920
C. R. Flemming-Williams		RAF	c.1917
Stanhope Forbes	1857–1948	Women's Work	1919
George Frampton	1860–1928	Women's Work	1919–1920
Robert Gibbings	1889–1958		Commission 1919–1920
Colin Gill			(see above, Table 4)

Graham Glen		RAF	1919
Jan Gordon	1882–1944	Naval Medical Table	1919
Joseph Gray	1890–1962		1918 drawings bought, work rejected by Ministry of Information 1919 commission from IWM.
Ronald Gray	1868–1951		1917 asked to paint replicas.
George Harcourt	1868–1947	Women's Work	1919
Alfred Hayward			(see above, Table 4)
W. Hatherall	1855–1928	Women's Work	1919
Adrian Hill★	b. 1895	War Trophies Section	December 1917–March 1919 paid salary through War Office.
Francis Hodge	1883–1949		Recommended by W. T. Wood, commissioned 1919, paid.
C. J. Holmes			(see above, Table 3)
William Hyde	1859–1925	Munitions	1919
Nellie Isaac		Women's Work	1919
Augustus John			(see above, Table 3)
Lucy Kemp-Welch	1869–1958	Women's Work	1919–1920
Phyllis Keyes		Women's Work	1919
Cecil King	1881–1942	Admiralty	1919, work acquired against his service pay, commissioned in 1919.
John Lavery			(see above, Table 1)
A. Neville Lewis			(see above, Table 6)
E. Bernard Lintott (secretary British Embassy, Petrograd)	1875–1959	Work ordered by Ian Malcolm, Russian Revolution	1918–1919
Guy Lipscombe	1881–1952		Commissioned 1919
Beatrice Lithiby	b. 1889	Women's Work	1919
Neville Lytton	1879–1951		Portrait 1920, Lee put a car at his disposal.
Ambrose McEvoy			(see above, Table 3)
Frank Mason	1876–1965	Admiralty	In Mediterranean, commissioned 1919.
Donald Maxwell★	1877–1936	Admiralty	October 1918–May 1919, salaried, Palestine and Mesopotamia.
Arthur David M'Cormick	1860–1943	Women's Work	Declined employment in 1917, commissioned 1919.
C. D. McGurk	b. 1894	?RAF	Paid for work 1919
Victoria Monkhouse		Women's Work	1918, 1919
D. Carey Morgan		Women's Work	1920
Oswald Moser	1874–1953	Naval Medical Section	1918–19, work rejected 1918
Nora Neilson-Gray	1882–1931	Women's Work	1919–1920
Edward Newling	b. 1890	RAF	1918–on service pay
William Nicholson			(see above, Table 2)
John Edwin Noble★	1876–1941	RA Veterinary Corps Section	1918–1919
Herbert Olivier (semi-official artist)	1861–1952	Present at Peace Conference, rejected by IWM and BWMC, sought to regularise his position.	Works presented 1922–3.
A. R. O'Reilly		RA Veterinary Corps	
William Orpen			(see above, Table 1)
Oscar Parkes	1885–1958	?Naval Medical Section	1919
Charles Pears★	1873–1958	Admiralty	January–November 1918, salaried.
Gyn Philpot			(see above, Table 6)

Stuart Reid		RAF	1919–1920
Louis Frederick Roslyn	1878–1940	RAF	1918
Walter Russell			(see above, Table 6)
Robert Henry Smith	fl. c.1910–30	Admiralty	1918–1919
Gilbert B. Solomon	1890–1954	RAF	1919
Howard Somerville	1873–1952		Portrait commission 1919, Canadian pictures.
A. O. Spare	1888–1956	Women's Work, also an RAMC artist	1919
C. T. Stabb			Commission for portrait 1919.
Ian Strang			(see above, Table 6)
A. Stuart-Hill			(see above, Table 6)
Campbell Taylor	1874–1969		Commission for portrait 1920.
Henry Tonks			(see above, Table 3)
Leon Underwood			(see above, Table 6)
Cecil and E. A. Walton	1860–1922, 1891–1956	Women's Work	Portrait finished by daughter 1921–2.
Louis Weirter/Whirter	1871–1932	RAF	1917–1918, 1919 employed by Canadians.
John Wheatley			(see above, Table 4)
Frederick Whiting	1874–1962		Portraits 1919–20.
Norman Wilkinson	1878–1971	Admiralty	Late 1917
Harold Williamson			(see above, Table 6)
Francis Derwent Wood	1871–1926		Recommended to IWM 1918 but not released by WO, Made portraits in Paris with IWM facilities. Wife donated work 1927.
Harold Wyllie	1880–1973	RAF	1919–1920

9b Royal Army Medical Corps Artists: Assembled by committee for Medical History of War, Medical Section IWM under the charge of Lt Col F. S. Brereton. Some work in IWM, others in Royal Army Medical College and elsewhere

Artist	Dates
David Baxter	1876–1954
Benjamin Clemens	1875–1957
A. N. Cotterell	
J. Hodgson Lobley	1878–1954
Hayden R. Mackey	b. 1883
Edwin Martin	
George Pirie	1863–1946
Gilbert Rogers, Officer in charge of RAMC artists	
A. O. Spare	1888–1936
Walter Spradbury	b. 1889
S. B. White	

9c Official Artists with Mesopotamian Expeditionary Force

Artist	Dates	Employment
V. C. Boyle		
S. Briault	1887–1955	
R. Cable		
Charles William Cain	1893–1962	1919.
Lionel Crane		
W. E. Judge	1892	
W. Pollard		
John Daniel Revel★	1884–1967	1918, salaried.
B. H. Wiles		
H. G. Wolfe		

10 War Office MI7b Artists

Artist	Dates	Employment
Bruce Bairnsfather		1917–
Frank Reynolds	1876–1953	1917–

11 Official artist for Glasgow Corporation

Artist	Dates	Employment
Fred Farrell		Sent to France December–January 1917, and about November 1918. Interviewed by Yockney August 1918.

12 European artists with war work in Canadian collections: Canadian War Museum, National Gallery of Canada, Canadian Senate.

Artist	Dates	Nationality	Type of work
Anna Airy	1882–1964		major canvas
Clare Atwood	1886–1962		major canvas
Ethel Barclay			portrait
Cyril Barraud	b. 1877		major canvas and other work
Alfred Bastien	1873–1955	Belgian	major canvases
David Bomberg	1890–1957		major canvas
Muirhead Bone	1876–1953		drawings
Frank Brangwyn	1867–1956		prints
Edgar Bundy	1862–1922		major canvases
D. Y. Cameron	1865–1945		major canvases
George Clausen	1852–1944		major canvas
Frank Dobson	1888–1963		portrait
Frederick Etchells	1886–1973		major canvas
Colin Gill	1892–1940		major canvas
Harold Gilman	1876–1919		major canvas
Charles Ginner	1878–1952		major canvas
Nina Hamnett	1890–1956		portrait
Edward Handley-Read	1869–1935		pastel drawing
Dudley Hardy	1866/7–1922		illustration
Herbert Hughes-Stanton	1870–1937		major canvas
Richard Jack	1866–1952		major canvases
David Jagger	d. 1958		canvas
Augustus John	1878–1961		unfinished major canvas
Eric Kennington	1888–1960		major canvas, drawings
James Kerr-Lawson	1865–1939		major canvases
Harold Knight	1874–1961		portraits
Laura Knight	1877–1970		major canvas
Wyndham Lewis	1884–1957		major canvas, drawings
Edward B. Lintott	1875–1951		portrait
Raymond Lintott	b. 1893		portrait
Flora Lion	1878–1958		portraits
William Logsdail	1859–1944		portraits
Ambrose McEvoy	1878–1927		portraits
Harrington Mann	1864–1937		portraits
Innes Meo			major canvas
Ivan Mestrovic	1883–1962	Yugoslavian	major relief sculpture
Gerald Moira	1864–1959		major canvases
Alfred Munnings	1878–1959		major canvas and numerous other works
Paul Nash	1889–1946		major canvas, a painting, prints and drawings
C. R. W. Nevinson	1889–1946		major canvases, prints
William Nicholson	1872–1949		major canvas
Julius Olsson	1864–1942		major canvas
William Orpen	1878–1931		portraits
Harold Piffard	1869–1939		portrait
Leonard Richmond	1878–1965		pastel drawings
William Roberts	1895–1980		major canvas
William Rothenstein	1872–1945		major canvas, drawings

Edvard Saltoft	1883–1939	Danish	prints
Charles Shannon	1863–1937		portrait
J. Byam Shaw	1872–1919		major canvas
Inglis Sheldon-Williams	1870–1940		major canvases
Clare Sheridan	1886–		sculptured bust
Charles Sims	1873–1928		major canvas, portrait
S. J. Solomon	1860–1927		portrait
Howard Somerville	1873–1927		portraits
G. Spencer-Pryse	1881–1956		prints
A. Stuart-Hill			portrait
Algernon Talmage	1871–1939		major canvases and other works
John Turnbull	1887–		major canvases
Edward Wadsworth	1889–1949		major canvas
Maurice Wagemans	1877–1927	Belgian	drawings
G. Spencer Watson	1869–1934		portrait
Louis Weiter/Whirter	1873–1932		major canvases
Norman Wilkinson	1878–1934		major canvases
F. D. Wood	1871–1926		sculpture
W. T. Wood	1877–1958		watercolours

Index to Lists of War Artists

Table 1   Wellington House Artists
Table 2   Efforts and Ideals Artists
Table 3   British War Memorials Committee Scheme 1
Table 4   British War Memorials Committee Scheme 2
Table 5   British War Memorials Committee, artist offered facilities
Table 6   Artists considered by BWMC whose work was acquired by IWM
Table 7   Artists whose works were purchased through the Bone Fund
Table 8a   Artists considered by BWMC
Table 8b   Other artists considered by BWMC and Wellington House
Table 9a   Artists employed or commissioned by IWM
Table 9b   RAMC artists
Table 9c   Artists with Mesopotamian Expeditionary Force
Table 10   War Office MI7(b) artists
Table 11   Glasgow Corporation artist
Table 12   European artists with work in Canadian collections

Adeney, Bernard   Table 4
Airy, Anna (Mrs Pocock) Table 6, Table 12
Aldin, Cecil   Table 9a
Allfree, Geoffrey   Table 9a
Arnold, Norman   Table 9a
Atwood, Clare   Table 6, Table 12

Bairnsfather, Bruce   Table 10
Barclay, Ethel   Table 12
Barraud, Cyril   Table 12
Bastien, Alfred   Table 12
Bateman, Henry   Table 8b
Baxter, David   Table 9b
Bayes, Walter   Table 3

Bechtel, B. Roberts   Table 8b
Becker, Henry   Table 8b
Beeton, Geneste   Table 9a
Bentley, Alfred   Table 8b
Bevan, Robert   Table 8b
Bomberg, David   Table 7, Table 12
Bone, Muirhead   Table 1, Table 12
Boyle   Table 9c
Brangwyn, Frank   Table 2, Table 12
Briault, S.   Table 9c
Brockhurst, Gerald   Table 8b
Brown, Gregory   Table 8b
Bryce, A. J. C.   Table 9a
Bundy, Edgar   Table 12

Cable, R.   Table 9c
Cain, Charles William   Table 9c
Cameron, David Y.   Table 3, Table 12
Carline, Richard   Table 9a
Carline, Sidney   Table 9a
Clausen, George   Table 3, Table 12
Clemens, Benjamin   Table 9b
Codrington, Isabel   Table 9a
Coke, Dorothy   Table 8a
Cole, Ernest   Table 8b
Collard, J.   Table 8b
Connard, Philip   Table 9a
Cooper, Alfred Egerton   Table 7
Cotterell, A. N.   Table 9b
Creelock   Table 8b
Cyriax, Tony   Table 7

Davis, G. Horace   Table 9a
Dawson, Montague   Table 9a
Dawson, Nelson   Table 9a

Dechaume-Geffroy, C.   Table 8b
Derrick, Thomas   Table 4
Dobson, Cowan   Table 9a
Dobson, Frank   Table 6, Table 12
Dodd, Francis   Table 1
Dodgson, John   Table 7
Douglas, Sholto   Table 9a
Dugdale, T. C.   Table 9a
Dulac, Edmund   Table 2

Epstein, Jacob   Table 7
Etchells, Frederick   Table 12
Everett, John   Table 8a
Eves, Reginald   Table 9a

Farrell, Fred   Table 11
Fergusson, John Duncan   Table 8a
Flemming-Williams, C. R.   Table 9a
Fletcher, Hanslip   Table 8b
Forbes, Stanhope   Table 9a
Fowler, Robert   Table 8b
Fox-Pitt, Douglas   Table 8b
Frampton, George   Table 9a

Garbe, Richard   Table 8b
Gertler, Mark   Table 8b
Gibbings, Robert   Table 8b, Table 9a
Giles, G. D.   Table 8b
Gill, Colin   Table 4, Table 12
Gill, Eric   Table 8b
Gilman, Harold   Table 12
Ginner, Charles   Table 12
Gordon, Jan   Table 9a
Graham, Glen   Table 9a
Grant, Duncan   Table 8b
Gray, Joseph   Table 9a
Gray, Ronald   Table 9a
Gregory, Leonard   Table 8b
Greiffenhagen, Maurice   Table 2
Guevara, Alvaro   Table 8b

Hacker, Arthur   Table 8b
Hamnet, Nina   Table 12
Handley-Read, Edward   Table 12
Harcourt, George   Table 9a
Hardy, Dudley   Table 12
Hartrick, A. S.   Table 2
Harvey, Harold   Table 8a
Hatherall, W.   Table 9a
Hayward, Alfred   Table 4
Hill, Adrian   Table 9a
Hill, Roderick   Table 8b
Hill, William   Table 8b
Hodge, Francis   Table 9a
Holmes, C. J.   Table 3
Hughes-Stanton, Herbert   Table 5, Table 12
Hyde, William   Table 9a

Isaac, Nellie   Table 9a

Jack, Richard   Table 12
Jackson, Ernest   Table 2

Jagger, C. S.   Table 4
Jagger, David   Table 8b, Table 12
Jamieson, Alexander   Table 8b
Japp, Darsie   Table 3
John, Augustus   Table 3, Table 12
Judge, W. E.   Table 9c

Kauffer, McKnight   Table 8b
Kemp-Welch, Lucy   Table 9a
Kennington, Eric   Table 1, Table 12
Kerr-Lawson, J.   Table 8b, Table 12
Keyes, Phyllis   Table 9a
King, Cecil   Table 9a
Knight, Harold   Table 12
Knight, Laura   Table 8b, Table 12
Kramer, Jacob   Table 8b

Lacey, E. H.   Table 8b
Lamb, Henry   Table 3
Lavery, John   Table 1
Ledward, Gilbert   Table 4
Lee, Rupert   Table 7
Lewis, A. Neville   Table 6
Lewis, Wyndham   Table 3, Table 12
Lintott, E. Barnard   Table 9a, Table 12
Lintott, Raymond   Table 12
Lion, Flora   Table 8a, Table 12
Lipscombe, Guy   Table 9a
Lithiby, Beatrice   Table 9a
Lobley, J. Hodgson   Table 9b
Logsdail, William   Table 12
Lowinsky, Thomas   Table 8b
Lumsden, E. S.   Table 8b
Lytton, Neville   Table 9a

M'Cormick, Arthur David   Table 9a
MacColl, D. S.   Table 7
Mackey, H. R.   Table 9b
MacLaren, Donald   Table 7
Mann, Harrington   Table 12
Martin, Edwin   Table 9b
Mason, Frank   Table 9a
Maxwell, Donald   Table 9a
McBey, James   Table 1
McEvoy, Ambrose   Table 3
McEvoy, Ambrose   Table 12
McGurk, C. D.   Table 9a
Meninsky, Bernard   Table 4
Meo, Innes   Table 8b, Table 12
Mestrovic, Ivan   Table 12
Moira, Gerald   Table 2, Table 12
Monk, William   Table 8b
Monkhouse, Victoria   Table 9a
Morgan, D. Carey   Table 9a
Morrice, J. W.   Table 8b
Morris, Carey   Table 8b
Moser, Oswald   Table 9a
Munnings, Alfred   Table 8a, Table 12

Nash, John   Table 4
Nash, Paul   Table 1, Table 12

Neilson-Gray, Nora	Table 9a	Slade, Adam	Table 8b
Nevinson, C. R. W.	Table 1, Table 12	Smith, Matthew	Table 8b
Newling, Edward	Table 9a	Smith, Robert Henry	Table 9a
Nicholson, William	Table 2, Table 12	Solomon, Gilbert B.	Table 9a
Noble, John Edwin	Table 9a	Solomon, S. J.	Table 12
		Somerville, Howard	Table 9a, Table 12
O'Reilly, A. R.	Table 9a	Spare, A. O.	Table 9a, Table 9b
Olivier, Herbert	Table 9a	Speed, Harold	Table 8b
Olsson, Julius	Table 12	Spencer, Gilbert	Table 3
Oppenheimer, Charles	Table 8a	Spencer, Stanley	Table 4
Orpen, William	Table 1, Table 12	Spencer-Pryse, G.	Table 1, Table 12
		Spradbury, Walter	Table 9b
Parkes, Oscar	Table 9a	Squire, Harold	Table 8a
Payne, Henry	Table 8b	Stabb, C. T.	Table 9a
Pearce, C. Maresco	Table 8b	Steer, P. Wilson	Table 3
Pears, Charles	Table 2, Table 9a	Strachan, Douglas	Table 8b
Pennell, Joseph	Table 1	Strang, Ian	Table 6
Philpot, Glyn	Table 6	Strang, William	Table 8b
Piffard, Harold	Table 12	Stuart-Hill, A.	Table 6, Table 12
Pirie, George	Table 9b	Sullivan, Edmund	Table 2
Pissarro, Lucien	Table 8b	Swynnerton, Annie	Table 8b
Pollard, W.	Table 9c		
Poole, Henry	Table 8b	Talmage, Algernon	Table 8b, Table 12
Proctor, Ernest	Table 8a	Taylor, Campbell	Table 9a
Pryde, James	Table 8b	Thomas, J. Harvard	Table 8b
		Toft, Alfonso	Table 8b
Raemaekers, Louis	Table 1	Tonks, Henry	Table 3
Reid, Stephen	Table 8b	Turnbull, John	Table 8a, Table 12
Reid, Stuart	Table 9a	Tweed, John	Table 8b
Revel, John Daniel	Table 9c		
Reynolds, Frank	Table 10	Underwood, Leon	Table 6
Richmond, Leonard	Table 12	Unwin, Francis S.	Table 7
Ricketts, Charles	Table 2		
Roberts, William	Table 4, Table 12	Wadsworth, Edward	Table 8b, Table 12
Rogers, Gilbert	Table 9b	Wagemans, Maurice	Table 12
Roslyn, Louis Frederick	Table 9a	Walcot, William	Table 8b
Rothenstein, William	Table 1, Table 12	Walton, Cecil, and E. A.	Table 9a
Rushbury, Henry	Table 4	Watson, G. Spencer	Table 12
Russell, Walter	Table 6	Weirter/Whirter, Louis	Table 9a, Table 12
Rutherston, Albert	Table 8b	Wheatley, John	Table 4
		White, S. B.	Table 9b
Sacre, Lester	Table 8b	Whiting, Frederick	Table 9a
Salisbury, Frank	Table 8b	Wiles, B. H.	Table 9c
Saltoft, Edvard	Table 12	Wilkinson, Norman	Table 9a, Table 12
Sargent, J. S.	Table 3	Williams, Margaret Lindsay	Table 8b
Schwabe, Randolph	Table 4	Williamson, Harold Sandys	Table 6
Seabrooke, Elliott	Table 7	Withers, Alfred	Table 8b
Shannon, Charles	Table 2, Table 12	Wolfe, H. G.	Table 9c
Shaw, J. Byam	Table 12	Wood, Francis Derwent	Table 9a, Table 12
Sheldon-Williams, Inglis	Table 12	Wood, Lawson	Table 8b
Shepperson, Claude	Table 2	Wood, W. T.	Table 4, Table 12
Sheridan, Clare	Table 12	Wright, John	Table 6
Sickert, Walter	Table 8b	Wyllie, Harold	Table 9a
Simpson, Charles	Table 8b		
Sims, Charles	Table 3, Table 12		

notes

ABBREVIATIONS

BBK, HLRO Beaverbrook papers, House of Lords Record Office
IWM   Imperial War Museum, Art Department
           BWMC: British War Memorials Committee
PRO   Public Records Office, The National Archive
           FO: Foreign Office papers
           INF: Ministry of Information papers
           T: Treasury files
TGA   Tate Gallery Archives

INTRODUCTION

1 Jane Marcus, 'Afterword. Corpus/Corps/Corpse: Writing the Body in/at War', in Helen Zenna Smith, *Not so quiet . . . Stepdaughters of War* (New York: Feminist Press, 1989), pp. 241–301.

2 See, for example, Charles Harrison, *English Art and Modernism, 1900–1939* (London and Indiana: Indiana University Press, 1981), and Richard Cork's two-volume *Vorticism and Abstract Art in the First Machine Age* (London: Gordon Fraser Gallery, 1976). This argument was repeated by various contributors to Paul Edwards, *Blast: Vorticism, 1914–1918* (Aldershot: Ashgate, 2000), such as the essays by Karin Orchard, Andrew Wilson and Cork. See also the introduction in Elizabeth Cowling and Jennifer Mundy, *On Classic Ground: Picasso, Léger, de Chirico and the New Classicism 1910–1930* (London: Tate Gallery, 1990), pp. 11–12. Richard Cork has commented that 'The 1920s was a quiet decade for all the former rebels, a time of retrenchment when the need to concentrate on placid subjects was matched by an equally strong desire to depict the observed world with greater exactitude and directness', Richard Cork, 'Machine Age, Apocalypse and Pastoral', in Susan Compton, ed., *British Art in the 20th Century: The Modern Movement* (London and Munich: Royal Academy of Arts, Prestel-Verlag, 1987), p. 71. See also the discussion in Jean Clair, 'Données d'un Problème', in Centre Nationale d'Art et de Culture Georges Pompidou, *Les Réalismes 1919–1939 Entre Révolution et Réaction* (Paris: Centre Georges Pompidou, 1981), pp. 13–14.

3 See both Joanne Bourke, *Dismembering the Male: Men's Bodies,* *Britain and the Great War* (London: Reaktion, 1996), and Graham Dawson, *Soldier Heroes: British Adventure, Empire and the Imagining of Masculinities* (London and New York: Routledge, 1994), who have also tended to frame their projects within a notion of redressing perceived errors in feminist research and theory. Dawson acknowledges a debt to feminist work but charges radical feminism, associated with the women's peace movement in the 1980s, with essentialism and with defining masculinity as homogenous and collective, almost as if it were a disorder. Bourke notes a reassertion of manliness in the inter-war years associated with male insecurity and a negative view of women's citizenship and autonomy. At the same time, however, she accuses feminism, meaning second-wave feminism in the 1970s, of ignoring 'the way . . . power structures oppress men', p. 14.

4 Avant-garde politics were closely imbricated with radical social and sexual politics not just in the pre-war period but throughout the conflict and after. See Lisa Tickner, 'English Modernism in the Cultural Field', in David Peters Corbett and Lara Perry, eds, *English Art 1860–1914: Modern Artists and Identity* (Manchester: Manchester University Press, 2000), p. 22.

5 Review of The Allied Artists' Association, in *The Egoist*, 1914, and letter to *The Egoist*, 1914, reprinted in Ezra Pound, *Gaudier-Brzeska: A Memoir* (New York: New Directions, 1970), pp. 30 and 37.

6 Evelyn Silber, *The Sculpture of Jacob Epstein with a Complete Catalogue* (Oxford: Phaidon, 1986), p. 33.

7 For example, David Bomberg joined up in November 1915,

William Roberts enlisted in early 1916, along with Wyndham Lewis. The pattern of artists volunteering for war service corresponds to a general pattern amongst professional workers. Until the introduction of conscription, one in four men of eligible age enlisted and self-employed professionals, and white collar workers were twice as likely to volunteer as manual workers. Around forty per cent of the occupational group covering artists was in the army by early 1916. See J. M. Winter, *The Great War and the British People* (Basingstoke and London: Macmillan Education, 1986), pp. 27 and 33–4.

8 Richard Cork, *Jacob Epstein: The Rock Drill Period* (London: Anthony D'Offay, 1973), p. 10.

9 Silber, *The Sculpture of Jacob Epstein*, p. 33.

10 Richard Cork, 'Vorticism and Sculpture', in Edwards, *Blast: Vorticism, 1914–1918*, p. 56.

11 See Evelyn Silber and David Finn, *Gaudier-Brzeska. Life and Art* (London: Thames and Hudson, 1996), p. 129.

12 This point is argued by Paul Peppis in '"Surrounded by a Multitude of Other Blasts": Vorticism and the Great War', *Modernism/Modernity*, vol. 4, no. 2, 1997, p. 61.

13 Jacob Epstein, *Let There be Sculpture: The Autobiography of Jacob Epstein* (London: Readers' Union, 1942 [London: Michael Joseph, 1940]), p. 44. He may have had other investments and also wrote 'Far from innovating, Gaudier always followed. . . . he . . . addressed me as Cher Maître', p. 45.

14 Wyndham Lewis 'The London Group. 1915 (March)', in Wyndham Lewis, *Blast: Review of the Great English Vortex* (*Blast II*) (Black Sparrow Press, Santa Barbara, 1981 [1915]), p. 78.

15 *Guardian*, 15 March 1915; *Observer*, 14 March 1915.

16 Lewis *Blast II*, p. 91.

17 Consequently, pre-war work by Ludwig Meidner, such as his Apocalyptic Cityscapes, or apocalyptic images by Kandinsky, are sometimes thought to have in some way unwittingly prophesised the war, rather than being embedded in more complex notions about European culture, industrialisation and war. For an account of the permeability of 1914–18 and ideas about the unstoppable force of industrialised war in nineteenth-century writings, see Daniel Pick, *War Machine: The Rationalisation of Slaughter in the Modern Age* (New Haven and London: Yale University Press, 1993).

18 Hal Foster, 'Prosthetic Gods', *Modernism/Modernity*, vol. 4, no. 2, 1997, pp. 6–7.

19 Paul Peppis, *Literature, Politics and the English Avant-Garde: Nation and Empire 1901–1918* (Cambridge: Cambridge University Press, 2000), p. 97.

20 'Note for Catalogue', *Vorticist Exhibition*, reprinted in Andrew Wilson and Phil Mertens eds., *Vorticism, Cahier*, no. 8/9 (Brussels: Internationaal Centrum voor Structuuranalyse en Constructivisme, 1988), p. 78.

21 Raymond Williams, 'The Politics of the Avant-Garde', in Tony Pinkney, ed., *The Politics of Modernism: Against the New Conformists* (London: Verso, 1989), pp. 50–51.

22 *Blast: Review of the Great English Vortex* (*Blast I*) (Black Sparrow Press, Santa Rosa, 1997 [1914]), p. 11.

23 See, for example, Bernard Smith, *Modernism's History: A Study in Twentieth-Century Art and Ideas* (New Haven and London: Yale University Press, 1998), p. 111. His source for this is Richard Cork's, *A Bitter Truth: Avant-Garde Art and the First World War* (New Haven and London: Yale University Press, 1994). Similar ideas were stated in the exhibition catalogue, Rainer Rother, ed., *Die letzten Tage der Menschheit. Bilder des Ersten Weltkrieges. Eine Ausstellung des Deutschen Historischen Museums, Berlin, der Barbican Art Gallery, London, und der Staatlichen Museen zu Berlin* (Preußischer Kulturbesitz in Verbindung mit dem Imperial War Museum, London, Berlin: Deutsches Historisches Museum/Ars Nicolai, 1994), of which Cork's project was part. In an introductory essay titled 'The bitter truth behind the propagated appearance [or pretence]' (Die bittere Wahrheit hinter dem propagierten Schein), Rainer Rother wrote that images from the First World War could be understood only within a framework of either disguising the unpalatable reality of war or uncovering a truth that had been glossed over, of either promulgating an aestheticisation or striving to resist deception. 'Ob ein Schein propagiert oder eine vertuschte Wahrheit aufgedeckt werden sollte: die Bilder des Ersten Weltkrieges haben ihre Unschuld verloren. Sie stellten dienstfertig den schönen Schein dar, oder sie gingen aufrecht gegen ihn an. Daß es noch Bilder des Krieges gäbe, die von solcher Alternative frei wären, ist seither Illusion', p. 9.

24 Peter Paret argues for the possibility of depicting 'the war's human costs' as expressing 'a fatalistic acceptance of what is regarded as inevitable'. 'The Artist as Staatsbürger: Aspects of the Fine Arts and the Prussian State before and during the First World War', *German Studies Review*, vol. 6, no. 3, 1983, p. 435.

25 I want to raise here a brief point of clarification about the terms 'avant-garde' and 'modernism'. Raymond Williams has identified three main phases in avant-garde and modernist art, beginning in the late nineteenth century. First, artists began to produce innovative work in opposition to the academies and to promote their work within the existing structures of the art market. Alternative groups, who were more radically innovative, then seceded to organise their own means of production, distribution and publicity. This led to fully oppositional groups who attacked not only existing cultural establishments but the whole social order. Avant-garde art proposed a rupture or break with tradition and a projection into a new future. Williams argues that it is not easy to separate the terms 'avant-garde' and 'modernism' and that the labels are often applied retrospectively, but he identifies 'modernism' with the second phase and 'avant-garde', the more militant term, with the third. Modernist artists conceived a new art to match a new social and perceptual world. Avant-garde artists tended to renounce received ideas about progression, 'a progress already repetitively defined', in favour of 'a militant creativity which would revive and liberate humanity'. Current literature on British art in this period uses the terms 'avant-garde' and 'modernism' together with 'modern' and 'progressive' interchangeably. I have in mind Harrison's *English Art and Modernism*, first published in 1981

and reprinted in 1994. Harrison writes, in the preface to his book, that he is using the term 'modernist' in the sense of retrospective and historical judgement and 'avant-garde' as a subordinate term suggestive of a nodal point in the development of the modern. More recently, Lisa Tickner has argued that distinguishing between modernism and avant-garde is ultimately not very useful; *Modern Life and Modern Subjects: British Art in the Early Twentieth Century* (New Haven and London: Yale University Press, 2000), p. 118. In London in 1914, there were several distinctive avant-garde groups and conflict within the avant-garde. The most radical of these, the artists associated with Wyndham Lewis and the Vorticists, also attacked the whole social order, sometimes identifying it with Victorian values, in writings like the journal *Blast*. In a sense, avant-garde art in London, when the war broke out, was at a point of transition between Williams's second and third phases. See Raymond Williams, 'The Politics of the Avant-Garde', pp. 50–51.

26 *The Times*, 10 March 1915. For Edward Storer, writing in *New Witness* on 11 March 1915, modernist art was not just the negation of art but a form of treason.

27 For example, Claude Phillips, art critic of the *Daily Telegraph*, argued that the Whitechapel exhibition, 'Twentieth-Century Art: (A Review of Modern Movements)', May 1914, revealed that modern art was now an established feature of the art scene and that it had to be treated and cured like an infection or a disease. For Phillips, modern art was the product of foreign influence by artists like Picasso, 'despotic monarch of the Cubists', while Duncan Grant had been corrupted by Matisse in ways that were 'grotesque and deformed'. Undated press cutting in Nevinson's Press Cuttings collection, Tate Gallery Archives (TGA), c.May 1914.

28 See the discussion in Stella Tillyard, *The Impact of Modernism, 1900–1920: Early Modernism and the Arts and Crafts Movement in Edwardian England* (London: Routledge, 1988), pp. 104 ff., and 106. In 1913, an exhibition of the art of the insane was held in London as part of a medical congress. This sparked a number of newspaper articles in the popular press associating modern art with insanity. T. B. Hyslop, Physician Superintendent at Bethlem Royal Hospital, had published an article in 1911, 'Post-Illusionism and Art in the Insane', in which comparisons between modern art and art produced in asylums were covertly made. See the discussion in John M. MacGregor, *The Discovery of the Art of the Insane* (Princeton: Princeton University Press, 1989), pp. 162–6.

29 Sam Hynes argues that literature detecting symptoms of a 'sickness' in English life and culture was retrospective and dated from the war but the evidence of pre-war art criticism contradicts this. *A War Imagined: The First World War and English Culture* (London: Bodley Head, 1990), p. 10.

30 *Manchester Guardian*, 13 March 1915.

31 *Outlook*, 31 July 1915.

32 In the 'War Number' of *Blast*, Lewis discussed Germany and made distinctions between different aspects of German culture in order to modify a rejection of all things German without appearing to be pro-German. Lewis also insisted on the vulgarity, brutality and obscenity of war against the self-deception, romanticism and idealism that he detected in liberal English views of the war; 'Editorial', 'War Notes', *Blast II*, pp. 5–6 and 9–16.

33 Nevinson wrote to the *Observer* in October 1914 that, with Berlin and Munich out of bounds, London would become the 'mecca' of European art and 'silence that vile saying of so many Parisian and English artists, "that the bankruptcy of Germany will mean their [the artists'] starvation"'. 4 October 1914.

34 *Globe*, 26 February 1915.

35 *The Times*, 10 March 1915.

36 *Evening News*, 13 March 1915.

37 *The Italian Futurist Painters* (London: Sackville Gallery, n.d. 1912), p. 23.

38 *Daily News and Leader*, 6 March 1915.

39 *Daily Telegraph*, 27 November 1915.

40 From the start of the war, there were sharp rises in prices, particularly for food, and artists, in common with the general population, began to feel the pinch. Artists' societies experienced reductions in sales and declining attendance figures at exhibitions from the early months of the war. The International Society, an artists' organisation that represented a more distilled version of the Royal Academy and the New English Art Club, reported a decline in income. For example, returns from the exhibition in October 1914 amounted to only £38 8s. (£38. 40), compared with £94 9s. (£94.45) from the spring show, and the Society decided, in view of the restricted gate, to cut down on the number of newspaper advertisements for the exhibition; minutes of a Council Meeting held at the Grosvenor Gallery on 22 October 1914, Minute Book of the International Society of Sculptors Painters and Gravers (TGA 738.3). The exhibition in spring 1915 made a loss of £117 0s. 5d. (£117.20) 'largely owing to the very small gate and lack of commission on sales', compared with a profit of £144 12s. 5d. (£144.62) in spring 1913; minutes Council Meetings held on 15 September 1915 and 8 August 1913 (TGA 738.3). Disappointment with the attendances and sales at wartime shows of the Society were reflected in reviews of the exhibitions. Henry Tonks wrote to D. S. MacColl in September 1914 that 'Already people are making application to the Artists Benevolent Society. It is a very serious question, and one you will be able to help in very much.' Quoted in Joseph Hone, *The Life of Henry Tonks* (London: William Heinemann, 1939), p. 111. Retrenchment in the art market was not entirely a consequence of general inflation curtailing disposable incomes. Audiences also stayed away from the nation's art galleries, as though art was not relevant to the war effort. At the Tate on Millbank, numbers dropped by a third: 182,705 visitors in 1915 compared with 242,195 in 1913. Papers on the closure of London museums and galleries PRO, (T 1 11922). Reviewing the state of the market in 1916, Frank Rutter noted that what had particularly suffered was the production of major ambitious works of art. People with large incomes were particularly cautious in their purchases and the market had preferred small works

at modest prices. Prosperity for artists was 'sporadic, not general,' and had favoured 'little fish only'; *Sunday Times*, 31 December 1916. Jan Gordon, writing under the nom de plume John Salis, noted that prices for portraits had declined by seventy-five per cent; 'The Reward of the Patriot', *New Witness*, 11 May 1916. The same general contraction was also experienced in Paris, as Malcolm Gee has shown: 'In the first two years of the war, the Parisian art market was stagnant . . . It was only in 1917 that the market showed real signs of coming to life again'; 'The Avant-Garde, Order and the Art Market, 1916–23', *Art History*, vol. 2, no. 1, March 1979, pp. 96–8. Much criticism in late 1915 and early 1916 commented on the lack of pictures of war by artists; for example, art had continued 'a calm enjoyment of its habitual detachment' from picturing events best left to the illustrated papers. *Westminster Gazette*, 30 November 1915.

41 *Sunday Times*, 5 March 1916.

42 Frank Rutter wrote, 'The pitiable horror of war has never been more powerfully emphasised in paint . . . Had this awful scene [La Patrie] been presented merely as an actuality it could only have been offensive, but Mr Nevinson has chosen the method of an epic poet rather than that of the sensational journalist and his pictorial rendering of the scene is dignified and hallowed by his original emotion remembered in tranquillity.' The work suggested that art dealt with 'real and serious things, the pity of war . . . , and it would be a monstrosity of criticism to permit threnody to a poet and not to a painter'; *Sunday Times*, 4 June 1916.

43 Reviewers assured readers that soldiers home on leave had confirmed its veracity, for example, *Yorkshire Post*, 26 September 1916; *Globe*, 28 September 1916; *Colour*, November 1916.

44 Cited in Richard Cork, 'Allies of the Avant-Garde: Patterns of Advanced Art in Britain 1910–1920', in Bowness, Collins, Cork, Darracott, et al., *British Contemporary Art 1910–1990: Eighty Years of Collecting by The Contemporary Art Society* (London: The Herbert Press, 1991), p. 28.

45 P. G. Konody, *Modern War Paintings by C. R. W. Nevinson* (London: Grant Richards Limited, 1917), pp. 20 and 21.

46 *Evening News*, 27 September 1916.

47 See Andrew Causey, *Paul Nash* (Oxford: Clarendon Press, 1980), p. 73.

48 Lawrence Bynion [sic], *The New Statesman*, June 1917 (TGA, TAM 38: Paul Nash Press Cuttings, Book 3).

49 *Daily Telegraph*, 12 May 1916.

50 Mary Bone, Introduction, in *Sir Muirhead Bone: Exhibition of Drawings from the Imperial War Museum and National Maritime Museum* (London: Imperial War Museum, 1966), and Lucy Masterman, *C. F. G. Masterman: A Biography* (London: Nicholson and Watson, 1939), p. 286. At the same time, Bone was in touch with Stephen Tallents at the Ministry of Munitions, as well as approaching the Medical Research Committee to make drawings for a medical history of the war. The main correspondence is in *Artists at the Front: Muirhead Bone* (IWM, G4010/27 and PRO, FO 395.47, News: General Files).

51 On the establishment of Wellington House see M. L. Sanders and Philip M. Taylor, *British Propaganda during the First World War, 1914–1918* (London: Macmillan, 1982) pp. 38–9 and Masterman, *Masterman*, p. 272.

52 In a letter to V. N., 16 December 1915, Masterman recounted how Lloyd George had raised the matter of propaganda in the Cabinet on 28 August 1914. The Prime Minister, Asquith, had replied that it was obviously Masterman's job. The work was meant to be part-time but Masterman found it totally preoccupying. Masterman Papers, University of Birmingham, Special Collections.

53 Frank Rutter, *Since I was Twenty-Five* (London: Constable and Co., 1927), p. 55.

54 See Seth Koven, 'From Rough Lads to Hooligans: Boy Life, National Culture and Social Reform', Andrew Parker, Mary Rosso, Doris Sommer, and Patricia Yaeger, eds., *Nationalisms and Sexualities* (New York and London: Routledge, 1992), and his 'The Whitechapel Picture Exhibitions and the Politics of Seeing' in Daniel J. Sherman and Irit Rogoff, eds., *Museum Culture. Histories, Discourses, Spectacles* (New York and London: Routledge, 1994). *From the Abyss: Of its Inhabitants, By one of them* was the title of a collection of essays by Masterman published in 1902.

55 These included a Captain Creelock, Arthur Hacker R. A., suggested by the *Illustrated London News*, and Jacob Kramer. The rejection of Kramer is discussed in Sue Malvern, '"War as it is": The Art of Muirhead Bone, C. R. W. Nevinson and Paul Nash, 1916–17', *Art History*, vol. 9, no. 4, December 1986, p. 504.

56 Winter, *The Great War and the British People*, p. 81.

57 Masterman, *Masterman*, p. 287.

58 Approximately thirty per cent of men aged 20 to 24 in 1914 died in the Great War. At the start of the war, Nash and Nevinson were 25 and Kennington 26. Their chances of being killed were about 1 in 3 or 1 in 4.

CHAPTER ONE

1 Report of the Work of the Bureau established for the purpose of laying before Neutral Nations and the Dominions the case of Great Britain and her Allies, 7 June 1915, p. 2 (PRO, INF 4/5).

2 Claud Schuster, chief executive officer until January 1916, wrote to Masterman on 4 December 1914 when he was preparing the First Report, '. . . I wish you could work into it . . . two . . . extracts warning us against indiscriminate propaganda. I am sure we are going to be pressed from all sources to do all sorts of silly things, and I should like the mind of the Cabinet to be prepared before hand'; Masterman Papers, Birmingham University, Special Collections.

3 Memorandum from Alfred Yockney, secretary to official war artists, to Masterman, undated (c. January 1918). James McBey (IWM 83/3).

4 Wellington House sought sanction from the Treasury to extend authorised expenditure to include Great Britain because it was considered useful to place Wellington House's

pamphlets on sale to the public in order to obtain the imprint of a London publisher and disguise a document's official origins, to serve public demand, to raise revenue and also because 'we have sometimes been influenced by the fact that a publication is valuable for the purpose of domestic propaganda'. It was intended to distribute free publications to the General Federation of Trades Unions or the Workers' Educational Union 'for purposes of domestic propaganda'; Claud Schuster, Wellington House, to Secretary to the Treasury, 17 September 1915 (PRO, T 1 11992: 22535).

5   Ernest Gowers, Wellington House, to Montgomery, Foreign Office, 29 May 1915 (PRO, FO 371 2559: Political M.G.(N) Files (Miscellaneous General (News)) 70104). Claud Schuster to Locock, Foreign Office, 12 November 1915 (PRO, FO 371 2576: War General no. 170797, 1915).

6   Fine Art Society to Alfred Yockney, 15 October 1918 (IWM, 282/6: Raemaekers, Louis).

7   Gowers to Montgomery, 11 November 1916 (PRO, FO 395 36: News, Spain Portugal no. 227831).

8   Steve Baker, 'Describing Images of the National Self: Popular Accounts of the Construction of Pictorial Identity in the First World War Poster', *Oxford Art Journal*, vol. 13, no. 2, 1990, p. 24.

9   Daniel Pick, *War Machine: The Rationalisation of Slaughter in the Modern Age* (New Haven and London: Yale University Press, 1993), p. 140. Emphasis in the original.

10 *The 'Land and Water' Edition of Raemaekers' Cartoons* (London: Land and Water, February 1916).

11 As E. J. Hobsbawm points out, in the study of language 'the first meaning of the word "nation" indicates origin or descent: "naissance, extraction, rang"'. He cites Froissart's 'je fus retourné au pays de ma nation en la conté de Haynnau' (I was returned to the land of my birth/origin in the country of Hainault); *Nations and Nationalism since 1870: Programme, Myth, Reality* (Cambridge: Cambridge University Press, 1990), p. 15.

12 Ruth Harris, 'The "Child of the Barbarian": Rape, Race and Nationalism in France during the First World War', *Past & Present*, no. 141, November 1993.

13 See, for example, the discussion in Richard Cork, *A Bitter Truth. Avant-Garde Art and the Great War* (New Haven and London: Yale University Press, 1994), pp. 203–4.

14 For example, in his catalogue of Nash's work, Andrew Causey does not cite *British Artists at the Front* as part of the painting's reproduction history, although this was the first public appearance of the image. Andrew Causey, *Paul Nash* (Oxford: Clarendon Press, 1980), p. 366.

15 Cork, *A Bitter Truth*, p. 198.

16 Margaret Nash, 'Memoirs of Paul Nash, 1913–1946' (TGA, 769.2.6: p. 24).

17 See, for example, Roger Fry, 'An Essay in Aesthetics', *New Quarterly*, April 1909 and *Vision and Design*, ed. J. B. Bullen (Oxford: Oxford University Press, 1981, pp. 12–27 [1920]).

18 Clement Greenberg, 'Avant Garde and Kitsch', in John O'Brian, ed., *Clement Greenberg: Perceptions and Judgments, 1939–1944*, vol. 1, *Clement Greenberg: The Collected Essays and Criticism* (Chicago and London: University of Chicago Press, 1986), p. 21.

19 T. J. Clark, *Farewell to an Idea: Episodes from a History of Modernism* (New Haven and London: Yale University Press, 1999), p. 305.

20 Francis Stopford, Introduction, 'The "Land and Water" Edition of Raemaekers' Cartoons (London: Land and Water, 1916), n. p.

21 It was consistently argued that 'the intrusion of a Government, or of persons inspired by Government, into the sphere of opinion, invariably excites suspicion and resentment'. Report, June 1915, p. 2 (PRO, INF 4/5).

22 Claud Schuster to Robinson, 3 December 1914 (PRO, INF 4/1B) and Report, June 1915, p. 2.

23 Second Report on the Work Conducted for the Government at Wellington House, 1 February 1916, p. 5 (PRO, INF 4/5).

24 Lucy Masterman, *C. F. G. Masterman: A Biography* (London: Nicholson and Watson, 1939), p. 275.

25 C. F. G. Masterman, *In Peril of Change*, quoted in Masterman, *Masterman*, p. 58.

26 See Stuart Hall and Bill Schwarz, 'State and Society, 1880–1930', in Mary Langan and Bill Schwarz, eds., *Crises in the British State 1880–1930* (London: Hutchison and Co Ltd., 1985): 'Their whole theorization was antipathetical to any analysis which privileged class relations for they reasoned that this was to succumb to the dictates of a singular social interest rather than elaborating a view of society which could accommodate the full spectrum of different interests.' pp. 22–3.

27 Robert Colls, 'Englishness and the Political Culture', in Robert Colls and Philip Dodd, eds., *Englishness: Politics and Culture 1880–1920* (London: Croom Helm, 1986), pp. 78 and 52.

28 Peter Chalmers Mitchell, 'Propaganda,' in *Encyclopaedia Britannica*, vol. 32, 1922, pp. 176–7. See also Raymond Williams on 'Advertising: the Magic System', in *Problems in Materialism and Culture* (London: Verso, 1980), p. 180. 'It was in the war itself, when now not a market but a nation had to be controlled and organised, yet in democratic conditions and without some of the older compulsions, that the new kinds of persuasion were developed and applied . . . The need to control nominally free men, like the need to control nominally free customers, lay very deep in the new kind of society.'

29 Colin Lovelace, 'British Press Censorship During the First World War', in George Boyce, James Curran and Pauline Wingate, *Newspaper History from the Seventeenth Century to the Present Day* (London: Constable, 1978), pp. 311–15.

30 'Belgium would be for [Lloyd George], as for almost all the others a way out of an impossible moral dilemma. It would allow him to abandon whatever traditional radical principles he had inherited . . . without ceasing to claim that heritage.' Zara S. Steiner, *Britain and the Origins of the First World War* (London: Macmillan, 1977), p. 235.

31 Arthur Marwick, *The Deluge: British Society and the First World War* (London: Macmillan, 1975 [1965]), p. 157.

32 J. H. Grainger, *Patriotisms: Britain 1900–1939* (London: Routledge and Kegan Paul, 1986), pp. 156 and 166 and the chapter 'Little Englanders'.

33 Alun Howkins, 'The Discovery of Rural England', in Colls and Dodd, *Englishness: Politics and Culture*.

34 Alex Potts, ' "Constable Country" between the Wars', in Raphael Samuel, ed., *Patriotism: The Making and Unmaking of British National Identity*, vol. 3 (London: Routledge, 1989), p. 163.

35 Masterman found the essence of 'Englishness' in a southern landscape and invoked a millenarian sense of impending death: 'Over [this] . . . vision of a secular decay Nature still flings the splendour of her dawns and sunsets upon a land of radiant beauty. Here are deep rivers flowing beneath old mills and churches; high-roofed red barns and large thatched houses; with still unsullied expanses of cornland and wind-swept moor and heather, and pine woods looking down valleys upon green gardens and long stretches of quiet down standing white and clean from the blue surrounding sea. Never perhaps, in the memorable and spacious story of this island's history has the land beyond the city offered so fair an inheritance to the children of its people, as to-day, under the visible shadow of its end.' C. F. G. Masterman, *The Condition of England* (London: Methuen, 1909), p. 208.

36 September 1914. 'This is No Case of Petty Right or Wrong', December 1915, *Edward Thomas: Selected Poems and Prose* (Harmondsworth: Penguin, 1981), p. 236.

37 'This England', *Edward Thomas: Selected Poems and Prose*, p. 164.

38 Potts, ' "Constable Country" ', p. 162.

39 'The first time I went out with Montague was in August 1916 . . . After visiting an advanced dressing station in the cellars of the Château of Contalmaison . . . we went back to a slope of the down behind and sat down to eat our lunch. Below us was the battle, and despite the mesmerism of Montague's calm elation at the scene, my sandwiches and my teeth didn't seem to keep proper time together'; Oliver Elton, *C. E. Montague: A Memoir* (London: Chatto and Windus, 1929), p. 138.

40 'I did not like to imagine war scenes and so only drew what I saw, and this only when I had a chance to digest it. This limited me very much and I am afraid resulted in rather prosaic work.' Bone to ffoulkes, IWM, 31 March 1929 (IWM, 43A/2: Muirhead Bone, February 1928–December 1935).

41 Charles Merewether, 'Traces of Loss', in Michael S. Roth, ed., *Irresitible Decay: Ruins Reclaimed* (Los Angeles: Getty Research Institute for the History of Art and the Humanities, 1997), p. 29.

42 Harry Salpeter: 'About Muirhead Bone: Cold and Restrained, He Still Ranks Among the World's Pre-eminent Etchers', *Coronet*, September 1938, p. 91.

43 Bone to Gowers, 1 September 1916 (G4010/27, IWM).

44 Steiner, *Britain and the Origins of the First World War*, p. 101.

45 C. E. Montague, 'The Western Front', in *The Western Front*, part I (London: Country Life and George Newnes, November 1916), n. p.

46 Montague, 'The Somme Battlefield', in *The Western Front*, part II, January 1917.

47 Montague, 'The Battle of Arras', in *The Western Front*, part VI, May 1917.

48 See the extended discussion in Paul Fussell, *The Great War and Modern Memory* (Oxford: Oxford University Press, 1977 [1975]), 'Arcadian Resources', p. 231ff.

49 Hewett, 2 June 1916, to a friend, in Laurence Housman, ed., *War Letters of Fallen Englishmen* (London: Victor Gollancz Ltd., 1930), p. 138.

50 Montague, 'The Western Front', in *The Western Front*, part I.

51 '1916–1917', Introduction to Montague, *The Western Front*, vol. I, June 1917.

52 Plate XXVIIb, *The Western Front*, part I.

53 Plate LII, *The Western Front*, part III.

54 'The Upper Hand', March 1917, *The Western Front*, part IV.

55 Montague, 'The Somme Battlefield'.

56
      Of the same lump (as it is said)
      For honour and dishonour made,
      Two sister vessels. Here is one.

      It makes a goblin of the sun.

      So pure, – so fall'n! How dare to think
      Of the first common kindred link?

I am indebted to Professor Raymond Wilson for searching out this reference.

57 Linda Nochlin, 'Lost and Found: Once More the Fallen Woman', in *Women, Art and Power and Other Essays* (London: Thames and Hudson, 1989), pp. 72–3.

58 See Michele J. Shover, 'Roles and Images of Women in World War I Propaganda', *Politics and Society*, no. 5, 1975, pp. 479–80.

59 Montague, 'The Somme Battlefield'.

60 C. E. Montague, 'Trench Scenery', February 1917, *The Western Front*, part II.

61 Montague, 'Trench Scenery'.

62 C. E. Montague, *Disenchantment* (London: Chatto and Windus, 1922), p. 8.

63 'Deserts', June 1917, *The Western Front, Part VII*.

64 C. E. Montague, *The Front Line* (London: Hodder and Stoughton, 1917), p. 3. 'I shall . . . suggest that ideology "acts" or "functions" in such a way that it "recruits" subjects among the individuals (it recruits them all), or "transforms" the individuals into subjects (it transforms them all) by that very precise operation which I have called interpellation or hailing, and which can be imagined along the lines of the most commonplace everyday police (or other) hailing: "Hey, you there!" ' Louis Althusser, 'Ideology and the State', in *Lenin and Philosophy and Other Essays* (London: NLB, 1977 [1971]), pp. 162–3.

65 For example, Robert Cumming misses the point when he asserts that Bone's pictures are neutral and without comment or distortion. This is a view of his work that Bone himself promoted, whilst, at the same time, Montague 'reveals the weakness of many a well-intentioned writer: he saw only what he wanted to see'; Robert Cumming, 'Recorder of a World at War: Sir Muirhead Bone

(1876–1953)', *Country Life*, vol. 163, no. 4207, 23 February 1978, p. 469.

66 C. E. Montague, 'War as it is', in *The Western Front*, vol. II, November 1917.

67 Montague, 'Trench Scenery'.

68 A publication to be called 'Britain's Fighting Forces' which would have reproduced works from several artists together was ruled out as too expensive and too complex. Dodgson to C. F. G. Masterman, 1 September 1917 (IWM: Western Front. English and General, M999 Part VII) and Yockney to Willson, 20 October 1917 (IWM, 266A/6: Nevinson 1917–1918).

69 Campbell Dodgson, 'The Artist', in *British Artists at the Front, Part One: C. R. W. Nevinson* (London: Country Life and George Newnes, 1918), n. p.

70 In biographical notes for Wellington House in 1917, Nash wrote 'Eventually failed for the Navy owing to mathematical inaptitude'. (IWM, 267A/6: Nash, Paul 1917–18).

71 'I do not think that . . . Nash learned very much, either from Professor or pupil.' John Salis (Jan Gordon), 'The Artist', in *British Artists at the Front, Part Three: Paul Nash* (London: Country Life and George Newnes, 1918).

72 Robert Ross, 'The Artist', in *British Artists at the Front, Part Two: Sir John Lavery* (London: Country Life and George Newnes, 1918).

73 'He [Lavery] evinced no taste whatever for discipline and betrayed no assiduity for study – those inevitable preludes to prosperity and virtue. . . . A distaste for arithmetic has always characterised the artistic temper, . . .' Ross, 'The Artist', *Sir John Lavery*.

74 Dodgson, 'The Artist', *C. R. W. Nevinson*, and Salis, 'The Artist', *Paul Nash*.

75 Campbell Dodgson, 'The Artist', in *British Artists at the Front, Part Four: Eric Kennington* (London: Country Life, 1918).

76 'There was general agreement among soldiers and civilians, art critics, and plain men . . . These were the pictures to make men come forward and do their duty for their country. They were full of life, manliness and force.' Dodgson, 'The Artist', *C. R. W. Nevinson*.

77 C. E. Montague, 'The Front's Foundations', in *British Artists at the Front, Part Two*.

78 ''Tis strange, – but true; for truth is always strange; / Stranger than fiction' Byron, 'Don Juan', canto XIV. CI.

79 Nash complained to his friend the poet Gordon Bottomley about Montague's preface: 'All that talk by Montague in the prevace [sic] is nonsense of course. Wire does & did grow as it is shown here, and I was neither mad nor drunk or trying to show an abnormal vision when I drew it. [sic] . . . I am afraid I don't look so beautiful & Blake-like as W. R. has drawn me but I like to think so'; Nash to Bottomley, 16 July 1918, in Claude Abbott and Anthony Bertram, *Poet and Painter: Letters between Gordon Bottomley and Paul Nash, 1910–1946* (Bristol: Redcliffe Press, 1990 [1955]), p. 98.

80 Byron's verse continues 'if it could be told, / How much would novels gain by the exchange! / How differently the world would men behold!' Byron, 'Don Juan', canto XIV. CI.

81 Montague, Plate VI, *British Artists at the Front, Part Two*.

82 John Rothenstein, *Paul Nash as War Artist*, in Margot Eates, ed., *Paul Nash: Paintings, Drawings and Illustrations*, usually called Memorial Volume (London: Lund Humphries, 1948), p. 17.

83 *Inverness Copse, Sunrise* [sic] (IWM, 267/6: 'Ref. photos P. Nash'). Dated as passed by Lee, 7 January 1918.

84 17 March 1917, reprinted in Paul Nash, *Outline: An Autobiography and Other Writings* (London: Faber, 1949), p. 189.

85 Nash to Rothenstein, May–July 1917 (National Art Library, Victoria and Albert Museum: MSS (Typewritten) English. Nash, Paul. Paul Nash Letters).

86 Nash to his wife, 13–16 November 1917, Nash, *Outline*, p. 211.

87 See the introduction by Andrew Causey to the reprint of Nash, *Outline* (London: Columbus Books, 1988).

88 Causey in Nash, *Outline* (1988), p. ix and xiii.

89 Herbert Read, *Outline* (1988), foreword, signed and dated July 1948, p. xx. In the memorial volume to Paul Nash, Read verified Nash's First World War paintings: 'I can testify, as one who often traversed it in those days, that The Menin Road [begun in 1918], for example, is, as a realisation of the scene, completely authentic.' p. 11.

90 'His comprehension of nature is a thing as born in him as his skeleton.' What Nash had done was to see nature 'not for its poetic sensuality, but for its poetic truths'. He had, said Gordon, 'drawn the veil [of nature] aside'. John Salis, 'The Artist', *British Artists at the Front, Part Three*.

91 Salis, 'The Artist'.

92 Montague, Plate I, *British Artists at the Front, Part Three*.

93 See the discussion in Lewis Johnson, *Prospects, thresholds, interiors. Watercolours from the National Collection at the Victoria and Albert Museum* (Cambridge: Cambridge University Press, 1994), p. 224.

94 Johnson has discussed how part IV of Ruskin's *Modern Painters* was written with the Crimean War in mind, where redemption and national destiny received its fulfilment in the formation of a national school of modern art, particularly landscape painting. The war dead, Ruskin's 'lost multitudes', return to haunt 'the willing brooks and peaceful vales of England' and by the repetition of dawn skies stained red, the nation, 'the redeemed land recaptures its dead as sacrifices to its own identity and project, its projected identity'; Johnson, *Prospects*, p. 10.

95 Geoffrey Grigson, 'A Metaphysical Artist', *The Listener*, 1 April 1948, p. 549.

CHAPTER TWO

1 J. E. Crawford Flitch, *The Great War: The Fourth Year: Paintings by C. R. W. Nevinson* (London: Grant Richards, 1918), p. 7.

2 Arnold Bennett, 'William Orpen at the Front' in *War Paintings and Drawings Executed on the Western Front by Major Sir William Orpen KBC, ARA* (London: Agnew's, 1918), p. 4.

3 *Graphic*, 8 May 1917.

4 *Graphic*, 11 May 1918.

5 *Second Report on the Work Conducted for the Government at Wellington House.* 1 February 1916, p. 7 (PRO, INF 4/5).

6 Papers relating to Yockney's appointment are in PRO, T 1 11992.

7 Campbell Dodgson to Watt, 25 May 1916 (IWM, G4010/27: 'Artists at the Front, Muirhead Bone'), Watt to Sheringham, 11 February 1918 (IWM, M999/2: part 1. 'The Western Front: Drawings by Muirhead Bone. American').

8 Masterman to Charteris, 2 November 1916, and to Bone, 7 November 1916 (IWM, M999: part 1, 'The Western Front').

9 Yockney to Sanderson, 20 February 1918 (IWM, M999/1: part VIII, 'The Western Front: Drawings by Muirhead Bone').

10 Yockney to Willson, 18 July 1917 (IWM, M999: part v, 'The Western Front: English and General'). Whitechapel Art Gallery, report by Campbell Ross, autumn 1917 (IWM, G3100/4: part III, 'Exhibitions: Muirhead Bone's Drawings').

11 Curator, Mapin Art Gallery, to Yockney, 11 August 1917, and Ryman, Oxford, to Yockney, 11 July 1917 (IWM, G3100/4: part III, 'Exhibitions: Muirhead Bone's Drawings').

12 Frances Carey and Anthony Griffiths, *Avant-Garde British Printmaking: 1914–1960* (London: British Museum Publications, 1990), p. 50. Of 3,300 prints sent to the States, 2,059 were returned. In 1922 the series was wound up. See (IWM, 381/8A: 'Art: Efforts and Ideals'). Cambridge University patriotically donated a set to the Harvard Club, New York, in memory of the Harvard graduates who had fallen in the army of the British Empire; 'British War Pictures', *Scribner's Magazine*, vol. 63, no. 6, June 1918, p. 642. The prints were thoughtfully provided by the Foreign Office, who originated the idea of the gift in response to a feeling that 'Harvard has rather drifted away from us lately', Butler to Gaselee, 25 October 1917 (PRO, FO 395 81: 'Britain's "Efforts and Ideals" Series of Prints').

13 20 February 1917 (IWM, 300/7: 'Henry Tonks').

14 See Robin Reisenfeld, 'The Revival, Transformation, and Dissemination of the Print Portfolio in Germany and Austria, 1890 to 1930', in Richard A. Born and Stephanie d'Alessandro, eds., *The German Print Portfolio, 1890–1930: Serials for a Private Sphere* (London: Philip Wilson Publishers, 1992).

15 Laurence Binyon, 'In Expressiveness', *New Statesman*, 4 August 1917.

16 P. G. Konody, *Observer*, 8 July 1917.

17 Charles Marriott, 'Art and War: A False Comparison', in *Land and Water*, 2 August 1917, p. 40.

18 Marriott, 'Art and War'.

19 Masterman had asked that the text accompanying the plates should be signed and addressed from GHQ 'otherwise the reader will think that it has been printed in England and made up by someone at home who has in his hand information from imagination rather than experience', Masterman to General Charteris, GHQ, 18 October 1916 (IWM, M999: part 1, 'The Western Front').

20 Masterman to Hutton-Wilson, 1 May 1917 (IWM, G4010/27).

21 P. G. Konody, *Observer*, 8 July 1917.

22 Campbell Dodgson, 'The Artist' in *British Artists at the Front, Part Four: Eric Kennington* (London: Country Life, 1918), n. p.

23 Robert Graves, 'The British Soldier' in *"The British Soldier": An Exhibition of Pictures by Eric Kennington (An Official Artist on the Western Front)* (London: Leicester Galleries, June–July 1918), p. 6.

24 Graves, *'The British Soldier' An Exhibition of Pictures by Eric Kennington*, p. 3.

25 Brendan Prendeville, *Realism in Twentieth-Century Painting* (London and New York: Thames and Hudson, 2000), p. 14.

26 Prendeville, *Realism*, p. 44.

27 This argument derives from the cinematic theory of suture where the point of view of the camera, far from offering the illusion of visual mastery to the spectator, determines and prescribes the subject's viewing position. See Kaja Silverman, *The Threshold of the Visible World* (New York and London: Routledge, 1996), p. 126. The 'made-to-order witness' is Hitchcock's.

28 Dodgson, 'The Artist', *Eric Kennington*, my emphasis.

29 *The Times*, 2 March 1918, and also the *Evening News*, 1 March 1918. Interestingly, this observation by *The Times* is not mentioned in Charles Doherty's article, 'Nevinson's Elegy: *Paths of Glory*', *College Art Journal*, vol. 51, no. 1, spring 1992. I do not agree with Doherty's romanticised interpretation of the censorship incident, for reasons that will become clear. A more accurate account is given in Jonathan Black, 'A Curious, Cold Intensity: C. R. W. Nevinson as a War Artist, 1914–1918,' in Richard Ingleby, Jonathan Black, David Cohen and Gordon Cooke, *C. R. W. Nevinson: The Twentieth Century* (London: Merrell Holberton, 1999), pp. 34–6.

30 'Home Publicity During the Great War National War Aims Committee', n. d. and anonymous, p. 3 (PRO, INF 4/4A).

31 It was noted at the Foreign Office, concerning the banning of the *Socialist Standard*, that 'no paper ought to be allowed to go abroad which is prejudicial to our interests or available for enemy propaganda. All these socialist papers are in reality "stop the war" papers, and in that respect they differ from the Harmsworth Press, detestable though the latter is.' Minute, 19 September 1916 (PRO, FO 395 47: 184609).

32 Minute, 21 November 1916 and 22 November 1916, Orage to Chief Postal Censor, MI9(a), 1 December 1916 (PRO, FO 395 54: 231816 and 251276).

33 'Military Press Control: A History of the Work of M. I. 7, 1914–1919', c.1938, p. 23 (PRO, INF 4/1B).

34 M. L. Sanders and Philip M. Taylor, *British Propaganda During the First World War, 1914–1918* (London: Macmillan, 1982), pp. 66–8.

35 It aimed 'To indicate, and where possible, specifically define the advantages of an Entente Peace, especially in relation to its effect on the daily lives of the people; to dwell on the democratic development and improvement in the lot of the working classes which State control and other war changes have already secured; to suggest the prospect of further improvement and greater freedom when the war is over;

generally to envisage the rewards of success.' Home Publicity During the Great War National War Aims Committee', pp. 2–3 (PRO, INF 4/4A). It frequently worked through public rallies and public meetings. 'Win the War Day' in Birmingham in September 1918 involved a procession of heavy vehicles including a tank along a route lined by Boy Scouts and 250,000 leaflets were dropped from aeroplanes. In August and September 1917, 1,298 meetings were held in fifty-four holiday resorts and in industrial areas 'with a view to counteracting pacifist propaganda which appears to be growing and in certain areas is securing a considerable measure of support'. It was noted that there was tendency for organised labour to stand aloof from local NWA committees. Meetings Department Report, G. Wallace Carter, 25 September 1917, NWAC Minutes and Reports, Wellington House File (PRO, T 102 16). The Committee relied on reports by its speakers for views of local conditions. Its activities take on a slightly ludicrous aspect in retrospect. Shipyards were known to be centres of industrial unrest and 'Wigan was recommended for special treatment as "the worst place for pacifists that I have had any experience of", the common allegation being that the war was a capitalists' quarrel.' 'Home Publicity', p. 5.

36 'The Organisation of the Services of Military Secrecy, Security and Publicity. Prepared by General Staff War Office.' October 1917, n. p. (PRO, INF 4/9).

37 Alan Sekula, 'The Instrumental Image: Steichen at War', in *Photography against the Grain: Essays and Photo Works, 1973–1983* (Halifax, Nova Scotia: The Press of the Nova Scotia College of Art, 1984), p. 33.

38 Brigadier Charteris, at GHQ, valued the introduction of photographic aerial reconnaissance because it removed the distortions of individual observers: 'It is a very necessary check on the exaggerated reports and the imagination of air observers. Photographs cannot lie – most air observers do.' When a limited number of official photographers were allowed at the front, Charteris took little personal interest in the censorship of their work because, as he explained, 'The photographs are quite harmless'; John Charteris, *At G.H.Q.* (London: Cassell & Co, 1931), pp. 77 and 144.

39 Jan Gordon, 'Art and the Camera', *New Witness*, 21 December 1916.

40 Bennett, 'William Orpen at the Front', p. 5.

41 *The Architect* put it 'The facts are there right enough, . . . but they are used significantly, and the impression made upon those who look at the drawings sympathetically is of that heightened kind which only a real artist can conjure up.' 30 March 1917. The *Daily Telegraph* put it more explicitly: 'When the camera has done its best with its gift of mechanical accuracy, the interpretation of all the bewildering things we have seen is left to ourselves. To give not only the thing seen but the spirit lying within it, so that it lives and thrills us with a new vision – that is the province of the imaginative and selective artist.' 27 July 1917.

42 Bennett, prefatory note in *'Void of War': An Exhibition of Pictures by Lieut. Paul Nash (An Official Artist on the Western Front)* (London: Leicester Galleries, 1918), my emphasis. In Andrew Causey's citation of this passage, the word 'true' is omitted, subtly and unintentionally altering the meaning of the text. *Paul Nash* (Oxford: Clarendon Press, 1980), p. 71.

43 Flitch, *The Great War: The Fourth Year*, p. 14 and pp. 8–9.

44 See Jane Carmichael, *First World War Photographers* (London: Routledge, 1989), pp. 141–2. The press also relied on amateur photographs and a 'disproportionate number of foreign photographs', p. 44.

45 Alain Sayag, ' "Wir sagten Adieu einer ganze Epoche", Apollinaire: Französische Kriegsphotographie,' and Bodo von Dewitz, 'Zur Geschichte der Kriegsphotographie des Ersten Weltkrieges,' in Rainer Rother, ed., *Die letzten Tage der Menschheit: Bilder des Ersten Weltkrieges. Eine Ausstellung des Deutschen Historischen Museums, Berlin, der Barbican Art Gallery, London, und der Staatlichen Museen zu Berlin – Preußischer Kulturbesitz in Verbindung mit dem Imperial War Museum, London* (Berlin: Deutsches Historisches Museum; Ars Nicolai, 1994), pp. 188 and 168.

46 Carmichael, *First World War Photographers*, p. 6.

47 Nicholson to Masterman, 16 October 1917 (IWM, Photography Department: Ministry of Information Papers Box One, File 3).

48 'Distrust and dislike of the press were endemic in the Service departments.' Colin Lovelace, 'British Press Censorship During the First World War', in George Boyce, James Curran and Pauline Wingate, eds., *Newspaper History from the Seventeenth Century to the Present Day* (London: Constable, 1978), p. 308; 'The Service Departments had long feared the press as a source of adverse publicity and criticism.' Sanders and Taylor, *British Propaganda*, p. 6.

49 George Boyce, 'The Fourth Estate: The Reappraisal of a Concept' in Boyce, Curran and Wingate, *Newspaper History*, p. 28.

50 Claud Schuster to Robinson, 3 December 1914 (PRO, INF 4/1B). As a later history of propaganda in First World War stated 'Arrangements were also made to obtain drawings . . . by first rate artists, partly for purposes of record, partly because of such propagandist value as the aesthetic appeal has amongst the aesthetic public.' (PRO, INF 4/4A: 'British Propaganda During the War 1914–1918. Secret. The History of Propaganda.' n.d. (c.1941) p. 6).

51 Sanders and Taylor, *British Propaganda*, p. 101.

52 Sanders and Taylor, *British Propaganda*, p. 171.

53 GHQ to Masterman, n.d. (November/December 1917) (IWM, 267A/6: Nash, Paul 1917–18).

54 Paul Nash, *Outline: An Autobiography* (London: Columbus Books, 1988), p. 178.

55 Foreign Office to Ivor Nicholson, Wellington House, 29 September 1917 (PRO, FO 395 80: 185451).

56 Nicholson to Masterman, 16 October 1917, Ministry of Information Papers (IWM, Photography Department).

57 29 September 1917 (IWM, 245A/6: Kennington, Eric 1917–1918).

58 29 October 1917 (IWM, 266A/6: Nevinson 1917–1918).

59 16 October 1917, Ministry of Information Papers (IWM, Photography Department).

60 3 December 1917 (IWM, 266A/6).

61 Lee to Yockney, 8 October 1919 (IWM, 323/7: 'G.H.Q.'). In one of those nice ironies of history, after the war Lee became managing director of a cutlery factory, where presumably he manufactured scissors.

62 Letter by Yockney to Dodgson, 21 November 1917 (IWM, 266A/6).

63 Added as a hand-written note to a letter of 27 November 1917 (IWM, 266A/6).

64 Lee, 24 April 1918 (IWM, 323/7). He also wrote that the 'facial expression of the man in the trenches or in rest billets is nothing like that of the same man when at home on leave – nor is it anything like the "Group of Brutes" – I hope the Huns wont get hold of it'; Lee to Yockney, 23 March 1918 (TGA, 72–4/13). See also Lee's letter to Yockney of 3 March 1918 (TGA, 72–4/12) when he also reiterates his belief that 'the Boche [will] make propaganda of it.' At the end of December 1918, Lee returned a small group of drawings that had been censored. One of these was a drawing by Martin Hardie, who had a loose association with Wellington House, of Kaffir's landing at Boulogne, and Lee wrote that it had been censored because one figure appeared to an officer and there were no Kaffir officers and because 'the native authorities here objected to the picture as accentuating the Kaffir features unduly'. 14 December 1918 (IWM, 323/7).

65 Annette Kuhn, Cinema, Censorship and Sexuality 1909–1925 (London: Routledge, 1988), pp. 23–5.

66 Nevinson to Lee, date stamped 27 November 1917 but not sent (IWM, 266A/6).

67 Daily Express, 7 March 1918.

68 Saturday Review, 16 March 1918.

69 C. E. Montague, plate VI, British Artists at the Front, Part 1, (London: Country Life, 1918), n. p.

70 Kuhn, Cinema, Censorship and Sexuality. I am indebted to Kuhn's study for the rigour with which she addresses issues of censorship and their effects. Similarly, in the USA at the trial to lift the ban of Joyce's Ulysses in 1933, the book was defined as a 'classic' in the canon of literature, with implications both for the limits of censorship of its language and content and for its assumed audience. See the account by Brook Thomas, 'Ulysses on Trial: Some Supplementary Reading', in Richard Burt, ed., The Administration of Aesthetics: Censorship, Political Criticism, and the Public Sphere (Minneapolis: University of Minnesota Press, 1994).

71 It was argued that if the Germans got hold of the painting 'they would seize upon [it] as evidence of British degeneration'. Yockney to Masterman, 4 December 1917 (IWM, 266A/6).

72 See Lovelace in Boyce, Curran and Wingate eds., Newspaper History, pp. 308–10, and Sanders and Taylor, British Propaganda, pp. 7–9.

73 'Propaganda by War Office During the Great War', p. 3 (PRO, INF 4/4a).

74 Nicholson to ffoulkes, Imperial War Museum, 28 November 1917 (IWM, 477/11: 'Imperial War Museum Ministry of Information HD/6').

75 Lee to Yockney, 2 May 1918 (IWM, 323/7).

76 Ideas, 3 April 1918. The Aberdeen Free Press said, 'There is nothing eccentric or freakish about these drawings', 28 March 1918, and Drawing described Nevinson as 'one of the Cubists who apparently has taken to shaping his cubes with commonsense'. April 1918.

77 3 December 1917 (IWM, 266A/6).

78 Craig Owens, Beyond Recognition: Representation, Power and Culture (Berkeley: University of California Press, 1992), p. 91.

79 Tatler, 13 March 1918 (my emphasis).

80 Nevinson to Masterman, 3 December 1917 (IWM, 266A/6).

81 Yockney to Lee, 5 December 1917 (IWM, 460/10: Artists at the Front. General Correspondence. G4010/17).

82 Outlook, 16 March 1918; Star, 28 February 1918. The Manchester Guardian described Nevinson as a 'lucky artist' who was able to have 'it' both ways, meaning presumably accreditation both as a rebel and an officially approved artist. The picture had been purchased by the Imperial War Museum and he had been able to exhibit it suitably veiled – 'That alone will bring big crowds to the exhibition.' Moreover, the newspaper also stated it was a show 'not to be missed', 2 March 1918.

83 Herald, 23 March 1918.

84 'He subordinates all these [pictorial] effects to his general criticism of the war – so far, that is to say, as the censor will let him. That tolerance is freely extended so far as the artist confines himself to exhibiting the instruments and the agents of war, and their work on mere fields and skies, which cannot retort, and refrains from suggesting the real purpose of these operations. That happens to be Death. But the idea that anybody (except Germans) ever gets killed in the war seems to have been too much for Sir Edward Cook or the gentleman who does the art censorship. In order that the fact many[sic] be well-screened from a sensitive public, a patch of brown paper covers all but the tell-tale feet and helmets of a couple of dead linesmen in "Paths of Glory." So my readers may see the Nevinson Exhibition, and come away from it quite happy and comfortable about its subject'; Nation, 9 March 1918. This produced a disclaimer from Nevinson denying that he was involved in any kind of act of defiance. Letter to the Editor, 16 March 1918.

85 Nation, 16 March 1918.

86 'Incident roundup', Index on Censorship, April/May, vol. 20, nos 4 & 5, 1991, p. 20.

87 See Daniel Pick's tracing of the deeper roots and complexities of the First World War in War Machine: The Rationalisation of Slaughter in the Modern Age (New Haven and London: Yale University Press, 1993), p. 189.

88 See the discussion in Martin Warnke, Political Landscape: The Art History of Nature (London: Reaktion Books, 1994), pp. 60–62.

89 Apollinaire phrased it 'Mon désir est là sur quoi je tire', which Paul Virilio glosses as 'a kind of telescopic tensing towards an imagined encounter, a "shaping" of the partner-cum-adversary before his probable fragmentation'. War and Cinema: The Logistics of Perception (London: Verso, 1989), p. 15.

90 Virilio, *War and Cinema*, p. 6.
91 Virilio, *War and Cinema*, pp. 5–6 and p. 11.
92 Introduction to the exhibition catalogue, Leicester Galleries, 1918, reprinted in C. R. W. Nevinson, *Paint and Prejudice* (London: Methuen, 1937), p. 107.
93 Jan Gordon, *Country Life*, 2 March 1918.
94 Flitch, *The Great War: The Fourth Year*, p. 19.
95 Flitch, *The Great War: The Fourth Year*, p. 21.
96 Virilio, *War and Cinema*, p. 18.
97 Tony Bennett, 'The Exhibitionary Complex', reprinted in Reesa Greenberg, Bruce Ferguson and Sandy Nairne, *Thinking about Exhibitions* (London and New York: Routledge, 1996), p. 84.
98 See the well-known account in Michel Foucault, *Discipline and Punish: The Birth of the Prison* (New York: Vintage Books, 1979), chapter on 'Panopticism'.
99 Bennett, 'The Exhibitionary Complex', p. 76.
100 'The most gratifying feature of Mr Nevinson's work is that he continues to regard each new task as a new experiment requiring its own particular treatment, and that he sternly refuses to be led by success into some form or other of hidebound convention.' P. G. Konody, the *Observer*, 10 March 1918. 'It is his [Nevinson's] habit to choose a "different style" on what seems an average of once a fortnight.' B. H. Dias (Ezra Pound), 'Art', *The New Age*, 17 January 1918. 'There are in the exhibition too many pieces of effective commonplace, no doubt mere task-work imposed on the artist, and the penalty of success.' *The Times*, 4 March 1918.
101 See J. M. Winter, *The Great War and the British People* (Basingstoke: Macmillan, 1985), p. 216.
102 The *Queen* reported that 'the Princess Royal spent quite a long time in the pretty little salons' at the Leicester Galleries, along with many society names: Lord Lansdowne, Balfour, Asquith, the Duchess of Marlborough, Lord Desborough, Lady Drogheda, Lady Tredegar, Lady Sligo, 30 March 1918.
103 He wrote 'the "Elect" of Bloomsbury . . . is pathetic and out of date' and decried 'the self-satisfied cliques, the petty groups and the jealous causeries of the superior "Intellectuals"' declaring that 'it is the duty of every sincere artist to have the courage of this bellicose ideal, giving his finest, singing his song from the roof-tops, even using a megaphone if necessary to overcome protesting howls, in order thoroughly to counteract the effect of that powerful section which can always be depended upon to give the public what it wants, and so, deliberately and cynically, to supply and cater for every low, mean instinct of the mob, blighting all hopes for democracy and compelling decent-thinking persons utterly to despair'. Preface to the exhibition catalogue, Leicester Galleries, 1918, reprinted in *Paint and Prejudice*, pp. 109–10.
104 *The Observer*, 3 March 1918.
105 *Burlington Magazine*, April 1918.
106 Hudson to Masterman, 26 October 1917 (IWM, 266A/6).
107 Frank Rutter, *Sunday Times*, 3 March 1918.
108 *Queen*, 25 May 1918.
109 See John Barrell, 'The Public Prospect and the Private View: The Politics of Taste in Eighteenth Century-Britain' in The

Birth of Pandora and the Division of Knowledge (Basingstoke: Macmillan, 1992).
110 Nash to Masterman, 3 April 1918 (IWM, 267A/6). It was a condition of his contract with the Leicester Galleries that Nash should organise the preface to his catalogue. Memorandum of an Agreement 22 December 1917, Ernest Brown and Phillips, Leicester Galleries, Lieut. Paul Nash (TGA, 7050 707–760).
111 Barrell, 'Public Prospect', p. 59.
112 *British Artists at the Front, Part Three: Paul Nash* (London: Country Life and George Newnes, 1918), plate xv.
113 *The Times*, 23 May 1915.
114 *Westminster Gazette*, 18 August 1918.
115 John Turner, Lt Royal Warwickshire Regiment, *Saturday Review*, 25 May 1918.
116 *Connoisseur*, August 1918; *New Age*, 11 April 1918; *Daily Express* and *Glasgow News*, both 19 September 1918.
117 *Daily Express*, 7 March 1918.
118 Harold Paget, Literary Agent to A. S. Watt, 10 March 1917 (IWM, M999, part IV, 'The Western Front: English and General').

CHAPTER THREE

1 Arnold Bennett, 'Officialism and War Painting', *New Statesman*, 20 December 1919, pp. 347–8.
2 Minutes, 2 March 1918, British War Memorials Committee (BWMC), BWMC I, IWM. At the meeting Beaverbrook referred to 'a national collection of war pictures by artists of great ability'.
3 See Brandon Taylor, *Art for the Nation* (Manchester: Manchester University Press, 1999), pp. 138–140 and 143; and National Gallery Millbank, *A Record of Ten Years: 1917–1927* (London: National Gallery Millbank; printed by Robert Maclehose and Co at the University Press, Glasgow, 1927), pp. 4–9; and Treasury, 'Minute. Constitution of a separate board of trustees for the National Gallery of British Art (Tate Gallery): deputation of the Royal Academy of Arts to the financial secretary to the Treasury, 1 August, 1917; qualifications for appointment of persons as trustees; future of the Chantrey bequest', 1917–1920 (PRO, T 1/12587).
4 Because he objected to being the only artist invited. Telegram, 1 May 1917 (PRO, T 1/12587).
5 He was 'considered exceptionally qualified'. Minutes, Tate Board, 16 November 1920 (TGA, TAM 72/5).
6 Minutes, Tate Board, 9 March 1921 (TGA, TAM 72/5). Frank Rutter, 'The Transformation of the Tate', in *Sunday Times*, 3 September 1922 lists Imperial War Museum works by Paul and John Nash, Stanley and Gilbert Spencer, Henry Lamb, Wyndham Lewis, Nevinson, and William Roberts, on view at the Tate.
7 A detailed account of the meetings of the British War Memorials Committee and Pictorial Propaganda Committee and the Ministry's correspondence with the Treasury and the Imperial War Museum is given in Sue Malvern, 'Art, Propa-

ganda and Patronage: An History of the Employment of British War Artists 1916–1919' (Ph.D. thesis, University of Reading, 1981), chapters 4 and 5. It also quotes extensively from the correspondence.

8 Pictorial Propaganda Committee, minutes of meeting held 24 July 1918. (IWM: Pictorial Propaganda Committee, Minute Book II).

9 An earlier enquiry in January 1917, after Lloyd George became Prime Minister, had resulted in the establishment of the Department of Information which absorbed Wellington House under John Buchan, but the work of Masterman's organisation had not been particularly altered. See papers in (PRO, INF 4/11).

10 J. D. Squires, *British Propaganda at Home and in the United States from 1914–1917* (Cambridge, Mass.: Harvard University Press, 1935), p. 38.

11 It accounted for approximately £433.851. *Copy of a report of proceedings at Wellington House*, 28 November 1917, p. 10 (PRO, INF 4/11).

12 Squires, *British Propaganda*, p. 39, and George North to Stephen Tallents, 23 March 1938 (PRO, INF 4/1A).

13 Arthur Spurgeon, Report on the Operations of Wellington House, 7 December 1917, p. 11 (PRO, INF 4/10).

14 John Buchan, Report of the Department of Information to Sir Edward Carson, September 1917, p. 8 (PRO, INF 4/1B).

15 Anonymous typescript, *British Propaganda During the War 1914–1918: The History of Propaganda*, n.d., p. 9 (IWM).

16 A. J. P. Taylor, *Beaverbrook* (Harmondsworth, Middlesex: Penguin Books, 1974), p. 110.

17 Taylor, *Art for the Nation*, pp. 195–6.

18 Maria Tippett, *Art at the Service of War: Canada, Art, and the Great War* (Toronto: University of Toronto Press, 1984), pp. 43–7.

19 Mond referred to the BWMC as 'a private organisation of your own'. Mond to Lord Beaverbrook, 29 May 1918. (HLRO, BBK E/19: 'War Memorials Committee. Pictorial Propaganda').

20 The political influence of the 'Press Lords' was initially coalesced by Chamberlain's Tariff Reform League formed in 1903. See Stuart Hall and Bill Schwarz, 'State and Society, 1880–1930', in Mary Langan and Bill Schwarz, *Crises in the British State, 1880–1930* (London: Hutchinson & Co, 1985), pp. 8–9; and Bill Schwarz, 'Conservativism and "caesarism", 1903–1922,' in Langan and Schwarz *Crises in the British State*, pp. 37–8.

21 Taylor, *Beaverbrook*, pp. x–xv.

22 Quoted in Lucy Masterman, *C. F. G. Masterman: A Biography* (London: Nicholson and Watson, 1939), p. 302. Rothermere felt that he and Beaverbrook 'should extract from the Canadian Government a message of thanks to you and me'. Beaverbrook to Masterman, 21 December 1920 (HLRO, BBK C/282: Rothermere 1912–1920).

23 See Taylor, *Art for the Nation*, pp. 107–8 and p. 131.

24 Bennett to Beaverbrook, 12 June 1918 (HLRO, BBK E/8).

25 Yockney to W. P. Mayes, 11 March 1960 (IWM, Miscellaneous Papers: 'Origins of an Art Collection. Notes. Corre-

spondence and Working Papers'). Bone's recollections (1931) also cited Bennett, Masterman and Ross but not Konody, quoted in Masterman, *Masterman*, pp. 304–5.

26 Quoted in Masterman, *Masterman*, p. 303.

27 He was close to the new Liberals, represented in the Nation group that included Masterman. Peter Clarke, *Liberals and Social Democrats* (Cambridge: Cambridge University Press, 1978), pp. 128–9.

28 In 1931, Bone described his 'undeviating determination to back any fresh and unacademic talent which chimed in so well with Masterman's uncommon originality of outlook in art as in everything else'. Quoted in Masterman, *Masterman*, p. 304.

29 Ross to BWMC, 8 April 1918 (IWM, BWMC I).

30 Ross to Beaverbrook, 12 June 1918 (HLRO, BBK E/8).

31 See Kinley E. Roby, *A Writer at War: Arnold Bennett, 1914–1918* (Baton Rouge: Louisiana State University Press, 1972), pp. 297–8; Margery Ross: *Robert Ross: Friend of Friends. Letters to Robert Ross, Art Critic and Writer, Together with Extracts from his Published Articles* (London: Jonathan Cape, 1952), p. 331; and Arthur Marwick, *The Deluge: British Society and the First World War* (London: Macmillan, 1965, 1975), p. 258. Ross attributed the celebrity of Billing's trial to disillusion with the war, writing to Charles Ricketts that 'The English, intoxicated into failure, enjoyed tearing poor Maud Allan to pieces, simply because she had given them pleasure, and kicking Oscar's corpse to make up for the failure of the Fifth army'; and to Cecil Sprigge that 'I have been used as a piece of mud . . . For a few days London forgot all about the war, in its excitement over the case'; Ross, *Robert Ross*, pp. 334–5. A recent account is Jodie Medd, ' "The Cult of the Clitoris": Anatomy of a National Scandal', *Modernism/Modernity*, vol. 9, no. 1, Jan, 2002.

32 Verbatim report of 'Maud Allan's Libel Case', *Weekly Dispatch*, 9 April 1918 (IWM, press cutting).

33 Grein to Donald, 22 March 1918 (PRO, INF 4/8); *Yorkshire Post*, 8 April 1918 and 9 April 1918; Donald to Beaverbrook, 9 April 1918 (PRO, INF 4/8); *Evening Standard*, 30 April 1918; T. L. Heath, Treasury to Ministry of Information, 15 July 1918 (PRO, T.121.1).

34 Ross to Charles Ricketts, 7 March 1918, in T. Sturge Moore and Cecil Lewis, eds., *Self Portrait: Taken from the Letters and Journals of Charles Ricketts, R.A.* (London: Peter Davies, 1939), p. 289.

35 Minutes, Tate Board, 15 October 1918 (TGA, TAM 72/5). In 1928, Conway of the War Museum wrote to the *New Age* that Ross 'never had any connection whatsoever with this museum'; *New Age*, 22 March 1928.

36 Bone to Thomas Bodkin, 4 April 1918, in James Hepburn, ed., *Letters of Arnold Bennett*, vol. III, 1916–31 (Oxford: Oxford University Press, 1970), p. 54; and Masterman, *Masterman*, pp. 303 and 305.

37 See Sue Malvern, 'War, Memory and Museums: Art and Artefact in the Imperial War Museum', *History Workshop Journal*, 49, 2000, pp. 201–2.

38 Yockney to Chairman, Pelham Committee, 27 May 1918

(IWM, G4099 Part 1); and Yockney to Maynard Keynes, 11 June 1918 and note, n.d. (IWM, 226/6: 'Grant, Duncan'). Grant's views of the war are discussed in Robert Skidelsky's biography of Maynard Keynes where he quotes from a letter by Grant, written to his father, in which he explains that he does not identify his enemies as foreigners but the masses anywhere, rather than the civilised of any nation; *John Maynard Keynes: Hopes Betrayed, Volume One, 1883–1920* (London: Macmillan London Ltd, 1983, 1992), p. 326.

39 Minutes of a resumed meeting, 21 March 1918 (IWM, BWMC I).

40 See, for example, the series of articles surveying war memorials in European history by A. E. Richardson and R. Randall Phillips, published in *Architectural Review* in 1915, such as 'Memorials of War – IV: Modern British', May 1915, pp. 95–104. The ritualistic burial of unknown soldiers in many European nations is discussed in Kenneth S. Inglis, 'Grabmäler für Unbekannte Soldaten', in Rainer Rother, ed., *Die letzten Tage der Menschheit: Bilder des Ersten Weltkrieges. Eine Ausstellung des Deutschen Historischen Museums, Berlin, der Barbican Art Gallery, London, und der Staatlichen Museen zu Berlin – Preußischer Kulturbesitz in Verbindung mit dem Imperial War Museum, London* (Berlin: Deutsches Historisches Museum; Ars Nicolai, 1994), pp. 409–22.

41 Martin Conway, 'Let us now praise famous men', *Country Life*, 24 July 1915, p. 134.

42 J. H. Watkins, 'The Canadian War Memorials Fund: History and Objectives', *Canada in Khaki*, 2, 1917, pp. 25–6, reprinted for the British War Memorials Committee, 4 March 1918.

43 Minutes, 21 March 1918 (IWM, BWMC I).

44 Minutes, 27 March 1918 (IWM, BWMC I).

45 Meirion Harries and Susie Harries state that 'The BWMC's approach to its task was systematic. It had no scruples telling artists exactly what to paint: the subject matter came first, and artists were chosen to serve it, not vice versa', *The War Artists: British Official War Art in the Twentieth Century* (London: Michael Joseph, 1983), p. 87. The facts do not bear this statement out. Lists of artists were prepared and discussed at the first Executive Committee meeting, on 7 March 1918, and the second, on 14 March 1918, at which meeting it was first proposed to draw up lists of subjects and match artists' names to subjects. By 14 March, all but seven of the artists eventually employed had been identified in one way or another. An elaborate process of consultation, negotiation and discussion with individual artists was undertaken so that what artists actually painted in the event was never dictated to them.

46 Harries and Harries, state that 'surprisingly, in view of Tonks' appointment, the Committee agreed [to Nevinson's request] as his subject a dressing-station scene; *War Artists*, p. 104. In fact, Nevinson had written to Masterman on 7 April 1918, expressing disquiet about the aeroplane subject he was painting for the Canadians and suggesting a Northern works or a camouflaged liner, and to Ross on 21 April 1918, stating that he wanted to paint a Field Casualty Station (IWM, 266A/6: 'Nevinson 1917–1918'). These two letters were discussed at the BWMC meeting of 24 April 1918 and Nevinson was to be asked to consider another subject. At the meeting of 1 May 1918, Bone reported that he had seen the artist and the title *The Harvest of Battle* was agreed. Nevinson did not 'refuse to accept the honorary commission as Second Lieutenant' as stated by Harries and Harries, *War Artists*, p. 104. Nevinson asked for a commission but the War Office turned the request down, as was usual for virtually all the artists, for instance Tonks. Nevinson to Masterman, 22 June 1918; Yockney to Nevinson, 26 June 1918 (IWM, 266A/6); Yockney to War Office, 14 May 1918; and Cubbitt, War Office, to Ministry of Information, 31 May 1918 (IWM, 300/7: 'Henry Tonks').

47 Ross to Yockney, 21 April 1918 (TGA, 724.193). Ross also interviewed Duncan Grant; Bone worked on Sargent, negotiated with Bayes and viewed Nash's sketches for his large canvas; and Konody talked to Airy and Philpot.

48 Nash to Yockney, 23 April 1918, and Yockney to Nash, 1 July 1918 (IWM, 267A/6).

49 Yockney to Lamb, 12 November 1918 (IWM, 253/6: 'Lamb, Capt. Henry B').

50 Memorandum, 8 April 1918 (IWM, BWMC I).

51 He also recalled an interview of Robert Ross writing 'I never quite understood what part Ross had in the Canadian War Paintings scheme'. Ross had no part in the Canadian scheme. William Roberts, *Memories of the War to End War, 1914–18* (London: Privately printed, 1974), p. 32.

52 See François Robichon, *L'armée française vue par les peintures 1870–1914* (Paris: Ministère de la Défense; Éditions Herscher, 1998), especially p. 19 on the golden age of military painting.

53 *Canadian War Records: Canadian War Memorials Exhibition*, Burlington House, January–February (London: Canadian War Memorials Fund, 1919), Introduction, n.p.

54 See Tippett, *Art at the Service of War*, pp. 28–30.

55 See R. H. Hubbard, 'The National Gallery of Canada, Ottawa. History,' TS, National Gallery of Canada, Ottawa, 1950; and Joan Sutherland Boggs, *The National Gallery of Canada* (Toronto: Oxford University Press, 1971).

56 See Dennis Montagna, 'Benjamin West's The Death of General Wolfe: A Nationalist Narrative', *American Art Journal*, vol. 13, no. 2, spring 1981, pp. 72–88; Annie Elizabeth Chennells Wolfe-Aylward, *The Pictorial Life of Wolfe* (Plymouth: Mayflower Press, 1927); and Jacques Monet, 'Canadians, Canadiens and Colonial Nationalism 1896–1914: The Thorn in the Lion's Paw', in John Eddy and Deryck Shreuder, eds, *The Rise of Colonial Nationalism: Australia, New Zealand, Canada and South Africa First Assert their Nationalities, 1880–1914* (Wellington: Allen and Unwin, 1988), especially p. 173.

57 Memorandum, 19 March 1918 (IWM, BWMC. I).

58 Deputation of the Royal Academy, Transcript, TS (PRO, T. 1. 12587).

59 Minutes, 3 April 1917 (TGA, TAM 72/5).

60 See Judith Collins, 'The Origins and Aims of the Contemporary Art Society', in Alan Bowness, Judith Collins and Joseph Darracott, eds, *British Contemporary Art 1910–1990:*

Eighty Years of Collecting by The Contemporary Art Society (London: The Herbert Press, 1991).

61 Denys Sutton, *Letters of Roger Fry* vol. 2 (London: Chatto and Windus, 1972), pp. 396–7. This letter is dated 20 May 1916 but a footnote by Sutton indicates that it is the Ministry show to which Fry is referring. The date is therefore incorrect. See also 'Pictures in Switzerland' (IWM, G1230/1031).

62 Minutes, 21 March 1918 (IWM, BWMC 1).

63 Paper, 8 April 1918, and minutes, 10 April 1918 (IWM, BWMC 1).

64 *The Housing of the Canadian War Memorials*, pamphlet, 1919, National Gallery of Canada, library. See R. F. Wodehouse, 'Lord Beaverbrook's Plan for a Suitable Building to House the Canadian War Memorials', *Organization of Military Museums of Canada Journal*, 7, 1978–9, pp. 1–8, and Laura Brandon, 'The Canadian War Memorial That Never Was', *Canadian Military History*, vol. 7, no. 4, 1998, pp. 45–54.

65 Minutes, 17 April and 8 May 1918 (IWM, BWMC 1). The John was purchased in May 1920 for £120 by the War Museum. It was earlier reproduced by Konody in an article about the Canadian paintings as 'Study for Detail in a Large Decorative Painting of War' ('The Canadian War Memorials', *Colour*, September 1918, p. 38) and is most likely part of his *Canadians Opposite Lens* which he never finished.

66 Notes, 22 May 1918 (IWM, BWMC 1).

67 TS, The Great Memorial Gallery, Liabilities for Pictures, n.d. (IWM, BWMC 1).

68 Bennett was a close friend of Rickards and wrote a memorial essay on the architect when he died in 1920. Holden was the architect of the Strand British Medical Association building, which contained controversial sculptures by Epstein, and may have been Bone's suggestion, although he was also the consulting architect for the Duveen Galleries at the Tate, designed by Romaine Walker (Tate Board Meeting Minutes, 5 October 1916 (TGA)). He was also the architect for Epstein's tomb for Oscar Wilde in Paris, which Ross commissioned. In 1918, Holden was in France, employed by the Imperial War Graves Commission to design cemeteries. In September 1918, after the British War Memorials Committee had ceased to function, Holden visited Jagger's and Ledward's studios with Yockney and Bone. Yockney, 17 September 1918, to Jagger, Lieut (IWM, C.S. 240/6). In his *Officialism and War Painting*, 1919, Bennett referred to Bone's 'great scheme' which 'exists only in Mr Bone's paper model of it' (p. 348) – confirmation that Holden never made any designs.

69 July 1918, Pictorial Propaganda Committee (IWM, Minute Book II).

70 Bennett to Beaverbrook, 31 July 1918; Needham to Beaverbrook (HLRO, BBK E/19).

71 See Evan Charteris, *John Sargent* (London: William Heinemann, 1927), p. 178.

72 The matter of what payments artists received under this Scheme is enormously convoluted. In April 1919, Yockney told Paul Nash that he had been paid a weekly detention allowance of £3 10s (£3.50) from 22 March to 3 May 1918 in addition to his army pay; from 15 June 1918 he had received £25 a month plus 10s 6d (52.5p) a day in lieu of army pay; and from September 1918 to February 1919 consolidated pay of £215 7s 6d (£215.28), rent for a studio at 10s (50p) per week and about £20 for materials. His period of full-time employment was counted as 15 June 1918 to 28 February 1919. He seems to have received no subsistence during May 1918. Yockney to Nash, 9 April 1919, and letter by Nash's wife to Gale Thomas, Ministry, 8 May 1918 (IWM, P 267A/6: NASH). Total payments to Paul Nash under Scheme 2 were listed as £318 10s 3d (£318.51). Yockney to Conway, 25 October 1919 (IWM, Finance File 324/7).

73 Gowers to Treasury, 14 July 1916 (PRO, 18975, T.I.11992).

74 There are two well-known surveys of pre-war salaries and incomes. Chiozza Money in 1904 counted rich people as those on incomes over £700 per annum and comfortable incomes as between £160 and £700. Bowlby's survey of changes in the distribution of income from 1880 to 1913 listed the average national wage in 1913 at £506 per annum. Higher incomes increased more rapidly than lower incomes. See the discussion in Harold Perkin, *The Rise of Professional Society: England Since 1880* (London: Routledge, 1990), pp. 29–31. By 1915, however, a salary of £400 per annum, while it allowed for security, left little for luxury and implied careful budgeting, see Arthur Marwick, *The Deluge: British Society and the First World War* (London: Macmillan, 1973), p. 128.

75 Yockney to ffoulkes, 6 February 1920 (IWM, 324/7).

76 *Canadian War Memorials Exhibition 1919*, p. 40. See also John Galt, *The Life, Studies, and Works of Benjamin West, esq., President of the Royal Academy of London, Composed from Materials Furnished by Himself* (London: Printed for T. Cadell and W. Davies, 1820), p. 50, and Edgar Wind, 'The Revolution in History Painting', *Journal of the Warburg and Courtauld Institutes*, 2, 1938, pp. 116–27.

77 Robert Antony Bromley, *A Philosophical and Critical History of the Fine Arts, Painting, Sculpture, and Architecture; and Occasional Observations on The Progress of Engraving, etc*, vol. 1. (London: Philanthropic Press, 1793), p. 58.

78 In 1909, Lord Stanmore, who had initiated the proposal, wrote 'The only historical pictures of any real value are, I think, those contemporary with the event represented.' Quoted in Alan Powers, 'History in Paint: The Twentieth-Century Murals', *Apollo*, vol. 135, no., 365, 1992, p. 318. These are also discussed in Clare A. P. Willsdon, *Mural Painting in Britain 1840–1940* (Oxford: Clarendon Press, 2000), pp. 94–108, although she does not cite this statement. Willsdon's text is flawed in that she claims, for example that the Canadian War Memorials paintings are in the Manitoba State Legislative Building and presumably has never made enquires to confirm this, she states that Gertler was 'discarded' by the British scheme when he was not (see p. 122), and misdates and misrecognises a cartoon published in *Punch* (see p. 132).

79 Arnold Bennett boasted about turning down most of the Academicians and 'even the inevitable Brangwyn'. Letter, 4 April 1918 in Hepburn, *Letters of Arnold Bennett*, p. 54.

80 'The ambition of this painting was to be history and to become history'; Ekkehard Mai, 'Mutations et évolution de la peinture d'histoire à la fin du XIXᵉ et au XXᵉ siècles', in Ekkehard Mai and Anke Repp-Eckert, eds., *Triumphe et mort du héros: La peinture d'histoire en Europe de Rubens à Manet* (Milan and Lyon: Electa/Musée des Beaux-Arts de Lyon, 1988), p. 162.

81 The most important project to revive and promote public art as part of art training in Britain was the Prix de Rome, established in 1912. See Alan Powers, 'Public Places and Private Faces: Narrative and Romanticism in English Mural Painting, 1900–1935', in J. Christian, ed., *The Last Romantics: The Romantic Tradition in British Art, Burne-Jones to Stanley Spencer* (London: Lund Humphries/ Barbican Art Gallery, 1989), pp. 63–9.

82 Virginia Woolf, *Roger Fry* (Harmondsworth: Penguin Books, 1979 [1940]), pp. 108–9.

83 'With the social and intellectual emancipation of the lower middle classes [who demanded] crude sensational effects [and] vivid appeals to a lazy curiosity', he argued that serious art had to be 'practised almost in secret like a proscribed religion'; Roger Fry, *Discourses Delivered to the Students of the Royal Academy by Sir Joshua Reynolds, K.T. With Introductions and Notes by Roger Fry* (London: Seely and Co. Ltd., 1905), pp. 347–8.

84 Reprinted in Roger Fry, *Vision and Design*, ed., J. B. Bullen (Oxford: Oxford University Press, 1981 [1920]), p. 21 and 15.

85 Widespread interest in early Renaissance art dated from the 1840s. See, for example, Camillo von Klenze, 'The Growth of Interest in the Early Italian Masters', *Modern Philology* vol. 4, no. 2, 1906. He writes 'at last depth and sincerity of feeling, and naïveté, became the watch-words of art-criticism, and [the Bolognese school, the Carraci, Guido Reni etc.] were banished', p. 3. In a statement that probably says more about Fry than Reynolds, Fry wrote that 'Reynolds was ahead of his generation in critical acumen; . . . in fact, on the verge of making the discovery of primitive art, and had he thought fit . . . to give free rein to these inclinations . . . he would have appeared as a pioneer in art criticism'; Fry *Discourses*, p. xii. Amongst students at the Slade, there was a cult of Botticelli. Nevinson describes being a member of a gang of students who called themselves 'the Neo-Primitives', making 'highly finished heads in the Botticelli manner' and the compensations of the Primitives Gallery in the Louvre. 'But', he writes, 'how we despised Rubens!'; *Paint and Prejudice* (London: Methuen, 1937), p. 33. Botticelli was the subject of two major monographs, by Herbert Horne in 1908 and Laurence Binyon in 1913.

86 The cartoons were on loan to the Victoria and Albert Museum after 1865 but, as John Sherman has pointed out, the prestige of the cartoons was at its lowest after the 1890s, in part because of the way they were hung, and neglected by students. See John Shearman, *Raphael's Cartoons in the Collection of her Majesty the Queen and the Tapestries for the Sistine Chapel* (London: Phaidon, 1972), pp. 160–66.

87 Paul Kristeller, *Andrea Mantegna* (London, Longmans, Green and Co., 1901), p. 435.

88 Fry, *Discourses*, p. xiii. In 1910, he wrote 'the biggest things demand the simplest language, and Cimabue could tell us more of divine, and Giotto more of human, love than Raphael or Rubens', 'The Grafton Galleries – 1', *Nation*, 19 November 1910, reprinted in J. B. Bullen, ed., *Post-Impressionists in England: The Critical Reception* (London and New York, Routledge, 1988), p. 123. In 'Retrospect', he discussed Raphael's *Transfiguration* of 1518–20 and wrote 'In Goethe's time rhetorical gesture was no bar to the appreciation of aesthetic unity. Later on in the nineteenth century, when the study of the Primitives had revealed to us the charm of dramatic sincerity and naturalness, these gesticulating figures appeared so false and unsympathetic that even people of aesthetic sensibility were unable to disregard them, and their dislike of the picture as illustration actually obliterated or prevented [their] purely aesthetic approval'; in *Vision and Design*, p. 209.

89 Wolfgang Kemp, 'Death at Work: A Case Study on Constitutive Blanks in Nineteenth Century Painting', *Representations*, 10, spring 1985, pp. 114 and 118.

90 John Barrell, *The Political Theory of Painting from Reynolds to Hazlitt: 'The Body of the Public'* (New Haven and London: Yale University Press, 1986), pp. 71, 99–101 and 112–13.

91 P. G. Konody, 'On War Memorials' in *Art and War: Canadian War Memorials* (Special Issue of *Colour Magazine*), London 1919, pp. 6 and 10–14.

92 Konody wrote 'We live in an age of individualism, . . . A completely homogenous plan, like the great decorative enterprises of the Renaissance could not be thought of. The aim was bound to be diversity rather than uniformity, but diversity kept under control.' Control, however, was to be exercised through 'unity of scale and decorative treatment'; *Art and War*, p. 15.

93 Kinney has argued that French painting in the 1860s was also a point of historical vacuum, when what was previously acceptable became inoperative. She argues that the role of genre is to orchestrate production and reception and they 'interrupt the presumed passage from raw social material into paint, channeling seemingly arbitrary arrangements of pigment into forms of address and instructions for comprehension.' Form has always mattered more than subject matter in reading genre or, more precisely, form is taken as content. But, as she points out, genres are sedimented and artistic form is inherently hybrid, because form is always renewing itself, 'adjusting archaic messages to different performative situations'. Fragments of something previously coherent survive in reinvented genres. New art is generated 'out of traditional modes of visualization', consequently, and especially in the modern period since around the 1860s or so, works are misunderstood; Leila Kinney, 'Genre: A Social Contract?' *Art Journal*, vol. 46, no. 4, 1987, p. 268. Kinney refers explicitly to Fredric Jameson's *The Political Unconscious* (1981) and to Mikhail Bakhtin. See especially, Bakhtin's 'Problems in Dostoevsky's Poetics' [1963], reprinted in P. Morris, ed.,

The Bakhtin Reader (London: Edward Arnold, 1994), pp. 188–9.

CHAPTER FOUR

1 William Orpen, *An Onlooker in France* (London: Williams and Norgate, 1921), pp. 65–6.

2 Wyndham Lewis, *Blasting and Bombardiering: Autobiography (1914–1926)* (London: Imperial War Museum, Department of Printed Books, 1992, Eyre and Spottiswood, 1937), p. 188.

3 Orpen to Beaverbrook, 22 May 1919 (HLRO, BBK C/262: Beaverbrook Papers, Series C Special Correspondence 1911–1964).

4 Quoted in Bruce Arnold, *Orpen: Mirror to an Age* (London: Jonathan Cape, 1981), p. 330.

5 Rothenstein to Max Beerbohm, 20 March 1918, in Mary M. Lago and Karl Beckson, *Max and Will: Max Beerbohm and William Rothenstein, Their Friendship and Letters 1893–1945* (London: John Murray, 1975), p. 106.

6 Orpen, *An Onlooker in France*, p. v.

7 Augustus Edwin John, *Chiaroscuro: Fragments of Autobiography, First Series* (London: Jonathan Cape, 1952), p. 93.

8 Michael Holroyd, *Augustus John: A biography* (Harmondsworth: Penguin, 1976), pp. 554–5.

9 Holroyd, *Augustus John*, p. 554.

10 William Rothenstein, *Men and Memories: A History of the Arts, 1872–1922*, vol. 2 (New York: Tudor Publishing Company, n.d.) p. 333.

11 Rothenstein, *Men and Memories*, p. 337.

12 Orpen, *An Onlooker in France*, p. 20.

13 Tonks to Yockney, 25 July 1918 (IWM 300/7: 'Henry Tonks'), and Joseph Hone, *The Life of Henry Tonks* (London: William Heinemann Ltd, 1939), pp. 143–4.

14 Lewis, *Blasting and Bombardiering*, pp. 137–8.

15 Daniel Pick, *War Machine: The Rationalisation of Slaughter in the Modern Age* (New Haven and London: Yale University Press, 1993), p. 8.

16 'Das ist ohne Frage, daß eine moderne Schlacht in ihre Ausdehnung und geistigen Bedeutung undarstellbar geworden ist. Jede Darstellung, die uns Soldaten, Stürme, Bewegungen, Geschütze, Schüsse, heroische Akte, Sieger und Besiegte zeigt, muß notwendig Episoden geben, die, mögen sie noch so menschlich erhebend oder erschütternd sein, doch nur winzige Kleinigkeiten, Ausschnitte des ungeheuren Geschehens darstellen, das die moderne Schlacht bedeutet, und umso kleinlicher, je naturgetreuer es ist. Eine malerische Darstellung aber, die ein möglichst großes Schlachtfeld zu überblicken versuchte, würde mehr als je alle Schlachtmomente aus den Augen verlieren, und man würde Menschen überhaupt nicht sehen, nur weites Feld, Ruinen, Dämpfe, Wolken, Himmel. Und je feiner ein Künstler, der den Auftrag erhält, uns Bild des Krieges zu entwerfen, ein solches Schlachtfeld malerisch auszubilden versteht, um so unwürdiger der großen Zeit wird er uns erscheinen, ein Aesthet und Genießer.

Eher werden wir die anklagenden Stimmen zu würdigen wissen, Darstellungen der Martyrien der Kämpfer und Verwundeten, der Gefangenen und Flüchtlinge. . . . Das Martyrium aber derer, die im Trommelfeuer auszuharren verpflichtet waren, kann keine Darstellung schildern, und die Masse, das Quantum des Leidens, das ein solcher Krieg über die Welt gebracht hat, lässt sich nicht einmal andeutungsweise auf engem Raum eines Bildes zusammendrängen.' Annegret Jürgens-Kirchhoff, *Schreckensbilder: Krieg und Kunst im 20. Jahrhundert* (Berlin: Reimer, 1993), p. 18.

17 Richard Cork writes that the employment of avant-garde artists was 'a grave threat to the integrity of their stylistic development', Richard Cork, *Vorticism and Abstract Art in the First Machine Age* vol. 2, (London: Gordon Fraser, 1976), p. 508. Charles Harrison also writes that Vorticist artists working on official commissions 'seem generally to have been unable to find ways of earning the money they sorely needed without involving themselves in what they must have seen as compromises'. Rather than resolving this as a matter of threat or coercion, Harrison argues that these war pictures are unsuccessful because they are 'evidence of the difficulty of reconciling two different sets of interests rooted in different forms of social practice', *English Art and Modernism 1900–1939* (New Haven and London: Yale University Press, 1994), p. 130.

18 On 12 December 1919, *Daily Mail* stated that no picture by Wyndham Lewis could match the fantastic circumstances that had deprived men of their humanness and that moreover the 'intellectual honesty' of the painters was a 'radical virtue'. The war had produced a 'youth made cruelly wise'. Reality had bitten into the soul of the artists who had emerged 'purged and sincere'; Raymond Coulson, *Evening Standard*, 2 February 1920.

19 'Their predilection for severe and formal design has served these men well in tackling such big problems, and the prescribed theme has brought back to modern art the serious consideration of subject matter and idea, for this occasion at least'; *Saturday Review*, 3 January 1920. The London *Times*, in an article titled 'Art's Fresh Start', stated that before the war the search for new ways of expression in art had lacked subject matter of sufficient consequence. The war itself had supplied such a subject and was an event that, in its magnitude and scale, must shatter continuity and produce change. As a result of first-hand experience as fighting men, several 'young painters have managed somehow to destroy that cut-off between the whole contents of the mind and the contents of a picture which has made modern painting so dull', 12 December 1919.

20 P. G. Konody declared that the exhibition was 'an event that may be destined to mark the dawn of a new era in British art'; *Observer*, 14 December 1919. The *Liverpool Post* stated that 'a revolution has come suddenly in British art, and the war has brought it about' for art had emerged 'strong and alert from the war, and has entered on a new epoch full of promise for the future'; *Liverpool Post and Mercury*, 12 December 1919. Similar sentiments were expressed by the *Daily*

Mirror (12 December 1919) and Sir Michael Sadler writing in the *Westminster Gazette*, 18 December 1919.

21 See Kenneth O. Morgan, *Consensus and Disunity: The Lloyd George Coalition Government, 1918–1922* (Oxford: Clarendon Press, 1979).

22 Charles Marriott, *Modern Movements in Painting* (London: Chapman and Hall, 1920), pp. 138–9.

23 R. H. Wilenski, 'The Nation's War Paintings at Burlington House', *Athenaeum*, 19 December 1919.

24 J. Middleton Murry, *The Nation*, 20 December 1919, pp. 419–20.

25 Andrew Rothstein, *The Soldiers' Strikes of 1919* (London: Journeyman, 1985 [1980]), p. 105. See also E. J. Leed, *No Man's Land: Combat and Identity in World War I* (Cambridge: Cambridge University Press, 1979), pp. 201–3. Klaus Theweleit examines veteran experience in Germany, in *Male Fantasies: Women, Floods, Bodies, History* (Cambridge: Polity Press, 1987) and *Male Fantasies, Male bodies: Psychoanalyzing the White Terror* (Cambridge: Polity Press, 1989).

26 Thomas Laqueur, 'Memory and Naming in the Great War', in John Gillis, ed., *Commemorations: The Politics of National Identity* (Princeton: Princeton University Press, 1994), p. 156.

27 Leed, *No Man's Land*, pp. 194–6.

28 Leed, *No Man's Land*, pp. 99–201 and 203–4.

29 Daniel J. Sherman, 'Monuments, Mourning and Masculinity in France after World War I', *Gender and History*, vol. 8, no. 1, 1996, p. 85.

30 Sherman, 'Monuments, Mourning and Masculinity', p. 85.

31 Leed, *No Man's Land*, pp. 202–3.

32 1 in 8 men were killed and 1 in 4 wounded between 1914 and 1918, see J. M. Winter, *The Great War and the British People* (Basingstoke: Macmillan, 1985), p. 72.

33 See Robert Rhodes, James *The British Revolution: British Politics, 1880–1939* (London: Methuen, 1978), p. 426; and Rothstein, *The Soldiers' Strikes*, 1985.

34 Ronald Paulson, *Representations of Revolution (1789–1820)* (New Haven and London: Yale University Press, 1983), p. 4.

35 *Saturday Review*, 3 January 1920; and *Sheffield Daily Telegraph*, 15 December 1919.

36 See the account in John Hatcher, *Laurence Binyon: Poet, Scholar of East and West* (Oxford: Clarendon Press, 1995), pp. 192–8.

37 See Roger Benjamin, 'The Decorative Landscape, Fauvism, and the Arabesque of Observation', *Art Bulletin*, vol. 75, no. 2, 1993, pp. 297–301.

38 Konody called them 'unnecessary soldier mannikins', *Observer*, 14 December 1919.

39 Nevinson to Yockney, 11 June 1919 (IWM, 266A/6: 'Nevinson 1917–1918').

40 Konody wrote that 'the group of figures, being pushed to the middle distance and below the horizon, do not tell at the normal distance from which a picture of such dimensions should be viewed'; *Observer*, 21 December 1919.

41 See Jane Carmichael, *First World War Photographers* (London and New York: Routledge, 1989), p. 9.

42 See Ralph Hyde, *Panoramania! The Art and Entertainment of the 'All-Embracing' View* (London: Lund Humphries and Barbican Art Gallery, 1988), pp. 169–72.

43 Nevinson to Yockney, 21 April 1918.

44 It was in fact a condition of the loan of the galleries imposed by the Royal Academy that no Academician could be prevented from showing an Imperial War Museum work in the summer exhibition. Lamb, Secretary of the Royal Academy, to Yockney, 30 January 1919, (IWM 21/1: 'Exhibition at Burlington House. Dec–Feb 1920').

45 *Belfast Evening Telegraph*; *Daily Express*, 28 March 1919.

46 Julia Kristeva, *Powers of Horror: An Essay on Abjection* (New York: Columbia University Press, 1982), pp. 2–3.

47 Canvases by artists such as Nash, Roberts, Spencer and Tonks, were shown with Sargent's *Gassed*. Four further works, including those by Lewis and Nevinson, were shown in an adjacent gallery opening off the Central Hall. Four reviewers commented at the time, however, on Lewis's absence from the main gallery. P. G. Konody, *Observer*, 21 December 1919; Michael Sadler, *Westminster Gazette*, 18 December 1919; *Saturday Review*, 3 January 1920; and B. H. Dias (Ezra Pound), *New Age*, 1 January 1920. It is important not to make too much of this, nor to imply that the works were in some way martyred. Articles by Reginald Grundy in the *Connoisseur* and the *Graphic* that have analysed the hostility to *A Battery Shelled* have over-stressed this critical reception, which was exceptional and out-of-step with the dominant mood. See Catherine Wallace, 'Art for Posterity? The Commissioned War Art of Percy Wyndham Lewis', *Imperial War Museum Review*, no. 6, 1992.

48 This interpretation is Paul Edwards's, and he also provides an excellent overview of how the picture has been analysed; Paul Edwards, *Wyndham Lewis: Art and War* (London: Lund Humphries, 1992), pp. 39–41.

49 He wrote in 1919: 'The eight-mile-wide belt of desert across France will be a green, methodic countryside in five years' time. The harsh dream that the soldier has dreamed – the barbaric nightmare – will be effaced by some sort of cosy sun tinting the edges of decorous lives.' and 'Ypres and Vimy . . . were deliberately invented scenes, daily improved on and worked at by up-to-date machines, to stage war.' 'The Men Who Will Paint Hell', *Daily Express*, 10 February 1919, reprinted in Walter Michel and C. J. Fox, eds., *Wyndham Lewis on Art: Collected Writings, 1913–1956* (London: Thames and Hudson, 1969), pp. 107–8.

50 Wilenski, 'The Nation's War Paintings'.

51 Christopher Prendergast, *Napoleon and History Painting: Antoine-Jean Gros's 'La Bataille d'Eylau'* (Oxford: Clarendon Press, 1997), p. 6.

52 Prendergast, *Napoleon and History Painting*, p. 8.

53 See the analysis by Jon Bird, 'Representing the Great War', *Block*, no. 3, 1980, p. 48.

54 Lewis, *Blasting and Bombardiering*, p. 138.

55 On his visit to France, Sargent could find only 'Anglo-American co-operation' happening 'in the abstract but not in any particular space within the limits of a picture' and renegotiated his subject to the scene of gassed soldiers he

had witnessed with Henry Tonks in exchange for agreeing to persist with a twenty-foot canvas; Sargent to Yockney, 4 October 1918, and Yockney to Bone, 5 November 1918 (IWM, 284/7: 'Sargent, John S.'). Sargent was the most important artist in the scheme, described as the 'keystone of the arch', and Bone insisted that the Committee 'must humour Sargent in every possible way!'; Yockney to Bone, 10 October 1918 (IWM, 284/7), and Bone to Yockney, 23 October 1918 (IWM, 39/2: 'Bone, Muirhead').

56 *Daily Graphic*, 30 January 1920 and 5 February 1920; 'Spurious Art', *Connoisseur*, vol. 56, no. 2, 1920.

57 'A False Dawn', *Athenaeum*, 9 January 1920.

58 Clive Bell, 'Wilcoxism', *Athenaeum*, 5 March 1920, reprinted in Clive Bell, *Since Cézanne* (London: Chatto and Windus, 1922), pp. 191–2.

59 Clive Bell, *Art* (London: Chatto and Windus, 1921 [1914]).

CHAPTER FIVE

1 All exhibited in the first Vorticist exhibition June 1915, Nevinson and Bomberg as guests. Bomberg held a startling solo exhibition at the Chenil Gallery in 1914. Nevinson had circulated a futurist manifesto with Marinetti.

2 See, for example, Richard Cork, *Vorticism and Abstract Art in the First Machine Age* (London: Gordon Fraser Gallery, 1976), and Charles Harrison, *English Art and Modernism, 1900–1939*, (New Haven and London: Yale University Press, 1994. London: Allen Lane, 1981).

3 See *The Globe*, 26 February 1915.

4 See correspondence in Timothy Materer, ed., *Pound/Lewis: The Letters of Ezra Pound and Wyndham Lewis* (New York: New Directions, 1985).

5 The standard account is Paul Fussell, *The Great War and Modern Memory* (Oxford: Oxford University Press, 1977, [1975]). The model dominates Richard Cork's *A Bitter Truth: Avant-Garde Art and the Great War* (New Haven and London: Yale University Press, 1994) with chapters such as 'Disillusion (1915–16)' or 'Despair and Redemption'.

6 Leo Bersani, *The Culture of Redemption* (Cambridge, Mass.: Harvard University Press, 1990), p. 22.

7 Michael Long, 'The Politics of English Modernism: Eliot, Pound and Joyce', in Edward Timms and Peter Collier, eds., *Visions and Blueprints: Avant-Garde Culture and Radical Politics in Early Twentieth-Century Europe* (Manchester: Manchester University Press, 1988), p. 98.

8 Francis Klingender, 'Content and Form in Art', in Betty Rea, *5 on Revolutionary Art* (London: Wishart, 1935), p. 38 and p. 40.

9 *Daily Express*, 8 March 1935.

10 See James Beechy, 'Defining Modernism: Roger Fry and Clive Bell in the 1920s', in Richard Shone, ed., *The Art of Bloomsbury* (London: Tate Gallery, 1999), pp. 30–51. A more rigorous account of Bloomsbury's entrenchment in the '20s can be found in Andrew Stephenson, '"Strategies of situation": British Modernism and the Slump, c.1929–1934',

Oxford Art Journal, vol. 14, no. 2, 1991, pp. 30–51. For the wider institutionalisation of modernism, see Matei Calinescu, *Five Faces of Modernity: Modernism, Avant-Garde, Decadence, Kitsch, Postmodernism* (Durham: Duke University Press, 1987), pp. 68–9.

11 10 October 1918, Denys Sutton, ed., *Letters of Roger Fry* (London: Chatto and Windus, 1972), p. 435.

12 It first came out in paperback in 1937. See Donald A. Laing, *Roger Fry: An Annotated Bibliography of the Published Writings* (New York: Garland, 1979), p. 11, who notes that some records on print runs are missing.

13 C. J. Holmes, '"Vision and Design"', *Burlington Magazine*, vol. 38, February 1921, pp. 82–4.

14 See John House, ed., *Impressionism for England: Samuel Courtauld as Patron and Collector* (New Haven and London: Yale University Press, 1994), in particular the essay by Andrew Stephenson, '"An Anatomy of Taste": Samuel Courtauld and Debates about Art Patronage and Modernism in Britain in the Inter-War Years', pp. 35–46.

15 Roger Fry, *Vision and Design* (Oxford: Oxford University Press, 1981 [1920]), pp. 6 and 10.

16 In Rea, *5 on Revolutionary Art*, p. 45.

17 D. S. MacColl, 'The Future of the National and Tate Galleries', *Nineteenth Century*, vol. 77, no. 460, June 1915, pp. 1392 and 1406.

18 Fry added 'Nearly everything from painting to book collecting is explained as a mere outcome of anal-eroticism' [but] the worst of it is that as everybody is thus shown to be anally-erotic one can't use it to score off anyone in particular'; Sutton, *Letters of Roger Fry*, p. 448.

19 Ernest Jones, *The Life and Work of Sigmund Freud*, abridged edn (London: Penguin, 1964), p. 487 and also pp. 515 and 542.

20 Hanna Segal, 'A Psycho-Analytic Approach to Aesthetics', *International Journal of Psycho-Analysis*, no. 33, 1952, p. 204.

21 Lyndsey Stonebridge, *The Destructive Element: British Psychoanalysis and Modernism* (Basingstoke: Palgrave/Macmillan, 1998), p. 72.

22 Sutton, *Letters of Roger Fry*, p. 434.

23 Stonebridge, *The Destructive Element*, p. 74.

24 For a discussion of mourning work, see Sigmund Freud, 'Mourning and Melancholia (1915)', in Angela Richards, ed., *On Metapsychology: The Theory of Psychoanalysis*, vol. 11, Penguin Freud Library (London: Penguin Books, 1984), pp. 247–68, and Rebecca Comay, 'Mourning Work and Play', *Research in Phenomenology*, vol. 23, 1993, pp. 105–30.

25 See, for example, the chapter on 'Modernity and Revisionist Modernism in the Twenties' where he writes 'Although modernity was extremely pressing as an issue [after 1918], in a number of ways the ability to address it directly in a public language of modernism was itself negated and replaced by a private and quietist 'modernism' with no such ambitions', David Peters Corbett, *The Modernity of English Art, 1914–30* (Manchester: Manchester University Press, 1997), p. 58.

26 See Introduction, note 2, p. 200.

27 See the discussion in Andrew Wilson, 'Introduction' to *Wyndham Lewis, 1882–1957* (London: Austin/Desmond Fine

28 Unidentified press cutting in Nevinson's press cuttings in the Tate Gallery Archives, probably an interview in *The Observer*, 22 May 1921.

29 An invaluable account that pioneered study of these interconnections, many of which would reward closer examination, was published by Alan Young, *Dada and After: Extremist Modernism and English Literature* (Manchester: Manchester University Press, 1981); on Sitwell see p. 43, Rodker pp. 87–9 and Hunt pp. 147–50.

30 See the issues for August 4 and October 27 1923.

31 See Eden and Cedar Paul, *Proletcult (Proletarian Culture)* (London: Leonard Parsons, 1921).

32 Harrison, *English Art and Modernism, 1900–1939*, p. 168.

33 Wyndham Lewis, *Blasting and Bombardiering* (London: Imperial War Museum, Department of Printed Books, 1992 [Eyre and Spottiswood, 1937]), p. 1.

34 TGA, 733.3.28: Notebook, p. 46.

35 Epstein to van Dieren, undated, quoted in Evelyn Silber, *The Sculpture of Jacob Epstein with a Complete Catalogue* (Oxford: Phaidon, 1986), p. 36.

36 Daniel Pick, *War Machine: The Rationalisation of Slaughter in the Modern Age* (New Haven and London: Yale University Press, 1993), pp. 190–91.

37 The evidence that the painting was not destroyed is in a letter from 1957 where Bomberg writes, 'This painting will one day be shown in a retrospective exhibition I hope, not too far removed that I shall be dead before it happens', draft unpublished letter to *The Times*, 11 April 1957 (TGA, 878.2.1).

38 Correspondence about Airy is in IWM, 27/2: 'Airy, Miss A'. There was a problem with Airy working for both the Imperial War Museum and the British committee and at one stage the size of her memorial commission was reduced from a large 'Uccello' to the less prestigious 60 × 42 inches. The artist reported that she had destroyed the rejected canvas, a picture of munitions girls leaving work.

39 See Richard Cork, *David Bomberg* (New Haven and London: Yale University Press, 1987), p. 2; Richard Cork, *David Bomberg* (London: Tate Gallery, 1988), p. 22; and Richard Cork, *Vorticism and Abstract Art in the First Machine Age* (London: Gordon Fraser Gallery, 1976), vol. 2, pp. 516–19 where he writes 'it turned out to mark a watershed in the development of his life's work. . . . For the first time in the whole of his outstandingly consistent career, his nerve had been broken . . . Bomberg's brief, heroic contribution to the progress of the avant-garde was now over. His revolution had run its course, ending in an agony of doubt, uncertainty and conflicting impulses from which he would never again fully emerge.'

40 Bone to Yockney, Christmas 1918 (IWM, 39/2). Yockney and Bone monitored the Canadian scheme carefully, often with Watkins at informal evening get-togethers, what Watkins called 'our Mutual Improvement in Art Society'; Watkins to Yockney, 28 September 1918 (IWM, 322/7: 'Canada').

41 It seems to have been George Frampton RA who orchestrated the campaign against Konody. Minutes, Council of the Royal Academy, 7 January 1919 and 25 January 1919, Royal Academy Archives. Konody was not hostile to abstract art. In 1921, Lawrence Atkinson exhibited 'Abstract Sculpture and Painting' with a catalogue essay by the critic.

42 The International Society suspended its German members in 1914 because it could not collect their fees, but voted to expel them only in July 1918. AGM, 22 July 1918. Minute Book of the International Society of Sculptors, Painters and Gravers (TGA, 73–8.4.33).

43 The letters were dated 28 (Roberts) and 29 (Bomberg) December 1917 and signed by Harold Watkins, on behalf of 'Officer i/c Canadian War Records'. The explanation for the condition was worded 'The reason for this request is that the Art adviser [Konody] informs us that he is not acquainted with your realistic work, and cubist work would be inadmissible for the purpose'. Roberts reprinted his letter in *Memories of the War to End War, 1914–18* (London: privately printed, 1974), p. 24. Bomberg's is in TGA, 878.2.2. Except for some minor differences in wording of the first sentence, the letters are identical.

44 Bomberg, draft letter to *The Times*, 11 April 1957 (TGA, 78.2.1).

45 Cork *Bomberg*, 1988, p. 82.

46 Letters between Bomberg and Yockney, dated 9 and 14 February 1920 (IWM, 150/4). Wadsworth's letter, 23 November 1918, is to be found at the IWM in a large 'elephant file' titled 'Artists considered'.

47 William Lipke, *David Bomberg: A Critical Study of his Life and Work* (London: Evelyn, Adams and Mackay, 1967), p. 48.

48 Herbert Read, *Arts Gazette*, 13 September 1919; *Jewish World*, 15 October 1919.

49 Bomberg to Sigfried Giedion, 26 July 1953 (TGA, 878.2.1). Bomberg gave numerous accounts of this encounter in letters to Lewis Mumford and Walter Gropius, dated July or September 1953.

50 See Cork, *Bomberg*, 1987, especially pp. 78–95, and Lisa Tickner, *Modern Life and Modern Subjects: British Art in the Early Twentieth Century* (New Haven and London: Yale University Press, 2000), pp. 177–8.

51 Cited in Lipke, *Bomberg*, p. 48 and in Fischer Fine Art, *Bomberg: Paintings, Drawings, Watercolours and Lithographs* (London: Fischer Fine Art, 1973) p. 26, where the statement is dated 1919. I have not yet found this statement in the Bomberg papers at the TGA.

52 Bomberg to his sister, Kitty, 9 April 1935 (TGA, 8811.1.1).

53 The description of the miners is in Bomberg's draft letter to *The Times*, 11 April 1957 (TGA, 878.2.1). Cork gives an account of the event depicted quoting Colonel Nicholson's history of the C. E. F., 1962, *Bomberg*, 1987, p. 113.

54 Watkin to Bomberg, 29 December 1917 (TGA, 878.2.2).

55 Tickner, *Modern Life and Modern Subjects*, pp. 175, 177 and 173.

56 Roberts, who came from an East End working-class background and was married to Jacob Kramer's sister, Sarah, was

a close friend of Bomberg's. Alice Mayes, letter to William Lipke, 27 June 1965 (TGA, 878.3.7).

57 *Observer*, 12 February 1928 (TGA, 878.9).

58 Bomberg, draft letter to *The Times*, 11 April 1957 (TGA, 878.2.1).

59 TGA, 7319; Bomberg to his sister, Kitty, 21 April 1939 (TGA, 811.1.1).

60 Quoted in Lynda Morris, *Henry Tonks and the 'Art of Pure Drawing'* (Norwich: Norwich School of Art, 1985), p. 17.

61 Bomberg to Roberts, 10 March 1957 (TGA, 878.2.1).

62 See the careful account in Tickner, *Modern Life and Modern Subjects*, pp. 279–80. Her statement that in 1912, 'all working-class [students at the Slade] were male *and Jewish*' (p. 149) needs to slightly qualified. Stanley Spencer, like Roberts, was not Jewish and was from a comparatively impoverished background rather than securely middle-class. See Roberts's own account of his origins, *William Roberts: Early Years* (London: privately printed, 1982 [1977]). Waite has argued that the effect of the First World War was to shift a complex hierarchy of class and status, with subtle gradations of status within both the middle and working classes, to a more simplified three-tier structure in which some higher working and lower middle classes lost status. B. A. Waites, 'The Effect of the First World War on Class and Status in England, 1910–1920', *Journal of Contemporary History*, no. 11, 1976, pp. 27–48.

63 See Eric J. Leed, *No Man's Land: Combat and Identity in World War I* (Cambridge: Cambridge University Press, 1979), pp. 94–6.

64 Roberts, *Memories*, p. 2.

65 Roberts, *Memories*, pp. 7, 14–15 and 20.

66 He completed and dated some finished drawings in August 1918 and discussed his large canvas with Bone in May. In November, he visited a shell dump in order to revive his impressions. Roberts to Yockney, 22 May 1918; Yockney to Captain Bowen, MI7c, 30 November 1918 (IWM, 277/6: 'Roberts, William'). The slighter sketches may have been exercises in recollection since Roberts did not revisit the front and probably represent his first works as a war artist, for instance *Rosières Valley* is possibly a first sketch for *Signallers*, dated August 1918.

67 Roberts to Yockney, 2 January 1919; Yockney to Colonel Fischer, War Office, 29 November 1918 (IWM, 277/6). In 1919 his son was born and in March of that year he reported that he had run out of savings; Roberts to Yockney, 15 March 1919. William Orpen, meeting him in May, found him 'in rather a pathetic state'; Orpen to Yockney 13 May [1919] (IWM, 39/2: 'Bone'). He was unable to hold an exhibition because he had sold most of his work to pay his way; Roberts to Yockney, 21 August 1919 (IWM, 277/6).

68 Roberts to Sarah, 11 November 1917, in *Memories*, p. 42.

69 Roberts to Sarah, 11 November 1917, in *Memories*, p. 42.

70 Leed, *No Man's Land*, pp. 68–72.

71 Roberts to Konody, 1 January [1918] Miscellaneous Collection. Letters to Konody from various artists after 1918 (some before 1914), IWM.

72 'Bobby writes me that he has practically got the Canadian job! That is Watkins (Records Office) has written him asking if he is willing to do the painting on spec: if not found suitable, no £250 but expenses paid. This since "their advisor" cannot guarantee his not doing a "Cubist picture" or something of that rot. He naturally accepts, with amertume, on any terms.' Lewis to Ezra Pound, 16 January 1918, in Rose, *Letters of Wyndham Lewis*, p. 97.

73 Roberts, *Memories*, p. 34.

74 Churchill is quoted in Robert Rhodes James, *The British Revolution: British Politics, 1880–1939* (London: Methuen, 1978), p. 428 and pp. 435–6.

75 Canadian War Memorials Fund, *Canadian War Records: Canadian War Memorials Exhibition*, Burlington House, January–February (London: Canadian War Memorials Fund, 1919), cat. no. 66, p. 12.

76 Canadian War Memorials Office, *Art and War: Canadian War Memorials*, with an article 'On War Memorials' by P. G. Konody (London: Colour Limited, 1919), plate XLIII. Lewis's most recent biographer attributes the comment to Lewis himself, but this is not very likely. Paul O'Keefe, *Some Sort of Genius: A Life of Wyndham Lewis* (London: Jonathan Cape, 2000), p. 209.

77 Wyndham Lewis, ed., *Blast: Review of the Great English Vortex* Santa Barbara: Black Sparrow Press, 1981 [London: John Lane, 1915], p. 91.

78 Sir Herbert Edward Read, University of Victoria Libraries Special Collections; Lewis, Percy Wyndham, 48.82, reprinted in Rose, *Letters of Wyndham Lewis*, p. 102.

79 Lewis, *Blasting and Bombardiering*, pp. 188–9.

80 Reprinted in Paul Edwards, *Wyndham Lewis: Art and War* (London: Imperial War Museum and Lund Humphries, 1991), pp. 141–2.

81 *Weekly Dispatch*, 16 February 1919.

82 Lewis to Quinn, 7 February 1919, in Rose, *Letters of Wyndham Lewis*, p. 104.

83 Lewis to Pound, 20 August 1917, Ezra Pound Papers, YCAL MSS 43 Box 29, Folder 1245, Beinecke Rare Book and Manuscript Library, Yale University, reprinted in Timothy Materer, ed., *Pound/Lewis: The Letters of Ezra Pound and Wyndham Lewis* (New York: New Directions, 1985), p. 96, based on the Cornell University collection.

84 Lewis to Pound, September 1917, Materer, *Pound/Lewis*, pp. 105–6. The reference to a French Salon painting is probably Henri Regnault's *Exécution sans jugement sous les rois maures de Grenade* of 1870, Musée d'Orsay, Paris.

85 Lewis, 'The Men Who Will Paint Hell', *Daily Express*, 10 February 1919, reprinted in Walter Michel and C. J. Fox, eds., *Wyndham Lewis on Art: Collected Writings, 1913–1956* (London: Thames and Hudson, 1969), p. 107.

86 Lewis, *Blasting and Bombardiering*, pp. 202–3.

87 Paul Fussell, *The Great War and Modern Memory* (London: Oxford University Press, 1977 [1975]), pp. 204–5.

88 Lewis, *Blasting and Bombardiering*, pp. 5–6.

89 Lewis 'The Men Who Will Paint Hell', 1919.

90 Ezra Pound Papers and Materer, *Pound/Lewis*, p. 86. The word 'aesthetic' is illegible in the Beinecke manuscript.

91 Hal Foster, 'Prosthetic Gods', *Modernism/Modernity*, vol. 4, no. 2, 1997, pp. 7 and 27.

92 Walter Benjamin, 'Theory of German Fascism', in *Walter Benjamin: Selected Writings, 1927–1934*, vol. 2 (Cambridge, Mass.: The Belknap Press of Harvard University Press, 1999), p. 312.

93 Jessie Dismorr, Frederick Etchells, C. J. Hamilton, William Roberts and Edward Wadsworth all contributed. Also exhibiting were Charles Ginner, Mcknight Kauffer, John Turnball and Frank Dobson.

94 Lewis wrote to McKnight Kauffer that 'Roberts told me on Sunday that at the London Group Meeting Fry was very excited [?] in his mind about x Group getting their show in before the London Group . . . It happens that the London Group have definitely chosen May: and that . . . we had better open on March 26th [1919?].' Rose, *Letters of Wyndham Lewis*, p. 115.

95 'The energy at present pent up (and much too congested) in the canvas painted in the studio and sold at the dealer's, and written up with a monotonous emphasis of horror or facetiousness in the Press, must be released. It must be used in the general life of the community. Thence, from the life outside, it will come back and enrich and invigorate the Studio,' Michel and Fox, *Wyndham Lewis on Art*, p. 131.

96 Wyndham Lewis, 'Tyros and Portraits', reprinted in Michel and Fox, *Wyndham Lewis on Art*, pp. 187–8.

97 Wyndham Lewis, 'The Children of the New Epoch', *The Tyro: A Review of the Arts of Painting, Sculpture and Design*, 1, 1921, p. 3; cited in David Peters Corbett, '"Grief with a yard wide grin": War and Wyndham Lewis's Tyros', in David Peters Corbett, ed., *Wyndham Lewis and the Art of Modern War* (Cambridge: Cambridge University Press, 1998), p. 104.

98 'I refuse to use the same technical method to express such contradictory forms as a rock or a woman', reprinted in C. R. W. Nevinson, *Paint and Prejudice* (London: Methuen, 1937), p. 125.

99 Michael Sadler, 'The Nevinson Palace of Varieties', *Westminster Gazette*, 4 November 1919. 'There is indeed so much variety that it is not easy to find the thread of individuality which binds all the different manifestations together', *Daily News*, 27 October 1919. He was described as 'almost . . . not an artist, but a troupe of artistes', *Athenaeum*, 31 October 1919. Charles Marriott said that Nevinson's disclaimer 'excites the uneasy feeling that his artistic methods during the war were those of exploitation rather than expression', 'Stunting in Art', *The Outlook*, 8 November 1919.

100 Claude Phillips wrote about his exhibition in 1921 that it 'will certainly amuse and stimulate the less earnest lovers of painting, while it will as surely leave unsatisfied those with whom no modernity (we *cannot* get away from the word), no light-hearted scorn of the conventional, will atone for aridity – for the lack of the deeper artistic emotion', *Daily Telegraph*, 4 October 1921. Konody said the pictures had been 'produced in hours of hopeless boredom', *Observer*, 2 October 1921. Hugh Stokes recommended that 'He should refuse to enter a picture gallery for at least a year. Then we

might have a chance of seeing a veritable Nevinson instead of innumerable clever *pastiches*', 'Nevinson's Pictures', *The Queen*, 15 October 1921.

101 *Sunday Chronicle*, 20 June 1920.

102 'Compared with the boom that set in towards the end of the war, and lasted until about 1920, we are in what some people might call a slump. It is merely the natural reaction from that period of exceptional activity', 'Down and Out Artists', *Westminster Gazette*, 28 September 1925. See also the introduction in Frances Carey and Anthony Griffiths, *Avant-Garde British Printmaking, 1914–1960* (London: British Museum Publications Ltd., 1990).

103 See Ian Jeffrey, 'C. R. W. Nevinson: Artist-Celebrity' in Kettle's Yard Gallery, *C. R. W. Nevinson, 1889–1946: Retrospective Exhibition of Paintings, Drawings and Prints* (Cambridge: Kettle's Yard Gallery, 1988–9), p. 59.

104 *Westminster Gazette*, 28 September 1925.

105 *World's Pictorial News*, 9 June 1923. 'His working garb already shows traces of the Mussolini influence', *Birmingham Gazette and Express*, 13 October 1923.

106 *Weekly Dispatch*, 9 March 1919.

107 *The Graphic*, 25 October 1919. In 1922, it was reproduced as *Strikers on Tower Hill*, *The New Leader*, 13 October 1922. Nevinson also exhibited a lithograph called *Night Shift, Merthyr*.

108 Nevinson to *Aberdeen Press and Journal*, 25 October 1924.

109 *The Tatler*, 15 October 1930.

110 *Daily Express*, 1 April 1930.

111 *Daily Record and Mail*, 25 August 1930.

112 *John O'London's Weekly*, 7 October 1922.

113 *Daily Express*, 14 March 1924.

114 Angus Burn, 'The Art of C. R. W. Nevinson', *The Graphic*, 15 March 1924, and *The Times*, 14 March 1924, and *The Westminster Gazette*, 14 March 1924.

115 *Westminster Gazette*, 13 March 1924.

116 *Daily Express*, 14 March 1924.

117 *The Illustrated London News*, 30 September 1933.

118 *Daily Sketch*, 26 July 1924.

119 *Observer*, 16 March 1924.

120 *Morning Post*, 14 March 1924.

121 *Daily Dispatch*, 14 March 1924.

122 *Daily News*, 10 November 1924.

123 *Daily Graphic*, 13 March 1924.

124 *Sphere*, 30 April 1927.

125 *Evening Standard*, Obituary, 9 October 1946.

126 Simon Watney, 'The Warhol Effect', in Gary Garrels, ed., *The Work of Andy Warhol: Dia Art Foundation Discussions in Contemporary Culture Number 3* (Seattle: Bay Press, 1989), p. 120.

127 Douglas Percy Bliss, *The Scotsman*, 8 October 1946.

128 Raymond Williams, 'The Politics of the Avant-Garde', in Tony Pinkney, ed., *The Politics of Modernism: Against the New Conformists* (London: Verso, 1989), p. 55 (originally published in Edward Timms and Peter Collier, eds., *Visions and Blueprints: Avant-Garde Culture and Radical Politics in Early Twentieth-Century Europe* (Manchester: Manchester University Press, 1988).

129 See Andrew Hewitt: *Fascist Modernism: Aesthetics, Politics and the Avant-Garde* (Stanford: Stanford University Press, 1993), pp. 29–30.

130 Fredric Jameson, *Fables of Aggression: Wyndham Lewis, the Modernist as Fascist* (Berkeley: University of California Press, 1979), pp. 14–16.

131 Mark Neocleous *Fascism* (Buckingham: Open University Press, 1997), p. 60. The literature on fascism and modernism is very extensive. An non-exhaustive list of such studies, and not including work on Stalinism, would include early writings such as Tom Gibbons, 'Modernism and Reactionary Politics', *Journal of Modern Literature*, 3, 1974, pp. 1140–57; Miriam Hansen, 'T. E. Hulme, Mercenary of Modernism, or, Fragments of Avantgarde Sensibility in Pre-World War I Britain', *Journal of English Literary History*, 47, 1980, pp. 355–85; as well as Jameson's work on Wyndham Lewis. General studies include various essays in Timms and Collier, *Visions and Blueprints*, 1988; Richard J. Golsan, *Fascism, Aesthetics, and Culture*, (Hanover, N.H., and London: University Press of New England, 1992); Andrew Hewitt, *Fascist Modernism: Aesthetics, Politics and the Avant-Garde*, 1993; Matthew Affron and Mark Antliff, eds., *Fascist Visions: Art and Ideology in France and Italy* (Princeton, N. J.: Princeton University Press, 1997); and Ruth Ben-Ghiat, *Fascist Modernities: Italy, 1922–1945* (Berkeley: University of California Press, 2001). Work on fascism and sexuality that is variously indebted to Klaus Theweleit's two-volume study of the Freicorps, *Male Bodies: Women, Floods, Bodies, History* and *Male Bodies: Psychoanalyzing the White Terror*, or writings such as Alice Kaplan, *Reproductions of Banality: Fascism, Literature, and French Intellectual Life* (Minneapolis: University of Minnesota Press, 1986); M.–A. Macciocchi, 'Female Sexuality and Fascist Ideology', *Feminist Review*, vol. 1, no. 1 1979, pp. 67–82; and Barbara Spackman, 'The Fascist Rhetoric of Virility', *Standford Italian Review*, vol. 8. no. 1–2.,1990, pp. 81–101, would include Hal Foster, 'L'amour fou', *Art in America*, vol. 74, January 1986, pp. 116–29, and his 'Exquisite Corpses', in Lucien Taylor, ed., *Visualizing Theory: Selected Essays from V. A. R. 1900–1994* (New York: Routledge, 1994), pp. 159–72, and 'Prosthetic Gods', *Modernism/Modernity*, vol. 4. no. 2, 1997, pp. 5–38.

132 In letters to Vanessa Bell, Fry wrote that 'Gertler . . . sent a large Yiddish translation of a Cezanne. Frankly I loathe Yiddish', 18 May 1917 (TGA, 8010.5.690), and, describing William Rothenstein's Canadian canvas of British troops standing guard on the banks of the Rhine, wrote 'It shows one the whole scheme of the British Empire upheld by the stern determination and the deep ethical sense of its German Jews', 17 March 1919 (TGA, 8010.5.780).

133 See the introduction in Corbett, *Wyndham Lewis and the Art of Modern War*, p. 6, and Geoff Gilbert, 'Shellshock, Anti-Semitism, and the Agency of the Avant-Garde', in the same volume, p. 86.

134 Paul Edwards, *Wyndham Lewis: Painter and Writer* (New Haven and London: Yale University Press, 2000), p. 199.

135 Harrison, *English Art and Modernism, 1900–1939*, p. 168.

136 TGA, 8811.1.1.

137 TGA, 878.4.12.

138 Foreword. The Chenil Gallery, July 1914, n.p.

139 Bomberg to his sister, Kitty, 13 March 1939 (TGA, 8811.1.1.)

140 There are several of these allegories including *With Nothing to Lose – Not Even Chains* of 1930, *They All Know The Way: A Symbolic Satire on Fascists, Socialists, Capitalists, Hedonists, Ascetics, Intellectuals, and Priests* of 1934 and *Ave Homo Sapiens* of 1935.

141 See Betsy Dokter and Carry van Lakerveld, eds., *Een Kunstolympiade in Amsterdam: Reconstructie van de tentoostelling D.O.O.D. 1936* (Amsterdam: Gemeentearchief, 1996).

142 Maude Royden, L. P. Jacks, A. E. Richardson, Marquis of Tavistock, C. R. W. Nevinson, Bernard Acworth and Bernard Denison Ross, *The Seven Pillars of Fire: A Symposium* (London: Herbert Jenkins, 1936), p. 187.

143 *Bystander*, 1 November 1939.

CHAPTER SIX

1 Walter Benjamin, 'Theses on the Philosophy of History', in *Illuminations* (New York: Schoken, 1969), p. 254.

2 See the account in Bob Bushaway, 'Name Upon Name: The Great War and Remembrance', in Roy Porter, ed., *Myths of the English* (Cambridge: Polity Press, 1992).

3 Bushaway, 'Name Upon Name', p. 155, and see Owen Chadwick, 'Armistice Day', *Theology*, 29, 1976, pp. 322–9.

4 Bushaway, 'Name Upon Name', p. 161.

5 See the discussion about cenotaphs in Alan Borg, *War Memorials: From Antiquity to the Present* (London: Leo Cooper, 1991).

6 D. S. MacColl, 'An Inscription', 1921, in *What is Art? and Other Papers* (Harmondsworth: Penguin Books Limited, 1940 [1931]), p. 234.

7 See Catherine Moriarty, 'Christian Iconography and First World War Memorials', *Imperial War Museum Review*, 6, n.d., p. 71, and Bushaway, 'Name Upon Name', p. 158.

8 Moriarty, 'Christian Iconography', p. 68.

9 Hansard, 20 May 1920, cited by Moriarty, 'Christian Iconography', p. 65.

10 Moriarty, 'Christian Iconography', p. 70.

11 See Moriarty, 'Christian Iconography', pp. 71–3 and Bushaway, 'Name Upon Name', pp. 148–9 and 159.

12 Paul Nash, *Outline : An Autobiography, and Other Writings* (London: Faber and Faber, 1949), p. 218.

13 See Andrew Causey, *Paul Nash* (Oxford: Clarendon Press, 1980), p. 357, for the reference to imagery of 1915–17.

14 John Rothenstein, 'Paul Nash as War Artist', in Margot Eates, ed., *Paul Nash: Paintings Drawings and Illustrations* (London: Lund Humphries, 1948), known as the Memorial Volume, p. 15.

15 Paul Nash, 'Outline' MS (TGA, 7050.2.12/1: p. 2).

16 See Clare Colvin, 'Introduction', in South Bank Centre, *Paul Nash: Places* (London: South Bank Centre, 1989), p. 31.

17 Colvin, 'Introduction', in South Bank Centre, *Places*, p. 29.

18 Ian Jeffrey, *The British Landscape, 1920–1950* (London: Thames and Hudson, 1984), pp. 10–12.

19 Jeffrey, *The British Landscape*, p. 7.

20 See Alex Potts, '"Constable Country" between the Wars,' in Raphael Samuel, ed., *Patriotism: The Making and Unmaking of British National Identity*, vol. 3, National Fictions (London: Routledge, 1989).

21 See Mary Beal, '"For the Fallen": Paul Nash's "Landscape at Iden"', *Burlington Magazine*, 1541, January, 1999, pp. 19–23.

22 See Alun Howkins, *Reshaping Rural England: A Social History, 1850–1925* (London: Harper Collins Academic, 1991).

23 Clare Colvin, *Paul Nash Book Designs* (Colchester: The Minories, 1982), p. 30.

24 Prose poems 'Winter' and 'Winter Wood', in Paul Nash, *Places: 7 Prints from Woodblocks Designed and Engraved by Paul Nash* (London: William Heinemann Ltd, 1922).

25 Colvin, 'Introduction', in South Bank Centre, *Places*, p. 6.

26 Causey, *Paul Nash*, p. 98.

27 See Colvin, *Paul Nash Book Designs*, p. 33.

28 Colvin, 'Introduction', in South Bank Centre, *Places*, p. 7.

29 Nash to Bottomley, about 23 August 1917, in Claude Abbott and Anthony Bertram, *Poet and Painter: Letters between Gordon Bottomley and Paul Nash, 1910–1946* (Brisol: Redcliffe Press, 1990 [1955]), p. 86.

30 Erwin Panofsky, 'Et in Arcadia Ego: Poussin and the Elegiac Tradition', in *Meaning in the Visual Arts* (Harmondsworth: Penguin Books, 1955), especially pp. 356–7. Paul Fussell also cites this reading of Panofsky's in *The Great War and Modern Memory* (Oxford: Oxford University Press, 1977 [1975]), pp. 245–6.

31 Lisa Tickner, *Modern Life and Modern Subjects: British Art in the Early Twentieth Century* (New Haven and London: Yale University Press, 2000), p. 75. John's *Atque in Arcadia Ego* was part of a set of drawings on the theme of gypsy courtship made in connection with John Sampson's Romani Poems published 1931. See Rebecca John and Mark Evans, *Themes and Variations: The Drawings of Augustus John, 1901–1931* (London: Lund Humphries; Cardiff: National Museums and Galleries of Wales, 1996), p. 69.

32 TGA 769.2.6: 'Memoirs of Paul Nash 1913–1946', pp. 12 and 19.

33 See the chapter 'The Golden Age and the French National Heritage' in James D. Herbert, *Fauve Painting: The Making of Cultural Politics* (New Haven and London: Yale University Press, 1992).

34 Abbott and Bertram, *Poet and Painter*, p. 86.

35 See the discussion in Colvin, *Paul Nash Book Designs*, pp. 38–50.

36 Nash, *Outline*, p. 148.

37 Benedict Anderson, *Imagined Communities: Reflections on the Origins and Spread of Nationalism* (London: Verso, 1983), p. 7.

38 Nancy Huston, 'The Matrix of War: Mothers and Heroes', in Susan Rubin Suleiman, ed., *The Female Body in Western Culture: Contemporary Perspectives* (London: Harvard University Press, 1986), p. 132. She cites Heraclitus, 'War is the mother of all things', and Clausewitz, 'War develops in the womb of State politics; its principles are hidden there as the particular characteristics of the individual are hidden in the embryo', p. 133.

39 Anderson, *Imagined Communities*, p. 5.

40 Andrew Parker, Mary Rosso, Doris Sommer and Patricia Yaeger, eds., *Nationalisms and Sexualities* (New York and London: Routledge, 1992), p. 5.

41 'The nationalist myth['s] . . . use of the past is therefore selective, singling out foundation myths and golden ages, and omitting unworthy episodes and embarrassing interpretations.' Anthony Smith, *Times Higher Education Supplement*, 8 January 1993, p. 15.

42 Quoted in Rothenstein, 'Paul Nash as War Artist, p. 16.

43 C. E. Montague, *Disenchantment* (London: Chatto and Windus, 1922), p. 176.

44 Montague, *Disenchantment*, pp. 7–8, 219, and 65.

45 Fussell, *The Great War and Modern Memory*, p. 246 and the discussion pp. 243–6.

46 Montague, *Disenchantment*, p. 172.

47 Montague, *Disenchantment*, p. 204.

48 Duncan Grant, 'Venus and Adonis', in *The Tate Gallery, 1970–72* (London: Tate Gallery, 1972), pp. 110–11.

49 Simon Watney, *The Art of Duncan Grant* (London: John Murray, 1990), p. 50.

50 Watney, *The Art of Duncan Grant*, p. 43.

51 Adrian Gregory, *The Silence of Memory: Armistice Day, 1919–1946* (Oxford: Berg, 1994), p. 46. David Lloyd argues that the priority given to women in memorial services held in 1920 was a consequence of popular pressure, not government initiative, *Battlefield Tourism: Pilgrimage and the Commemoration of the Great War in Britain, Australia and Canada, 1919–1939* (Oxford: Berg, 1998), pp. 79–80.

52 Causey, *Paul Nash*, p. 128.

53 Roger Cardinal, *The Landscape Vision of Paul Nash* (London: Reaktion Books, 1989), pp. 29–30.

54 Iain Gale, 'Back to the Land', *The Independent*, 25 June 1993, p. 15.

55 Paul Nash, 'Aerial Flowers', reprinted in *Outline*, pp. 262 and 265.

56 Causey, *Paul Nash*, pp. 11–12 and 18.

57 Fussell, *The Great War and Modern Memory*, chapter eight.

58 Elizabeth Bronfen, 'Death Drive (Freud)', in Elizabeth Wright, ed., *Feminism and Psychoanalysis: A Critical Dictionary* (Oxford: Blackwell, 1992), p. 56; and see Elizabeth Bronfen, *Over her Dead Body: Death, Femininity and the Aesthetic* (Manchester: Manchester University Press, 1992), pp. 32–3.

59 R. H. Wilenski, *Stanley Spencer* (London: Ernest Benn, 1924), pp. 25–6.

60 Andrew Causey, 'Stanley Spencer and the Art of his Time' in Royal Academy, *Stanley Spencer RA* (London: Royal Academy of Arts; London: Weidenfeld and Nicolson, 1980), p. 29.

61 Jeffrey, *The British Landscape*, p. 13.

62 Florence Spencer, quoted in Kenneth Pople, *Stanley Spencer: A Biography* (London: Collins, 1991), p. 68.

63 In Duncan Robinson, *Stanley Spencer, 1891–1959: An Exhibition Organised by the Arts Council* (London: Arts Council, 1976), and Royal Academy, *Stanley Spencer RA*.

64 John Rothenstein, *Modern English Painters, volume II: Lewis to Moore* (London: Macdonald and Jane's, 1976), p. 165.

65 Stanley Spencer (TGA, 733.3.83: Notebook).

66 Stanley Spencer, in about 1928 (TGA, 733.3.28: Notebook, p. 124).

67 Robinson, *Stanley Spencer 1891–1959*, p. 6.

68 Royal Academy, *Stanley Spencer RA*, p. 58.

69 Spencer Letter to Yockney, 12 and 27 July 1919, (IWM, 290/7:'Pte Stanley Spencer').

70 Walter Benjamin, *Illuminations* (New York: Schocken Books, 1968), p. 84.

71 Spencer to Lamb, 24 March 1915 (TGA, TAM17: Lamb).

72 'He felt no compunction in continuing where he had left off, despite the length of time that had elapsed.' Richard Carline, *Stanley Spencer at War* (London: Faber and Faber, 1978), p. 110.

73 Spencer to Lamb 20 July 1917 (TGA, TAM15: Lamb).

74 Spencer, 'Notebooks' in Judith Nesbitt, ed., *Stanley Spencer: A Sort of Heaven* (Liverpool: Tate Gallery, 1992), p. 20.

75 Robinson, *Stanley Spencer, 1891–1959*, p. 6.

76 Spencer quoted in Carline, *Stanley Spencer at War*, p. 112.

77 Causey in Royal Academy, *Stanley Spencer RA*, p. 24.

78 Nesbitt, *Stanley Spencer: A Sort of Heaven*, p. 32.

79 Spencer to Desmond Chute, Summer 1916, The Spencer-Chute Correspondence, Stanley Spencer Gallery, Cookham. See also Timothy Hyman, Patrick Wright, Adrian Glew and Tate Britain, *Stanley Spencer* (London: Tate Gallery, 2001).

80 The 1923 designs were made at Henry Lamb's home in Poole, Dorset and early plans included raising a subscription amongst Spencer's friends and patrons. See letters to Richard Carline and Henry Lamb (TGA, TAM 19 and TAM 15).

81 See the discussion by Duncan Robinson in The National Trust, *Stanley Spencer at Burghclere: The Oratory of All Souls Sandham Memorial Chapel Berkshire* (London: The National Trust, 1991).

82 Letter to Carline, reprinted in Carline, *Stanley Spencer at War*, p. 182.

83 'It is rather interesting to think of pictures in the way musicians think of music. The early Italians would sometimes do a series of pictures related one to the other. . . . the dramatic integral relation, such as one has in a sonata in music, between the first, second and third movements . . . each . . . being a picture . . . A Predella is rather like a Prelude to a fugue . . . I feel there is a fine architectural element in this', lecture given in 1922, quoted in Carline, *Stanley Spencer at War*, p. 138.

84 Timothy Hyman, 'Stanley Spencer: The Sacred Self', in Jane Alison, ed., *Stanley Spencer : The Apotheosis of Love* (London: Barbican Art Gallery, 1991), p. 30.

85 Stanley Spencer (TGA, 733.3.28: p. 38).

86 Stanley Spencer (TGA, 733.3.28: p. 40).

87 See the discussion in Keith Bell, *Stanley Spencer: A Complete Catalogue of the Paintings* (London: Phaidon, 1992), pp. 52 and 59.

88 Quoted in Carline, *Stanley Spencer at War*, p. 173.

89 Carline, *Stanley Spencer at War*, p. 184.

90 Carline, *Stanley Spencer at War*, p. 192.

91 Carline, *Stanley Spencer at War*, p. 195.

92 R. H. Wilenski, *English Painting* (London: Faber and Faber, 1933), p. 280.

93 Benjamin, *Illuminations*, p. 102.

94 Brian Wallis, 'Telling Stories: A Fictional Approach to Artists' Writings', in Brian Wallis, ed., *Blasted Allegories: An Anthology of Writings by Contemporary Artists* (New York and Cambridge, Mass.: The New Museum of Contemporary Art and MIT Press, 1989 [1987]), p. xii.

95 Robinson, *Stanley Spencer, 1891–1959*, p. 6.

96 In *Nation and Athenaeum*, 12 March 1927, quoted in Royal Academy, *Stanley Spencer RA*, 1980, p. 92. Richard Carline recollected that Roger Fry, who had included one of Spencer's works in his second post-Impressionism exhibition before the war, did not support Spencer and was, on occasions, rude to him. Carline, *Stanley Spencer at War*, p. 32.

97 Roger Fry, *Vision and Design*, ed., J. B. Bullen, (Oxford: Oxford University Press, 1981 [1920]), p. 115 et seq.

98 See Susan Handelman, *Fragments of Redemption: Jewish Thought and Literary Theory in Benjamin, Scholem, and Levinas* (Bloomington and Indianapolis: Indiana University Press, 1991), p. 132.

99 Fry, *Vision and Design*, p. 118.

100 Quoted in Carline, *Stanley Spencer at War*, p. 148.

101 John Ruskin, 'Giotto and his works in Padua' [1853–1860] reprinted in E. T. Cook and Alexander Wedderburn, eds., *The Works of John Ruskin*, vol. 24 (London: George Allen, 1906), p. 43.

102 Quoted in Bell, *Stanley Spencer: A Complete Catalogue*, p. 52.

103 See the discussion about Berlin Dada and censorship in Maud Lavin, *Cut with the Kitchen Knife: The Weimar Photomontages of Hannah Höch* (New Haven and London: Yale University Press, 1993), p. 24.

104 'The political significance of a work of art is never given once and for all, it does not have a fixed ontological status, but must be reaffirmed and fought for over and over again', Jutta Held, 'How do the Political Effects of Pictures Come About? The Case of Picasso's *Guernica*', *Oxford Art Journal*, vol. 11, no. 1, 1988, pp. 38–9.

105 See Jane Alison, 'The Apotheosis of Love' and ' Early Spencer was an early Italian; the pure milk of Trecento and Quattrocento fed into him, and his art was programmed for altarpieces and frescoed chapels. . . . From the beginning . . . the language of the Church-House was less Italian, than Northern; the blubbered faces of early German art, the scurrying crowds of Breughel, but also English humorous imagery in all its forms – end-of-pier, cartoons, caricatures. One of the great shifts of twentieth century taste, after three centuries dominated by classical decorum, has been the rehabilitation of the grotesque – part of a general questioning of the Ideal. Early Italian art had served Spencer's innocence; now in his fallen state, the Northern grotesque suddenly came into full play, as the visual language appropriate to experience'; Hyman, 'Stanley Spencer: The Sacred Self', pp. 11 and 29–30.

106 'To me there are two joys the joys of innocence and religiousness and the joys of change and sexual experience and while these selves seem unrelated and irreconcilable still I am

convinced of their ultimate union', Spencer, 1940, quoted in Antony Gormley, 'The Sacred and Profane in the Art of Stanley Spencer' in Robinson, *Stanley Spencer, 1891–1959*, p. 21.

107 Spencer to James Wood, 3 March 1918 (TGA, TAM 19).

108 Craig Owens, 'The Allegorical Impulse: Towards a Theory of Postmodernism', in *Beyond Recognition: Representation, Power and Culture* (Berkeley, L. A. and Oxford: University of California Press, 1992), p. 53.

109 Owens, *Beyond Recognition*, p. 71.

110 R. H. Wilenski, *English Painting*, p. 280.

111 Spencer to Lamb, 1915 (TGA, TAM 15).

112 Owens, *Beyond Recognition*, p. 55.

113 Marcia Tucker, 'Director's Forward' in Wallis, *Blasted Allegories*, p. viii.

114 Spencer (TGA, 733.2.28: p. 9).

115 Carline, *Stanley Spencer at War*, p. 182. The operation subject was outlined in a letter to Chute: 'And have the incision in the belly in the middle of the picture & all the forceps radiating from it like this [sketch]. It is wonderful how mysterious the hands look wonderfully intense. There was something very classical about the whole operation. Major Morton looked away from the incision when he was searching & feeling in it. What is so wonderful also is the stillness in the theatre & outside the swift silent steps of those "fetching & carrying" I would like to do a figure either side of picture of operation of a nurse & a man with fresh [?] looking sterilisers. This does not sound much but leave it to me'; Spencer to Chute, summer 1916, Spencer–Chute correspondence.

116 Spencer (TGA, 733.3.28: Notebook, p. 34).

117 Spencer wrote later: 'During the war, when I contemplated the horror of my life and the lives of those with me, I felt that the only way to end the ghastly experience would be if everyone suddenly decided to indulge in every degree and form of sexual love, carnal love, bestiality, anything you like to call it. These are the joyful inheritances of mankind'; quoted in Maurice Collis, *Stanley Spencer: A Biography* (London: Harvill Press, 1962), pp. 138–9.

118 Spencer to Chute, 17 November 1926, Spencer–Chute correspondence.

119 The Trustees of the artist's estate have refused permission for this painting to be reproduced. Details of the painting and where it has previously been reproduced are listed here. Full details of the work can be found in Tate Gallery, *The Tate Gallery 1972–4: Biennial Report and Illustrated Catalogue of Acquisitions* (London: Tate Gallery, 1974).

Stanley Spencer, *Double Nude Portrait: The Artist and His Second Wife ('The Leg of Mutton Nude')*, 1936–7, oil on canvas, 91.5 × 92.7, Tate Gallery, London.

Exhibited: *Stanley Spencer*, Merradin Gallery, March–April 1972 (ex cat.) *Stanley Spencer RA*, Royal Academy, Sep-

tember–December 1980, cat. 178; illus. p. 151; *Stanley Spencer. The Apotheosis of Love*, London, Barbican Art Gallery, January–April 1991, cat. 21, illus. pp. 62–3; *Stanley Spencer*, Norwich Castle Museum, May–August 1991, cat. 8, illus. (London: Tate Gallery Publishing); *Stanley Spencer. A Sort of Heaven*, Tate Gallery, Liverpool, March 1992–January 1993, illus. p. 45; Fiona MacCarthy, *Stanley Spencer: An English Vision* (New Haven and London: Yale University Press) 1997 Hirshorn Museum, Washington, October 1997–January 1998; Centro Cultural/Arte Contemporáneo, Mexico City, February 1998–May 1998; California Palace of Legion of Honor, San Francisco, June–September 1998, illus. pl. 35; *Stanley Spencer*, Tate Gallery, 22 March–24 June 2001, (The Art Gallery of Ontario, 14 September–16 December 2001; The Ulster Museum. 25 January–7 April 2002), cat. 58, illus. p. 153.

Reproduced: Edward Lucie-Smith, *Eroticism in Western Art* (London: Thames and Hudson, 1972) pl. 173; Simon Wilson and Robert Melville, *Erotic Art of the West* (New York: G. P. Putnam, 1973) pl. 53; Tate Gallery, *The Tate Gallery 1972–4. Biennial Report and illustrated Catalogue of Acquisitions* (London: Tate Gallery, 1974) p. 273; Duncan Robinson, *Stanley Spencer: Visions from a Berkshire Village* (Oxford: Phaidon, 1979), pl. 49; Duncan Robinson, *Stanley Spencer*, (Oxford: Phaidon, 1990), pl. 58; Keith Bell, *Stanley Spencer* (London: Phaidon, 1992), cat. 225, illus. p. 333.

120 See its catalogue entry in Royal Academy, *Stanley Spencer RA*, pp. 151–2, and Andrew Stephenson, *Visualising Masculinities* (London: Tate Gallery, 1992), n.p. Spencer wrote that he wanted his nude paintings 'to show the analogy between the Church and the prescribed nature of worship, and human love'. See the catalogue entry in *The Tate Gallery 1972–4: Biennial Report and Illustrated Catalogue of Acquisitions* (London: Tate Gallery, 1975), p. 238.

121 Caroline Walker Bynum, 'The Body of Christ in the Later Middle Ages: A Reply to Leo Steinberg', in *Fragmentation and Redemption: Essays on Gender and the Human Body in Medieval Religion* (New York: Zone Books, 1992), p. 109.

122 'Introduction' in Margaret Randolph Higonnet, Jane Jenson, Sonya Michel, and Margaret Collins Weitz, eds., *Behind the Lines: Gender and the Two World Wars* (New Haven and London: Yale University Press, 1987), p. 4.

123 Duncan Robinson, 'Introduction' in The National Trust, Stanley Spencer at Burghclere, p. 8.

124 See Bernard McGinn, 'Revelation', in Robert Alter and Frank Kermode, eds., *The Literary Guide to the Bible* (London: Fontana Press, 1987).

125 Spencer to Chute, 6 September 1918, Spencer–Chute correspondence.

126 Spencer to his sister Florence, 10 October 1918. (TGA, 733.1.750–776).

Photograph Credits

Every effort has been made to trace copyright holders of the works illustrated. In most cases the illustrations have been provided by the owners or custodians of the works; other sources and additional credits follow:

index

Aberdeen Free Press, 209 n. 76
Adelphi Gallery, 118
Admiralty, 53
Adorno, Theodor, 37
aeroplane, 47, 56–7
Affron, Matthew, 220 n. 131
Agnew's, 18, 37, 70
Airy, Anna, 114, 218 n. 38
Aitken, Charles, 80
Aitken, Max, *see* Beaverbrook
Aldington, Richard, 154
Alison, Jane, 223 n. 105
Allan, Maud, 74, 211 nn. 31, 32
allegory, 118, 173–7, 221 n. 140
Allied Artists Association, 10, 17, 200 n. 5
Alma-Tadema, Lawrence, 79
Althusser, Louis, 205 n. 64
American Civil War, 55
Anderson, Benedict, 158, 222 n. 37
Angell, Norman, 54
anti-Semitism, 114, 146, 221 n. 132
Antliff, Mark, 220 n. 131
Apollinaire, Guillaume, 55, 209 n. 89
Architect, 208 n. 41
armistice, 76, 93, 99, 114, 122, 151
Arnold, Bruce, 215 n. 4
Arras, 26, 91, 152
art criticism, 5, 15; reception of war art, 37; on Nash, 64, 87; and *The Nation's War Paintings,* 93-8, 106-07, 145; critical consensus, 6, 10, 12–13, 15–17, 93, 141
art market, 7, 12, 13, 110; retrenchment in, 202-03 n. 40; post-war slump, 220 n. 102
artistic persona, 29-30
Artists International Association, 147
Asquith, Herbert, 14, 21, 72, 203 n. 52
Athenaeum, 106, 217 nn. 57, 58, 220 n. 99

Atwood, Clare, 81
audiences, 6, 13, 21; intended for official art, 38–41, 44–5; voters, 47; for film, photography and art, 52–4, 55; for modern art, 57, 60; for Nash and Nevinson, 64–7, 87; 'broken transactions of looking', 89, 93 n. 93, 214; for history painting, 94–9, 101, 104, 106, 173; made-to-order witness, 45, 207 n. 27; viewers, 24–5, 44, 94, 112, 175
Australia, 34
avant-garde art, and the outbreak of war, 1–13, 15, 21, 30, 54, 60, 63, 70, 86, 93, 107, 109, 111–13, 118, 141; and the 30s, 145–9, 153; and sexual politics, 200 n. 4; clarification, 201–02 n. 25; compared to the art of the insane, 202 n. 28; *see also* modern-ism

Baden-Powell, Robert, 75
Baker, Steve, 204 n. 8
Bakhtin, Mikhail, 214–15 n. 9
Barbusse, Henri, 97, 104
Barnett, Canon and Henrietta, 13, 73
Barrell, John, 63–4, 87, 210 n. 109, 214 n. 90
battle painting, 76, 86, 88, 92
Bayes, Walter, 61; *The Underworld,* 61, fig. 49
Beadle, James, *Dawn – Waiting to Go Over,* 37, 44-45, 67, fig. 27
Beal, Mary, 222 n. 21
Beaverbrook, Lord (Max Aitken), 47; as Minister of Information, 69–75, 81, 91, 211 nn. 19, 22
Beechy, James, 217 n. 10
Belfast, 30
Belfast Evening Telegraph, 216 n. 45
Belgium, 17–18
Bell, Clive, 48, 106–07, 122, 217 nn. 58, 59
Bell, Keith, 223 n. 87
Bell, Vanessa, 111, 221 n. 132
Belloc, Hilaire, 23
Ben-Ghiat, Ruth, 220 n. 131
Benjamin, Roger, 216 n. 37
Benjamin, Walter, 110, 139, 151, 164, 170, 177, 220 n. 92, 222 n. 1, 223 n. 70

Benn, Gottfried, 146

Bennett, Arnold, 22, 37; on Orpen and Nash, 48, 54, 69, 71; and the British War Memorials Committee, 73–5, 78, 81, 206 n. 2, 208 n. 42, 210 n. 1; and Rickards, 213 n. 68, 213 n. 79

Bennett, Tony, 57, 210 n. 97

Bentham, Jeremy, 57

Bersani, Leo, 110, 139, 149, 217 n. 6

Bird, Jon, 216 n. 53

Birkenhead, Lord (Frederick Smith), 144

Billing, Pemberton, 74, 211 n. 31

Binyon, Laurence, 35, 44, 64, 100, 203 n. 48, 207 n.15

Black, Jonathan, 207 n. 29

Blake, William, 31

Blast. A Review of the Great English Vortex, 4, 7, 139, 201 nn. 14, 22; 'War Number', 202 n. 32, 219 n. 77

Bliss, Douglas Percy, 220 n. 127

Blomfield, Reginald, 79, 152

Bloomsbury Group, 106, 109,111, 210 n. 103, 217 n. 10

Boccioni, Umberto, 61

bodies, 1–5, 27, 31, 34; and modernity, 44–5; in Paths of Glory, 50, 54, 56–7, 75; and graves, 98; cadaver, 102, 139; and memorials, 151; landscape-as-body, 33–4

Boer War, 23

Boggs, J. Sutherland, 211 n. 55

Bolshevism, 99

Bomberg, David, 5, 76, 82, 109–13; post-war work, 114–122, 123, 134, 141, 146–7, 153; joining up, 200 n. 7, 218 nn. 37, 43, 49; Figure, fig. 87; Figures, fig. 88; In the Hold, 118, 120, fig. 85; Mud Bath, 118, 120; Players, fig. 86; Russian Ballet, lithograph, 115, fig. 80; Stairway: Drawing no. 3, fig. 89; Study for Sappers at Work. A Canadian Tunnelling Company fig. 82: Sappers at Work: A Canadian Tunnelling Company, 76, 83, 114, 120, 218, nn. 38, 53, fig. 83; Study for a Memorial to T. E. Hulme, 118, fig. 84

Bone, Muirhead, first employed, 13–14, 17, 21; at the Front, 24–9, 38, 41, 49, 55–6, 67; and the British War Memorials Committee, 71–2, 74, 78, 81, 82, 114, 147, 154; and Spencer, 164, 169; seeking official employment, 203 n. 50; at the front, 205 nn. 39, 40, 205 n. 65; press responses, 208 n. 41, 211 n. 29, 213 n. 46; and memorial gallery, 213 n. 68, 218 n. 40; The Battle of the Somme, 24, fig. 16; Distant View of Ypres, 24; The Great Crater, Athies, 25, fig. 17; Road Liable to be Shelled, 27, 29, fig. 18; The Western Front, 17, 21, 24–9, 30, 38, 42, 44, 48, 72, 155, 159, 164

Borg, Alan, 221 n. 5

Bottomley, Gordon, 157, 206 n. 79

Bourke, Joanne, 200 n. 3

Boyce, George, 208 n. 49

Brangwyn, Frank, 14, 41, 72, 86

Braque, Georges, 146

Bristol Trade Unions Conference, 17

Britain's Efforts and Ideals, 14, origins and reception 41–4, 72; donated to Harvard, 207 n. 12

British Artists at the Front, 17–18, 21, 29, 35, 37, 41–2, 44, 48, 49, 52; Paths of Glory, 54–5, 64, 72, 141, 159, fig. 13, 204 n. 14, 206 n. 68

British Museum 13, 73

British War Memorials Committee, 67, establishment and employment of artists 69–85, 91–4, 98, 106–08, 109–110, 114, 165, 177, 210 nn. 2, 7, 212 n. 46; Pictorial Propaganda Committee, 69, 75, 81, 210

British retreat from Mons, 23

Bromley, Robert, 85, 213 n. 72

Bronfen, Elizabeth, 162, 222 n. 58

Brown, Eric, 78

Brücke, Der, 42

Bryce Report, 17

Buchan, John, 14, 47, 52, 71–2, 211 n. 9

Burckhardt, Jacob, 12

Burlington Magazine, 61, 210 n. 105

Burn, Angus, 220 n. 114

Bushaway, Bob, 151, 221 n. 2

Bynum, Caroline Walker, 176, 224 n. 121

Byron, Lord (George Gordon), 31,206 nn. 78, 80

Calinescu, Matei, 217 n. 10

Cambridge University, 207 n. 12

Cameron, D.Y., 41, 76–7, 91, 100, 104, 114; The Battlefield of Ypres, 99, fig. 74

Canada, 47, 54, 72; nationalism, 76, 109, 113, 120; and Lewis 132–5, 139; and Wolfe, 211 n. 56; Canadian Houses of Parliament, 81, fig. 62; Canadian War Records Office, 72

Canadian War Memorial Fund, 5; establishment, 70, 72–3, 76–8, 81, 85, 89, 91, 104, 114, 154, 213 nn. 64, 78

Cardinal, Roger, 161; n. 53, 222

Carey, Frances, 207 n. 12, 220 n. 102

Carline, Hilda, 158, 174

Carline, Richard, 223 nn. 72, 96

Carmichael, Jane, 208 n. 44, 216 n. 41

Causey, Andrew, 33, 156, 159, 162, 164, 203 n. 47, 204 n. 14,206 n. 28, 208 n. 42, 221 n. 13, 222 n. 60

Cavell, Edith, 18, 35

Cenotaph, see memorials

censorship, 23; of artists, photographers and Nevinson's Paths of Glory, 37–58, 89, 144, 209 nn. 64, 70, 71, 86; press censorship, 53; film censorship, 52

Chantrey Bequest, 79

Charteris, Evan, 213 n. 71

Charteris, John, 72, 208 n. 38

Chavanne, Puvis de, 101

Chenil Gallery, 147

child art, 140

Church of England, 152–3, 176

Churchill, Winston, 132

Chute, Desmond, 176–7, 223 n. 79, 224 n. 115

Clair, Jean, 200 n. 2

Clark, T. J., 21, 112, 204 n. 19

Clarke, Peter, 211 n. 27

Clausen, George, 14, 41, 72, 75, 81, 114

Collier, Peter, 221 n. 27

Collins, Judith, 212 n. 60

Collis, Maurice, 224 n. 117

Colls, Robert, 204 n. 27

Colnaghi's, 41

Colour, 203 n. 43

Colvin, Claire, 155, 221 n. 16

Comay, Rebecca n. 24, 217

communism, 5, 145–6

Connoisseur, 65, 217 n. 56

Contemporary Art Society, 10, 80, 141

Conway, Martin, 71, 75, 211 n. 35, 212 n. 41

Coppard, George, 123

Corbett, David Peters, 112, 217 n. 25, 220 n. 97, 221 n. 133

Cork, Richard, 114, 200 n. 2, 201 nn. 8, 23, 203 n. 44, 204 n. 13, 215 n. 17, 217 nn. 2, 5, 218 n. 39

Cornwall, 23

Coulson, Raymond, 215 n. 18

Country Life, 18, 38
Courbet, Gustave, 86, 105
Courtauld, Samuel, 110
Cowling, Elizabeth, 200 n. 2
Creelock, 203 n. 55
critical consensus, *see* art criticism
Crystal Palace, 103
Cubism, 7, 124, 145, 202 n. 27
Cumberland, Gerald, 141
Cumming, Robert, 205 n. 65
Curzon Report, 70

Dada, 107, 112, 223 n. 103
Daily Chronicle, 71
Daily Express, 52, 65, 72, 103, 110, 134, 143, 216 nn. 45, 49, 217 n. 9
Daily Herald, 54
Daily Graphic, 3
Daily Mail, 45, 215 n. 18
Daily Mirror, 70, 216 n. 20
Daily News and Leader, 202 n. 38, 220 n. 99
Daily Telegraph, 12, 202 nn. 27, 39, 203 n. 49, 208 n. 41
Dante (Dante Alighieri), 103, 174
Dark, Sidney, 65
Daumier, Honoré, 61
Dawson, Graham, 200 n. 3
Defence of the Realm Act, 22–3, 53
demobilisation, 99
Department of Information, 14, 20, 47, 71, 211 n. 9
Derain, André, 146
Derrick, Thomas, 41; on Nevinson, 50, 57, 70, 76
Desborough, Lord (William Grenfell), 64
De Stijl, 112, 118
Détaille, Édouard, 67, 78
Dewitz, Bodo von, 208 n. 45
Dix, Otto, 122, 139
Dodd, Francis, 14, 29, 72, 82
Dodgson, Campbell, 13-14; and Nevinson, 29–30, 41–2, 44–5, 70, 73, 206 n. 76
Doesburg, Theo van, 112
Doherty, Charles, 207 n. 29
Dokter, Betsy, 221 n. 141
Dolores, 144–5
Donald, Robert, 71, 74
Doré Gallery, 4
Douglas, Alfred, 74
Dulac, Edmond, 41, 72
Duveen, Joseph, 70

Edwards, Paul, 146, 200 n. 2, 216 n. 48, 219 n. 80, 221 n. 134
Egoist, 200 n. 5
Eiffel Tower, 57
Emergency Powers Act, 98
Englishness, *see* national identity
Epstein, Jacob, 1–4, 109, 113, 144–5, 201 n. 13, 213 n. 68, 218 n. 35; *Rock Drill*, 1–4, 201 n. 13, figs. 3 and 5
Etchells, Frederick, 114–15
Evening News, 202 n. 36
Evening Standard, 215 n. 18

Farquarson, Joseph, 79
fascism, 5, 21, 98, 110, 141, 145–6; and sexuality, 221 n. 131
feminism, 200 n. 3

Fine Art Society, 17, 41
Flanders, 6, 63, 65, 154
Flitch, Crawford, on Nevinson, 37, 48, 56, 141, 206 n. 1
food rationing, 60
Foreign Office, 17, 49, 53, 71, 207 n. 12; and *Socialist Standard*, 207 n. 31
Foster, Hal, 4, 139, 201 n. 18, 220 n. 91, 221 n. 131
Foucault, Michel, 57, 210 n. 98
Frampton, George, and Konody, 218 n. 41
France, 6, 10, 12, 14, 24, 32, 48, 75–6, 86, 91, 101, 109, 134, 151, 153
Franco-Prussian War, 78, 86, 103
Fraser, Claude Lovat, 155
French Revolution, 100
French, Viscount, 47
Freud, Sigmund, 111, 162, 217 n. 24
Freytag-Loringhoven, Baroness Else von, 113
Fry, Roger, 20–21, 48; and the National Art Collections Fund, 79–80; on Reynolds, 86–7, 106–07; and critical orthodoxy, 110–12, 140; and Lewis, 146; and Spencer, 170-3, 204 n. 17; and Ministry of Information, 213, 214 nn. 83, 85, 88, 217 n. 12; and Freud, 217 n. 18; and anti-Semitism, 221 n. 132; and Spencer, 223 n. 96; *Vision and Design*, 110–11, 214 n. 84
Fussell, Paul, 159, 162, 205 n. 48, 217 n. 5, 219 n. 87
Futurism, 6, 10, 120, 146, 149, 202 n. 37

G.H.Q., and artists, 13–14; Montague at, 23–6, 30, 38; artists and photographers at, 49–50, 72, 207 n. 19
Gale, Iain, 222 n. 54
Galerie des Batailles, Versailles, 88
Galsworthy, John, 22
Gatling, Richard, 55
Gaudier-Brzeska, Henri, and Epstein, 1–4; at the London Group, 5–6, 63, 109, 113, 141, 201 n. 13; *A Mitrailleuse in Action*, 10, fig.10; *One of our Shells is Bursting*, 10, fig. 9
Gee, Malcolm, 203 n. 40
Germany, 18, 21–2, 24; compared with England, 27–8, 34, 37; print market, 41–2, 46, 54; 1918 offensive, 72, 74, 76, 86, 93, 98, 102, 109; defeat, 111, 112, 146, 159, 218 n. 42; Kultur, 21
Gertler, Mark, 109, 144, 147; and Fry, 221 n. 132; *The Queen of Sheba*, 158, fig. 132
Gibbons, Tom, 220 n. 131
Gilbert, Geoff, 221 n. 133
Gill, Colin, 122
Gill, Eric, 110
Gilman, Harold, 109
Giotto, 165, 172
Glasgow, 24
Glasgow News, 65
Glew, Adrian, 223 n. 79
Globe, 202 n. 34, 203 n. 43
Glover, Edward, 111
Golsan, Richard, 221 n. 131
Gordon, Jan, and Paul Nash, 29–31, 33; on war photography and art, 47–8, 55, 64, 203 n. 40, 206 n. 90, 208 n. 39, 210 n. 93
Goupil Gallery, 10, 12, 134
Gowers, Ernest, 204 n. 5
Goya y Lucientes, Francisco José de, 10, 88, 103, 134, 139
Grafton Galleries, 47
Grainger, J. H., 204 n.32
Grant, Duncan, 75, 109, 158-59, 202 n. 27; and conscientious objection, 211–12 n. 38, 222 n. 48; *Venus and Adonis*, 202 n. 27, fig. 133
Graphic against official artists, 37–8, 44, 106, fig. 26, 216 n. 47

Graves, Robert, 37; on Kennington, 44–5, 134
Greenberg, Clement, 21, 111, 204 n. 18
Gregory, Adrian, 222 n. 51
Greiffenhagen, Maurice, 41
Grein, J. T., 74
Griffths, Anthony, 207 n. 12, 220 n. 102
Grigson, Geoffrey, 35, 206 n. 95, 220 n. 102
Gros, Antoine-Jean; *La Bataille d'Eylau*, 105, fig. 79
Group X, 139, 220 nn. 93, 94
Grosz, George, 113, 122
Grundy, Reginald, 106, 216 n. 47
Guardian, 4, 6, 17, 26, 55, 71, 153, 201 n. 15, 209 n. 82
Gulf War, 55

Hacker, Arthur, 203 n. 55
Haig, Douglas, 72
Hall, Stuart, 204 n. 26, 211 n. 20
Hambleden, Viscount, 75
Hammann, Richard, 92
Handelman, Susan, 223 n. 98
Hansen, Miriam, 220 n. 131
Hardie, Martin, 209 n. 64
Harris, Ruth, 18, 204 n.12
Harries, Meirion and Susie, 212 nn. 45, 46
Harrison, Charles, 112–13, 146, 200 n. 2, 201 n. 25, 215 n. 17, 217 n. 2
Hartrick, A. S., 41, 72
Harvard University, 207 n. 12
Hatcher, John, 216 n. 36
Held, Jutta, 223 n. 104
Hepburn, James, 211 n. 104
Herbert, James D., 222 n. 33
Hewett, Stephen, 26
Hewitt, Andrew, 221 n. 129
Higonnet, Margaret Randolph, 224 n. 122
Hind, C. Lewis, 10
Hinterglasmalerie, 11
history painting, 5, 69, 75, 77; Ross's view on, 80; theories of, 85–9, 92, 94, 101, 107, 109, 149, 213 n. 78
Hobhouse, L. T., 22
Hobsbawn, E. J., 204 n.11
Hobson, J. A., 22
Hoerle, Heinrich, 113
Holden, Charles, 81, 166, 213 n. 68
Holmes, C. J., 79–80, 110, 217 n. 13
Holroyd, Malcolm, 215 n. 8
Home Front, 17; film censorship, 52
Home Office, 14
homosexuality, 74–5
Hone, Joseph, 205 n. 40
House, John, 217 n. 14
Howkins, Alun, 205 n. 33, 222 n. 22
Hubbard, R. H., 212 n. 55
Hudson, Edward, 50, 61
Hueffer, Ford Madox (Brown, Ford Maddox), 6
Hulme, T. E., 118
Hunt, Sidney, 113
Huston, Nancy, 222 n. 38
Hyde, Ralph, 216 n. 42
Hyman, Timothy, 223 nn. 79, 84
Hynes, Sam, 202 n. 29
Hyslop, T. B., 202 n. 28

Ideas, 53
Illustrated London News, 49
Imperial War Graves Commission, *see* memorials
Imperial War Museum, 52, 55; and the British War Memorials Committee, 69–71, 75, 115, 145, 211 n. 35
imperialism, 23, 63, 73, 75
Independent Labour Party, 46, 109
Independent Theatre Society, 74
Inge, W. .R.,18
Inglis, Ken, 212 n. 40
International Society, 202 n. 40, 218 n. 42
Irish Home Rule, 23, 73

Jack, Richard, 76, 81; *The Second Battle of Ypres*, 76, fig. 53
Jackson, Ernest, 41, 72; *United Defence against Agression (England and France, 1914)*, fig. 34
Jacobson, Bernard, 161
Jagger, C. S., 69, 82; *The Battle of Ypres*, fig. 64
James, Robert Rhodes, 219 n. 74
Jameson, Fredric, 146, 214 n. 93, 220 n. 130
Japp, Darsie, 76
Jeffrey, Ian, 141, 154, 220 n. 103, 221 n. 18
Jewish World, 118
John, Augustus, 14; and *Britain's Efforts and Ideals*, 41, 72, 81, 91, 110, 134, 145, 147, 157, 222 n. 31; *The Canadians opposite Lens*, 76, fig. 54, 213 n. 65; *Chiaroscuro*, autobiography, 215 n. 7; *The Dawn*, fig. 31; *Fraternity*, 81, fig. 63; *Lyric Fantasy*, fig. 131
Johnson, Lewis, 206 nn. 93, 94,
Jones, Ernest, 111, 217 n. 19
Joyce, James, 112, 209 n. 70
Jünger, Ernst, 139, 146
Jürgens-Kirchhoff, Annegret, 92, 215 n. 16

Kaplan, Alice, 221 n. 131
Kassak, Lajos, 112
Keane, John, 54–5
Kemp, Wolfgang, 87, 214 n. 89
Kennington, Eric, 10–12; first employed, 14–15, 18, 21; *British Artists at the Front*, 29–30, 37, 41, 44–5; at the Front, 49–50, 72, 114, 203 n. 58; *The Cup Bearer*, fig. 35; *The Kensingtons at Laventie*, 10–12, 30, fig. 12; *Making a Soldier: In the Trenches*, fig. 33; *Raider with a Cosh*, fig. 20
Keynes, Maynard, 75
Kinney, Leila, 89, 214 n. 93
Kipling, Rudyard, 35, 151
Klein, Melanie, 112, 157
Klenze, Camillo von, 214 n. 85
Klingender, Francis, 110, 217 n. 8
Konody, P. G., 4, 7, 10, 44, 60, 61, 70, 73, 76, 77, 88, 114; on Bomberg, 122, 124, 133, 141, 203 n. 45, 210 n. 100, 92, 214; 215 n. 20, 38, 216 nn. 40, 47, 218 n. 41, 219 n. 76, 220 n. 100
Korda, Alexander, 149
Koven, Seth, 203 n. 54
Kramer, Jacob, 203 n. 55, 218 n. 56
Kristeller, Paul, 87, 214 n. 87
Kristeva, Julia, 103, 216 n. 46
Kuhn, Annette, 52, 209 nn. 65, 70

Lakerveld, Carry von, 221 n. 141
Lamb, Henry, 76–7, 165, 174, 223 n. 103; *Irish troops surprised by a Turkish bombardment*, 104, fig. 78
Land and Water, 17–18

Laqueur, Thomas, 216 n. 26
Lautréamont, Comte de, 112
Lavery, John, 14, 17, 29–30, 72
Lavin, Maud, 223 n. 103
Leder, Carolyn, 164
Ledward, Gilbert, 69, 82
Lee, A. N., 50–53, 209 nn. 61, 64, 219 n. 62
Leed, E. J., 98, 124, 216 n. 25, 219 n. 63
Leicester Galleries, 7, 18, 33, 37, 47, 61, 141, 210 n. 110
Lewis, Wyndham, 4–6, 12, 69, 82, 91–2, 94, 109–13, 115, 124, 132–41,
    146, 153; joining up, 201 nn. 7, 14, 16, 202 nn. 25, 32, 216 n. 49,
    219 n. 72, 220 nn. 94, 95; *Abstract Composition*, 140; *Action or
    Artillery*, fig. 105; *Battery Salvo: A Canadian Gun Pit*, fig. 106;
    Battery Pulling in (II), 138; *A Battery Shelled*, 94–6, 99, 104–06, 133,
    138, fig. 69; *Blasting and Bombardiering*, autobiography 104, 134, 215
    n. 2, 216 n. 49, 218 n. 32; *A Canadian Gun Pit*, 132, fig. 104; *Drag
    Ropes*, 138, fig. 107; *Drawing of the Great War No. 1*, fig. 108; *Great
    War Drawing No. 2*, fig. 110; *Guns* exhibition 134, 139; *Kermesse*,
    86, fig. 65; *Laying*, 138; *L'Ingenue*, fig. 114; *The Menin Road*, fig.
    108; *Officers and Signallers*, fig. 112; *A Reading of Ovid (Tyros)*, fig.
    115; *Shell Humping*, fig. 109; *Study for To Wipe Out*, fig. 113; *The
    Tyro*, 141; *see also* Blast
liberal 14; attitudes to war and propaganda, 17–24, 26, 57, 64, 67, 69,
    82, 86; conceptions of the state 73, 87, 146, 211 n. 27
Liberalism, *see* liberal
Lima, Bertram, 70–71
Lion, Flora, 29
Lipke, William, 218 n. 47
Little Review, 113
Liverpool Post, 215 n. 20
Lloyd, David, 222 n. 51
Lloyd George, David, 14, 93, 203 n. 52, 211 n. 9
London Group, 1, 5–7,
London Regiment, 10
Long, Michael, 110, 217 n. 7
Lovelace, Colin, 204 n. 29, 208 n. 48
Lutyens, Edwin, 151–2

Macciocchi, M. A., 221 n. 131
MacColl, D. S., at the Tate, 79–80, 111, 152, 217 n. 17, 220 n. 40, 221
    n. 6
MacGregor, John M., 202 n. 28
made-to-order witness, *see* audiences
Mai, Ekkehard, 214 n. 80
Maillol, Aristide, 158
Malcolm, Ian, 75
Malevich, Kazimir, 113
Malvern, Sue, 203 n. 55, 210 n. 7, 211 n. 37
Mantegna, Andrea, 87
Mapin Art Gallery, 41
Marcus, Jane, 1, 200 n. 1
Marey, Etienne-Jules, 55
Marinetti, Filippo Tommaso, 4, 61, 146
Marriott, Charles, 44, 93, 207 n. 17, 216 n. 22, 220 n. 99
Marwick, Arthur, 23, 204 n. 31
Marsh, Eddie, 14, 122
masculinity, and modernism, 1–5, 27; and Nash's *We are Making a
    New World* 35, 45; and painting, 60–61, 91; unmanned, 97, 109,
    158–9, 176, 200 n. 3; veterans, 98–9, 113
Masterman, C. F. G. , 13–14, 17, 21, 23, 38, 42; relationship to artists,
    49–53, 69, 71, 73, 75, 153, 165; origins of Wellington House, 203 n.
    52, 203 n. 54, 205 n. 35; and GHQ, 207 n. 19, 211 n. 27; *The Con-
    dition of England*, 14, 205 n. 35

Masterman, Lucy, 15, 203 n. 50, 204 n. 24
Materer, Timothy, 217 n. 4
Matisse, Henri, 86, 146, 158
Mayes, Alice, 114
Mayes, W. P., 211 n. 25
McBey, James, 14, 41, 72, 82
McGinn, Bernard, 224 n. 124
Medd, Jodie, 211 n. 31
Medusa, 18
Meidner, Ludwig, 201 n. 17
Meissonier, Ernest, 86
memorials, 55, 73, 75–76; to T. E.Hulme 118; 151–4, 159, 212 n. 40,
    222 n. 51; Cenotaph, 99, 151–2; mourning, 112, 217 n. 24;
    poppies, 26, 151, remembrance, 25–6, 77, 85, 100, 151–3, 157; Tomb
    of the Unknown Warrior, 151–2, 159; War Graves Commission, 98,
    151, 213 n. 68
Meninsky, Bernard, 84, 158
Merewether, Charles, 26, 205 n. 41
Michelet, Jules, 12
Ministry of Defence, 55
Ministry of Information, 29, 37, 47, 67; Beaverbrook and, 69–75, 164
Mitchell, Peter Chalmers, 22–3, 204 n. 28
Modernism, and the avant-garde, 1–5; and degeneracy, 5, 21, 38, 44,
    49, 54, 57, 60, 65, 70, 86, 109–13, 146; and avant-garde, 201–02 n.
    25; reactionary modernism, 110, 146; *see also* avant-garde art
Moira, Gerald, 72
Mond, Alfred, 70, 75, 211 n. 19
Monet, Jacques, n. 56, 212
Money, Chiozza, 213 n. 74
Montagna, Dennis, 212 n. 56
Montague, C. E., 26; and *The Western Front*, 29–30, and *British Artists
    at the Front*, 31–5, 45, 64, 75, 153, 159, 161, 165, 169; *Disenchantment*,
    159, 222 n. 43; *War as it is*, 28
Morgan, Kenneth O., 216 n. 21
Moriarty, Catherine, 221 n. 7
Morning Post, 145
Munnings, Alfred, 91
Murry, John Middleton, 96–8, 104, 107, 216 n. 24
Mussolini, Benito, 141, 149, 220 n. 105
mutiny, 46, 98

Nash, John, 76, 94, 100; *Oppy Wood*, 100, fig. 75
Nash, Margaret, 18, 20, 32–3, 156–9, 204 n.16
Nash, Paul, 12; first employed, 14–15, 17; and *British Artists at the
    Front*, 21, 29–35, 37, 48, 49; uncensored, 53, 57, 60; and Nevinson,
    63–7, 69, 72, 76, 84, 94, 100, 110, 114–15, 144, 147, 153; post-war,
    154–62, 165, 203 n. 58; education, 206 nn. 70, 71, 206 n. 79, 221 n.
    12, 222 n. 55; *Black Poplar Pond, Iden*, 155; *The Caterpillar Crater*,
    33, fig. 24; *Chaos Decoratif*, 101, fig. 76; *Chestnut Waters*, 154, 161–
    62, fig. 135; *Crater Pools, Below Hill 60*, 31, fig. 21; *Dark Lake*, 154;
    Dark Lake, Iver Heath, 155; *Existence*, 37, fig. 28; *The Field of Pass-
    chendaele*, 34; *Garden Pond, Wittersham*, 155, fig. 127; *Hill 60, From
    the Cutting*, 33, fig. 23; *The Lake*, 154, 159, fig. 134; *Landscape, Year
    of Our Lord, 1917*, 33, 63, fig. 51; *MeetingPlace, Buntingford*, 155, 162,
    fig. 126; *The Menin Road*, 96, 101, fig. 70; *Night Bombardment*, 154;
    Outline autobiography 33, 123, 154, 158, 161–2, 206 n. 84, 208 n.
    54; *Paths into the Wood, Whiteleaf*, fig. 129; *Places*, 154–8; *Ruin.
    Sunset*, 64, fig. 52; *Sunrise, Inverness Copse*, 31, 34–5, fig. 22; *Tail-
    piece, Iden*, fig. 130; *Very Light*, 63, fig. 50; *Void of War*, exhibition
    37; *We Are Making a New World*, 18–21, 31, 33, 35, fig. 15; *White
    Cross*, 154, fig. 125; *Winter Wood, Hamden*, fig. 128
The Nation, 22, 54, 209 n. 84
National Art Collections Fund, 79–80

National Gallery, London, 70, 81, 110
national identity, 4–6, 12, 13, 17–18; and landscape, 23–4, 54, 154–5, 158–9, 204 n. 11, 222 n. 41; Englishness, 17, 26–9, 33, 153, 154–5; 'South Country', 23
Needham, 71, 81–2
Neocleus, Mark, 146, 221 n. 131
Neuville, Alphonse de, 67, 78; *Le Cimetière de Saint-Privat*, fig. 55
Nevinson, C. R. W., in the early years of the war, 5–12; first employed, 14–15, 17, 21; and *British Artists at the Front*, 29–30, 37–8, 41, 44, 47; at the Front and exhibition in 1918, 49–67, 69, 72, 76, 100, 104, 109–13, 115; after the war, 141–5, 153, 165, 202 n. 33, 203 n. 58, 206 n. 76, 210 n. 103, 212 n. 46, 214 n. 85, 220 n. 98, 221 n. 140; *After a Push*, 60, fig. 46; *Amongst the Nerves of the World*, fig. 119; *The Arrival*, figs. 4, 5; front cover of *British Artists at the Front, Part One, C. R. W. Nevinson*, fig.19; *Bursting Shell*, 7, 65, fig. 7; *The Doctor*, 10, fig. 11; *Exodus A. D. A Warning to Civilians*, novel 147; *Flooded Trench on the Yser (Deserted Trench)*, 6–7, fig. 6; *The Food Queue*, 60, 63, fig. 47; *Glittering Prizes*, 144, fig. 120; *The Great War: The Fourth Year*, book 37; *A Group of British Soldiers*, 52, 60–61, 64, 65, fig. 38; *The Harvest of Battle*, 76, 96–7, 99, 101–04, 141, 144, 145, 212 n. 46; frontispiece, fig. 71; *Lilies of the Café*, fig. 117; *Looking at Battle from New Points of View*, 37–8, 55, fig. 29; *La Mitrailleuse*, 10, 80, 141, fig. 8; *Modern War Paintings by C. R. W.Nevinson*, book, 7, 10; *Nerves of an Army*, 55, fig. 39; *Night; Light; Crowd: An Interpretation*, 10; *Paths of Glory*, censored, 37, 45, and 50–53 (207 nn. 29,82, 84), 56, 60, 142; censored, fig. 25, fig. 37; *La Patrie*, 47, fig. 36; *Paint and Prejudice* autobiography, 210 n. 92, 210 n. 103; *Portrait of a Pretty Girl*, 144; *Reliefs at Dawn*, 60: *Returning to the Trenches*, 2, 6, figs 1, 5; *The Road from Arras to Bapaume*, 60 *Roads of France*, 55–56, figs. 40–43: *Soul of a Souless City*, fig. 118; *Throwing a Bomb*, 60, fig. 45; *The Twentieth Century*, 149, fig. 121; *Violence: An abstraction* 10; *War Profiteers*, 60, fig. 48; *The Workers*, 142, fig. 116
Nevinson, Henry, 14, 54
The New Age, 46
New Witness, 202 n. 26
New English Art Club, 13, 60, 79
New York, 141, 143
Newnes, George, 18
Nicholson, Ivor, 38, 49, 53
Nicholson, William, 14, 41, 72
Nietzsche, Friedrich, 18
Nochlin, Linda, 27, 205 n. 57
Northcliffe, Lord (Alfred Harmsworth), 70–71

Observer, 145, 201 n. 15, 210 n. 104
O'Connor, T. P., 142
Official artists, 5, 10, 12; beginnings, 13–15, 17, 37–8, 49–54, 69, 91, 113, 149, 153; and payment, 213 n. 72
Official Secrets Act, 22
O'Keefe, Paul, 219 n. 76
Ophelia, 31
Orage, A. R., 46, 207 n. 32
Orpen, William, 14, 18, 37; untruthfulness, 48, 70, 72, 81, 91–2, 206 n. 26; and Roberts, 219 n. 67; *Blown-up* 97–8, fig. 73; *An Onlooker in France* war memoir, 91, 215 n. 1; *Shell-shocked*, 52
Ottawa, 78
The Outlook, 54, 202 n. 31
Owen, Wilfred, 162
Owens, Craig, 53, 174, 209 n. 78, 224 n. 108

pacifism, 46–7, 98
Paget, Harold, 210 n. 118

Palace of Westminster, 85
Palestine, 76, 110, 146
Pankhurst, Sylvia, 113
Panofsky, Erwin, 157, 222 n. 30
Paret, Peter, 201 n. 24
Parker, Andrew, 222 n. 40
Parliament, 14, 22, 47, 71
Passchendaele, 24
Paul, Eden and Cedar, 218 n. 31
Paulson, Ronald, 100–01, 216 n. 3
Pears, Charles, 72
Pearson, Lionel, 166
Pennell, Joseph, 41, 72, 143
Penny, Edward, 85, 201 n. 19
Peppis, Paul, 4, **20** nn.12, 19
perception, 55
Perkin, Harold, 213 n. 74
Phillips, Claude, 6, 12, 141, 202 n. 27, 220 n. 100
photography, 12, 14, 24; in the *Graphic*, 37–8, 44; and propaganda, 47–50; panoramic, 102–03; aerial reconnaissance, 47, 56, 208 n. 38; *Bild und Filmamtes*, 48; Section Photographique de l'Armée, 48
Piero della Francesca, 104
Picasso, Pablo, 86, 140, 146, 202 n. 27; *Guernica*, 175
Pick, Daniel, 18, 55, 113, 201 n. 17, 204 n. 9, 209 n. 87
Ploughshare, 141
Pople, Kenneth, 222 n. 62
pornography, 52
Potts, Alex, 23–4, 155, 205 n. 34, 222 n. 20
Pound, Ezra, 3, 46, 60, 65, 113, 134, 138, 146, 155, 210 n. 100, 216 n. 47, 219 n. 83
Powers, Alan, 213 n. 78, 214 n. 81
Poynter, Edward John, 79
Prendergast, Christopher, 105, 216 n. 48
Prendeville, Brendon, 44–5, 207 n. 25
Press, 23, 26, 37; photographers, 49, 55, 73, 93; and the army, 208 n. 48; 'Press Lords', 211 n. 20
Prix de Rome, 214 n. 81
proletcult, 113
propaganda, 13–15; and Wellington House, 17–22, 35; and artists, 48–9; reorganisation in 1918, 71–2, 74, 80, 82, 203 n. 2, 204 n. 21; history, 208 n. 50; Crewe House, 71; M.I.5, 47; M.I.7, 207 n.33; National War Aims Committee, 46–7, 207–08 n. 35; Pictorial Propaganda Department, 38
prostitution, 60
psychoanalysis, 111–12
publishers, 2
Puni, Ivan, 112

Québecquois, 78
Queen, 63, 210 n. 102
Quinn, John, 134

Raemaekers, Louis, 17–18, 21, 26, 35, 67, 72; *Thrown to the Swine. The Martyred Nurse*, 18, fig. 14
RAF, 30
Raphael, 87, 214 n. 86
Read, Herbert, 33, 118, 133, 155, 206 n. 89, 218 n. 48, 219 n. 78
Regnault, Henri, 219 n. 84
Reisenfield, Robin, 207 n. 14
Rembrandt van Rijn, 103
Renaissance, and humanism, 4; premonitions of a national renaissance, 12; fashions for, 87; 'the new renaissance', 92–4, 98, 106 (215-12 n. 20), 176; early Renaissance, 214 n. 85

Renoir, Pierre Auguste, 158
Reynolds, Joshua, 85; *Discourses*, 86, 214 nn. 85, 88
Richmond, William, 30
Rickards, E. A., 81, 213 nn. 64, 68
Ricketts, Charles, 41, 211 n. 34; *Italia Redenta*, fig. 30
Rider-Rider, William, 102–03
Roberts, William, 5, 6, 12, 76–8, 82, 84, 86, 94, 109–13, 114; war
    service and war painting, 122–32, 134, 141, 153, 158, 164; joining
    up, 201 n. 7; and Canada, 212 n. 51, 218 nn. 43, 56, 219 n. 72; and
    official employment, 219 nn. 66, 67; *Brigade Headquarters: Signallers
    and Linesmen*, fig. 95; *The Cinema*, 132, fig. 102; *Died of Wounds*,
    fig. 101; *During a Battle*, fig. 94; *The First German Gas Attack at
    Ypres*, 76, 120, fig. 90; *The Gas Chamber*, fig. 93; *A Group of British
    Generals*, fig. 98; *Gunners: Turning Out*, fig. 96; *Infantry Duckboard
    being Shelled*, fig. 97; *Memories of the War to End War*, autobiogra-
    phy 123; *On the Wire – Inspired by 'With a Machine Gun to
    Cambrai'*, fig. 91; *Rosières Valley*, fig. 92; *A Shell-Dump*, 94–6, 99,
    fig. 68; *Signallers*, fig. 99; *Taking the Oath*, 132, fig. 103; *Tommies
    Filling their Water Bottles*, fig. 100
Robey, Kinley E., 211 n. 31
Robichon, François, 212 n. 52
Robinson, Duncan, 165, 170, 176, 222 n. 63, 223   n. 81
Rodin, Auguste, 149
Rodker, John, 112, 115
Romney, George, 78, 85; 'Portrait of Joseph Brant (Thayendanegea)',
    78, fig. 56
Rosenberg, Isaac, 118
Ross, Margery, 211 n. 31
Ross, Robert, and Lavery, 29–30; at the Tate, 70; and the British War
    Memorials Committee, 73–81, 82; on Lavery, 206 n. 72; and
    Billing, 211 n. 31; and Tate Gallery, 211 n. 35; and artists, 212 nn.
    47, 51
Rossetti, Dante Gabriel, 27, 205 n. 56
Rosso, Mary, 222 n. 40
Rothenstein, John, 31, 110, 154, 157, 206 n. 82, 221 n. 14, 222 n. 64
Rothenstein, William, 14; and Paul Nash, 29–30, 32, 41, 72, 81, 91–2,
    114, 164, 215 nn. 5, 10, 221 n. 132,
Rother, Rainer, 201 n. 23
Rothermere, Lord (Harold Harmsworth), 70–71, 211 n. 22
Rothstein, Andrew, 216 n. 25
Royal Academy, 53, 54, 61, 79, 85, 103, 114, 132, 139, 145, 174; and
    Tate Gallery, 210 n. 3, 216 n. 44; *The Nation's War Paintings*, 5, 12,
    69, 71, 78, 93, 98, 103–04, 106–07, 122, 141, 165; press reception,
    215–16 nn. 18, 19, 20; arrangement of canvases at the Royal
    Academy, 216 n. 47
Royal Army Medical Corps, 76, 113, 141, 164
Royal Berkshire Regiment, 166
Royal Field Artillery, 122
Royal Ulster Constabulary, 132
Rubens, Peter Paul, 87
Ruskin, John, 173, 206 n. 94, 206 n. 94, 223   n. 101
Russell, Bertrand, 54
Russian Revolution, 98, 112, 145
Russolo, Luigi *La Revolta*, 6, fig. 2
Rutter, Frank, 10, 13, 118, 202 n. 40, 203 nn. 42, 53, 210 n. 107, 210
    n. 6

Sackville Gallery, 6
Sadler, Michae,l 10, 141, 164, 216 nn. 20, 47, 220 n. 99
salaries and incomes, 213 n. 74
Salisbury Plain, 26
Salpeter, Harry, 205 n. 42

Sampson, John, 222 n. 31
Sanders, M. L., 203 n. 51
Sandham, Lieutenant Henry Willoughby, 176
Sargent, John Singer, 69, 70, 81–2, 92, 106; and Tate Gallery, 210 n. 4;
in France, 216–17 n. 55; *Gassed*, 97, 99, 103–05, fig. 72
Saturday Review, 52, 60–61, 65, 215 n. 19
Sayag, Alain, 208 n. 45
Schuster, Claud, 203 n. 2, 204 n. 4
Schwabe, Randolph, 76
Schwarz, Bill, 204 n. 26, 211   n. 20
Schwitters, Kurt, 113
Scott, C. P., 26, 71
Second World War, 30, 33, 54, 60, 69, 111–12, 151, 162, 164, 175
Segal, Hannah, 112, 217 n. 20
Sekula, Alan, 47, 208 n. 37
Select Committee on National Expenditure, 71
Senefelder Club, 41
Seurat, Georges, 86
Shannon, Charles, 41, 72; *The Rebirth of the Arts*, fig. 32
Sherman, Daniel, 98–9, 216 n. 29
Sherman, John, 214 n. 86
Shepperson, Claude, 72
Shover, Michele, 205 n. 58
Shropshire, 23
Sickert, Walter, 78
Silber, Evelyn, 200 n. 6, 201 n. 11
Silverman, Kaja, 207 n. 27
Sims, Charles, 76–7, 81, 84, 91; *Sacrifice*, fig. 60
Sistine Chapel, 176
Sitwell, Sacheverall, 112
Slade School of Art, 30, 78, 86, 122, 214 n. 85, 219 n. 62
Smith, Anthony, 222 n. 41
Smith, Bernard, 201 n. 23
Smith, Helen Zenna, 200 n. 1
socialism, 46
Somme, 24, 26, 45, 55–6, 92
Sommer, Doris, 222 n. 40
'South Country', *see* national identity
Soviet Union, 98–9, 113, 146
Spackman, Barbara, 220 n. 131
Spanish Civil War, 147, 162
Spencer, Gilbert, 94
Spencer, Stanley, 69, 77, 86, 94, 104, 110, 113, 114, 132, 153, 158; and
    Burghclere, 162–77; 223 n. 83, 223–4 n. 106, 224 n. 115; make love
    not war, 224 n. 117, 224 n. 120; *Ablutions*, 166, 176; *Bedmaking*,
    158, 166, 174; *Burghclere Chapel*, 132, 153, 164–77; *Camp at Karasuli*,
    166, 175, figs. 145–6; *Convoy Arriving with Wounded*, 122, fig. 137;
    Double Nude Portrait, 176, 224 n. 119; *Dug out or Stand-to*, 166, 168;
    Filling Tea Urns, 166, figs. 139, 141; *Filling Water Bottles*, 166, fig.
    175; *Firebelt*, 166; *Frostbite*, 166, 175; *Kit Inspection*, 166; *Map-reading*,
    166, 175, 177; *Moving Kitbags*, 166; *Port Glasgow Resurrection Series*,
    164, 175; *The Resurrection, Cookham*, 168, 170, 174, fig. 143; *Resur-
    rection of the Soldiers*, 166, 168, 175, fig. 138; *Reveille*, 166, 168, fig.
    142; *Riverbed at Todorova*, 166, 175, fig. 147–48; *Scrubbing the Floor*,
    166, 175, fig. 140; *Sorting the Laundry*, 175; *Swan-upping at Cookham*,
    115, 165, fig. 81; *Tea in the Hospital Ward*, 166, 175; *Travoys Arriving
    with Wounded*, 87, 164–5, fig. 66; *Unveiling Cookham War Memorial*,
    162, 170, fig. 136; *Washing Lockers*, 166, 175, fig. 144
Spencer-Pryse, Gerald, 72
Sphere, 145
Squires, J. D., 211 n. 10
Star, 142, 143

Steiner, Zara S., 204 n. 30
Stephenson, Andrew, 217 nn. 10, 14, 224 n. 120
Stokes, Hugh, n. 100, 220
Stonebridge, Lyndsey, 112, 217 n. 21
Stopford, Francis, 21, 204 n. 20
Storer, Edward, 202 n. 26
Sullivan, Edmund, 72
Sunday Times, n. 42, 203;

Tallents, Stephen, 203 n. 50
Tate, Board of Trustees, 70, 79
Tate Gallery, 10; establishment, 70, 73–4; and the Chantrey Bequest, 79–80, 110, 121–22, 141, 174, 210 n. 3; and Imperial War Museum, 210 n. 6, 213 n. 68
Tate, Henry 73
Tatler, 142
Taylor, A. J. P., 211 n. 16
Taylor, Brandon, 210 n. 3
Taylor, Philip M., 203 n. 51
Theweleit, Klaus, 216 n. 25, 221 n. 131
t'Hoff, Robert van, 118
Thomas, Brook, 209 n. 70
Thomas, Edward, 23, 205 n. 36; *This England*, 24; *This is No Case of Petty Right or Wrong*, 24
Tickner, Lisa, 118–20, 157, 200 n. 4, 202 n. 25, 218 n. 50, 219 n. 62, 222 n. 31
Tillyard, Stella, 202 n. 28
The Times, 5; 'Artists and the War', 12, 23, 38, 45, 60, 64, 202 n. 26, 210 n. 100, 215 n. 19
Timms, Edward, 220 n. 131
Tippett, Maria, 211 n. 18
Tonks, Henry, 41, 76, 78, 91–2; in Russia, 99, 202 n. 40, 219 n. 60
topography, 24–5, 64, 158
Toynbee, Arnold, 13
Treasury, 13–14, 49, 67, 69; and the British War Memorials Committee, 71 and 73–5, 83, 84, 204 n. 4; and Tate Gallery, 210 n. 3
Trotsky, Leon, 52
Tucker, Marcia, 224 n. 113
Turnbull, A., 114
Turner, J., 210 n. 115
Twentieth Century Art. A Review of Modern Movements, see Whitechapel Art Gallery

Uccello, Paolo, 10, 81, 96, 134, 139; *Battle of San Romano*, 81, 88, 92, fig. 59
Underwood, Leon, 122
United States of America, 17, 67, 71

Varley, Frederick, *For What?*, 139, fig. 111
Velasquez, Diego, 81, 103; *The Surrender of Breda*, fig. 58
Verdun, 55
Vereshchagin, Vasily, 10, 88; *Apotheosis of War*, fig. 67
Victory Parade, 99
viewer, *see* audiences
Vildrac, Charles, 110, 112
Virilio, Paul, 55–7, 209 n. 89
Vorticism, 3-4, 139, 202 n. 25, 217 n. 1

Wadsworth, Edward, 5, 109, 113, 115, 218 n. 46
Waites, B. A., 219 n. 62
Walden, Herwarth, 112
Walker, Edmund, 78
Wallace, Catherine, 216 n. 47
Wallis, Brian, 223 n. 94
war and gender, 5; and rape, 18, 27, 44, 99, 176, 222 n. 38; *see also* masculinity
War Artists Advisory Committee, 164
War Office, 23, 30, 46; and Nevinson, 52, 69, 72, 75; M.I.7(a) 53; M.I.7(b), 46, 53
War Pictorial, 38, 72
Warhol, Andy, 145
Warnke, Martin, 209 n. 88
Watkins, Harold, 76, 114, n. 40, 218; and Bomberg and Roberts, 218 n. 43
Watney, Simon, 220 n. 126, 222 n. 49
Watt, A. S., 13, 22
Weekly Dispatch, 211 n. 32
Wellington House, establishment of, 13–15, 17, 23, 37–8; *Britain's Efforts and Ideals*, 41–2, 44, 47; and artists, 49–53, 65, 67; and Imperial War Museum, closure, 70–73, 82, 91, 153, 165, 203–04, 211 nn. 9, 11,
Wells, H. G., 22, 54, 149
Werner, Anton von, 86
West, Benjamin, 85; *The Death of General Wolfe*, 78, 85, fig. 57, 212 n. 56
Westminster Abbey, 78
Westminster Gazette, 64, 203 n. 40, 220 n. 102
Whitechapel Art Gallery, 13, 41, 73, 80, 147, **20** n. 27; *Twentieth Century Art. A Review of Modern Movements*, 4, 6
Wigan, 26
Wilde, Oscar, 71, 74–5, 211 n. 31, 213 n. 68
Wilenski, R. H., 94–5, 98, 105, 162, 170, 174, 201–02 n. 25, 216; 222 n. 23, 59, 223 n. 92
Williams, Raymond, 4, 145–6, 201–02 nn. 21, 25, 204 n. 28, 220 n. 128
Willsdon, Clare A. P., 213 n. 78
Wilson, Andrew, 217 n. 27
Wind, Edgar, 213 n. 76
Winter, J. M., 201 n. 7, 210 n. 101, 216 n. 32
Witt, R. C., 79
Wodehose, R. F., 213 n. 64
Wolfe-Aylward, A. E. C., 212 n. 56
Wood, W. T., 18
Wright, Patrick, 223 n. 79

Yaeger, Patricia, 222 n. 40
Yockney, Alfred, appointed to Wellington House, 38, 52, 70, 73, 76, 81, 84–5, 114–15, 165; appointment, 207 n. 6; and Tate Gallery, n. 5, 210
Yorkshire Post, 203 n. 43
Young, Alan, 218 n. 29
Ypres, 24, 26, 134